CU01025126

To Eoin,

Thanks for the

Computer Rescue!

Jim McL

A Makeshift Majority

The First Inter-Party Government, 1948–51

DAVID MCCULLAGH

IPA
INSTITUTE OF PUBLIC
ADMINISTRATION

First published 1998
Institute of Public Administration
57–61 Lansdowne Road
Dublin 4
Ireland

ISBN 1 872002 69 2

British Library Cataloguing-in-Publication Data
A catalogue record for this book is available from the British Library.

Cover design by Creative Inputs, Dublin
Typeset in 11/13 Caslon by Carrigboy Typesetting Services, County Cork
Printed by ColourBooks, Dublin

CONTENTS

ACKNOWLEDGEMENTS

This book would not have happened without the help, encouragement and advice of Senator Maurice Manning. He not only encouraged me to begin an MA and helped select a topic, but also advised me to convert my thesis to a PhD, and put me in touch with a publisher. I am deeply grateful for his help.

Professor Tom Garvin later took over the supervision of the thesis, and his incisive comments and stimulating conversation greatly aided progress. At the Institute of Public Administration, Tony McNamara and Kathleen Harte guided me through the process of publishing a book, while Finbarr O'Shea did a superb job of editing the text. Ed Mulhall read a draft and made useful comments as well as directing me towards some material that was new to me.

Research was carried out in a number of archives – University College Dublin; the National Archives of Ireland; the Public Record Office in Kew, London; and the Public Record Office of Northern Ireland, whose Deputy Keeper gave permission to quote from material held there. The staff in all these institutions were unfailingly courteous and helpful. I also spent many happy hours in the cuttings library of the *Irish Press*, now sadly no more, the library and archives of RTÉ, the University College Dublin library, and the National Library. Many thanks also for accommodation during research to Pat and Anne Smyth in Belfast and Fionnuala Smyth in London.

A number of people who were closely connected with the events in this book have spoken or written to me, and I would particularly like to thank Liam Cosgrave, Patrick Lynch, Risteárd Mulcahy, Louie O'Brien, and Ken Whitaker, all of whom shed useful light on many areas.

On a more mundane level, a small army of friends helped to rescue drafts from computers that were obsolete, or had finally had enough of my mistreatment. Thanks to Adrienne and Robert Thompson, Cathal Guiomard, Aileen O'Meara, and Eoin Fahy.

I hope my parents Robin and June will feel that this book at last justifies my stubborn refusal to study something useful at college (if only I'd done Law!). Many thanks for their support, of all kinds, over the years.

Finally, I want to thank my wife, Anne-Marie Smyth, to whom this book is dedicated. She has patiently endured my mental and physical absences over a period of six and a half years as I researched, wrote and rewrote the text, and encouraged me to (finally!) finish it. I promise never to mention the subject again.

INTRODUCTION

Fifty years after its creation, the first inter-party government is popularly remembered, if at all, for the Mother and Child debacle and perhaps for the 'declaration' of the Republic. Neither event gives much cause for the first Costello administration to be particularly well thought of in the popular memory.

That's a shame, because there is much more to the story of that government than the country's first (only?) Church–state crisis and the comedy of errors which accompanied the breaking of the last link with the British Commonwealth.

Not all of that story reflects credit on those involved: when we come to consider the treatment of the civil service and the Battle of Baltinglass in Chapter Two, or relations with Northern Ireland in Chapter Four, or the attitude towards the Catholic Church in Chapter Seven, the contemporary reader may not know whether to be amused or appalled.

But there is enough on the credit side of the ledger – the housing drive, the massive investment in agriculture, the new thinking about economics – to suggest that the first inter-party government deserves recognition as a reforming administration. Not least, there is the fact that a coalition could come together and survive for three and a half years, involving as it did the radical, republican Clann na Poblachta, the conservative, Commonwealth-inclined Fine Gael, two separate Labour parties and the farmers of Clann na Talmhan, with six Independents thrown in for good measure. One can see why Seán Lemass should dismiss it contemptuously as 'a makeshift majority' and why most observers predicted it wouldn't last a year. But despite its variegated appearance it survived for three and a half years. For those interested in the role of coalitions in Irish politics, there could hardly be a better case study.

Of course, while the number of parties involved made this a unique experiment, it was also Ireland's first experience of a new form of administration – coalition. There has been no real tradition of coalition government in the English-speaking world, largely thanks to the use of first-past-the-post electoral systems which favour the development of two major parties. Britain's traditional distaste for multi-party governments was expressed in the middle of the nineteenth century by Benjamin Disraeli, who told the House of Commons that 'England does not love Coalitions.'[1] This distaste has continued in the twentieth century, with coalition governments in Britain existing only in wartime (1915–22 and 1940–5) or periods of extreme economic emergency (1931–2).

In its exported form, the Westminster system also led to single-party government in Canada, Australia and New Zealand (up to 1996), while in the United States – the largest English-speaking democracy – there is no question of an executive coalition because, by definition, only one party can be represented in the Presidency (although legislative coalitions are observed in Congress – despite an electoral system which favours a two-party system, party discipline is relatively weak, leading to a blurring of party lines as informal legislative coalitions are built on different issues, a process known as 'log-rolling').

Even those countries with a British cultural heritage which have used proportional representation (PR) have tended not to opt for the list systems used in almost all other countries.[2] Ireland and Malta both use the single transferable vote form of PR (PR–STV) for national elections, while Australia uses it for elections to the Senate, the Tasmanian House of Assembly and the Legislative Assembly of the Australian Capital Territory. However, the use of PR has not necessarily led to coalition – Malta initially had a multi-party system, but in the last thirty years two parties have monopolised both votes and seats,[3] while virtually all of the seats in Tasmania are won by two parties.[4]

The one exception to this trend is New Zealand. Once described as 'a virtually perfect example of the Westminster model of democracy',[5] New Zealand voted in 1993 to adopt a variant of the German additional member system, known as mixed-member proportional (MMP), largely because 'it combined the virtues of full proportionality with New Zealand's tradition of single-member constituencies'.[6] The first MMP election, held in October 1996, led to the formation of New Zealand's first coalition government.[7]

The Maltese and Tasmanian experiences suggest that the historical rarity of coalitions in Ireland may not be as unusual as it appears at first sight. Perhaps it is the legacy of British rule, or perhaps it is something in the nature of PR–STV, but Ireland accepted coalition only very slowly. The first such arrangement was formed a quarter of a century into the state's history. Indeed, in the first fifty years of that history (1922–73), coalitions held power for just six and a half years, with single-party Cumann na nGaedheal or Fianna Fáil administrations being in office the rest of the time. However, a change has since taken place: in the third quarter-century of self-government in Ireland (1973–98), single-party administrations held power for only seven years, and, given the electoral reality that Fianna Fáil appears unlikely to win an overall Dáil majority, it seems that coalitions will be the norm from now on.

Ireland is also unusual from another standpoint, that of ideology. Standard coalition theory suggests that coalitions should form between parties that are adjacent on a policy scale. The first five coalitions (1948–51, 1954–7, 1973–7, 1981–2, 1982–7) involved Fine Gael and Labour, with the addition of extra parties in the first two cases, with Fianna Fáil excluded. Yet Fianna Fáil occupies a position between Fine Gael and Labour on any left–right scale. The sixth and ninth coalitions (1989–92, 1997–) were made up of Fianna Fáil and the Progressive Democrats – and the PDs are surely to the right of Fine Gael. The seventh coalition (1993–4), Fianna Fáil and Labour, was the only ideologically connected coalition on a left–right scale, but was quickly replaced by another Fine Gael/Labour government (1994–7), this time with the addition of Democratic Left.

Of course, a left–right divide is not the only conceivable cleavage, and in Ireland at the time of the formation of the first coalition, the Anglo-Irish Treaty of 1921 could be seen as more important.[8] But here too there are problems: Clann na Poblachta was more republican than Fianna Fáil, as was Clann na Talmhan and to a lesser extent elements of Labour, while Fine Gael was at the opposite end of this particular spectrum.

But if the Treaty *per se* did not provide a rational basis for the first inter-party government, a connected issue could be seen as providing the glue which held five parties and a group of Independents together – dislike of de Valera. Maryann Valiulis has described the opposition view of de Valera as 'the man they could never forgive': 'Other Republicans could be forgiven [by Fine Gael]. They were men of principle, men who had been led astray, men who did not understand. . . . But Eamon de Valera was different. He was the man the leaders of the Opposition could never forgive – and never trust again.'[9] She claimed that the Civil War became, for the Free State side, 'both a perceptual prison and a perceptual prism', because it defined the parameters of political debate and because it coloured their views of all subsequent events.[10] For instance, Richard Mulcahy, leader of Fine Gael, held de Valera personally responsible for the Civil War.[11] Thus, even the extreme republicans of Clann na Poblachta were more acceptable to Fine Gael than the former chief they felt had betrayed them.

If this dislike of Fianna Fáil, and particularly of de Valera, is the relevant spectrum, then Fine Gael was clearly the most strongly opposed, followed by Clann na Poblachta, for entirely opposite reasons. The opposition of Labour and Clann na Talmhan was largely due to the fact that Fianna Fáil had been in power for sixteen years. Elements of National Labour (on the party's national executive and in the Congress of Irish Unions) were actually favourably disposed towards Fianna Fáil, as will be seen in Chapter One.

Both aspects of Ireland's position as a 'deviant' case when it comes to coalition theory (i.e. the rarity of coalitions before 1973 and the ideological make-up of the coalitions that have been formed) can be seen to have arisen from the dominant political position of Fianna Fáil. The Civil War provided the initial cleavage in Irish politics; when it later became less salient, Fianna Fáil's strong electoral position allowed it to remain aloof from coalition making. At the same time as this situation pushed the opposition parties together, memories of the Civil War also fuelled the dislike which many felt for de Valera and his party – whose removal from office became an overriding aim, justifying compromises on policy in order to keep coalitions together.

Spending time on the opposition benches, facing the same government, also tended to increase the areas of agreement among the other parties. Cumann na nGaedheal was not close to Labour. Fine Gael became (relatively) close. The cynical could argue that simple hunger for office overcame differences. But in part those differences were lessened by the imperative to combine forces in the legislature to oppose the government of the day. The first inter-party government added to the pressures forcing Fine Gael and Labour, in particular, closer together. The second such experiment followed quickly, before a fallow period for coalitions of sixteen years. But once the initial ice had been broken, it became easier to conceive of coalition arrangements in future.

Many years later, before a spell in Government Buildings rescued his own political fortunes, John Bruton was asked about the possibility of Fine Gael returning to office. Admitting that it could only do so as part of a coalition involving at least three parties, he praised the first inter-party government as 'one of the most successful governments this state ever had', adding that although it only lasted three years, 'it is an example that once there is a will to co-operate . . . a government will go extremely well'.[12]

His enthusiasm was perhaps due to one of the most important long-term effects of the change of government in 1948 – the rescue of Fine Gael from seemingly terminal decline. The similarities with 1994 and the formation of the Rainbow Coalition can also be seen in the fate of the junior partners in the arrangement – in both 1951 and 1997, electoral reward for Fine Gael meant disaster for their coalition allies.

Quite apart from the electoral consequences, the first inter-party government provides a fascinating case study, with the number of parties involved making it unique in Irish experience. No subsequent Taoiseach has had to perform a juggling act comparable to that carried out by John A. Costello. But many could have learned from his methods. So too could the leaders of smaller parties. If the first inter-party government has any overriding message, it is that junior partners in coalition governments need to convince at least some of the members of the larger party before they can make significant policy advances.

Recent events in Irish politics suggest that coalition governments are here to stay. A look at the first such administration may, therefore, prove timely.

ONE

PUT THEM OUT!

I drove into Tuam and I saw there the large physique of a man, a civic guard, who was standing on the footpath. I pulled in diagonally and lowered my window.

'Guard, is there any news from Dublin?'

'At ten past five this afternoon, Mr John Aloysius Costello was elected Taoiseach of this country.'

I knew by the way he said it, that this really meant something to him and I said: 'Guard, would you like a drink?'

'We'll have two.'

'Will you wait a minute, until I park this car?'

'Leave it where it is. We have freedom for the first time in sixteen years.'

We had more than one drink that day.

Patrick Lindsay[1]

As Patrick Lindsay and his friendly garda celebrated the election of John A. Costello as Taoiseach on that February day in 1948, they were marking more than the end of sixteen years of Fianna Fáil rule. Nineteen-forty-eight was one of the crucial years of Irish democracy. Just as 1922 showed that the majority had the right to decide the future of the state, and 1932 proved that the losers of the Civil War could with time reverse that defeat through democratic politics, so 1948 indicated to the opponents of Fianna Fáil that it was, after all, possible to beat Dev.

The change of government was important in another way. It was the first time that an 'alien' concept, coalition, had been tried out in Ireland. That coalition was regarded as abnormal is amply demonstrated by the new government's insistence on the term 'inter-party'.

But despite its novelty the first Costello administration proved to be a revelation. It was expected to last a year. Instead it remained in office for nearly three and a half. While there is much to criticise in those forty months, there is also much to praise.

Entering the 1948 election, Fianna Fáil could have been forgiven for overconfidence, particularly given the weakness of Fine Gael and the disarray in the Labour ranks. But there were reasons for caution too – the emergence of a new republican party which echoed many of the themes of an earlier Fianna Fáil was one; signs of increased co-operation among the opposition parties was another. In any event, after sixteen years in power, Fianna Fáil's position was relatively weak, quite apart from the general impression that the party was jaded.[2]

Between 1939 and 1946, the cost of living index rose by about two-thirds, but the average weekly earnings of industrial workers rose by only one-third.[3] After the war, the Minister for Finance, Frank Aiken, acted on the assumption that inflation would prove temporary, as it had following the First World War, and food subsidies were introduced to help the public with essential supplies. But the inflation persisted, and the subsidies ate up an increasing share of taxation, leading eventually to the Supplementary Budget of 1947, a highly unpopular measure which increased taxes on beer, cigarettes and cinema tickets.

Then there was a series of 'scandals' which, it was claimed, demonstrated a certain ethical laxity on the part of Fianna Fáil ministers. In fact, it was more a sign of carelessness (and arrogance) after so many years in office, and of the opposition's eagerness to use anything to discredit the government. Dr Con Ward, the Parliamentary Secretary to the Minister for Local Government and Public Health, was forced to resign after an inquiry into his involvement with a bacon factory in Monaghan. Seán Lemass was tainted by allegations that a friend had been involved in irregularities on the stock market. And then there was the proposed sale of Locke's Distillery in Kilbeggan, Co. Westmeath to foreign nationals, where Eamon de Valera was supposed to have sold out the national interest for the sake of a gold watch.[4]

A Department of the Taoiseach memo noted the 'significant and interesting fact that these allegations of corruption against the government are timed, to a remarkable extent, to coincide with pending by-elections . . . The allegations re. the reported sale of Locke's Distillery were first made in the Dáil . . . within a week of the by-elections which are taking place today . . .'[5]

In the event, a tribunal of inquiry into the sale of Locke's found no evidence against anyone, except Independent TD Oliver J. Flanagan, one of the first to make allegations of corruption. The tribunal called him 'very uncandid and most disposed to answer questions unthinkingly and as if he were directing his replies elsewhere than to the Tribunal'.[6]

Flanagan was unabashed, telling de Valera three days after the report came out that 'people are not surprised at report . . . right will win out eventually'.[7] In the event, Flanagan got the highest first preference vote in the country in the 1948 election – 14,369, or over 30 per cent of the vote in a five-seat constituency.[8] He celebrated his victory with another telegram to de Valera: 'Leix–Offaly's answer to Locke Tribunal leaves no doubt as to belief in existence of corruption. Eagerly awaiting assembly of Dáil Éireann to reopen this and other similar public scandals.'[9]

A long-running teachers' strike in 1946 also proved to be a disaster for Fianna Fáil, not just because it alienated a normally favourable sector, but because it became, in the words of one observer, 'an electoral runway rolled out in front of a new party waiting to take off'.[10] It was this new party, wearing the radical and republican clothes of an earlier Fianna Fáil, which swung the balance towards the opposition in 1948.

During its sixteen years in office, Fianna Fáil moved towards the centre. But while this move served to deprive Fine Gael of support, it also opened ground to Fianna Fáil's left.[11] Clann na Poblachta, which tried to occupy this ground, grew out of protest at the government's treatment of republican prisoners. At the beginning of 1945, lawyers Con Lehane and Seán MacBride set up the Republican Prisoners Release Association. Its constitution stated that it 'has no connection with any political party, and its appeal is directed to all freedom-loving men and women who believe in the right of Ireland to be free from foreign aggression in any form'.[12]

Both of its founders had Irish Republican Army links. MacBride had been co-opted as chief of staff of the IRA in 1936 but was later defeated in an election for that post at an IRA convention[13] and left the organisation shortly afterwards. Lehane had been imprisoned for IRA membership in 1935[14] and was interned for a short time during the Emergency, despite his association with MacBride and the group which left the IRA with him.[15] Clann TD Jack McQuillan later claimed that six of his colleagues elected in 1948 had strong IRA links: MacBride, Lehane, John Tully, Patrick Kinnane, Michael Fitzpatrick and Joseph Brennan. He also claimed that 'the Clann was run by the IRA men who had been around MacBride'.[16] It should be stressed that these were former rather than current IRA members[17] – participation in electoral politics was not consistent with 'army' membership.

The prisoner problem raised by the Prisoners Release Association became more acute for the government when Seán McCaughey, a prisoner in Portlaoise, refused food from 19 April 1946, and liquids five days later. The embarrassment was compounded by the fact that McCaughey, a Northerner in a Southern jail, was on hunger strike at the same time as David Fleming, a Southerner in a Northern jail.[18]

At the beginning of May, seventeen TDs and three senators petitioned the government to release McCaughey 'so that his life may be saved', but he died in the early hours of 11 May.[19] In the same month, Fleming was released by the Stormont government.[20] On 29 May, a motion in the name of Michael Donnellan of Clann na Talmhan calling for an investigation by a select committee of the Dáil into McCaughey's treatment was defeated by sixty-six votes to fourteen, with Fine Gael supporting the government, and Labour and the Farmers behind Donnellan.[21]

The following day, Noel Hartnett, a Fianna Fáil activist who was close to MacBride, was banned from acting as a radio compère by the Minister for Posts and Telegraphs, P.J. Little, because of his role in the hunger-strike agitation.[22] This pushed him further into MacBride's camp, where his political experience was to prove crucial. Hartnett moved into the lodge of MacBride's home[23] and was referred to jocularly as 'the Shadow of the Shadow of a Gunman'.[24]

MacBride's performance at the McCaughey inquest was a triumph, forcing the prison medical officer to admit that he 'wouldn't treat a dog in that fashion'. The Fianna Fáil Minister for Justice, Gerald Boland, attacked MacBride in the Dáil, claiming that 'he trapped this man into making a remark which was not quite correct . . . I saw juries being handled by Mr MacBride myself at another inquest, and I must say my feeling was one of pity for the jurors. I would not expect them to give any other verdict than the verdict they gave . . .'[25]

Speaking to a Fianna Fáil meeting in Roscommon a month later, Boland laid down the gauntlet to the Prisoners Release Association. 'Is it too much to ask them to repudiate terrorism and put a programme before the people for the next General Election? If they get the support of the majority the government will be handed over to them as peacefully as the late government handed it to us, or they could help the party which seems to support them in the Dáil, Clann na Talmhan, to try to get a majority.'[26]

It was a challenge MacBride was ready to accept, and on 6 July 1946, Clann na Poblachta was formed. MacBride outlined his ideas at a meeting in the Mansion House in Dublin early in 1947. He told his audience that if there was to be any hope of ending partition, social and economic conditions in the South would have to be made at least equal to those in the North.[27] He also called for Northern elected representatives to be allowed enter the Dáil, a point underlined by the presence at the meeting of the Republican MP for the Falls in Belfast, Harry Diamond.[28]

The new party was to be radical as well as republican. MacBride said that 'if we get a republic in name it would mean nothing unless it ensured economic and social freedom for all the people of the country. We have to ensure that no section of the people will be exploited by another section.'[29] The Clann called for full employment, based on a minimum wage related to the cost of living, with the state undertaking the responsibility of providing work 'for every man and woman in the country who is willing and able';[30] but at the same time it adopted a social welfare plan devised by Bishop John Dignan of Clonfert, at least in part to answer allegations of communism.[31]

At around this time, an official in the United States legation in Dublin reported that 'in the overall picture of Irish politics' the Clann did not 'loom large', although 'there is the possibility that it might become part of a bloc of malcontents made up of the Labour Party and several of the Farmers' groups. This could be of importance, inasmuch as there is no upper middle class in Éire which could be relied upon to support the government if such a movement became widespread.'[32] The party's growing confidence was demonstrated in May 1947, when it decided to contest two of the three upcoming by-elections, as well as every constituency in the next general election.[33]

There was a fairly clear division within the party between, on the one hand, the republicans and, on the other hand, radicals like Noël Browne, attracted by the Clann's social policy. It is sometimes suggested that the republicans wanted to use the radicals to extend their electoral appeal. For instance, Browne claimed that the Clann only wanted him to help elect his running mate in Dublin South-East, Donal O'Donoghue, a former quartermaster-general in the IRA under MacBride. However, this should be taken with a pinch of salt, as Browne had already secured a high profile within the party. A more concrete example was Roscommon, where the Clann's general secretary Michael Kelly shared the party ticket with county footballer Jack McQuillan. Kelly was reported to have said that 'with McQuillan's boots and my brains, I'll be elected in Roscommon!'[34] This rivalry between the two factions eventually destroyed the Clann. But it should be noted that the radicals were not entirely innocent in generating bad feeling – John A. Murphy has noted the 'condescending attitude of some progressives to the simple nationalist faith of the republican rank-and-file'.[35]

De Valera used the threat from the new party to try to extract concessions from the British, telling Commonwealth Secretary Philip Noel-Baker in November 1947 that the effective opposition to his party was on the left, and that MacBride 'would always concentrate attention on grievances against Great Britain . . . For this reason, it was desirable to remove such grievances.' Specifically, de Valera asked him to consider the release of IRA prisoners in order to stop Clann na Poblachta using them to 'stir up hostility',[36] which was a bit rich as the Clann had its roots in protest against the treatment of prisoners by the Dublin government!

Another relatively new arrival on the political scene was Clann na Talmhan, which contested its first general election in 1943. Supported by smaller farmers, especially in the west, its emergence has been called 'a symptom of the frustration and impotence of small farmers who felt themselves ignored and misunderstood by a remote government and bureaucracy and exploited by big business and rapacious unions'.[37] Michael Donnellan, who was elected to the Dáil and the party leadership in 1943, only held the post for one year, resigning because he felt 'that honours should rotate'.[38] His successor as party leader was the Mayo South TD, Joseph Blowick, who had also entered the Dáil in 1943.

Although at first the party voiced an equal distaste for the two main parties, the evidence of transfer patterns indicates that its supporters had a greater dislike for Fianna Fáil, presumably because it was in government. In the general election of 1944, Fine Gael got almost six times as many Clann na Talmhan transfers as Fianna Fáil, and a similar pattern was seen in 1948.[39] However, the rise of Clann na Talmhan took votes off both major parties, with Fine Gael's vote in Connaught–Ulster falling from 33 to 23 per cent in the 1943 election, while Fianna Fáil fell from 52 to 42 per cent.[40]

A problem faced by Clann na Talmhan was its confinement to the western seaboard. The party attempted to overcome this by merging with the Farmers' Federation of Leinster, which represented large farm interests.[41] But the outcome of this experiment proved that farming and land differed so widely across the country that farmers nationally had little in common.[42] In the words of one observer, 'the Western representatives of Clann na Talmhan [are] following a bold and challenging line on the question of land division, while the midland supporters tend to abandon the party in favour of the ultra-conservative Fine Gael. There is no unifying element to make a farmers party an enduring political force.'[43] The large farm element quickly departed, leaving Clann na Talmhan to represent small farmer interests in the west[44] and to remain 'essentially a conservative party'[45] with no major party aspirations.[46]

One reason for the emergence of these new parties was the weakness of the main opposition party, Fine Gael, the successor to Cumann na nGaedheal, the party of government of the state's first decade. Its image was not improved by the fact that when William Cosgrave retired in 1944 the new leader, Richard Mulcahy, didn't even have a seat in the Dáil. The quality and commitment of other members of the front bench can be gauged from the search for a leader in the Dáil. James Dillon, who had left Fine Gael because of his opposition to neutrality, declined an approach from Patrick

McGilligan to become leader, deputy leader, or even a member of the front bench as long as the war lasted, 'gladly as I would serve in any of these capacities in different circumstances, under Dick Mulcahy's leadership'.[47]

A further sign of weakness was Fine Gael's failure to contest four of the five by-elections in 1945 because, according to Mulcahy, the party simply couldn't find candidates prepared to stand.[48] The reluctance of potential candidates may be explained by the results: in all five by-elections Fianna Fáil received more than 50 per cent of the vote, with the highest proportion – 67.9 per cent – being won in the only contest featuring a Fine Gael candidate.[49] Part of the problem was the antipathy towards constituency work which W.T. Cosgrave bequeathed to his party – many members of the front bench considered it 'undignified' to organise branches and contest local elections. This attitude dated back to the days of Cumann na nGaedheal, when 'organisation' consisted of 'sending letters to influential men asking their aid'.[50] Despite Mulcahy's efforts, travelling the country on an autocycle (a bicycle with a small motor attached), it was hard to change this attitude.[51]

In April 1947, the party's deputy leader, Dr T.F. (Tom) O'Higgins, wrote to newspapers suggesting 'some form of amalgamation or association' between Fine Gael, Clann na Talmhan, Independent Farmers and Independents. The *Irish Times* interpreted this as 'a coalition of Opposition parties', but in fact O'Higgins seemed to be suggesting a new party.[52] Liam Cosgrave, the most promising young TD in the party, responded in an outspoken letter to Mulcahy. He agreed that Fine Gael was incapable of forming a government on its own, but felt that a 'coalition or merger is extremely unlikely, if not an impossibility'. After criticising the commitment of the front bench, the state of party organisation and the lack of clear policy formulation, Cosgrave concluded: 'I cannot any longer conscientiously ask the public to support the party as a party, and in the circumstances I do not propose to speak at meetings outside my constituency.'[53] It was an extraordinary vote of no confidence in the future of Fine Gael.

However, it was not all gloom for the party. In November 1947, Mulcahy wrote out a list of thirteen younger candidates he hoped would contest the next general election. Eight of them did in fact run, and four were elected – Tom jun. and Michael O'Higgins, Eamonn Rooney and Seán Collins – while the other four performed well enough: John Douglas got 10 per cent of the first preference vote, Thomas Roe got 12.5 per cent, while Patrick Lindsay and James Trainor scored just over 5 per cent each.[54]

Michael Gallagher sees the number of new candidates as a signal that Fine Gael's fortunes had actually turned before the party entered government in 1948. In 1944, the party nominated only twenty-five candidates who were not outgoing TDs, with one being elected. In 1948, sixty candidates were not outgoing TDs, and thirteen were elected. 'Between 1938 and 1944 the Fine Gael label had not been enough to ensure the election of a candidate not already entrenched and with his own personal following, but the influx of new TDs in 1948 suggests that, despite the fact that Fine Gael's overall percentage vote declined, the purely party vote increased between 1944 and 1948. If this is indeed the case, then Fine Gael's revival pre-dated the 1948 election and was not simply a consequence of Fine Gael's membership of the inter-party government.'[55] However, it should be noted that there had been a very heavy rate of attrition among the Fine Gael deputies elected in 1944: three had died, one became a judge, two didn't contest the 1948 election, and two ran as Independents. Four sitting Fine Gael TDs lost their seats in 1948, but all had suffered extensive constituency revisions.[56] These twelve absentees, along with a larger Dáil, explain why thirteen new Fine Gael deputies were elected – there was plenty of space for them, even with the existing 'purely party vote'.

While Fine Gael appeared to be suffering from anaemia, Labour's problems were even more severe, with the party divided into two bitterly opposed factions. The split came when Labour was doing better politically than for many years – becoming the largest group on Dublin Corporation in the 1942 local elections and having its best general election showing since 1927 the following year, going from nine to seventeen deputies. One of the newly elected TDs was James Larkin sen., and the Irish Transport and General Workers' Union (ITGWU) immediately demanded his expulsion from the parliamentary party. Party leader William Norton failed to calm the situation, and the ITGWU disaffiliated in January 1944. Five of the eight TDs backed by the union left the party to form the National Labour Party, under the leadership of James Everett of Wicklow.[57] The split in political Labour in 1944 was followed by the division of congress, with Irish-based unions forming the Congress of Irish Unions (CIU) in April 1945, leaving the Irish Trade Union Congress (ITUC) in the hands of the amalgamateds, or British-based unions.

Although rooted in personalities, the split was represented in starkly ideological terms, with the ITGWU claiming that Labour had been infiltrated by communists: 'The Labour Party has allowed the virus of Communism to enter its system too deeply to permit of any hope of its recovering its independence as the political expression of Irish working class interests.'[58] This was somewhat ironic, as one activist recorded that 'the leaders of the Labour Party . . . regarded even the mention of Connolly's name with deep suspicion. Socialism, too, was a dirty word . . .'[59] The split almost halved the Labour vote – in the 1944 election, the main party won eight seats and 8.7 per cent of the vote, a drop of just under seven percentage points, while National Labour got 2.7 per cent and four seats.

The opposition, then, was not in great shape to fight an election in February 1948. Labour was split, Fine Gael appeared to be in danger of imminent collapse, and Clann na Poblachta needed more time to put an organisation in place to fight a general election. But under the surface, there were signs that the opposition parties were beginning to consider a co-operative approach, which would prove the undoing of Fianna Fáil. The fact that Mulcahy had taken over from Cosgrave also helped – Cosgrave 'was accustomed to leading a government comprising a single party with deputies loyal to him and to the common policy. A multiplicity of parties in government would, to him, have been unthinkable.'[60]

There is some evidence in transfer patterns to support the view that voters saw the logic of co-operation.[61] In the 1945 presidential election (the first such contest), Patrick McCartan ran as an Independent, with the support of Labour, Clann na Talmhan, and some Independents. He won 19.6 per cent of the vote, compared to 30.9 per cent for Fine Gael's Seán MacEoin and 49.5 per cent for Seán T. O'Kelly of Fianna Fáil. The most significant pointer for the future was the destination of his transfers – over 55 per cent of which went to MacEoin, compared to 12.8 per cent to O'Kelly, and 31.8 per cent non-transferable.[62]

Clann na Poblachta's victory in two of the three by-elections in October 1947 – with Seán MacBride in Dublin County and Patrick Kinnane in Tipperary – was due to transfers from the other opposition parties. More than half of Labour's transfers went to the new party, while 47.7 per cent of Fine Gael's did likewise[63] – astounding on the face of it, given their positions on the left–right scale.

As we have seen, Fine Gael was unable to contest four of the five by-elections in 1945. However, by the first half of 1947 party morale was beginning to pick up. The Fine Gael organisation in Tipperary was anxious to have the by-election caused by the death of William O'Donnell of Clann na Talmhan held as quickly as possible. Mulcahy resisted the pressure to move the writ for the by-election himself, preferring to wait until Clann na Talmhan did so, as tradition demanded. His replies to the pleas of local activists made it clear that his motive was not reluctance to face the electorate: rather he wanted to have the maximum possible co-operation among the opposition parties. In May 1947 he wrote to the secretary of the Tipperary constituency executive: 'I cannot myself see that anything but harm would be done both for the Tipperary by-election and for our hope of harmoniously gathering general strength to beat Fianna Fáil in the general election if I, as leader of Fine Gael, move this writ.' He told another local activist two days later that to do so would 'do damage between the farmers and ourselves'.[64]

Although Tom O'Higgins had suggested combination of the opposition parties, it was Mulcahy himself who did most to bring this about, although there was little support from other prominent party members – even his son wrote to him from London warning that such an idea was impractical.[65] There had been various moves towards forming a new 'National Party' in 1947, centred on disgruntled members of Fine Gael and Clann na Talmhan who attempted to draw James Dillon into the arrangement. Mulcahy firmly rejected such moves. 'Even if Fine Gael was to go down . . . I would prefer to stick to Fine Gael going down flying a clear unmistakable flag than bury its tradition in any kind of [new] Party . . .'[66]

Dillon – still an Independent TD – continued to try to bring Clann na Talmhan closer to Fine Gael, and he reported this attempt to the American legation in November 1947, adding the observation that Labour would support such an alliance, as would Clann na Poblachta, 'in the negative sense that Seán MacBride's bitterness towards de Valera is intense'.[67] However, within a month Dillon informed his friends that his attempt had failed.[68] But by then, the country was on the verge of a general election.

Worried by the threat from the new party, Seán MacEntee, the Minister for Local Government, introduced the Electoral Amendment Bill 1947, which, despite a decline in the population, increased the number of TDs from 138 to 147, the maximum allowed under the constitution. He also increased the number of three-seat constituencies from fifteen to twenty-two and abolished the three seven-seaters, moves which favoured the largest party. The revision was 'an explicit effort . . . to distort the effect of electoral preferences by lowering average constituency size'.[69] The average number of TDs per constituency was reduced from 4.1 to 3.7.[70] MacEntee justified his actions in the Dáil by claiming that it was necessary to 'provide . . . a government which will be stable and capable of acting with authority, decision and leadership . . .'[71] These changes, and their effects, are discussed in more detail below.

In another attempt to wrong-foot Clann na Poblachta, de Valera decided to hold an election before the new party was ready, and fifteen months before it was necessary, announcing the decision to go to the country on 21 December, two days after the Locke Tribunal reported.

The campaign, not surprisingly given the time of year, was fought in bad weather. There were floods throughout the country at the beginning of January,[72] while later in the month there were snow falls of two to six inches, with heavy drifts in places and ice-bound roads.[73] A more serious problem for the parties, particularly Fine Gael, was the mortality rate among candidates. James Hughes, the Fine Gael TD for Carlow–Kilkenny, collapsed and died while addressing an election meeting;[74] Sligo Fine Gael TD Martin

Roddy died a week later;[75] the death of Eamonn Coogan, the second Fine Gael TD for Carlow–Kilkenny, led to the election being postponed in that constituency until 10 February;[76] and on the eve of polling day, Fianna Fáil candidate John J. Keane died at his home in Connemara. Voting in Galway West had already begun on the islands, so it had to continue, and if Keane had been elected there would have been a by-election.[77]

When nominations closed on 21 January, there were 406 candidates for the 146 seats (excluding the Ceann Comhairle), a record number, and one not surpassed until 1987, when 466 candidates went forward.[78] Both elections saw the emergence of new parties – the Progressive Democrats in 1987 and Clann na Poblachta in 1948, which ran ninety-three candidates, more than any other party except Fianna Fáil.

While the Clann na Talmhan candidates and many of the Independents were naturally farmers, and more than half of the Labour candidates were either trade union officials or workers, the candidates of the other parties were slightly more diverse. The largest categories in Fianna Fáil were farmers (43) and businessmen (32), while in Fine Gael businessmen were in the lead (30), followed by lawyers and farmers (both 19). Surprisingly for a party derided in some circles as the political wing of the Law Library, only fourteen of the Clann na Poblachta candidates were lawyers, compared to twenty teachers, fifteen farmers, and fourteen businessmen.[79] These figures indicate that Clann na Poblachta, at least in this period, was a broad-based party similar to Fianna Fáil and Fine Gael, rather than being confined to a single class.[80]

The main thrust of the Fianna Fáil campaign was that 'everything is coming right for us!'[81] and that 'the Dev you know is better than the devil you don't'.[82] In case such bland optimism was not enough, the governing party used the odd political 'stroke' as well. The Minister for Health, Dr Jim Ryan, announced just over a week before the election that he was going to allow the health authorities to make weekly payments to 'people who are being treated for certain infectious diseases or who are probable sources of infection'. This gesture to the TB vote was expected to cost the Exchequer a quarter of a million pounds a year.[83] The Fianna Fáil programme promised a 'reasonable measure of compulsory tillage, with a reduced tillage quota and with full freedom as to the crops to be grown'[84] – clearly an attempt to make the best of an unpopular policy.

Fine Gael was expected to 'make the most determined effort in 15 years to unseat the Government'.[85] The party's main concerns were the reduction of the cost of living, through lower state expenditure which would lead to tax cuts, and 'an end to jobbery'.[86] Patrick McGilligan in his election notes stressed the removal of the Supplementary Budget taxes, through reducing expenditure on 'Aer Lingus, Cosmic Rays, Tourist Hotels, Army'. He also condemned the 'socialist ideas' contained in the Sinn Féin Funds Bill and the 1947 Health Act.[87]

Clann na Poblachta made quite a stir with the first party political broadcast, an eight-minute film covering emigration, unemployment, and food prices, among other issues. According to cameraman Brendan Stafford, nothing in the film was faked. 'We showed it as it was. If we showed bare-footed newsboys, there were bare-footed newsboys – we didn't ask them to take their shoes off.'[88] Noel Hartnett narrated the film, while Noël Browne discussed TB. One reason for the success of the project was the enthusiasm of cinema owners. By early February, they were claiming that the Supplementary Budget tax on tickets had cut audiences by a quarter,[89] and as a result were 'only too happy' to show the Clann's film.[90]

MacBride also wanted to use radio; he wrote to de Valera on 13 January claiming that the bad weather made it difficult for parties to get their message across at public meetings. 'Owing to the time of year at which it has been decided to hold a General Election, I would suggest that ample time should be afforded on the Radio to enable the policies to be set forth fully for the information of the people.' The secretary of the Department of the Taoiseach, Maurice Moynihan, replied two days later that 'it is not considered desirable to depart from the long standing rule that the national broadcasting service should not be used for the purpose of political party controversy'.[91]

Among Clann na Poblachta's aims, set out in an election leaflet for Dublin South-Central, were the elimination of jobbery; a comprehensive social insurance scheme; full employment; abolition of slums; a reduced cost of living through subsidies for essential foodstuffs; provision of sanatoria for TB victims; free education up to and including university level; and freedom and independence for all Ireland as a democratic republic.[92]

There were wildly exaggerated forecasts of Clann na Poblachta's electoral prospects: the *Irish Times*'s political correspondent predicted the party would become 'the third largest – if not the second largest – to emerge from the contest'.[93] The party received extensive media attention. The *Irish Times*, which backed Fine Gael rather than the Clann, gave more prominence on its front page to the latter than to the former, or even to Fianna Fáil.[94] MacBride's final rally in Dublin's city centre was reported on the front page, side by side with de Valera. Mulcahy, speaking in Clonmel, was relegated to page three.[95] But no amount of media coverage could overcome the Clann's organisational weakness – the party had an average of only six branches in each constituency.[96]

Labour leader Bill Norton told his final rally in Dublin that Labour would use its position after the election to reduce and control prices, extend social services, conduct an inquiry into education, form a National Housing Council to build houses for ordinary people, and increase agricultural and industrial production.[97] The party also advocated the nationalisation of the transport company, Córas Iompair Éireann (CIÉ), and the flour-milling industry.

The main themes of the opposition, then, were the rising cost of living, especially the Supplementary Budget, and the alleged 'squandermania' of the government which was supposed to have caused it. Plans for a transatlantic air service, the size of the army, and recent increases in ministerial salaries were subjected to attack by all the opposition parties. (It should be noted in relation to the last point that the new government at its first meeting decided to keep such remuneration at the new, increased, level.[98]) Fianna Fáil was also accused of 'jobbery', or giving positions within the gift of the state only to party supporters.

Fianna Fáil's response was to accuse Clann na Poblachta of communism. Seán MacEntee's fondness for this task led the *Irish Times* to describe him as a 'political Don Quixote tilting gaily at Communist windmills and smelling Bolsheviks behind every bush . . .'[99] De Valera also warned of the dangers facing the electorate, reminding them that 'the individual ought to keep a firm grip on his liberty . . . the road to a slave state and serfdom is broad and easy, but the road to sturdy independence is not'.[100]

The Clann managed to hit back with the 'Russian jewels scandal'. This matter first came to light on 18 January, when Patrick McCartan, the former presidential candidate now running for the Clann in Cork, revealed that a Soviet representative in the USA in 1919–20 gave an agent of the Irish Republic jewels as security against a loan of between ten and twenty thousand dollars.[101] McCartan had been in America at the time with de Valera, where they disagreed about relations with the Soviets. McCartan favoured developing links with the USSR, while de Valera was opposed.[102] De Valera confirmed that the loan had not been repaid and that the jewels were in the possession of the government, after being handed over by a 'private individual' after Fianna Fáil came to power in 1932.[103] In fact, the jewels had been brought back to Ireland by Harry Boland and given to Michael Collins, but following an argument between the two men, they were returned to Boland the same evening. The jewels were retained in the Boland family until 1932.[104]

Fine Gael's Dan Morrissey worked up a fine head of steam, accusing de Valera of helping 'in laying the foundations of Communism',[105] while James Dillon said that Fianna Fáil had made Ireland 'a pawnshop for the Bolshevists'.[106] The Soviets finally repaid the loan in September 1949,[107] after representations by MacBride.[108]

Of course, the Clann was not the only target for anti-communists, with the split in the Labour Party leading to more red-baiting. National Labour leader James Everett claimed there was 'intrigue and infiltration among members of the Labour Party, and those who had spent time in Moscow and had been fighting for Marshal Tito were the real rulers behind the scenes'.[109] Labour TD William Davin had already said that if Everett could name any Labour candidates who had associations with 'the mysterious Communist Party in this country', he would be given the opportunity to prove his case before a civil or ecclesiastical court.[110]

While the North rarely intruded on the campaign, there was limited discussion of the link with the Commonwealth. Both Labour and Clann na Poblachta made clear their antipathy to the External Relations Act 1936, which was central to this link. One of Norton's attacks on the Act led the British representative in Dublin, Lord Rugby, to note that while 'there is no real feeling against the working of the . . . Act . . . it does furnish the opponents of any government with a cheap form of attack. Mr de Valera seems particularly sensitive to it . . .'[111]

Fine Gael's position was less clear on this issue, despite Mulcahy's commitment that the party would not change the Act: 'Any final form for the Irish state or description of it can be settled only when partition has passed away and the Irish people as a whole from Fair Head to Mizen Head wish to decide.'[112] Rugby noted that this speech came a day after Tom O'Higgins attacked the External Relations Act. 'It is indicative of the way in which the Fine Gael party mismanage their affairs that General Mulcahy . . . should now come out with the firm pronouncement . . . in favour of not altering the present constitution in relation to external affairs, while one of his leading henchmen . . . has taken the contrary line . . .'[113]

Rugby felt that the constant attacks on the Act might persuade de Valera to promise to remove it during the election campaign. 'The threat to him comes from the Left . . . It might well be good tactics to rob the Left of their programme and to steal their thunder. If he does away with the . . . Act . . . he will remove a point of attack against his government and take a good card out of his opponents' hand . . .'[114] However, despite the fact that legislation to repeal the Act had been prepared,[115] de Valera held his hand on the issue during the campaign.

One other issue received a lengthy airing – coalition. It was quite obvious that the only way there would be a change of government was through some form of coalition, the only previous example of which had been the participation by the leader of the Farmers' Party, Michael Heffernan, in the 1927–32 Cumann na nGaedheal administration, as Parliamentary Secretary to the Minister for Posts and Telegraphs.[116] Heffernan was allowed to attend meetings of the Executive Council (Cabinet) for a period, on the grounds that 'he never knew about certain things till they were decided'.[117] However, this arrangement held few pointers for a coalition involving separate and distinct parties: a merger with Cumann na nGaedheal had been considered *before* the September 1927 election,[118] and the Farmers were later absorbed by the larger party.

During the campaign, the spectre of coalition was frequently raised by Fianna Fáil. De Valera began the year by saying that coalitions 'had worked out disastrously in many countries',[119] claiming that this form of government 'had led to dictatorship in certain European countries'.[120] He called on the opposition to 'have their bargains now in the open, and do not let the people be asked to vote for them in the dark. That is what they are doing and they know it.'[121] Lemass also warned against coalition, saying that while 'other people may be prepared to haggle and bargain to get a make-shift majority for a coalition government with any or no policy, Fianna Fáil would not have any part of such manoeuvres'.[122]

Fianna Fáil in Dublin South-East warned the electorate that 'the five opposition parties are appealing to voters to bring about a change of government while they admit frankly they do not know, themselves, what the consequences would be . . . One of the Fine Gael candidates for this area . . . conceded that it would be necessary for such a government as he visualised to refrain for some years from dealing with problems about which "acute party differences exist" . . .'[123]

Not surprisingly, the opposition was less keen to talk about coalition, although Fine Gael senator, Gerry Sweetman, did point out that 'any talk of a party getting a clear majority in this election was merely a red herring to deceive the people. It was not going to happen.' He also claimed that the experience of recent years had shown that government by a party with a clear majority tended to 'become dictatorial', and that it was not necessary 'that the party forming the government should have a clear majority of its own',[124] which was just as well for Fine Gael!

Labour's Bill Norton said he was prepared to consider coalition, with the right partners. He would welcome the assistance of any progressive party in forming a government in the new Dáil that was prepared to 'implement a vigorous policy of expansion of production, to arrest emigration, to control prices and to provide a plan for social security'.[125] One of the Clann na Talmhan candidates, M.J. Finan, declared that 'his party would co-operate with the opposition group to give a good coalition government to the people if they indicated by their votes that they were tired of the Fianna Fáil adminis-tration'.[126]

The prospect of a coalition was being discussed in detail in the *Irish Times* by the middle of January, where it was suggested that Fianna Fáil might seek the support of National Labour, 'as on many questions the Congress of Irish Unions and National Labour have given critical support to the government in the past and have not been critical of the government during the election campaign. Fianna Fáil canvassers in many country areas are said to be advising their supporters to give their second preference votes to National Labour.' The paper also predicted that an agreement on a common programme between Clann na Poblachta and Labour, if they had enough TDs between them, 'is considered to be almost certain'.[127]

De Valera and MacBride held rival meetings in Dublin on the eve of polling, one at Nelson's Pillar, the other at the Bank of Ireland. Although Fianna Fáil attracted more of the twenty thousand people in attendance, neither meeting 'could claim to have been enthusiastic . . . Judging by the crowds surging in opposite directions over O'Connell Bridge, the predominant feeling was that something more interesting must be happening at the other meeting.'[128] Summing up the campaign, the *Irish Times* found that de Valera had drawn much smaller crowds than in 1944 and had stressed the need for strong government; Mulcahy was hampered by bad organisation and based his campaign on tax cuts and the abolition of squandermania; MacBride generated enthusiasm but no wild cheering, which was charitably attributed to the fact that 'the crowds were thinking, instead of bursting into enthusiasm for a single individual'.[129] Fianna Fáil predicted it would win a majority, while Fine Gael said it would hold what it had, and add to it. The former was wrong, while the latter was proved right by the slimmest of margins; but neither was as inaccurate as the Clann na Poblachta official who forecast that 'the government are going to get the greatest pasting ever. We expect to have at the lowest 45 and at the highest 75 seats.'[130]

Because of the delayed voting in Carlow–Kilkenny, there was no certainty about the final result even after all other seats had been filled. The *Irish Times* noted that 'Clann na Poblachta polled surprisingly few votes in most constituencies, many of their candidates losing their deposits'.[131] The *Irish Press* felt that 'the outstanding feature of the election was the complete collapse of Clann na Poblachta as a serious party contestant', also noting with some satisfaction that 'Clann na Talmhan has been reduced to a small local group'.[132]

Despite the nine extra Dáil seats available, Fianna Fáil lost eight seats – going from seventy-six to sixty-eight – and dropped seven percentage points nationally, to 41.8 per cent. The party's vote decreased in all regions, but the most catastrophic decline was in Dublin, where it fell by an alarming thirteen percentage points.

The extensive constituency revisions carried out before the election failed to protect Fianna Fáil's position, largely because the drop in its first preference vote caused by the intervention of Clann na Poblachta prevented it taking the second seat in some of the new three-seat constituencies. But despite this, the precision of the surgery carried out on some of Fianna Fáil's main problem areas was impressive. The party's worst performance in 1944 had been in Leitrim, where it was beaten into second place (with just 26.8 per cent of the vote) by Independent Ben Maguire. Another poor area was Sligo, where Fine Gael received more first preferences. Under the boundary revision, these two three-seaters were combined into one five-seat constituency. The area had elected two Fianna Fáil TDs, three Fine Gael and one Independent in 1944. In 1948, despite winning just 30.3 per cent of the vote in the new constituency, its lowest share of the vote nationally, Fianna Fáil managed to retain two seats, while Fine Gael lost its third seat.

However, efforts to improve Fianna Fáil chances in the Cork region, where the party's first preference vote was relatively poor in 1944, backfired. The two four-seaters, one five-seater and one three-seater were reorganised into one five-seat and four three-seat constituencies, a gain of one seat. In 1944 Fianna Fáil won eight seats in Cork, compared to two each for Fine Gael, Labour, Clann na Talmhan and Independents. The assumption was that Fianna Fáil could take a second seat in each of the three-seaters. But in the event, Cork returned six Fianna Fáil, three Fine Gael, four Labour, one National Labour, two Clann na Talmhan, and one Independent TD.

Dublin was also redrawn, with one seven-seat, two five-seat and two three-seat constituencies, a total of twenty-three seats, becoming three five-seat and five three-seat constituencies, a total of thirty seats. The five-seat Dublin County constituency was divided into two three-seaters, Dublin County north of the city, and Dún Laoghaire/Rathdown to the south; without the intervention of Clann na Poblachta, Fianna Fáil could have expected to win two seats in the first, and possibly in the second. The removal of the seven-seater obviously favoured the larger parties, but Fianna Fáil's problem in Dublin was the dramatic drop in its vote caused by the intervention of Clann na Poblachta, a situation which no amount of redrawn boundaries could help. Despite the extra seats, Fianna Fáil won just eleven seats in Dublin, compared to fourteen in 1944, while Fine Gael gained two to eight, Labour gained one to three, there was one extra Independent, and Clann na Poblachta took six.

A far more successful piece of boundary revision occurred in Galway, where a four-seater and a three-seater became three three-seat constituencies, a gain of two seats compared to an increase in the electorate of just 3,000. One of the constituencies, Galway South, returned Ceann Comhairle Frank Fahy automatically and so became in effect a two-seater. With 64.3 per cent of the vote, Fianna Fáil won both seats in contention. The party also won two seats in the other Galway constituencies, compared to one Fine Gael and one Clann na Talmhan TD. In 1944, there were five Fianna Fáil TDs from Galway, again with one each for Fine Gael and Clann na Talmhan. The redrawing of the boundaries added two to the Fianna Fáil total.

Fine Gael's share of the national vote also dropped, by just over half a percentage point, bringing it below 20 per cent (19.8 per cent) for the first time, although the party managed to win an extra seat, giving it thirty-one TDs (in a larger Dáil, of course – the party's percentage of seats fell from 21.7 to 21.1 per cent).

Nationally, the votes for the two Labour parties were more or less unchanged, at 8.7 for Labour and 2.6 per cent for National Labour. But the electoral results were extremely encouraging, with Labour winning fourteen seats, an extra six, while the National Labour total increased by one to five. The Labour vote was up marginally in Leinster and Munster but dropped two percentage points in Dublin.

Clann na Talmhan's vote was halved, from 10.8 to 5.6 per cent, and the party won seven seats, a loss of four (although two former

Clann na Talmhan deputies, Patrick O'Reilly in Cavan and Patrick Cogan in Wicklow, were returned as Independents). All the party's seats were now in just five counties – Cork (2), Kerry, Galway, Mayo (2), and Roscommon.

On its first outing, Clann na Poblachta gained the support of 13.2 per cent of the voters and won ten seats. The party had a particularly strong showing in Dublin, winning 19.3 per cent of the vote and six seats, making it the third largest party in the capital. But the party's performance was not simply a metropolitan affair – the Clann got 9 per cent of first preferences in Leinster, 12 per cent in Munster and 14 per cent in Connaught–Ulster, and won seats in Cavan, Roscommon and the two Tipperary constituencies.[133]

However, this was far from the total expected by MacBride, and the decision to put up so many candidates served merely to split the Clann vote, losing the party a number of seats. In four constituencies, the Clann candidates secured a higher proportion of the first preference vote but lost out to a single candidate from another party – to Labour in Dublin County (17.3 per cent against 15.9 per cent) and Dublin North-Central (18.1 per cent against 16.3 per cent), to National Labour in Kerry North (16.5 per cent against 16.3 per cent), and to Fine Gael in Kerry South (20.3 per cent to 18.9 per cent). Part of the problem was that the Clann did not have established candidates in most constituencies, so many were selected in the weeks immediately before the election[134] and were considered at the time 'nonentities selected at short notice'.[135] With no idea of how popular various candidates might be, the party was forced to run more than might otherwise have been the case. The number of candidates was a sign of weakness, rather than strength.

Another demonstration of the folly of putting up so many candidates is that thirty-three of those running for the Clann, one-third of the party slate, lost their deposits, compared to twenty Fine Gaelers, fifteen Labour, four National Labour, and six each from Clann na Talmhan, Fianna Fáil and Independents.[136] This helps explain the disparity between the Clann's nationwide percentage of the vote and the number of seats it won. The Clann contested every constituency – the only other party to do so being Fianna Fáil, as Fine Gael had no candidate in Monaghan. So even votes that had no prospect of electing a candidate were being added to the Clann's national tally. For instance, the party won 9 per cent of the vote in Leinster, but didn't win a single seat, while in Munster, outside the two Tipperary constituencies, it won 11.2 per cent of the vote and no seats.

However, while those votes might have been wasted from the Clann's point of view, they were extremely valuable to other anti-government, and particularly Labour, candidates. When Fianna Fáil, Fine Gael and Labour candidates were in the field, Labour got 39.5 per cent of Clann na Poblachta transfers, while Fine Gael got 18.1 per cent and Fianna Fáil got just 10 per cent.[137] This transfer pattern helps to explain the very strong performance by Labour. Despite the fact that Clann na Poblachta won 2 per cent more of the national vote than the two Labour parties combined, it won nine fewer seats.

The other opposition parties also transferred against Fianna Fáil. Of particular interest was the transfer pattern of National Labour voters. When both Fianna Fáil and Labour candidates were available, 20.7 per cent of National Labour votes went to the former, compared to 33.6 per cent to the latter.[138] This suggests that the party's voters did not share the Congress of Irish Unions' preference for Fianna Fáil.

It was not immediately clear to Fianna Fáil that it had lost the election. Even two decades later, Seán Lemass still blamed the loss of power on the betrayal of the National Labour Party, which had 'fought the election on the basis they were going to support a Fianna Fáil government, and certainly Fianna Fáil, plus the Labour Party, had a majority'.[139] While the electoral intervention of Clann na Poblachta had served to deprive Fianna Fáil of a majority in the Dáil, the intentions of the National Labour Party would now determine whether there was to be a change of government.

Shortly before polling in the delayed election in Carlow–Kilkenny, Richard Mulcahy said that Fine Gael would resolutely oppose the re-election of de Valera as Taoiseach, and that his party was 'prepared to co-operate with other parties in forming a government which . . . will, with a full co-operative spirit, review and take action in those most urgent matters . . . the cost of living, government extravagance, taxation, the housing shortage, and emigration'.[140] The following day, MacBride told an election meeting, in reference to Fianna Fáil, that 'all parties and Independents sought support for a mandate to put them out. The people have given that mandate.'[141]

On the day of the Carlow–Kilkenny count, after discussing the matter with Dan Morrissey,[142] Mulcahy wrote to the leaders of the other opposition parties, inviting them to a meeting in Leinster House on Friday, 13 February. All except National Labour attended.[143] Bill Norton said at this meeting that Labour would not accept the leader of any other party – in other words, Mulcahy – as head of a government. Eventually, Fine Gael's John A. Costello was agreed as a compromise Taoiseach. The Fine Gael TD for Wexford, Sir John Esmonde, was also apparently considered,[144] and Seán MacEoin's name was mentioned in the early stages of the negotiations,[145] presumably because of the cross-party support his presidential candidacy had attracted. But even if others were mentioned, Costello's was the only name seriously considered.[146]

According to Seán MacBride, 'Clann na Poblachta insisted that Mulcahy must not be Taoiseach because of his close identification with the events of the Civil War . . .'[147] However, this objection was never actually articulated in public – Norton's suggestion let MacBride off the hook, as it was presumably intended to. That the Clann's objections to Mulcahy lay in the events of the early 1920s was somewhat ironic, given their stated hope of getting away from Civil War politics. But feeling in the new party ran deep. One of the republican element in the Clann was heard to refer to Mulcahy as a 'bloody murderer'.[148]

Some have argued that Mulcahy did not particularly want the job of Taoiseach, that he was happier as a 'backroom boy' in Education,[149] but he certainly had the right, as leader of the largest party, to have his name considered. Whether due to lack of ambition, or to eagerness to remove Fianna Fáil, his selfless decision not just to stand aside, but to actively encourage Costello to take the post of Taoiseach, must stand as one of the most noble gestures in Irish politics. Mulcahy had turned down the chance to head a government before, when after the death of Michael Collins, Kevin O'Higgins wanted him to become leader. On that occasion, Mulcahy put winning the Civil War above political advancement.[150] This time, his determination to oust de Valera outweighed whatever personal ambition he possessed. This outcome was perhaps fortunate: Mulcahy's biographer has noted that he demonstrated a 'single mindedness which left him oblivious to tensions in the cabinet',[151] while his personality was based on 'the virtues of self-help, self-discipline, hard work and personal reserve'[152] – hardly the characteristics necessary for the delicate task of keeping such a diverse coalition together.

MacBride had a difficult enough time persuading his party to go into coalition with the former enemy, without having to vote for Mulcahy as Taoiseach.[153] Members of Fine Gael were not overly enthusiastic about embracing the Clann either. Garret FitzGerald, then a young party activist, has written of his 'deep hostility' to MacBride, adding that 'not having adult memories of the sixteen years of Fianna Fáil government, I did not fully share the conviction of older people in the opposition parties that an alliance with MacBride's party was a price worth paying in order to provide an alternative government'.[154] However, the desire to elect a new government was the main objective for most party members, irrespective of its make-up.[155]

Policy was also discussed at the meeting on 13 February, according to MacBride: 'I think I was the first to enunciate policy. I was aware at the time that this was awaited anxiously by Fine Gael and others.' The four points he insisted on were more public investment in Irish resources; a doubling of forestry planting; the release of Hospitals Trust funds to build hospitals and sanatoria; and a very substantial increase in social welfare benefits. 'There was a sigh of relief because I had not mentioned the External Relations Act or the political prisoners, although I had campaigned on those issues in the election. Everybody around the table agreed to the points I had proposed. Norton . . . came in then with, I think, something about transport, that was the sum total of the discussion on policy. I specifically did not raise the two outstanding questions because while I had campaigned on those issues the others had not, and I felt it would be putting an impossible strain on them to ask them to agree to things for which they had not campaigned.'[156] As far as Noël Browne was concerned, the Clann had limited aims in the new government, and he claimed MacBride promised him that as soon as TB was controlled and the hospital building programme under way, they would go to the country for an increased mandate for the party.[157]

MacBride appears to have been the first to christen the experiment, when he said 'what is visualised is not a coalition government, but rather an inter-party government . . . The only alternative would be the Fianna Fáil party dictatorship which has been emphatically rejected by the people.'[158] One of the negotiators told the *Irish Times* that the new administration 'would not be a party government, and in the event of a defeat it would not necessarily resign. Many questions would be left to a free vote of the members present [in the Dáil] and the government would abide by the result.'[159]

On Saturday, 14 February, the day after the initial meeting, Labour's parliamentary party and administrative council met for two hours and decided to participate.[160] At the same time, James Dillon met with a group of like-minded Independent deputies – Alfie Byrne, Alfred Byrne jun., Patrick Cogan, Charles Fagan and Oliver J. Flanagan – and the six agreed their support for the new experiment.[161] Leading members of Fine Gael, meanwhile, met in Mulcahy's home in Rathmines to discuss their attitude,[162] while Clann na Talmhan also decided to participate. That evening, the prospective ministers from Fine Gael, Labour and Clann na Talmhan, along with Dillon and MacBride (who came alone as he wanted to find out what second department his party would hold before deciding who should fill the job), met in the Mansion House.[163] This meeting agreed the structure and personnel of party representation, and Costello was formally invited to become Taoiseach.[164] He had first been told he was being considered on the Saturday morning. In the afternoon MacBride told him that all the parties would join in forming a government if he led them; no one else would be acceptable. Norton too was insistent on Costello taking the job.[165]

Costello later claimed to have been 'appalled' at the idea of taking the office. 'I never wanted to be Taoiseach . . . I think my resolve was shaken mainly by the appeals made to me by O'Higgins at Mulcahy's home.'[166] He told one of his closest advisers that he hadn't even wanted to become a minister or Attorney General.[167] Mulcahy later said that Costello had been asked to leave all that his life meant to him, professionally and personally, 'within 24 hours'.[168] On the Sunday, 15 February, after a game of golf, Costello went to see his friend Arthur Cox, who told him: 'You have been in politics for 30 years, and you cannot refuse the top post. If you play with fire you must expect to get burned some time.'[169] Costello accepted the nomination as Taoiseach later that day.[170]

The method of his selection made Costello's job more difficult. It produced a position where 'the Prime Minister was not the leader of any political party and was, instead, as much the creation of his Ministers as their leader'.[171] Brian Farrell has noted that Costello's position 'marked a major change in the customary relationship of Taoiseach and Cabinet'.[172] He was not a party leader, had no choice in who became a minister, and had none of the patronage normally enjoyed by a Taoiseach. For instance, the only senior appointment directly made by Costello was that of the Attorney General, his friend Cecil Lavery; he did not even nominate the 'Taoiseach's Eleven' to the Seanad (in a series of replies to Fine Gael hopefuls seeking nominations, Costello said that he was 'not a free agent in this respect'[173]); and when T.J. (Tim) Murphy died, it was the Parliamentary Labour Party which elected his successor as Minister for Local Government.[174] As a result, Costello was not in a position to impose discipline on his Cabinet, or even on Fine Gael.

On the other hand, the new Taoiseach was more sympathetic than many in Fine Gael to the other parties. He had persuaded MacBride to take up constitutional politics, through what has been described as 'the freemasonry of the Law Library',[175] and his father had been friendly with Jim Larkin,[176] which gave him an understanding of the second largest party in the government. Labour also approved of the liberal social views he had shown on the boards of a number of hospitals.[177] In a conversation at the time of the formation of the second inter-party government in 1954, James

Larkin jun. said to Costello: 'Don't you know that we would do anything for you?'[178]

Seán Lemass later described him as a person who 'did not have deep rooted political convictions',[179] and this too may have been an advantage in the situation in which he found himself. Even Noël Browne acknowledged that he was a very fair chairman of government meetings. And when he wanted to be, Costello could be decisive and effective in getting things done; for example, his work on the consolidation and codification of laws, an area in which he had been interested while in opposition, resulted in the setting up of a department within the Attorney General's office to deal with law reform and consolidation.[180] The chief medical officer in the Department of Health had this to say of Costello's brief spell as minister after Browne's resignation: 'When he had decided what he wanted to do, he sent for the Secretary of the Department and . . . gave him his orders. As he was Taoiseach as well as Minister for Health and had a positive determined manner, no one dared to say anything.'[181]

However, Costello, like some of his ministers, could with justice have been accused of lacking the common touch. Patrick Lindsay recalled travelling with Costello and Dillon to Áras an Uachtaráin to return their seals of office after the defeat of the second inter-party government. Their car passed a famous Dublin pub, and Dillon remarked that the only pub he had been in was his own in Ballaghadereen, while Costello said he had only been in a pub once, to which Lindsay replied, with typical bluntness: '****. I now know why we are going in this direction today and why we are out of touch with the people.'[182]

One of those closest to the Taoiseach described him as 'kind and generous, qualities often masked by a manner, blunt and gruff . . . his experience as a lawyer was not always an advantage. Acceptance of the law's delays did not foster an overnight conversion to consistent punctuality. The vehement rhetoric of the Courts did not necessarily match the changing moods of the Dáil, and he sometimes found it hard to avoid flowery diction and the purple patch.'[183] One of his Cabinet colleagues described him as 'a saint',[184] which was just as well given all he had to put up with.

Now that the proposed government had a Taoiseach, attention focused on its composition. One list speculated that Costello would take Justice as well as being Taoiseach; MacBride as Minister for Finance; Norton in Posts and Telegraphs, Dillon in Industry and Commerce and Mulcahy in Local Government; Joseph Blowick as Minister for Agriculture, with Seán MacEoin tipped for Defence, James Larkin jun. for Education, Patrick McGilligan for External Affairs, Tom O'Higgins for Health and Social Welfare, and Patrick Cogan as Minister for Lands.[185] Noël Browne considered this to be 'black propaganda', particularly the reference to Larkin,[186] and the list appeared in the papers on the morning of a crucial meeting of the National Labour Party, which was hardly coincidental.

McGilligan made a note during the negotiations showing Mulcahy as Minister for Finance, and later as Minister for External Affairs. He had the names of Brendan Corish (Labour), Oliver J. Flanagan (Independent) and Con Lehane (Clann na Poblachta) written down, presumably as parliamentary secretaries. There was also a suggestion that the portfolios of Industry and Commerce and External Affairs should be put together.[187] However, it appears that Mulcahy himself opted for Education,[188] and even if he hadn't, the junior partners in the coalition wanted McGilligan to take Finance, a view first expressed by Labour TD Bill Davin and backed by Norton and MacBride.[189]

But before portfolios could be given out, the inter-party government needed a majority – which made the support of the five National Labour TDs, under strong pressure to re-elect de Valera, vital. The *Irish Times* reported on 7 February that de Valera was likely to be supported by National Labour and some Independents,[190] repeating this prediction two days later,[191] and stating just over twenty-four hours before the Dáil met that 'it is virtually certain now that the National Labour Party will vote for Mr de Valera as Taoiseach and for the continuation of the Fianna Fáil regime'.[192] However, it seems that Fianna Fáil was wary of the National Labour leaders. One retired politician observed that 'nobody trusts them. Lemass knows they would sell out on him in the morning if it suited the interests of those in charge of the ITGWU that they should do so.'[193]

In fact, the ITGWU-dominated Congress of Irish Unions wanted the party to vote for Fianna Fáil, as it was the only other party favouring 'an Irish self-contained Trade Union movement'. The five National Labour TDs were instructed to vote for de Valera at a meeting on 13 February.[194] While Costello called Mulcahy the 'father' of the inter-party government because he made the first move in bringing the parties together, for him James Everett was 'the hero – no man was under heavier pressure to support the then Government, both from his union and from Fianna Fáil'.[195] Everett himself claimed, with pardonable exaggeration, that no five men in Irish history had a more serious decision to make than the National Labour TDs.[196]

On 17 February, in a three-hour meeting, Everett, Dan Spring and James Hickey told a second meeting of the CIU/National Labour Party joint committee that they had been instructed by their supporters not to vote for de Valera, because of his government's treatment of rural workers, road workers, pensioners and other low-paid sections of society. It was suggested that the five TDs should meet Gerry Boland to see if a deal could be struck, but Spring and Everett refused, and the deputies left the meeting.[197] Everett then went to Leinster House to tell Mulcahy that they would be supporting the opposition.[198] Makeshift or not, the inter-party government now had a majority.

The CIU later emphasised that the five TDs had been advised not to vote against Fianna Fáil, but decided 'at the last moment' to do so.[199] The five TDs explained that while they had consulted the joint committee, 'no arguments then put forward ... were ... sufficiently convincing to induce us to accept ... a position of instability and political dissatisfaction which would inevitably lead to another and early general election'. They claimed an inter-party government was 'the only means of escape from the Emergency Budget taxes, the means test, the unsatisfactory social services, emigration due to low wages, ... and all the other evils which induced the majority of the electorate to declare for a change of government'.[200] It was also, given Fianna Fáil's stated opposition to coalition, the only way for James Everett to get a Cabinet post.

Years later, Seán Lemass recalled that 'up to the night before the Dáil met we did not realise there was going to be a majority against us. Even then, we did not believe it was going to last very long because it was such a makeshift sort of government.'[201] Once it was known that National Labour would support the inter-party group, de Valera paid a private visit to President Seán T. O'Kelly on the evening of the 17th.[202]

At nine o'clock the same night, Mulcahy issued a statement to the press on behalf of Fine Gael, the two Labour parties, the two Clanns, and the Independents in the inter-party group, outlining their agreed policy 'in view of the defeat of the Fianna Fáil party in the general election, and desirous of offering the people an alternative government on an inter-party basis . . .'[203] The parties had agreed ten points of policy:

1. Increased agricultural and industrial production.
2. Immediate all-out drive to provide houses for the working and middle classes at reasonable rates. Luxury building to be rigidly controlled.
3. Reduction in the cost of living.
4. Taxation of all unreasonable profit-making.
5. Introduction of a comprehensive social security plan to provide insurance against old age, illness, blindness, widowhood, unemployment, etc.
6. Removal of recent taxes on cigarettes, tobacco, beer and cinema seats.
7. Immediate steps to provide facilities for the treatment of sufferers from tuberculosis.
8. Establishment of a Council of Education.
9. Immediate steps to launch a National Drainage Plan.
10. Modification of means test as at present applied to old age, widows and orphans, and blind pensions.

When the Dáil met, the outgoing Ceann Comhairle, Frank Fahy, was nominated for the post again by de Valera, seconded by Mulcahy, and re-elected, leaving Fianna Fáil with a strength of sixty-seven. De Valera's nomination as Taoiseach was defeated by seventy votes to seventy-five. Four Independents supported him – Thomas Burke, John Flynn, Ben Maguire and Michael Sheehan – while one of his party, Thomas Brennan of Wicklow, was absent through illness. Eight Independents voted against de Valera – the six who had formed a group led by James Dillon, as well as Patrick O'Reilly and William Sheldon.[204]

Costello was then nominated by Mulcahy, who spoke of establishing a 'fruitful harmony' among men with different backgrounds and outlooks. He said Costello's 'character and ability . . . pointed him out . . . to a number of groups in the House and in the country as the man to hold together and to bind that spirit and to lead it to achievement'[205] – a generous tribute considering Mulcahy himself had not been so chosen. The nomination was seconded by Norton, while MacBride, Blowick and Dillon all spoke in his support. Two Independents who had supported de Valera, Maguire and Burke, abstained on the vote for Costello, and he was supported by the same eight who had voted against the outgoing Taoiseach, and was thus elected by seventy-five votes to sixty-eight. 'Hand-clapping and some cheering broke out when the Speaker [*sic*] announced the results, and Mr Costello was surrounded for a moment or two by well-wishers.'[206] Costello later told reporters that the new administration had been 'elected as a representative government and our policy will be national rather than a party one. Our first concern will be directed to agriculture in an effort to increase production and to raise the standard of living of the rural community.'[207]

There had been no contact between the Department of the Taoiseach and the new government before the Dáil assembled, and the civil servants didn't even know the names of the new ministers until they were announced by Costello in the Dáil.[208] As soon as Costello was elected, he was met by Maurice Moynihan, secretary of the Department of the Taoiseach, and James McElligott, secretary of the Department of Finance (who happened to know the new Taoiseach), at the exit from the Dáil chamber. McElligott introduced Costello to Moynihan, and the three men went to the Taoiseach's room, where de Valera congratulated Costello and, after a short conversation, left the room. Costello, accompanied by Moynihan, by his son-in-law Alexis Fitzgerald, and by a Fine Gael staff member, Captain Michael Byrne (who was commissioned a commandant on 27 February and appointed aide-de-camp to the Taoiseach), then went to Áras an Uachtaráin where he was officially appointed by the President.

The Cabinet proved to be an interesting blend of the talents available. With thirteen members, it was the largest Cabinet to date, all others under W.T. Cosgrave and de Valera having had ten or eleven members. Costello became Taoiseach without any other portfolio. His party leader, Richard Mulcahy, became Minister for Education, a relatively minor post, but one on which he had often spoken during the general election campaign. Fine Gael also took the portfolios of Finance (Patrick McGilligan), Industry and Commerce (Dan Morrissey), Justice (General Seán MacEoin) and Defence (Dr Tom O'Higgins). The leader of the Labour Party, Bill Norton, became Tánaiste and Minister for Social Welfare, while his party colleague Tim Murphy became Minister for Local Government, where he would oversee the housing drive until his untimely death in April 1949, when he was succeeded by Michael Keyes. Jim Everett, the National Labour leader, took over Posts and Telegraphs, while Joe Blowick of Clann na Talmhan became Minister for Lands, and Independent James Dillon was Minister for Agriculture. Seán MacBride became Minister for External Affairs, and Noël Browne was Minister for Health. Only Mulcahy and McGilligan had previous ministerial experience, while Costello had been Attorney General.

As was common at the time among leading politicians, many of the new ministers had a 'national record'. Mulcahy, of course, played a crucial role in both the War of Independence and the Civil War, while MacEoin, the 'Blacksmith of Ballinalee', was a heroic figure, still technically under sentence of death by the British. O'Higgins had also served with distinction, while Everett had been an IRA member and a justice of the Republican Courts. MacBride had fought on the other side during the Civil War, and there was a certain sensitivity towards this – an outline of his Civil War record was removed from the official biography issued by the Government Information Bureau.[209] It was not surprising that there was some tension over the Civil War – republicans had murdered Tom O'Higgins's father and brother.

There was also a shared legal background among some ministers. Cecil Lavery, the new Attorney General, completed a quartet of leading barristers serving in the government, the others being Costello, MacBride and McGilligan.[210] A number of important cases – the Sinn Féin Funds case, Dillon's legal challenge to the 1947 Health Act, and the Foyle/Bann Fisheries litigation – were affected by the sudden removal of their talents.[211] Lavery was appointed to the Supreme Court in April 1950, and was replaced as Attorney General by Charles Francis Casey.[212]

The appointment of Lavery involved Costello in his first major disagreement with his civil servants, when he decided to overturn significant rules regarding the office. The Executive Council had decided in December 1936 that any fees paid to the Attorney General for the performance of his duties should be paid to the Exchequer.[213] After talking to Lavery, Costello instructed that as the monies involved were so small, the matter should be left to the Attorney General to decide what to do with the fees,[214] later instructing that such fees 'should be retained by the Attorney General as part of his personal income'.[215]

Another convention, set by the Cabinet in January 1946, was that the Attorney General should not take private work.[216] Again, Costello overruled this, insisting that 'the Attorney may engage in such private practice as, in his discretion, he might deem not to be incompatible with the duties of his office'.[217] He later justified this by arguing that it was in the public interest to have a leading member of the Bar in the position, and that 'it would be unreasonable to expect such a person to make the considerable sacrifice of income that would be involved in accepting the office of Attorney General without the right to engage in private practice'.[218] The detail of the notes prepared by Moynihan indicates the depth of his feelings about this reversal of policy.

Costello also insisted on the revival of the tradition that the chief justice formally welcome Lavery and 'summon him to his place as leader of the Bar', observing that this had been the practice on each of his appointments to the position, although the last time it had been done appeared to be in 1936.[219] Lavery had been a very high earner at the Bar (as, indeed, had Costello) and he lost a considerable part of his income when he agreed to become Attorney General, even though the government at its first meeting decided to increase his salary to £3,000 a year, the same as the Taoiseach.[220] It was perhaps natural for Costello to wish to cushion the blow as much as he could – but it was still a highly questionable decision in the circumstances, and one that would certainly be regarded as improper today.

The three parliamentary secretaries were not appointed until 24 February – 'apparently because the new Government had not made up their minds regarding the individuals to be appointed'.[221] Brendan Corish of Labour was to be Parliamentary Secretary to the Minister for Local Government; Fine Gael's Liam Cosgrave was appointed to the Taoiseach and to the Minister for Industry and Commerce; and Michael Donnellan of Clann na Talmhan was Parliamentary Secretary to the Minister for Finance. Labour also received the post of Leas Cheann Comhairle for Patrick Hogan,[222] giving each party an almost exact 'match' of parliamentary strength to jobs within the government.

Of course, it is important to note that portfolios have different values for different parties. Labour was obviously most interested in Social Welfare and Local Government, where the new social security scheme and the housing drive were major commitments. Dillon in Agriculture and Blowick in Lands were dealing with areas important to their constituents – Dillon was to say twenty years later that 'it was the apotheosis of my whole public life. I never wanted to be anything but Minister for Agriculture.'[223] MacBride's interest in diplomacy and the constitutional question would be best served in External Affairs,[224] while Browne could implement Clann policy in Health. But Fine Gael, as the major party, held the most important economic portfolios, Finance and Industry and Commerce. As would become clear, no radical change in economic policy was possible without the support of these departments, particularly the former.

Fianna Fáil was stunned to be out of office, with one outgoing minister, Tomás Derrig, condemning the 'naked opportunism' of National Labour and the 'so-called Republicans'.[225] Lemass said: 'We are leaving you this country in good shape . . . Make sure that you hand it back that way.' His biographer notes that he 'was too angry to conceal his emotions. His voice was shaking with rage and his face was contorted with disappointment as he shouted across the floor of the chamber.'[226] De Valera later referred to the inter-party government as a 'fraud against democracy'.[227]

On the Tuesday after his election, Costello addressed the nation on Radio Éireann. 'The groups that comprise the government have their own separate policies and individuality which they will continue to maintain. Over a wide field of action they are in complete agreement . . . The chief of these fundamental objectives upon which there is complete agreement is our determination to assert the right of the Irish nation to complete territorial unity and to absolute freedom . . . [But] the average citizen at present is primarily concerned with the problems of making ends meet . . . These economic considerations must take priority over all political and constitutional matters.'[228] That prediction was quickly to prove incorrect.

TWO

ELASTIC GOVERNMENT

Any points on which we have not agreed have been left in abeyance.
John A. Costello[1]

Each of us watches the other like a cat watches a mouse, but each does what he thinks best in the interests of Ireland.
Seán MacEoin[2]

A s might have been expected, the new type of government introduced in 1948 caused considerable strains on a political and administrative system based on the 'Westminster model' and therefore used to single-party government. There were significant tensions in Cabinet, with ideological dividing lines being drawn between parties (or more particularly, between Fine Gael and the rest). The coalition arrangement also led to breaches of Cabinet procedure, the virtual abandonment of collective responsibility, and serious tensions with the civil service, while the need to ensure continuing support from Clann na Poblachta led to a number of concessions to republican opinion. But while such developments were seen as regrettable by those who looked to Westminster for their standards in public life, the flexible way in which John A. Costello and his colleagues adapted the machinery of government to suit their situation helped the inter-party government to retain, and to use, power.

Costello later acknowledged the unique problems he faced. 'In the original coalition or inter-party government there were difficulties which did not exist as much in the second . . . In the first one I had four [*sic*] parties and six Independents who were looking to be represented in the Cabinet. That caused very considerable difficulties because all the interests had to be considered . . .'[3] However, as one of his closest advisers later wrote, 'John Costello had no difficulty in persuading himself that the national interest demanded maintaining the unity of his government to keep Fianna Fáil out of office.'[4] Opposition to Fianna Fáil meant that anything done to keep the inter-party government in power could be interpreted as being in the 'national interest'.

Costello rejected suggestions that there had been distrust between ministers from different parties: 'If a coalition is formed it is formed on the basis of goodwill . . . the general idea would be "We have come together, we had better stay together", and that desire to stay together which is natural particularly in politics and very particularly in government will tend to tease out . . . all problems of that kind and all personal jealousies . . . I certainly found no such [problems] . . . in my experience in two administrations.'[5]

Not surprisingly, perhaps, this view was not shared by Noël Browne, who pointed out that 'a compromise where you are in a minority is likely to be the compromise which suits the majority . . . in this process of Cabinet government you have two very important things, you have first of all Cabinet responsibility, that is you must accept responsibility for whatever the majority in Cabinet decides, and secondly you then have majority decisions. Now on different matters Fine Gael would concede here and there but on the fundamentals there was no compromise. . . . On . . . important social and economic and financial issues the dominant policies that come out of a multi-party situation are those of the biggest party.'[6]

Within the Cabinet, the first to feature more than one party, there were clashes of personality and ideology. The most obvious was the bitter feud between the two Clann na Poblachta ministers, but according to both Costello and Browne there was also animosity between Fine Gael members of the Cabinet. Costello was later to claim that, apart from the Mother and Child controversy, 'there was no inter-party disagreement within the Cabinet, though there were differences between Fine Gael men',[7] and Browne supported the latter point, saying 'there was much hostility between the individual Fine Gael Ministers, though it dissolved when faced with outside opposition in the Cabinet'. In particular, he pointed to James Dillon's habit of picking on Dan Morrissey and to Richard Mulcahy being 'treated with a mixture of levity and contempt'[8] by his party colleagues.

Mulcahy could be a difficult colleague. W.T. Cosgrave reportedly found him 'a pain in the neck',[9] and he had a sometimes uneasy relationship with Costello, later ensuring that the latter did not succeed him in the leadership of Fine Gael.[10] One later Cabinet colleague said that the relationship between the two men was 'strained', pointing to the difference between Mulcahy, who 'with the rigidity and austerity of his army training, was not well placed to obtain or inspire the best in a voluntary organisation', and Costello, who was 'warm and generous' and 'ever ready to help in any situation . . .'[11]

Mulcahy, of course, was very conservative, as was his party colleague Seán MacEoin. Another conservative influence was Gerry Sweetman, the Fine Gael party whip, who was close to Mulcahy.[12] Costello and Tom O'Higgins had much in common, and along with Patrick McGilligan, they were rather more liberal on many matters.[13]

Dillon played a role in Cabinet like a modern-day Cassandra: 'When anything requiring a decision arose, if James wasn't happy that we had examined all aspects of the matter, he would preface his remarks by saying "I want to sound a Three Bell warning", and when James sounded the "Three Bell warning", we all listened with respect and in the majority of cases accepted his judgement.'[14]

Joseph Blowick was a somewhat inarticulate man. One commentator referred to his inability to say what the government's view was on a private member's bill affecting his department: 'Mr Blowick can plead . . . that he is unused to public speaking, and found it difficult to break the ice on this occasion.'[15] One regular attender at meetings of ministers at this time cannot remember a single contribution by the Minister for Lands.[16] There was also a certain amount of tension between Blowick and Seán MacBride, according to Clann na Poblachta TD Jack McQuillan. 'Blowick was just as keen as MacBride on afforestation and resented very much the fact that MacBride tried to cash in on what he was doing.'[17] His colleagues had little respect for Blowick. When it was suggested to Dillon on one occasion that it was dangerous for a large number of ministers to fly in the same plane (probably to the trade talks in London in June 1948), he 'expressed with audible relish his conviction that the country's government could be left in no more safe hands than those of Mr Joseph Blowick . . .'[18]

James Everett appeared to be mainly interested in constituency matters, and one of his colleagues was to claim that during Cabinet meetings, he took 'no part in discussion except when an item came up concerning Wicklow in any shape or form. His contributions were then brief, to the point, invariably self-interested, and usually acted on.'[19] His departmental secretary described him as 'a simple man who concealed his inadequacies by putting officials in the front line'.[20]

T.J. (Tim) Murphy, formerly a trade union official and journalist, had been Labour TD for Cork West since 1923. He was to prove an extremely hard-working Minister for Local Government – so much so that his health suffered, and he collapsed and died while addressing an inter-party meeting in Fermoy in April 1949. The Parliamentary Labour Party elected Michael Keyes to replace him. Keyes had been a railway worker and trade union official, and had been elected to the Dáil for his native Limerick in June 1927, but lost his seat in the general election the following September. He was re-elected in 1932 and held a seat until his death in 1957. He was to be Minister for Posts and Telegraphs in the second inter-party government.

Dr T.F. (Tom) O'Higgins had served as director of medical services in the Free State army before taking up politics. He was deputy leader of Fine Gael from 1932 to 1948. He served as Minister for Defence from 1948 to 1951, and as Minister for Industry and Commerce for a brief period in 1951. He retired from politics in 1954, and his son (Tom jun.) became Minister for Health in the second inter-party government.

Fine Gael's Seán MacEoin was first elected to the Dáil in 1921, but decided to concentrate on his army career, eventually becoming chief of staff in 1928. He resigned the following year to successfully contest a by-election. He also ran (unsuccessfully) against Seán T. O'Kelly in the 1945 presidential election. MacEoin was a kindly man, one of the few members of the Cabinet to receive a kind word in Noël Browne's autobiography. He was also deeply pious, and is reputed to have coined the phrase 'I don't want to get a belt of a crozier' when describing Church–state relations (the comment was made in relation to a controversy concerning proposals to legalise adoption which he, as Minister for Justice, had to deal with).

Dan Morrissey, a former road worker who became a Labour TD and later joined Fine Gael, was faced with what Costello described as 'the hardest task of the lot' in the Department of Industry and Commerce.[21] It was made harder by the fact that he succeeded Seán Lemass, who did not rate him highly, writing in May 1948: 'He does not seem to have made up his mind as to where he is going in the matter of industrial development . . . My personal view is that he will neither remove any existing protective duties [n]or recommend any new ones.'[22] Morrissey also suffered from poor health.

Browne, by his own account, was treated by his colleagues with patience and courtesy, but rarely taken seriously[23] – perhaps because of the age difference involved; he was just thirty-two, compared to the average age of the Cabinet, fifty-one. MacBride didn't take his party colleague into his confidence before Cabinet meetings, and Browne felt that time spent at Cabinet could more productively have been spent elsewhere. Browne was something of a surprise choice – Con Lehane had more call on one of the Clann seats at Cabinet, and was certain that he would get one. MacBride's decision caused Lehane such disappointment that he became a focus for discontent within the party, particularly among the former IRA members.[24]

Browne himself suspected that MacBride thought of him as 'an unknown nonentity appointed to an unimportant department', and therefore less likely to question his leader's decisions.[25] However, the reason for MacBride's surprise choice was almost certainly his desire to conduct the campaign against tuberculosis effectively. Having secured funding for the Department of Health to tackle the disease, MacBride felt he needed a doctor to oversee the spending of the money.[26] Even before the election, Browne's value as a medical expert was realised by the Clann – he had a major role in the party's propaganda film, outlining the steps necessary to deal with TB. Lehane didn't appear at all.[27]

William Norton played a key role in keeping the government together, a role appreciated by Costello who later said 'any time I ever had any trouble, any problems to solve, and there were many, I always sent for my friend Bill Norton for his sage and wise advice and counsel, and it was never lacking'.[28] The Tánaiste brought two important skills to his job – skill as a negotiator, and a feel for issues likely to cause the government trouble.[29] Browne interpreted

Norton's role differently, sarcastically describing him and O'Higgins as 'the wonderfully plausible peace makers of the Government'.[30] He claimed Norton supported the conservatism of Fine Gael, and that Costello would turn aside any radical objections by the Minister for Health by saying: 'But the Labour leader, Mr Norton, agrees, what's your difficulty Dr Browne?'[31] Lemass said of Norton, some years after his death, that 'as a leader of the Labour Party he was not seriously committed to any particular political philosophy. He was leading a Party like a cricket player with a bat, ready to hit any balls thrown at him.'[32] However, another assessment was that he 'exhibited a high degree of the skill that consists in making the rough ways of government smooth – a skill that Browne was wrong in dismissing as simple lack of principle'.[33]

The most fundamental clash within the Cabinet was between Patrick McGilligan and Seán MacBride. McGilligan was to prove an innovative minister and had become quite progressive on financial and economic matters, which should have made his relations with MacBride easier. However, MacBride was intent on 'putting his spoke into the Finance wheel',[34] by making forays into policy areas which were not part of his External Affairs brief. McGilligan resented this, but didn't confront it, probably in the interests of coalition harmony.[35] His first line of defence was to stall, by objecting to the tabling of External Affairs memoranda at Cabinet. When MacBride's views finally came up for discussion, the Minister for Finance would absent himself, claiming illness, thus preventing a discussion and leading to the postponement of the relevant item on the agenda.[36]

McGilligan, at fifty-nine the oldest member of the Cabinet, had been Minister for Industry and Commerce from 1924 to 1932, with the Shannon Scheme, which harnessed the river at Ardnacrusha hydro-electric station, as his main achievement. The scheme led to him being viewed as 'a dangerous socialist' by some of the sillier elements in the business world at the time.[37] He managed to get the scheme through Cabinet by discussing it when the Minister for Finance, Ernest Blythe, was absent, so that Finance 'was unaware of how far the project had developed until an advanced stage had been reached'.[38] He was also Minister for External Affairs from 1927 to 1932.

McGilligan has often been criticised for a statement in the Dáil in 1924, during a debate on unemployment: 'There are certain limited funds at our disposal. People may have to die in this country and may have to die through starvation.'[39] However, reading the full debate makes it clear that McGilligan was not being as heartless as that quote on its own suggests; in response to a question from Dan Morrissey, then a Labour TD, he said that the government had acted to reduce hunger, adding 'I do not say it goes far enough'.[40] It should also be remembered that the remark was made just after a destructive civil war when the future of the state itself did not look at all secure.

During the long period in opposition he had pursued an academic career, becoming professor of law at University College Dublin in 1934,[41] as well as reading widely in economics and international finance. There were conflicting views of his prowess. Browne, while acknowledging McGilligan's brilliance in many areas, claimed that as the Budget approached 'he appeared to melt into an orgy of inaction and self-pity, skipping Cabinet meetings or arriving late . . . Because of his clear panic on these occasions, the Cabinet decided to establish a subcommittee . . . who would help formulate his Budget.'[42] However, Costello recalled him reading out his Budget from notes on the back of an envelope which, when the manuscript of the speech was available later, was seen to be a comprehensive and complete summary.[43] This recollection accords with that of one of McGilligan's civil servants, T.K. Whitaker, who recalled that for his first Budget speech, the minister said he didn't want a prepared script, just two pages of figures from which to ad lib.[44]

Whitaker felt that McGilligan was the most intelligent minister he had served under, although 'his shrewd, critical, questioning approach was hampered by the tensions of the inter-party government'.[45] One official who worked closely with him suggested that he quickly grew tired of the routine in Finance, and would have preferred to be Attorney General[46] – a post which he occupied in the second inter-party government. Because of his reluctance to face MacBride directly, he tended to 'lie low a bit', was seldom in the department, and was even difficult to contact at home.[47]

Ronan Fanning claimed that McGilligan was reluctant to put forward the views of Finance (invariably against any plans to increase spending) because 'if McGilligan said no, he was often denying the demands, and sometimes the ideology, of a party other than his own, with the consequences which that entailed for the unity of the coalition. This factor alone was not conducive to Finance's resorting to the traditional method of sending memoranda to the government in order to defeat policies originating in the spending departments.'[48] However, as we shall see below, there were nonetheless constant battles between McGilligan and the spending ministers.

His principal opponent in Cabinet, Seán MacBride, was believed by some of his colleagues to have 'fallen in love with the trappings and aura of politics and, above all, of Cabinet office', and to have overestimated his ability to outwit the other members of the government.[49] His rather reserved personality was also a problem, while one civil servant who worked closely with him complained that 'he treated his Civil Servants as if they were members of his party, and the members of his party as if they were Civil Servants'.[50] In an assessment drawn up for President Harry Truman, the Central Intelligence Agency (CIA) referred to MacBride as 'the outstanding personality of the present government . . . Like Costello a brilliant and successful barrister, he is noted for his forceful advocacy and remarkable talent for cross-examination. He is probably the best debater in the Dáil. He is definitely of Prime Ministerial calibre. He is charming, affable and intelligent, an excellent diplomat.'[51]

Although MacBride was successful in increasing the stature of External Affairs, he failed to secure fundamental change in the Department of Finance, and in October 1949 he went so far as to tell Patrick Lynch he would resign unless 'a material improvement occurred' in the performance of the government. He also toyed with the idea of the creation of a Department of National Development covering the investment of Marshall Aid funds, with himself as minister. Lynch reported the conversation to Costello,[52] who presumably recognised it as an empty threat. In any event, MacBride's influence within the government was on the wane from around this time, largely because of his failure to overcome Finance.

With such a potentially explosive mix of elements, it is not surprising that the inter-party government would adapt Cabinet conventions designed for single-party administration. One newspaper editorial noted that the return of Fianna Fáil in 1951 would mean a return to collective Cabinet responsibility, which had been abandoned under Costello. 'Individual Ministers could say what they liked outside the Dáil, with the inevitable result that divergence of opinion became public property. Therein lay the essential weakness of the Inter-Party experiment, although in most other respects, the idea was admirable.'[53]

The convention of collective responsibility was established in Ireland as early as August 1922, when the Provisional Government decided that members and ex-members of the government should not publish 'the reasons or alleged reasons of the Government for adopting certain policies or lines of actions';[54] a fortnight later, it was further decided that all Cabinet decisions 'should be regarded as unanimous, and should be treated as strictly confidential'.[55]

W.T. Cosgrave reinforced this secretive approach two years later, when he refused to give details of Cabinet discussions to the Army Inquiry Committee, on the grounds that the Executive Council acted collectively, and once a decision was made it was regarded as unanimous. 'Previous divergence of views, individual opinions, arguments pro or con, all become merged in the decision which becomes, not the decision of a majority, but the decision of all, binding every member of the Council equally whatever may have been his previous attitude . . . The course of the discussion . . . and the interchange of individual views are matters of the utmost confidence . . . It would be against every canon of public policy to permit any breach of a protection so vital to the full and anxious exploration of the problems of government by responsible Ministers.'[56]

In fact, there are three cases of objections by some members of the Executive Council to decisions being recorded in the minutes, all of them in 1923,[57] but from then on the convention of collective responsibility applied, and this conservative approach was passed from Cumann na nGaedheal to Fianna Fáil with the help of the civil service. From the outside a single-party Cabinet could indeed seem unanimous in its views. Luckily for the historian, the tensions engendered by a multi-party coalition served to open a few cracks in the edifice of collective responsibility.

Joe Blowick not only breached collective responsibility, but turned it on its head, ignoring an express decision of the Cabinet and announcing the opposite in public, thus forcing his colleagues to reverse course. The issue was a pay increase for forestry labourers. In July 1948, the Cabinet agreed to Blowick's proposal to pay them two shillings a week over the rate for agricultural labourers, despite strong objections from Finance; but the cost was to be met out of savings in the Department of Lands' budget.[58] In November, Cabinet reaffirmed this decision, despite Blowick's failure to find the money within his department.[59] Five days later, answering questions in the Dáil, Blowick said that he would pay the increases as soon as possible, backdated to 15 March; a fortnight later, he promised that the money would be paid before Christmas.[60] Not surprisingly, Finance took a dim view of this, but the government was forced to bring in a Supplementary Estimate to pay for the wage increases, the only alternative being to lay off 1,500 men, leaving just 250 working in state forests in the entire country. This blatant disregard for the normal procedures of government cost £7,500 – not a huge sum, but significant when, because of extra planting not approved by Finance, the Department of Lands' budget was expected to run out before the end of January.[61]

While this case was kept within government circles, other disagreements were aired in the Dáil as well as outside. Shortly after the formation of the government, McGilligan said in the Dáil that politics worked on compromise, 'that men having differing views came together and hammered out a policy. We will probably have to do so openly here in the Dáil. I do not think that is an unwise procedure.'[62] Again, in March 1950, he asked a rhetorical question: 'Have we got to the stage when, on a matter which may be an important point of policy when it is decided, we cannot have freedom of speech? Have we got to the stage when men, because they join the Government circle, must all . . . when they go out of the council chambers, speak the same language?'[63]

That ministers were not expected to speak the same language was made clear by Costello in October 1949, in response to complaints by the governor of the Central Bank, Joseph Brennan, about a speech in which MacBride attacked the bank. Brennan sought a public assurance from McGilligan that the speech did not represent government policy. McGilligan didn't reply, but Costello told Brennan that in an inter-party arrangement 'it was considered permissible for a Minister in an individual or party capacity to give public expression to views which might not necessarily be those of the government as such'.[64]

When James Dillon suggested the establishment of a customs union between Britain, the USA, Canada, Australia and Ireland, Costello said in the Dáil that Dillon 'was expressing his own views and not those of the Government. Since he was speaking as an individual, and not for the Government, the question whether his views in this matter have the approval of the Government does not arise, nor does the question of Government policy.'[65]

In October 1949, MacBride advocated multilateral trade arrangements within the Organisation for European Economic Co-operation (OEEC),[66] contrary to the expressed opinions of Costello and McGilligan, who were anxious to protect sterling. Lemass commented in the Dáil that 'there is perhaps a suspicion in some quarters that the Minister for External Affairs acts in these matters independently of his colleagues or even in conflict with them'.[67] In a lighter moment, Lemass suggested that Costello should 'arrange to have some signal given, such as the flying of a flag over Government Buildings, whenever a Minister is speaking in a manner in which he is expected to be taken seriously'.[68]

In January 1950, Everett breached collective responsibility in a quite blatant manner, calling for the abolition of the Labour Court because of the growing unrest among workers about it. 'No matter who or what is responsible for the failure of the Court . . . it is certain that it cannot continue to function or to be of any value to the community if it hasn't the confidence of the workers.'[69]

An *Irish Times* editorial called his behaviour 'questionable', suggesting he should have either said he was speaking in a personal capacity (which would hardly have met the charge of breaching collective responsibility), or if he had the backing of the government, announced that the Cabinet disapproved of the Labour Court and its workings.[70] The court itself was stung by the remarks, requesting a meeting with Costello (then on pilgrimage to Rome) to discuss

Everett's attack.[71] At the end of the month, Everett insisted that he had 'no apology' to make for his attack on the court.[72]

After a meeting with Costello early in February,[73] the Labour Court made a public statement as 'it is not in the public interest that the errors they [Everett's two speeches] contain should be allowed to remain uncorrected . . . The Court will continue to try faithfully to discharge its statutory duties and will not allow itself to be influenced by any suggestion that its duty is merely to secure the settlement of a dispute in accordance with the desires of one party, whether employers or workers.'[74]

Seán MacEntee claimed the Cabinet was flouting the constitutional provision of collective responsibility, as 'Minister after Minister has openly attacked his colleagues and criticised them for the conduct of their particular Department . . . Their conduct has become a public scandal . . . If the present Taoiseach had any sense of his constitutional obligations, he would request [Everett] to resign, and, if he refused to comply, would dismiss him.'[75]

In the same month, ministers found themselves in opposite lobbies in the Dáil twice in the same day. The first vote was on an amendment to the Land Bill, which would have excluded foreigners from receiving full compensation for land purchased by the Land Commission. The amendment was proposed by Bernard Commons of Clann na Talmhan. His party leader Joe Blowick told him that his proposal was not the way forward, while Dillon suggested that it would be unconstitutional. Nevertheless, Browne was one of twenty TDs who supported the amendment (which was opposed by eighty-one). Following the vote, Fianna Fáil baited Norton with this division, with MacEntee calling out: 'Face the country; you are split from top to bottom.'[76]

The second vote that day involved a section of the Transport Bill which would have compensated the directors of CIÉ and the Grand Canal Company for loss of office (due to the nationalisation of CIÉ which is discussed in Chapter Six) with two years' fees. In a free vote, the section was defeated by ninety-nine votes to ten; those in favour of the section were Morrissey, Mulcahy, MacEoin, O'Higgins, Cosgrave, Patrick O'Donnell, Eamonn Rooney and Maurice Dockrell (all Fine Gael) and Independents Dillon and William Sheldon.[77] This division was attacked by Fianna Fáil's

Tomás Derrig, who said the constitution required the government as a body to take responsibility not just for its acts as a government, but also for the acts of individual ministers. 'Mr Costello might tell the people . . . that voting on opposite sides was merely another proof of the wonderful freedom the government had brought about, whereby every Minister could vote as he liked. If it was like that in the Dáil, what must it be like when Government decisions were made in Cabinet?'[78]

In March 1951, as the inter-party government moved closer to dissolution, another *Irish Times* editorial discussed collective responsibility, claiming that the principle had been 'abandoned at a fairly early stage' and adding: 'The government has been able to stand all the strains that have been put upon it precisely because it is so elastic. If Mr Costello had attempted to discipline his Ministers, as they would have been disciplined by a party leader, he and they would have been out of office long ago.'[79]

The inter-party government also faced problems with the administrative system. The government's first task was to ensure its control over a civil service which had spent sixteen years dealing with Fianna Fáil and which had become used to having its own way.[80] In 1971, after another lengthy period of Fianna Fáil rule, Costello was to complain of what he saw as an overreliance on officials. 'Civil servants, in my view, are getting too much control. The Fianna Fáil Government have landed themselves into the hands of the civil servants. Their policies are now Civil Service policies.'[81] It was an assessment that could equally have applied in 1948.

Noël Browne wrote that on taking office he was 'convinced that the civil service would set out to control its Minister', although he admitted that, given the superior education and experience of senior civil servants over their political 'masters', there were sound reasons for this! 'I resented and feared the possibility of being "managed" . . .' Browne put his stamp of authority on his department when he insisted on a senior official being transferred after he was overheard telling another department to ignore 'one of the Minister's hare-brained schemes'.[82]

MacBride was especially prone to distrust the civil service – reportedly his first words to his new departmental secretary, Frederick Boland, were: 'Mr Boland, give me a list of all the British agents working in your department.'[83] Ironically, the British believed that the Irish were spying on them, with their representative in Dublin, Lord Rugby, concluding after one meeting with MacBride and Boland that the two men had 'been listening very carefully to our telephone conversations with the Commonwealth Relations Office'.[84]

One consequence of MacBride's distrust of senior officials was of key importance: the exclusion from Cabinet meetings of Maurice Moynihan, who as secretary of the Department of the Taoiseach normally took minutes at such meetings. After eleven years of service to de Valera, it was felt that Moynihan was biased, and so he only attended the first two government meetings, along with one other which will be discussed below. After Cosgrave was appointed Parliamentary Secretary to the Taoiseach, he or Costello took notes of the decisions at meetings,[85] and then passed them on to Moynihan for processing. An added problem was that because of the extraordinary length of many government meetings, it was sometimes not entirely clear when a decision had actually been made.[86] It was a situation ripe for confusion, and was a contributory factor to the two most controversial episodes during the government's term of office, the declaration of the Republic and the Mother and Child crisis.

Patrick Lynch felt this exclusion proved 'a grave handicap' and was 'cruelly unfair' to Costello, who did not share MacBride's distrust of Moynihan. 'If Maurice Moynihan had been allowed to function normally . . . [it] would have eased the strain on the Taoiseach and relieved him of many tedious matters of routine that were time-consuming and no part of the normal functions of a head of government.'[87] Despite his exclusion from government meetings, Moynihan made the best of the situation, and proved invaluable to Costello, who had a high regard for him. The Taoiseach's tendency to act on the spur of the moment was somewhat tempered by the civil servant's caution.[88]

The semi-state bodies didn't escape scrutiny by the new government. Dan Morrissey caused a bitter row by accusing C.S. (Todd)

Andrews of favouring Fianna Fáil members with jobs in Bord na Móna, where he was managing director – the minister eventually had to back down over this issue. However, Morrissey's suspicion of those with Fianna Fáil links claimed a victim in Percy Reynolds, the chairman of CIÉ, who was replaced by a civil servant, Ted Courtney, apparently for purely political reasons.[89] Also pushed out because of his politics was Jack O'Brien, the director of the Tourist Board.[90]

However, the most serious breach between the permanent and elected governments occurred in February 1951, when the secretary of the Department of Social Welfare, Dan O'Donovan, was dismissed for failing to act on instructions given to him by Norton, by the Taoiseach, and by the government as a whole. The cause of this row was Seán O'Driscoll, an official in the Department of Social Welfare. O'Driscoll had entered the civil service in 1935 and had been seconded to the Civil Service Executive and Higher Officers Association in May 1942 as its secretary.[91] On the change of government in 1948, he returned to the department as head of the information section. However, O'Donovan was unhappy with O'Driscoll's performance, claiming that he was frequently not available for duty and had never explained what he was doing when not following the secretary's instructions.[92] Accordingly, O'Donovan sacked him.

Norton instructed O'Donovan to reinstate O'Driscoll, which the secretary refused to do, as he felt it was not in the interests of the civil service. The instruction was repeated by Norton, and by Costello, five times without effect. O'Donovan offered to move department, as long as O'Driscoll was disciplined, and had also offered to pay O'Driscoll's salary for January, despite his objections to doing so as accounting officer, if Norton gave him a written direction to do so. Norton made it clear to him that one of them would have to go.[93]

On the afternoon of 12 February, the Cabinet directed O'Donovan to comply with the instructions he had been given.[94] When he refused again, the government that evening removed him from his position as secretary and from the civil service. It is a sign of the seriousness of the situation that for the first time in three years, Maurice Moynihan was allowed to attend the Cabinet meeting.[95] In a lengthy statement to the Dáil, Costello said that the central issue was whether O'Donovan was prepared to obey an express order from his minister, from the Taoiseach, and from the government. 'The Secretary has the right and duty to make proper submissions to his Minister, within the scope of his functions, but, having done so, he has imposed on him the clear duty of loyally obeying the Minister's direction and carrying his decision into effect promptly and without question.'[96]

But according to O'Donovan, the Taoiseach and the government did not have the power to authorise him, as accounting officer, to pay O'Driscoll's salary, while Norton had refused to give him the authority to do so.[97] This interpretation of procedure was deemed correct by one of the experts – Joe Brennan, governor of the Central Bank and also O'Donovan's cousin. He advised that Norton had 'blundered' and 'fails to understand the issue'. Brennan argued that the issue was not the authority of the government, but rather the authority of the Dáil. The *policy* of expenditure was decided by the party majority supporting the government; but O'Donovan, as accounting officer, was responsible to the Dáil on a non-party basis for the *regularity* (or propriety) of expenditure. If Norton wanted to overrule the objections of the accounting officer, he should do so in writing. 'The subsequent intervention of the Taoiseach and the Government was a scandalous piece of bullying as they had no *locus standi* whatever for overruling or otherwise directing you in your capacity as Accounting Officer.'[98]

The unseemly row was given a full airing in the Dáil, where Seán MacEntee claimed that Norton had been after O'Donovan since he refused to help the minister's solicitors during his 'unprofitable action against the *Irish Press*'.[99] He also alleged that O'Driscoll had often been absent from his office and uncontactable. Norton made the clearly correct assumption that MacEntee had been briefed by O'Donovan, and promised to 'ram' MacEntee's words down his throat if the matter was discussed in public.[100] The following week, Norton denied MacEntee's suggestion that a 'sinecure' had been created for O'Driscoll because he was a member of the Labour Party. He insisted that O'Driscoll was efficient and hard-working, and that he had been a friend of O'Donovan's, until the secretary went 'scalp-hunting'.[101]

The only previous dismissal of such a senior civil servant had been that of E.P. McCarron, secretary of the Department of Local

Government, in 1936, after Seán T. O'Kelly, his minister, said he had lost confidence in him.[102] The assistant secretary of the Department of Social Welfare, William Maguire, replaced O'Donovan.[103] However, O'Donovan was reinstated in the civil service in September 1951 as an adviser to the new Minister for Social Welfare, Jim Ryan; there was no precedent for such a post.[104] The appointment was made on the understanding that he would regain his job as secretary of the department when Maguire retired, although this was not made public.[105] But while O'Donovan had regained his job as secretary by the beginning of 1953,[106] when the second inter-party government came to power in June 1954, he was sent on leave, under protest.[107] In August, the government decided to terminate O'Donovan's appointment as secretary, although this time he was appointed secretary to the President, a move which satisfied all concerned.[108]

Less dramatic were the continual battles between civil service and government to maintain the proper procedures in relation to the workings of the Cabinet. Civil servants were very keen to maintain the convention that submissions to the government came from ministers, rather than from their departments. This matter was raised in the strongest terms by Moynihan in February 1949, after Noël Browne submitted a memorandum attacking a submission 'from the Department of Finance' on his proposals for extra staff. Among other things, Browne accused the department of being facetious, impertinent, aggressive, and even deliberately misleading – charges he could hardly have levelled at McGilligan!

In a minute to Costello, Moynihan pointed out that: '(a) it is a Minister who submits a memorandum to the Government; (b) an attack on the tone, content or phraseology of such a memorandum is an attack on a document which is the production of the responsible Minister, whether he drafted it with his own hand or whether he adopted a draft prepared for him by his officials; and (c) attacks by Ministers on officials for the tone, content or phraseology of a document for which their own Minister has taken responsibility must tend to destroy the whole basis on which a Civil Service composed of honest, conscientious public servants is built'.[109]

The theme of ministerial authorship was taken up by Moynihan's assistant secretary, Nicholas Nolan, the following month. Nolan advised a colleague to be careful in the phrasing of memos to departmental secretaries informing them of government decisions, insisting that these should refer to 'the memorandum submitted by the Minister', rather than to 'your Department's memo', on the grounds that the Department of the Taoiseach should not 'lend any semblance of foundation to a suggestion that memoranda for the Government are submitted by Departments rather than by Ministers. The recent submission by the Minister for Health . . . shows how necessary it is to make the true position in this regard clear beyond all measure.'[110]

Another battle continually waged by Moynihan and his officials was against ministers – particularly MacBride – submitting proposals on subjects outside their areas of concern. The proper course for a minister wishing to make his views known on a matter not covered by his departmental responsibilities was to write to the responsible minister, not to submit a memorandum to government on it. Moynihan warned Costello that 'if the facts and opinions affecting a proposal are to be properly and adequately represented to the Government, the proposal must be submitted by the Minister in charge of the Department mainly concerned, who has at his immediate disposal the knowledge and experience of expert advisers. Only in this way can there be a reasonable assurance against decisions that might give rise, in practice, to serious administrative and financial difficulties and that might cause irreparable damage before they could be amended.'[111]

One example of MacBride stepping outside his responsibilities was his attempt to submit a memorandum on the establishment of a committee to investigate industrial protection in January 1949.[112] Moynihan immediately objected to the memo being included on the agenda for the following day's government meeting, on the grounds that this 'would open the way to the creation of chaos in the arrangements for the transaction of Government business', because the matter was within the purview of the Minister for Industry and Commerce, Dan Morrissey, rather than MacBride. 'The whole basis of the Cabinet Procedure Instructions . . . is that proposals for consideration by the Government must be submitted by the Minister in charge of the Department primarily concerned.'[113] Moynihan noted that Costello had read and approved his memo, and that the Taoiseach was treating MacBride's communication as one to himself as head of government from a minister holding personal views on a problem which had been discussed at a government meeting.[114]

Costello later told Moynihan that MacBride's submission had been due to 'unusual circumstances', in that it had been understood that any minister with suggestions should communicate them to government. But the Taoiseach accepted that the Cabinet procedure rules were 'proper and necessary . . . and should be enforced'. Costello spoke to MacBride about the matter, explaining why the submission was not put on the agenda.[115]

In August 1950, Browne, through one of his officials, raised a number of questions with the Department of the Taoiseach relating to government procedure. He wanted to know the number of members of the government required to form a quorum; whether decisions of the government are arrived at on the basis of majority votes; and which ministers were present at a meeting on 15 August. The reply stated that no quorums were specified for meetings of the government; that decisions were based on collective responsibility rather than majority voting; and that Costello, MacBride, O'Higgins, Morrissey and the Attorney General, Charles Francis Casey, were present at the meeting in question. Browne's official rang back the following day to confirm the attendance.[116] It's not clear exactly what Browne's point was, as the only decision recorded concerned the raising of the status of representation between Ireland and France to ambassadorial level.[117]

Patrick Lynch observed that the number of informal meetings, added to the strain imposed by the lack of proper minute taking, caused serious problems. 'Often there were ad hoc meetings of Ministers; these could be tantamount to government meetings because they frequently took decisions . . . if Mr Cosgrave were not present the procedure for recording a decision for transmission to the Secretary to the government could easily be overlooked . . . A government decision is not vitiated if not minuted, but the omission can lead to misunderstanding, confusion and even recrimination, particularly in an inter-party or coalition government.'[118]

Ministers were, on occasion, frustrated by the speed of decision making. Each proposal had to be submitted to other departments concerned for observations. Once a proposal was finally approved, the general scheme of the legislation was drawn up and circulated again for observations, while the final form of the Bill to be introduced in the Dáil also had to be circulated. Other departments could therefore stall progress by delaying their responses; the most obvious example of this behaviour involved Norton's social welfare plans.[119] In November 1949, following suggestions by ministers, Costello submitted an amendment to the Cabinet Procedure Instructions to deal with this problem. Ministers who felt other departments were stalling could inform the secretary of the Department of the Taoiseach, who would consult the Taoiseach on whether he wished to direct that the original memo containing the proposal should be circulated without the observations of the offending department. The proposal was approved by Cabinet, but there is no evidence to suggest it was particularly effective.[120]

The use of Cabinet committees by Costello has been noted by a number of political scientists; although not a new innovation,[121] it seems that they were more widespread in the first inter-party government than in previous administrations. It has been suggested that the committee system may have helped to put a check on ministers, who in the Irish system had been used to a certain level of autonomy. The committee became a way of overcoming this autonomy, as well as weak government discipline.[122] This point is supported in a negative way by the Mother and Child affair: a Cabinet committee dealing with this issue would have kept the government fully informed of Browne's progress, and would have made it more difficult for his colleagues to disown the scheme later.

The range of issues on which committees were set up is indicated in the Cabinet minutes – six in 1948, nine in 1949, sixteen in 1950, and one in 1951, covering subjects as diverse as Irish tests for civil servants, the fate of refugees on a ship in Cork harbour, grain storage, and teachers' salaries. A number of points can be made about them. McGilligan was on most of them (and certainly any that dealt with increases in expenditure, as most did); Costello or

Norton was nearly always in the chair; and of the thirty-two committees mentioned, Fine Gael (along with Dillon) had an absolute majority on twenty-two, made up half the members on a further five, and were in a minority on only five committees (those dealing with civil defence, employment, roadworks, Irish tests in the civil service, and the memorial to the national struggle).

Some of the more important committees deserve closer scrutiny. In February 1948, the new government set up a Cabinet Economic Committee, made up of Costello, Norton, MacBride, Mulcahy, Dillon, McGilligan, Morrissey and Cosgrave, with Patrick Lynch as secretary.[123] At its first meeting, it decided to concentrate on short-term problems first, particularly those relating to the forthcoming Budget, and that it could later turn to long-term issues.[124] But apart from dealing with alternative jobs for unemployed turf workers and the Anglo-Irish trade negotiations, little seems to have been achieved. According to the file of minutes, it met only seven times, with its last meeting in June discussing the imminent trade talks in London.[125]

In February 1949, a Cabinet committee of Costello, Norton, McGilligan and O'Higgins was set up 'to examine all outstanding Estimates for 1949–50, to make any cuts possible and settle them by 18/2/49'.[126] At the Cabinet's next meeting, this time limit was removed and it was confirmed that the committee on the Estimates would 'consider all outstanding Estimates for decision', as well as deciding on Department of Health staffing proposals.[127]

In February 1950, a Cabinet committee of Costello, Norton, McGilligan and Dillon was set up to examine the draft Estimates for the year ended 31 March 1951 and 'to devise a programme of capital works to be undertaken by the state over a period of years'.[128] This committee quickly began to be given other topics for consideration: food subsidies, the dairy industry,[129] rural electrification,[130] teacher training colleges,[131] spending on roads,[132] cement production,[133] and the dairy industry (again).[134]

On 14 March, it was decided that the Estimates Committee would remain in being, to continue devising a programme of capital works, and to keep departmental spending under review to avoid the necessity of Supplementary Estimates.[135] Thus, the Estimates Committee had become extremely powerful – and in doing so had usurped some of the functions of the Minister for Finance. The exclusion of MacBride is also significant; if economic decisions were now being taken by this committee rather than the full Cabinet, the Clann na Poblachta leader's attempts to influence policy could more easily be ignored.

The use of committees was typical of the 'elastic' approach which Costello adopted – both from necessity and from personal preference. If a dispute between ministers could not be resolved in Cabinet (despite the marathon length of many meetings), it was logical to send the issue into a committee, where agreement might be reached. But this tactic often simply delayed a decision, the prime example being the long-running saga of the social welfare scheme.[136] And on many issues delay facilitated the more conservative elements in the government who opposed change and the Department of Finance which opposed extra expenditure. But given the divisions in the government, there would appear to have been little alternative to the cautious, consensual approach pursued by Costello. The result of trying to push through a scheme which was strongly opposed by elements within the Cabinet was either delay until the government fell (Norton's social welfare scheme) or the withdrawal of public support at the first available opportunity (Browne's Mother and Child scheme).

If the government was to remain united, the strains within the individual parties caused by the formation of the coalition would have to be addressed. Nowhere was this strain more pronounced than within Clann na Poblachta. There have been suggestions that three Clann na Poblachta deputies were reluctant to vote for a Fine Gael Taoiseach at all, even Costello, but in the end loyalty to MacBride led them to do so.[137] Captain Peadar Cowan later claimed that his motion not to take ministerial office seemed likely to be passed by the party's executive, until MacBride threatened to have those who opposed him driven from the party. 'A few members changed sides after this speech and my motion was narrowly defeated.'[138] MacBride was the only one of the original thirteen IRA men on the executive to vote in favour of entering government,[139] and the motion was only carried by eighteen votes to sixteen.[140]

A couple of weeks after the formation of the government, the British representative, Lord Rugby, claimed that MacBride was 'committed to a move to the Right', and that although he 'has brought his ten henchmen along with him so far . . . the new party as a party is a blank cartridge. Already party members in the country are declaiming about being sold and are resigning. How many of the ten men elected to the Dáil will remain obedient to the Coalition Whip?'[141] Although there is more than a hint of wishful thinking in this, it is certainly true that MacBride needed movement on issues close to republican hearts to justify taking office.

In later life MacBride said that he entered politics 'because I was so dismayed with political internments and executions . . . Because of the Clann's involvement all the political prisoners were released. Military courts and executions became a thing of the past.'[142] He claimed that the Minister for Justice, Seán MacEoin, approached him shortly after the election of the government, to say he had discussed the political prisoners with Costello. 'They appreciated that I had not raised the question, but they would favour the release of all of them. He asked me to go through the list and indicate which I felt should be released – there could be borderline cases who had committed crimes which were not politically motivated. I spent a couple of hours with him doing this. It was wrongly reported in the press that I had issued an ultimatum on the releases.'[143]

Thus, the appeasement of the republicans in Clann na Poblachta was one of the first concerns of the new government. At its second meeting, the release of Liam Rice and Eamonn Smullen from Portlaoise Prison was approved,[144] and two days later they were freed.[145] Within a fortnight, another three, Seán McCurtain, Henry White and James Smith, were also released.[146] Later, another six prisoners jailed by the Special Criminal Court were freed.[147]

Costello once famously asserted that the Blueshirts would be 'victorious in Ireland . . . [as] the Blackshirts were victorious in Italy . . . [and] the Hitlershirts . . . [were] victorious in Germany'.[148] Now the former leaders of a movement set up to fight the IRA were releasing republicans from prison. Costello insisted that the decision to release the five prisoners from Portlaoise was made by himself and MacEoin alone, on the grounds that continuing to hold them would only lead to resentment and unrest, and denied that 'any member of a particular party had anything to do with the decision . . . It had nothing whatever to do with anything that brought about the formation of the present government. The matter was never mentioned; it was not part of the agreed policy. No pressure was brought to bear upon us from any outside source whatsoever.'[149]

Another issue for republicans was the reburial of IRA prisoners executed during the Emergency. On 10 August 1948, the Cabinet agreed to MacEoin's proposal that this should be allowed if the local bishop approved and there was to be no cost to the state. The Cabinet also insisted that no demonstrations of any kind, apart from religious services, should be held.[150] MacEoin made his proposal following a request from the mother of Richard Goss, one of the six prisoners executed during the war.[151]

The policy of appeasing republicans seemed to pay off: in his report for 1948, MacEoin told the government that 'political' prisoners had been released, the remains of the six executed men had been exhumed and handed over to their relatives, and the treatment of all prisoners had been improved. 'The Minister is happy to be able to report that the year was particularly free from political disturbance of any kind and that there was every evidence of the dawn of that new era of which the Taoiseach has so often spoken.'[152] Another interpretation has been offered by J. Bowyer Bell, a historian of the IRA, who wrote that apart from the release of prisoners and of the bodies of executed IRA men, 'most important came the end to police harassment and intimidation'.[153] Bell suggested that the breathing space gained thanks to MacBride allowed the IRA to come back from the brink of extinction and reorganise – thus laying the seeds for the Border Campaign of the late 1950s.

The need to placate the smaller parties led Costello into a serious error at the end of 1950 – the 'Battle of Baltinglass' – which stained the integrity of a government elected at least in part on an anti-corruption platform. The incident was sparked by the decision to transfer Baltinglass Post Office in County Wicklow from Helen Cooke to Michael Farrell – a decision taken by Minister for Posts and Telegraphs and local TD James Everett against departmental advice.[154] The Cooke family had run the post office in the village since 1880. Helen Cooke was the niece of Katie Cooke, who had inherited the running of the post office from her father. However, when the elder Miss Cooke attempted to transfer the office to her niece, she was made aware of a new regulation which limited succession rights to direct blood relatives.

On 30 November, Cooke was told that the post office was to be awarded to Farrell, the 27-year-old son of a former Labour councillor who was close to Everett. Half of the thousand local residents attended a public meeting in support of Cooke, and when Posts and Telegraphs officials tried to transfer the office on 1 December, they were prevented from doing so by a large crowd of townspeople.[155]

On 5 December, about one hundred and fifty people attended a Labour Party meeting calling on the government to implement the appointment of Farrell as sub-postmaster. The majority of residents 'blacked out their houses as a protest' against the meeting.[156] Everett claimed in the Dáil the following day that Farrell was the most suitably qualified candidate, and that only a direct relative could inherit the sub-postmaster job. Fianna Fáil's Paddy Smith said the affair was 'dirty, low-down political corruption' and accused the Leas Cheann Comhairle, Patrick Hogan, of being a partisan political hack. Joe Blowick had to restrain Oliver J. Flanagan from crossing the House to 'have words' with Smith.[157]

The affair was politically damaging enough on its own, but it also began to cost the government vital parliamentary support. Independent TD Patrick Cogan wrote to Costello on 8 December to say he wouldn't support the government until the wrong was righted. 'The battle of Baltinglass is everybody's battle now. It is a battle for clean administration and decent public life; it is a fight for justice for the defenceless, and for impartiality in the exercise by Ministers of their executive functions.'[158]

On 11 December, a large force of gardaí protected the Posts and Telegraphs engineers as they disconnected Cooke's premises and connected Farrell's. Michael Farrell claimed it was a case of 'big shots' against farmers and working men. Helen Cooke said she would go to England to look for work.[159] Several telephone poles between Baltinglass and Dublin were cut down following the moving of the post office, while many of the townspeople boycotted Farrell.[160]

While Costello refused to give time for a private member's motion calling for an inquiry into the Baltinglass case, the local branch of Clann na Poblachta dissolved itself in protest at the situation.[161] The branch complained that 'the party, during the election campaign, made it known that it would not stand for anything but clean government; you now stand by and allow a grave injustice to be done on two defenceless women. The appointment of Michael Farrell . . . is one of the many glaring cases of political jobbery that are being enacted during the Inter-Party Government's term of office.'[162] A more serious portent of the effect of the scandal was a speech by leading Clann na Poblachta member Noel Hartnett to a party meeting in Dundrum, challenging Everett to say whether he had acted on the advice of his officials. If he had not, Hartnett said, he should resign.[163] A few days later, The O'Mahoney, a former Fine Gael TD, resigned from that party in protest at the Baltinglass situation.[164]

Farrell resigned as sub-postmaster on 21 December, on the grounds that the situation was being used to launch 'base and unwarranted' attacks on Everett. The minister accepted his resignation with regret, but promised to bring in an independent system of appointment as soon as possible.[165]

Having disposed of Farrell, the Baltinglass activists renewed their efforts on behalf of Helen Cooke, sending four cars on a nationwide tour to gain support for her.[166] Early in January 1951, Everett established a permanent selection board of department officials to fill vacancies for sub-postmasters;[167] later in the month, Helen Cooke was appointed sub-postmistress of Baltinglass.[168]

On 8 February, Hartnett resigned from Clann na Poblachta over the Battle of Baltinglass, although he did not publish his letter of resignation for another two months. In many ways this widening of the split in the Clann, and the loss of Hartnett, 'an invaluable bridge between the republican zealots and the social reformers',[169] was the most important result of the episode.

In his letter, Hartnett claimed that coalition had led 'to compromise on those principles of political honesty and clean administration which we induced our supporters to believe were fundamental to our policy'. He claimed that issues were not judged on their merits for the country, but purely on whether they would cause an election or be popular with the electorate. 'This may be "real-politik" but it is nevertheless amoral.' He further complained of 'an Inter-Party mentality leading to confusion of thought and the virtual abandonment of any fundamental political or social philosophy', and of 'the love and loyalty which to the detriment of principle now seems to bind us to the leaders of the other parties in the Government'.[170] One of those closest to Costello at the time felt that the Taoiseach's defence of Everett demonstrated that 'concessions on petty issues in accumulation can eventually impinge on one's concept of principle'.[171]

While the parties in the inter-party arrangement faced threats to their identities, there were also advantages to coalition, the most obvious being the reunification of the Labour Party in June 1950. Fianna Fáil, in opposition for the first time in sixteen years, also faced opportunities as well as dangers. In Lemass's words, 'we embarked on a very vigorous reorganisation campaign . . . so that by 1951 we had a much more effective organisation than we had in 1948';[172] but he also told his son-in-law, Charles Haughey, that 'the hardest thing to do in politics was to keep a party together in opposition'.[173]

The best way to keep the party together, it seemed, was to attack the government at every available opportunity. One journalist, not unsympathetic to Fianna Fáil, observed 'the mood was such that the party would have opposed the Ten Commandments had they been introduced by a coalitionist Moses'.[174] De Valera lectured his parliamentary party that 'strength lies in unity. To say the contrary, and to hold that there is some special virtue in a "heap of uncementing sand" is a pretence which deceives only those who want to be deceived . . .'[175]

Despite the government's attempts to bring the term 'inter-party' into everyday language, Fianna Fáil speakers continued to refer to it as a coalition[176] and to deny its legitimacy. For instance, Lemass reasserted in May 1948 his belief that the government 'is in office on false pretences; that it secured control by a trick. The Irish people did not want them there and would remove them if they got the chance.'[177]

At the end of February 1948, Lemass joined the board of the Irish Press as managing director[178] and became heavily involved in the work of the group, particularly the launch of the *Sunday Press.* 'It was for me a very pleasant experience, I must admit. In a personal sense . . . I was disappointed when it came to an end and we had to go back into Government again.'[179]

The *Press* was a very effective instrument in the hands of Fianna Fáil. Costello told the Dáil in May 1949 that forty-seven statements had been issued by the Government Information Bureau or individual departments correcting the accuracy of reports in Irish newspapers since the government took office – six each in the *Irish Independent* and the *Irish Times*, four in the *Cork Examiner*, three in the *Evening Mail*, two in the *Evening Herald*, and no less than twenty-six in the *Irish Press*.[180]

On 16 February 1949, the *Irish Press* claimed that Bill Norton 'occupies most of his time with party matters and leaves his Department to run itself'. Norton began a libel action against the paper in April.[181] Lemass admitted that he supplied the notes which were written up by a journalist for publication. He told the High Court that 'the general view was that his [Norton's] function was not so much to administer the Department of Social Welfare but to look after the government and hold it together in so far as there was a danger of dissension arising in it'.[182] This, of course, was not the same as devoting oneself to party matters, and could be regarded as part of Norton's legitimate duties as Tánaiste. Norton won his libel case, but was awarded just £1 in damages.[183] As a result, a gleeful MacEntee took to referring to the Tánaiste as Billy the Quid.

This first Irish coalition, then, adapted the machinery of government to provide a more 'elastic' administration. This was made necessary by the differences within Cabinet, whether caused by policy or personality. The customary Cabinet procedures were stretched – meetings went on inordinately long as consensus was sought; collective responsibility was breached again and again; and many issues were referred to Cabinet committees in the hope that agreement would be reached, or that the question could simply be forgotten. These changes led to tensions with the civil service, culminating in the sacking of a departmental secretary, but fortunately the permanent government proved able to adapt. Party considerations also forced change on the Cabinet. The need for all parties to maintain their separate identities led to frequent public statements which could be regarded as undermining the stability of the government. It also led to Fine Gael finding itself supporting concessions to republicans, as well as Everett's blatant political jobbery in Baltinglass.

Perhaps the most surprising outcome is that the system was able to survive the strains placed upon it, despite the fact that an often divided government faced a single-party opposition backed by a powerful newspaper group. The first inter-party government remains a striking example of how a system, even one unused to coalitions, can be adapted to cope with a new and unexpected type of administration.

THREE

STEALING THE LONG
MAN'S CLOTHES

*The repeal of the External Relations Act will take the gun out of Irish
politics and will give us complete independence with a Republican form
of government.*

John A. Costello[1]

*We . . . are convinced that the standard of political honesty in Ireland has
been lowered grievously by the action of Mr Costello and his Fine Gael
colleagues.*

Irish Times editorial[2]

The first indication of the new government's attitude to
constitutional questions was, appropriately, entirely symbolic.
Outside the Houses of the Oireachtas in Leinster House
was a large statue of Queen Victoria, 'a work of intense, though no
doubt unintentional, ugliness . . . popularly known as "Ireland's
revenge"'.[3] The statue of the Famine Queen had remained unmo-
lested despite Fianna Fáil's sixteen years in office, but the new
government decided to remove it, ostensibly to provide more car
parking space.[4] The government was fully aware of the symbolism
involved, as was made clear when the Northern-based National
Union of Protestants offered to buy it – Seán MacBride objected to
the statue being re-erected on Irish soil.[5]

Symbolism was important in the late 1940s, when the state was
only a quarter of a century old. Although sovereignty had been
demonstrated by neutrality during the Second World War, the
constitutional position remained ambiguous. Eamon de Valera had
tried to have things both ways, with his 1937 constitution in effect

introducing a republic while the 1936 External Relations Act left a door open to the Commonwealth. This was the culmination of a promise he made in 1933: 'Let us remove these forms one by one, so that this State that we control may be a republic in fact; and that, when the time comes, the proclaiming of the Republic may involve no more than a ceremony, the formal confirmation of a status already attained.'[6] The irony was that his Civil War opponents were now to bring about that formal confirmation.

With the obvious exception of the Mother and Child crisis, the declaration of the Republic was the most controversial episode in the life of the first inter-party government. Critics ranging from *Irish Times* editor R.M. (Bertie) Smyllie to Noël Browne claimed that John A. Costello declared a Republic, without Cabinet approval, while on a visit to Canada. If true, such an action would demonstrate Costello's unfitness to be Taoiseach. In fact, he did nothing of the sort. He merely confirmed the truth of a newspaper story predicting the repeal of the External Relations Act – a decision which had been taken by the Cabinet (although not properly recorded) and communicated to the British. However, it is true that Costello's decision to tell the truth at his fateful press conference placed his government in diplomatic difficulty, and was not welcome to his Cabinet colleagues. Apart from this excess of honesty, Costello can also with some justice be accused of allowing the situation to slip out of control once he had confirmed that the Act was to be repealed, with results we shall examine.

The External Relations Act was introduced in December 1936 by de Valera as part of his continuing campaign to dismantle the 1921 Anglo-Irish Treaty settlement. The Act, which authorised the British King to sign letters of credence for Irish diplomats, was opposed by Fine Gael and Labour. On its introduction, Costello said that he didn't care what the constitutional position was going to be, 'provided we know definitely where we stand'. He said he could understand membership of the Commonwealth, or 'a decent declaration of a republic. But I cannot understand the indecency which is being perpetrated on this country by this Bill . . . whether we are in the Commonwealth, whether we are a republic, or whether we are neither one thing nor the other – a state unknown hitherto to political theory – I want at least that it should be definite . . .'[7]

By 1947, the External Relations Act was increasingly becoming an embarrassment. It was one of the targets of Clann na Poblachta, and de Valera had decided to get rid of it, although he had no plans to formally change the status of the state. A draft of a Bill to do so, the Presidential (International Powers and Functions) Bill, had been drawn up by the Attorney General, Cearbhall Ó Dálaigh, in November 1947. But the draft Bill did not make any reference to the state being a republic.[8] The British representative in Dublin, Lord Rugby, suggested to de Valera in October 1947 that 'he would be very unwise to lay hands on the External Relations Act . . . if left alone it still might prove a useful bridge over difficulties not yet in sight . . .'[9] As we saw in Chapter One, de Valera left the Act alone during the election campaign, although Rugby was under no illusions that if returned to office he would finally take action.[10]

Fine Gael's confused attitude during the 1948 election campaign has already been noted, with party leader Richard Mulcahy coming out in favour of keeping the External Relations Act while Tom O'Higgins said he favoured its removal.[11] However, the repeal of the Act was not necessarily inconsistent with some continuing association with the Commonwealth. Mulcahy had for a long time been staunchly in favour of maintaining the Commonwealth connection. At the February 1946 Fine Gael ard fheis, for instance, he stated that 'Ireland's political liberties, its military security and its hope of ending partition are firmly bound up with our membership of the British Commonwealth'.[12] However, the views of other leading figures in Fine Gael were more complex. Costello believed that Ireland had ceased to be a member of the Commonwealth when it stopped attending Commonwealth conferences (regular meetings of Commonwealth leaders).[13] He was also anxious, as he never tired of pointing out, to 'take the gun out of Irish politics', a desire prompted by his distaste for the repressive measures he had been involved with as Attorney General.[14] Patrick McGilligan had become frustrated 'at the failure of membership to restore Irish unity or even to permit unity within the 26 counties . . . His motivation was Irish freedom not dominion equality nor unfettered commonwealth partnership, though he saw no objection to the third, providing the first was accepted . . .'[15]

Rugby warned the Commonwealth Relations Office at the end of January 1948, just days before the general election, that 'the annulment of the External Relations Act will not be long delayed. No party has left the door open for any other course . . . I should not be sorry to see this strange device removed . . . it is now clear that it will not provide the bridge to closer associations, as was once hoped.' He predicted that the introduction of the British Nationality Bill in the House of Commons would give Dublin the excuse to repeal the Act.[16]

However, while Rugby believed the Act was certain to be repealed, MacBride seemed to accept that no public mandate had been received to do so. During the debate on Costello's nomination as Taoiseach on 18 February, MacBride told the Dáil that Clann na Poblachta could not 'claim that in this election we secured a mandate from the people that would enable us to repeal, or seek to repeal, the External Relations Act and such other measures as are inconsistent with our status as an independent republic. These, therefore, have to remain in abeyance for the time being . . .'[17] Rugby concluded that Fine Gael opinion was having its effect, and that 'it is probable . . . that this question will not come up in an urgent form'.[18] Three days later he added information, from 'a wholly reliable source', that while Costello 'does not like the Act he does not propose to interfere with it'.[19]

But a significant straw in the wind was James Dillon's comment on the day of the government's election. 'I observe that Deputy MacBride contemplates a long postponement of some objectives near his heart, but I am more optimistic than he.' He went on to suggest that Ireland would shortly be called upon to 'take her place with those nations who seek to defend the liberty of the world . . . In accepting that invitation, we may see a sovereign, independent and United Ireland delivered from the nauseating frauds of a dictionary republic sooner than we anticipate.'[20] In this passage, Dillon was indicating his approval for the repeal of the External Relations Act, but also his wish to see an end to neutrality, a matter that was to prove more controversial.

One of the key questions was whether Ireland was still a member of the Commonwealth, or already a republic, in 1948. The opinion of an Attorney General more than a decade later is interesting: 'The Republic of Ireland Act, 1948, did not in any way alter the constitutional position of the state. That could be done only by an amendment of the Constitution. Accordingly, if the state is now a Republic . . . it has been such since the Constitution of 1937 came into operation.'[21]

But at the time Frederick Boland, secretary of the Department of External Affairs, insisted that the repeal of the External Relations Act was an important change in the state's status. Before repeal 'we had indeed a republican constitution, but superimposed on it we had an act under which functions, which in the case of other countries are always performed by the head of state, were performed for us by the British King. To call the state a Republic, as long as that act remained in force, was to say the least of it controversial. It is that act which is now being repealed. We will then have . . . a republic indistinguishable from any other republic in the world.'[22]

Two issues were critical to the declaration of the Republic: trade and citizenship. The former was covered by the Anglo-Irish Trade Agreement, negotiated in June 1948 and signed in July, which gave Ireland rights of access to the British market independent of Commonwealth membership. Citizenship had also been the subject of talks between London and Dublin, in connection with the British Nationality Bill. After objections by Dublin to the terms of the Bill which seemed to claim Irish nationals as Commonwealth citizens, the Bill was eventually amended to read that 'any law in force in any part of the UK and Colonies . . . shall . . . continue to have effect in relation to citizens of Éire who are not British subjects in like manner as it has effect in relation to British subjects'.[23] MacBride, speaking in the Dáil in July 1948, said that a 'very serious effort to meet our viewpoint was made by Mr Attlee's government and embodied in the Bill which has just passed the British House of Commons. Some of the provisions of the Bill . . . still fall considerably short of our viewpoint; such, for instance, as the imposition of a non-Irish status on our fellow countrymen in the Six Counties . . . [The Bill's] importance lies . . . not so much in its actual practical effect as in the indication it gives of a real desire to understand our viewpoint.'[24]

MacBride could have added, in view of the controversy about to break out over citizenship in relation to the repeal of the External Relations Act, that its importance also lay in Britain granting rights to Irish citizens who were expressly held not to be British subjects.

Indeed, it is hard to see how the British could have seriously argued that repeal altered the position as set out in their own legislation. The British Lord Chancellor put precisely this view – that the Nationality Act conferred rights independently of Commonwealth membership – to the Prime Minister, Clement Attlee, on 9 October 1948.[25] This did not, of course, stop the British from trying to argue the opposite case. It is also worth noting that the British Home Office felt that the declaration of the Republic would have to be followed by 'extensive amendment' of the Nationality Act, and that in particular 'the provisions of the Act that Éire citizens are not aliens . . . will have to be repealed'.[26] As we shall see, this view was not in the end accepted by the British government.[27]

But while the Nationality Act clarified, at least for the time being, certain questions, others remained open, in particular whether Ireland was still a member of the Commonwealth. In an attempt to find out, Derry MP Sir Ronald Ross asked in the House of Commons in April 1948 if the Irish government had been consulted about the alteration in the official title of the King, who was also Emperor of India, following the change of status of India and Pakistan. Patrick Gordon-Walker, the Under Secretary of State at the Commonwealth Relations Office, replied that Dublin had been informed of the change the previous June. When he was pressed as to whether Ireland was a dominion, and in what capacity it had been consulted, Gordon-Walker replied: 'Naturally, as a member of the British Commonwealth.'[28]

Captain Peadar Cowan was also seeking a definition of the state's status. Throughout the summer of 1948, Cowan – who, as we shall see in Chapter Eight, was expelled from Clann na Poblachta in early July – repeatedly tried to get a clear answer from the government. His questioning in the Dáil was highly embarrassing, and fears that he might introduce a private member's motion to repeal the External Relations Act played an important part in government actions. In Jack McQuillan's opinion, this harrying of ministers was 'Peadar's way of getting the boot into MacBride'.[29] In July, MacBride told Cowan that 'we are certainly not a member of the British Commonwealth of Nations', a proposition with which de Valera agreed. But MacBride added: 'As Deputy de Valera knows well, there are certain functions performed by heads of state, and we lack such a head at the moment. We have, for external purposes, no head of state.'[30]

A week later, Cowan asked Costello how and under what circumstances Ireland ceased to be a member of the Commonwealth. The Taoiseach referred to the constitutional position of Ireland as a sovereign, independent, democratic state associated with the Commonwealth, and said that the process by which Ireland ceased formally to be a member was one of gradual development. Cowan pressed him as to whether Ireland had ceased to be a member, to which Costello replied: 'It has ceased to be formally a member but it is associated with the other members.'[31] In response to further questioning from Cowan on 5 August, Costello insisted that the association with the Commonwealth was a free one, which, 'by virtue of its freedom, can be terminated by unilateral action'.[32]

The following day, Norton told the Dáil that it 'would do our national self-respect good, both at home and abroad, if we were to proceed without delay to abolish the External Relations Act'. De Valera responded 'Go ahead', adding 'You will get no opposition from us.'[33] De Valera, the architect of the Act, said that because of the confusion caused, and 'the play which has been made for political purposes with it here', it might be best to transfer the power of signing letters of credence to the President. 'If the present Administration want to do that, they will not find any opposition over here.'[34]

According to Costello, 'these remarks made it urgent for the Government to reach a decision. Accordingly, absolutely on my own motion, I raised the matter with the Government. An express, unanimous decision to repeal the External Relations Act was taken by the Government, which decided that the legislation should be introduced immediately the Dáil re-assembled.' Costello claimed that all ministers except Noël Browne were present, and although he wasn't sure if the decision was recorded, 'that the decision was definitely taken I have no doubt'.[35] Patrick Lynch later said he believed the decision had been taken 'at an ad hoc meeting of ministers in Leinster House late at night' before Costello left for Canada. He also said that no consideration had been given to possible reaction from London, because 'there had been no discussion with civil servants'.[36] It should be noted again that repeal of the External Relations Act did not necessarily imply a change in the relationship with the Commonwealth. Even if Costello's recollection is correct, the fact that such an important decision wasn't recorded, either by Costello or by Cosgrave, raises serious questions about the way the government was run.

As to why the government's decision was not announced immediately, Costello was later to claim that it had been decided to defer an announcement until the late autumn, because 'it was rather a drastic decision . . . and we had decided to issue a National Loan in the autumn, and it was better that there should not be any disturbance in the political atmosphere . . .'[37] Costello's recollection is definitely at fault on the question of the loan, as the last national loan had been raised in March 1948 and the next was not issued until the following year.[38]

MacBride denied that any pressure had been put on Costello by Clann na Poblachta. He said that when the constitutional position was discussed in Cabinet in the summer of 1948 – as it was in connection with letters of credence, the British Nationality Act, and the Commonwealth Prime Ministers' Conference, as we will see below – he expressed the view that the External Relations Act 'was a constant source of constitutional difficulties and an irritant, and that it should be repealed. There was no question of pressurising by any member of the government on this issue; there was no disagreement. The discussions that took place were mainly concerned with the consequential steps that would be necessitated by the repeal of the Act.'[39] This assertion was backed by Frederick Boland, MacBride's departmental secretary, who said that the government 'had discussed it I know twice in the Cabinet and there was a consensus . . . that the act would go, but there was no decision as to when and how the job would be done'.[40] Again, this indicates that agreement on repeal of the External Relations Act did not extend to agreement on leaving the Commonwealth.

MacBride was later to claim that he had, in his first six months in office, taken a number of 'ancillary steps' which made the repeal of the Act inevitable. The first was the appointment of the new Argentine minister, who arrived in Dublin with letters of credence addressed to the King. 'I consulted the Cabinet and said we should change the practice and letters of credence should be addressed to the President. There was immediate agreement that this was a piece of nonsense and so the Argentinian Minister got a fresh letter addressed to the President. Seán T. was like a peacock at the ceremony. Press and photographers were present, but the press never realised the significance of it. I was waiting for the British reaction; I had not said a word to the British. I believe to this day the British did not notice it.'[41] This was hardly surprising – MacBride's own memorandum to the government said that while the letter was addressed to the President, this would not entail any change in the ceremony. The letter would still be accepted by the Taoiseach, although on this occasion, Costello would personally deliver it to O'Kelly.[42] The ceremony in Áras an Uachtaráin was not, therefore, as important as MacBride claimed, a point underlined by his own department, which said the first direct presentation of credentials to the President was by the Belgian minister in September 1949.[43]

But despite MacBride's hyperbole, the fact that the letter of credence was formally addressed to the President was significant. Ian McCabe notes that MacBride 'bounced' the Cabinet into accepting this by-passing of the Act, presenting a memorandum on the subject five days before the official presentation of the credentials, too late for his actions to be reversed; however, two weeks later the Cabinet formally granted MacBride authority to appoint a chargé d'affaires to Lisbon 'subject to section 1 (1) of the External Relations Act',[44] indicating a return to normal procedure.

The second step in MacBride's subversion of the Act involved the negotiations on the British Nationality Act, discussed above. The third was the reply to Attlee's invitation to the Commonwealth Prime Ministers' Conference which was to be held in London in October. MacBride's reply was that the government did not regard Ireland as a member and could not attend unless provision could be made for the discussion and solution of partition. Naturally, Attlee replied that this was not possible.

MacBride later claimed that McGilligan and other ministers were in favour of the repeal of the External Relations Act. 'The firm attitude of the Fine Gael members was that it was a monstrous piece of double-talk.'[45] MacBride told Rugby shortly after Costello's Canadian announcement that repeal of the Act had been brought up in Cabinet by Fine Gael, 'who had had such a grim time in the period of the Cosgrave government defending what they did not really believe in that they had decided this time not to find themselves in that position against a virulent Opposition'.[46]

Rugby appeared to accept that Fine Gael was responsible, suggesting that the party 'had a sudden brain-wave that they could steal the "Long Man's" clothes . . . They are all somewhat bewildered by their own sudden illogical iconoclasm and must now find high sounding phrases to justify it.'[47] But there was at least some logic to Fine Gael's position – after all, it was still the party of Michael Collins, the proponent of the Treaty as a stepping stone. McGilligan had been an important figure in the development of the Commonwealth; in a discussion with King George V in 1931, he compared the (British) constitution to a balloon, adding: 'We are pulling it from the outside. I hope no-one will get hurt if we ever let go.'[48] Costello was later to argue that the 1931 Statute of Westminster, the crowning achievement of the Cosgrave government in the diplomatic field, 'justified all the arguments that [Arthur] Griffith and Collins had put forward in the Treaty debates. It received its fullest implementation in the Republic of Ireland Act which enabled us to clear out of the Commonwealth in quite a lawful manner.'[49] Thus, it could be argued, Fine Gael was able to regain the mantle of Collins, which had been appropriated by de Valera in office.

The Cabinet met on 19 August, for the last time before Costello's departure to Canada. It decided that Ireland should not be represented as a member at the Commonwealth conference, although 'consideration of the question whether Ireland should be represented at the meeting, otherwise than as a member of the Commonwealth, for the purpose of any particular subject, was deferred, pending the receipt of further information in that connection which the Minister for External Affairs undertakes to procure'.[50] Patrick Lynch has pointed to the wording of this decision as proof that 'on the day before the Taoiseach left Dublin for Canada the government did not consider Ireland a member of the Commonwealth'.[51] Although there was no record of a decision to repeal the Act, this had been anticipated by Lord Rugby, who advised London shortly before Costello's trip to Canada that 'I have no doubt that it has been decided to repeal the [External Relations Act]. I expect this to happen soon after the reassembly of the Dáil in November . . .'[52]

The Cabinet also approved Costello's speech to the Canadian Bar Association. MacBride believed this to be the only occasion on which the script of a speech was read and approved at a Cabinet meeting.[53] Costello left for his North American tour on 22 August, arriving in New York on the 27th[54] and in Canada three days later.[55]

Two issues were later blamed for Costello's 'impulsive' decision to make the announcement. The first was the failure to toast the President of Ireland following a dinner. According to Costello, the Irish high commissioner, John Hearne, had made it clear that the Taoiseach would not attend the dinner unless the toast was made.[56] Rugby believed that the failure to give the toast was part of a pattern, taking in a similar incident during the trade talks in London, and also Irish attempts to have visiting British dignitaries placed in the position of having to give the toast to the President: this happened to the Lord Chancellor, Benjamin Jowitt, and to the British army showjumping team, during visits to Dublin in the summer of 1948. Rugby felt that these incidents formed 'a chain of events which . . . played a great part in bringing on the developments which led to the repeal of the External Relations Act'.[57]

The second upset for Costello in Canada involved the placing of a silver replica of Roaring Meg, one of the guns used to defend the siege of Derry in 1689, in front of him at a dinner given by the Governor General, Lord Alexander. Two decades later, Costello still remembered the incident: 'I decided to make no comment, although I considered the matter to be in bad taste. I felt that any protest would only disturb and embarrass the Prime Minister and that while the display was tactless it was not intended to be provocative.'[58] Patrick Lynch recalled that Alexander actually pointed out the Roaring Meg silverware to Costello. Lynch also wrote that Costello 'normally a good talker, found the going hard because the Governor General was a man of few words and limited conviviality'.[59] In contrast, Alexander later told the *Irish Times* that 'every effort was made to please John A. Costello, and a green, white and orange flower arrangement was placed in front of him'.[60]

If Alexander was unfriendly, and it appears that Costello believed this to be the case, the Taoiseach only had himself to blame. He had declined an invitation to stay at Government House, and this may have appeared as a snub.[61] Hearne had advised Costello that 'it is usual for visiting Prime Ministers and their wives to be guests of the Governor General at Government House during their stay in Ottawa', but Costello replied 'subject . . . to your advice in the matter, I must say that I should prefer if arrangements could be made for our stay elsewhere'.[62]

In his speech to the Canadian Bar Association in Montreal on 1 September, Costello said of the External Relations Act that 'the in-accuracies and infirmities of these provisions are apparent. The Crown was the symbol of free association and not the symbol of co-operation; the formalities of the issue of Full Powers to negotiate or sign treaties are ignored and the statutory provisions deal only with the appoint-ment and not with the reception of diplomatic representatives.'[63] The speech as drafted (by Frederick Boland) had nothing about the Act in it. After reading the draft, Costello commented: 'It's fine, but there's too much of the smell of Empire about this.'[64] The speech, according to Patrick Lynch, who accompanied the Taoiseach on the visit, was 'extraordinarily well received . . . it was soon obvious that the subject of his address would stir up a good deal of comment'.[65]

The *Sunday Independent* of 5 September reported that Ireland was to repeal the External Relations Act. The story came as a surprise to members of the government – Richard Mulcahy was visibly taken aback when the paper was brought into him as he ate his breakfast, either by the contents of the story or by the fact of publication.[66] Costello said the story 'worried and surprised me. It seemed to me to be quite obvious that the story was not just intelligent anticipation, but was the result of a leak from some person with inside know-ledge.'[67] In fact, he privately blamed MacBride.[68]

Hector Legge, the editor of the *Sunday Independent*, always claimed that his article was the result of 'obvious journalistic intuition', with no leak involved.[69] It would seem more than a little strange that, however good his intuition, a journalist of Legge's calibre would not attempt to check such a story with his sources – and he was a close friend of both Seán MacBride and James Dillon. MacBride's personal secretary, Louie O'Brien, believed that MacBride inspired the story, along with Legge and another journalist on the *Sunday Independent*. She claimed to have found out the truth by accident a number of years after the event from the other journalist involved. In her view, MacBride was frustrated by the lack of progress on the repeal of the External Relations Act. The other members of the government were in favour of repeal – but at some stage in the future. According to Louie O'Brien, they had not made a formal decision and were not prepared to go ahead with repeal until more urgent matters had been dealt with. Thus, she claimed, the *Sunday Independent* story was planted by MacBride to force their hand.[70]

MacBride later said he believed Costello's speech to the Canadian Bar Association heralded the announcement of the repeal of the Act.[71] If he briefed journalists on this point, it explains the *Sunday Independent* story. MacBride also told Lord Rugby on 7 September that the government intended to do away with the Act.[72] What MacBride had not bargained for was Costello's decision to publicly confirm the story at a press conference.

Costello was contacted on the evening of the *Sunday Independent* story by one of the Ottawa papers and asked for a comment. 'I of course said that I did not have anything to say about it at that time, but I had arranged long before I came to Canada a press conference for the following Tuesday . . . I knew that the first question that I would be asked was . . . was it true. I was thousands of miles away from my colleagues, the responsibility fell to me . . . if I had denied it of course it would have been a lie, if I had said no comment it would have been clear that I meant yes, so I made up my mind that in all circumstances telling the truth is best . . .'[73] According to Patrick Lynch, MacBride sent a telegram to Costello early on the Monday morning, advising him to make no comment on the *Independent* story,[74] while both Lynch and Hearne urged him not to refer to the impending repeal.[75] However, Louie O'Brien claimed that MacBride encouraged Costello to do the opposite during a telephone conversation: 'Look, the easiest thing to do is to say yes, because you actually have nothing against it, now have you?'[76]

Whatever advice Costello received, at the press conference in Ottawa he repeated the statement he had made to the Canadian

Bar Association, that the External Relations Act was full of inaccuracies and infirmities, and that the only thing to do was to scrap it. Costello said that the decision had already been taken by Cabinet.[77] This revelation bemused most of the journalists present, who had no idea what the Act was all about, until one of their number asked if repeal meant that Ireland was leaving the Commonwealth.[78] Costello said it did, adding that he saw no reason why Ireland could not continue in association with Britain, but not as a formal member of the Commonwealth.[79] This forthright statement went further than was absolutely necessary, and it surprised Lynch, who asked the Taoiseach if his action had been wise. Costello replied simply: 'no qualifications'.[80]

Frederick Boland felt that the announcement had been made in a 'burst of indiscretion', and reported that all he could answer the flood of phone calls to his office with was 'our Prime Minister has simply made an awful gaffe'.[81] He opined: 'Jack Costello had about as much notion of diplomacy as I have of astrology . . . You can safely say, if de Valera had remained in power, we would have remained in the Commonwealth, but all references to the Crown etc. would have been eliminated from the Act.'[82]

Boland claimed he told MacBride about the announcement as he dined in the Russell Hotel with Rugby, and that the minister was 'amazed'.[83] Rugby said MacBride was 'not a little surprised – indeed perturbed – by this sudden unconventional development'.[84] However, MacBride was later to insist that Costello's confirmation 'was no surprise to me or to any Minister'. He added that he had met Rugby that day because he 'did not want him to be in an awkward position regarding the press conference. I do not know how he could have been so misinformed about the feeling of the Cabinet. Possibly he felt he should have known and didn't know.'[85]

Rugby's correspondence told a different story. As we have seen, he had already informed London of the government's intention to repeal the Act; but on 9 September he wrote that MacBride had told him 'as a personal confidence that neither he nor any member of the Cabinet here had any idea that Mr Costello was likely to make any statement in Canada on the subject of the External Relations Act . . . I am sure that Mr MacBride is sincere in this.'[86]

In his memoirs, Attlee stated that he believed Costello's statement in Canada was 'not premeditated . . . he declared for cutting the last link which bound Éire to the Commonwealth, and could not then retreat from this position'.[87]

But Rugby stated the position with more precision when he wrote that while 'it is true that there was a firm intention to repeal the act . . . the procedure had not been discussed' by the Cabinet.[88] The British annoyance at Costello's announcement was not caused by what he said – it was when and how he said it. Reporting on a conversation with MacBride, Rugby reiterated in December that while 'it was true that in their general line of policy they had a plan to get the Act removed . . . they had no immediate intention of going ahead. They would have consulted us and certainly would not have come out with a statement likely to embarrass the Imperial Conference.'[89]

Proof that the British expected repeal is provided by an August meeting which discussed issuing a warning against any tampering with the Act. Cabinet Secretary Sir Norman Brook, Commonwealth Secretary Philip Noel-Baker and Lord Rugby decided to find out how the older Commonwealth members felt about the prospect of any Irish action. The aim was to let the Irish know 'before it is too late, that the repeal of the External Relations Act would be regarded by the older members of the Commonwealth as ending her membership of the club', although, showing a grasp of the realities of Irish politics, the meeting concluded that such a warning 'would probably have no effect'.[90]

A note prepared in the Department of the Taoiseach in 1957 for de Valera concluded that 'no *formal* decision was taken on the matter prior to the 9th September 1948. It is, however, reasonable to assume that the Taoiseach would not have made the statement in Ottawa . . . and that the Minister for External Affairs would not have submitted proposals in the matter to the Government on the following day – in the absence of the Taoiseach – unless the matter had been discussed and approved (informally) by the Government sometime before the Taoiseach made his visit to Canada. Nowhere, however, is there any suggestion that the Taoiseach should be authorised to introduce the Bill [to repeal the Act] when he saw fit.' The same note also points out that the authority to introduce the

Bill in the Dáil 'would appear to have been given to the Minister for External Affairs (by whom the various drafts of the Bill had been submitted)' rather than to Costello.[91]

Noël Browne also believed that Costello had not received Cabinet approval for the repeal of the Act, arguing that any minister requiring a Cabinet decision 'would formally submit a written request for permission to act, supported, usually, by documentary justification for such action . . . Such, without doubt, would have been the case were the government to take such an important decision as to decide formally to repeal the External Relations Act.'[92]

A letter from Costello to Norton, written a few days after the press conference, is worth quoting at some length:

> Dear Bill,
>
> . . . As you well know, I very nearly, if not actually, 'declared' the Republic – in Ottawa above all places. I will explain when I return why I decided to state publicly that we intended to repeal the External Relations Act. It was really the article in the *Sunday Independent* that decided me, although I had intended to tell Mr Mackenzie-King . . . of our intentions in this regard.
>
> Actually, it turned out to be good tactics. I have had several talks with him, a most cordial character. He fully understands and accepts my point of view and we have in him a very good friend and one who will advocate us when he is in London next month.
>
> I will reserve until I get home a full account of our conversations which were most interesting and helpful. I understand that the Canadian Cabinet considered the matter too, and as my final interview with him, which lasted for three hours, was after the meeting, I think we can assume that we have the backing of the government, certainly as long as he is a force in it . . .'[93]

The reference to declaring the Republic in 'Ottawa above all places' shows that Costello's action was certainly not premeditated; but the letter also shows that the Taoiseach believed he was merely enunciating government policy, and that he felt his hand had been forced by the *Sunday Independent* story.

The Cabinet met for an hour and a half on 9 September. The ministers present considered a memo from MacBride of the same date accompanying a rough draft of a Bill, entitled the Powers and Functions of the President (External Relations) Bill 1948. MacBride's draft Bill was much wordier than the final result, and included the change of name of the state as section 4 (2): 'If and insofar as it may be necessary or expedient to refer to the State in any instrument as aforesaid whether granted, issued, received or concluded before or after the passing of this Act, the State shall be or be deemed to be described as the "Republic of Ireland".'[94]

A certificate of urgency accompanying the memo and draft stated that the matter had to be dealt with at that meeting because 'Government approval is required urgently in order to allow time for the drafting of the contemplated Bill', adding that it hadn't been submitted earlier because 'recent developments have made it imperative that a decision should be arrived at immediately'.[95] This demonstrates again that while the Cabinet may have informally agreed to repeal the Act, it had not reached a formal decision. Now, however, approval was given for the drafting of a Bill repealing the External Relations Act and providing for 'the exercise and performance by the President of the powers and functions which, in accordance with that Act, are at present capable of being exercised and performed by the King who is recognised by the States of the British Commonwealth of Nations'.[96]

When Costello arrived back in Cobh at the beginning of October, he was met by MacBride and Mulcahy, who both congratulated him on the success of his visit, although Mulcahy indicated his less than whole-hearted support with the rather sour comment to Patrick Lynch that Costello 'has been drinking some very heady wine in Canada'. Later Lynch travelled back to Dublin with MacBride and discussed the issue at length over lunch in Abbeyleix. MacBride gave no indication that he was unhappy with the announcement, talking instead about the favourable impression made by Costello.[97]

Costello told reporters that legislation to abolish the Act would be introduced in the next Dáil session, adding that there would be 'a better conception of the Commonwealth without the Crown'. At a public meeting in Patrick Street in Cork some hours later, he stressed the desire for better relations with Britain: 'We believe that that desire will give us within the next few months complete unity here, and will sweep away the causes of bitterness among the people.'[98]

Browne claimed that a 'caucus meeting' of the Cabinet was held soon after Costello's return from Canada,[99] at which the Taoiseach apologised for his 'unconstitutional' action in deciding to repeal the Act without approval. Browne claimed that Costello offered to resign but that he, in MacBride's absence abroad and speaking for Clann na Poblachta, dismissed the suggestion. 'With varying degrees of enthusiasm the members of the Cabinet remaining assured Costello that he must not resign.'[100] Browne gave his version of events on radio in 1976, but was contradicted by the surviving members of the Cabinet – Dillon, Morrissey, MacBride and McGilligan. Hector Legge later claimed that no such meeting was held, citing the views of Dillon, MacBride, Lynch and Declan Costello, son of the Taoiseach.[101]

Ian McCabe notes that the draft minutes for the Cabinet decision approving Costello's actions in Canada and the US ask if 'the decisions are to be dated for Thursday, October 7th', which supports Browne's claim that a meeting was held.[102] There is an even more telling piece of evidence in the archives. Because of the number of government meetings which were being held without decisions being made, it was decided within the Department of the Taoiseach to keep a record of times and attendances at meetings which would otherwise be unrecorded. Thanks to this, there is written proof that a meeting of ministers was held in the Taoiseach's house on Thursday, 7 October at 8 p.m. although there is no indication of who was there or what they discussed.[103]

The meeting, and the alleged offer to resign, have become controversial because both sides of the argument have accepted Noël Browne's interpretation – if Costello offered to resign, it was because he realised that he had acted unconstitutionally by declaring a Republic without Cabinet approval. We already know that Costello was apologetic about the manner in which he handled the press conference because of his letter to Norton. But that letter also made it clear that Costello felt he was simply confirming a decision that had already been taken. Thanks to notes written by civil servants, we know that a meeting definitely took place, despite the denials of a number of people closely connected with Costello. However, it would seem to have been poorly attended. Given Costello's tendency to speak 'off the cuff', it is not impossible that he would have made an offer to resign, but not necessarily for the reasons advanced by Browne. He had earlier that day received the British *aide-mémoire* that is discussed below. If Costello was taken aback by the strength of the British reaction, he might have felt bound to offer his resignation to allow the government to reverse course. Such an offer of resignation would not necessarily have been made, or heard, as a serious one – but it would show ministers in stark terms what the alternatives were.

That Costello regretted his actions seems to be supported by the assessment of Lord Rugby, who told the Commonwealth Relations Office on the same day, 7 October, that 'Mr Costello was rather on the defensive in regard to his recent pronouncement . . . I said that we had been and still were rather in the dark about it all . . . He finally assured me once again that the repeal of the External Relations Act would be a constructive move in the field of friendly relationships. He added significantly "think what my position would have been if a private member had brought in a motion for its repeal. I dreaded that." '[104] Eight days later, Rugby was even more scathing: 'Mr Costello has conducted this business in a slapdash and amateur fashion . . . When the Government came into power . . . the stated policy was "no constitutional change" . . . one by one loose individual pronouncements have started an unexpected, unnecessary and unfortunate drift, which has certainly not increased general confidence in the government and the man at the wheel.'[105]

The Cabinet met officially on 11 October, and 'the action taken by the Taoiseach during his visit to Canada and the United States of America was approved'.[106] This can be read either as proof that the Cabinet had not previously approved repeal, or as a confirmation of the previous policy in the light of its being made public and the British response. This response, handed to Costello by Rugby on 7 October, warned that if the repeal of the Act was held to make Ireland a foreign country, 'there would flow from that relationship important consequences particularly in the field of preferences and nationality. In both of these matters the UK have international treaty obligations under which they are bound to give most favoured nation treatment to a number of foreign countries which would preclude us from affording to Éire that special treatment which on other grounds we would wish to accord to her.' The British then requested discussions with the Irish before 'the Éire government take a step which may bring these results'.[107]

The Cabinet's reply agreed to talks, but suggested the inclusion of the Commonwealth governments. The Irish desire for friendly relations and for the continuance of trade preference and citizenship rights was stressed, and the hope expressed that 'there should be no insuperable difficulties in doing this, provided that the British government and Commonwealth governments also share this desire'. It added that the Irish relationship with the Commonwealth should be based on the exchange of these rights, rather than 'on forms implying dependence or limitation of sovereignty', finishing off with a declaration that the decision to repeal the External Relations Act 'is not open to revision or modification'.[108]

This note was handed to Rugby by MacBride on 12 October. Clement Attlee replied to Costello two days later, following discussions with representatives of Canada, Australia and New Zealand, then in London for the Commonwealth Prime Ministers' Conference. 'These, with the UK, are the Commonwealth countries with the largest Irish populations and on that account the most closely interested in the practical consequences flowing from the repeal of the External Relations Act. All these Ministers are most anxious to have an opportunity while they are in London of discussing the position with Éire Ministers.' Attlee then invited Costello, and any minister he wished to bring with him, to meet them over the weekend in Chequers, as this was the only time they would be in London but free from the business of the Commonwealth conference.[109]

It was initially planned to send Norton, MacBride and Attorney General Cecil Lavery to the talks,[110] but the delegation was changed to MacBride and McGilligan.[111] On 17 October, the two Irish ministers met Attlee, Canadian Prime Minister designate Louis St Laurent, Australian Minister for External Affairs Herbert Evatt, New Zealand Prime Minister Peter Fraser, Lord Chancellor Jowitt and Commonwealth Secretary Noel-Baker at Chequers. Cabinet Secretary Sir Norman Brook had warned the British side that if

common citizenship was recognised as the link between Common-
wealth members, rather than allegiance to the Crown, a 'two-tier'
Commonwealth could be created. He advised a firm line with the
Irish.[112]

However, the Commonwealth representatives failed to back the
British in their warnings of the dire consequences of Ireland leaving
the Commonwealth[113] – which justified the Irish insistence on
including them. MacBride later claimed that the British didn't
realise that Evatt and his Canadian counterpart Lester Pearson
were pro-Irish; Fraser was an unknown quantity, but New Zealand
was regarded by the Irish as a 'Union Jack' country. However, when
MacBride met Fraser for the first time, at Chequers, the New
Zealand Prime Minister leaned over and said: 'How is your dear
mother? I used to attend her anti-recruiting meetings when I was
in the docks in Glasgow.' He also asked after James Connolly's
children, adding 'I knew him well.'[114]

The British feared that the Chequers meeting had done little
good, as they received a report from journalist A.P. Ryan of the
London *Times* that while Irish officials were pessimistic, the
ministers believed that 'the difficulties . . . could perfectly well be
overcome with good will on both sides . . . they were all lawyers
themselves and knew very well that there were always ways around
legal difficulties.' An official in Rugby's office added that Frederick
Boland had hinted to him 'that what was said at Chequers has not
penetrated into the minds of the Éire Ministers'.[115]

Following the Chequers meeting, the Cabinet approved a note to
be sent to the British, Canadian, Australian and New Zealand governments. It said that while Ireland was not a member of the
Commonwealth, it recognised 'the existence of a specially close
relationship arising not only from ties of blood and kinship but from
traditions and long established economic, social and trade arrangements based on common interests'. It further claimed that the rights
and privileges involved were based on long-standing tradition rather
than being new ones, and therefore they would not lead to claims
for similar treatment under most favoured nation clauses.[116]

Seán Lemass said that while Fianna Fáil welcomed the government decision to repeal the External Relations Act, the party 'reserved
its right to criticise the manner in which the whole business had been

managed by the Coalition government'.[117] Dillon told Wexford Chamber of Commerce that the repeal of the Act was part of the government campaign to eliminate fraud and dishonesty from public life, adding that the Act had 'imposed upon all our people the disgusting necessity of living a lie, pretending to be one thing inside Ireland and to be quite another; smuggling the diplomatic representatives of friendly foreign states into the country and dispatching their letters of credence furtively to London while they were escorted to the Phoenix Park'.[118] Seán MacEntee derisively said that watching a man 'who hitherto may have been regarded as the John Bull of Irish politics draping himself in the habiliments of Tone, would make a skeleton merry'.[119] An editorial in the *Irish Times* came to the conclusion that Dillon was protesting too much; neither he nor Fine Gael had made repeal an issue during the election campaign: 'there can be very small doubt that the government's decision . . . represents part of the price that must be paid for Clann na Poblachta's continual loyalty to the Coalition'.[120]

This comment prompted Costello to hold a press conference, at which he claimed the decision was the unanimous view of all the parties and all the members of the government. 'There is no shadow of a foundation for the statements that were repeated twice in the *Irish Times* that the Bill represented some sort of a pound of flesh or something of that kind, by Mr MacBride and his party for the continuance of their participation in the government. That suggestion is given here by me on behalf of my colleagues, including Mr MacBride, an absolute and unqualified denial.'[121]

He refused to answer detailed questions, on the grounds that discussions were continuing and that the Dáil should hear the details first. The *Irish Times* commented with some justice that if he were such a stickler for etiquette, he would hardly have announced the proposal while in Canada.[122] In fact, according to Rugby, MacBride had insisted that Costello should not answer questions 'as he felt strongly that nothing but harm could come from unrestrained questions'.[123] The *Irish Times* editorial after the press conference went on to question Costello's denial of pressure from Clann na Poblachta: 'We find it hard to understand why none of the Fine Gael members of the Cabinet mentioned the act in their general election speeches . . . We wish the government well in its adventure;

but we must admit frankly that we are disappointed that secession from the Commonwealth would be the work of a Cabinet with John A. Costello at its head.'[124] MacBride said the impetus for repeal came from the Taoiseach. 'Mr Costello's initiative in the matter was due, I believe, to the appreciation by him of the historical factors and of the need to place the sovereignty of this state beyond dispute. The decision of the Government was unanimous.'[125]

At least some Fine Gael activists felt betrayed by the decision, and blamed MacBride. Garret FitzGerald and his wife Joan had reassured the inhabitants of Dublin's Waterloo Road that Fine Gael supported the Commonwealth during the election campaign, and in his memoirs FitzGerald records his 'disillusionment', adding: 'I attributed the dynamic of this decision to MacBride . . .'[126]

Meanwhile, the drafting of the Bill to repeal the External Relations Act continued. At the end of October, the Department of External Affairs circulated copies of the Executive Powers of the State (International Relations) Bill 1948 as prepared by the parliamentary draftsman. The name of the state was now dealt with in section 1 (2): 'In any instrument relating to the executive power of the state in or in connection with its external relations, the state may be referred to as the Republic of Ireland (or the Irish Republic).'[127] The secretary of the Department of the Taoiseach, Maurice Moynihan, had his doubts about section 1 (2). He felt that restricting the scope of the Bill to international relations might imply that the name of the state would be the Irish Republic only in relation to foreign affairs, or that a separate Bill would have to be introduced to deal with the name of the state internally. He also wanted to know if it was constitutionally proper to give the state a title other than Éire or Ireland.[128]

In his explanatory submission to the government, MacBride said that the section was necessary in order to clear up confusion about the exact title of the state for formal diplomatic documents, and also 'to make quite clear, both to foreign powers and to our own people, the character and scope of the constitutional change which the enactment of the Bill will effect. Its omission might be used to suggest some difference between our position and that of India which – although she expects to maintain her existing trade and other arrangements with the Commonwealth – is described in the draft Constitution . . . as a "sovereign, independent Republic".' MacBride said that the section was deliberately permissive because 'the use of mandatory terms might be argued to be an attempt to amend indirectly Article 4 of the Constitution'.[129]

Costello was also looking closely at the Bill, scribbling on his copy a separate section on the name of the state, reading simply: 'The description of the State shall be the Republic of Ireland.'[130] This suggested amendment was agreed on 9 November, although it was noted that the long title of the Bill would have to be changed to take account of this section.[131] The parliamentary draftsman suggested on 11 November that the short title too should be changed because of the new section, to the Republic of Ireland Bill 1948.[132]

The British Cabinet met on 12 November and agreed a tough *aide-mémoire*, warning that their legal advice was that repeal of the External Relations Act would make Ireland a foreign country for most favoured nation purposes, and that this would have severe implications for trade and the treatment of nationals.[133] This note was shown to the Commonwealth leaders in Paris later that day for their approval. In the event, 'Dr Evatt would have none of it, and he was supported, though in less outraged tones, by Mr Pearson'. Without Commonwealth support, the British were forced to send a rather more conciliatory note the following day.[134]

The new note was handed to MacBride on 13 November by Rugby. It said that the British were still unable to find a way to deal with the difficulties that had been outlined at Chequers. A not very subtle threat was included: 'The last thing that the UK government would wish would be to be hurried into taking action in advance to deal with the very difficult situation which will arise in international law when the proposed repeal of the External Relations Act takes effect.' The note went on to urge either a delay in the introduction of the Bill (due on 17 November), or else the setting of a date for its coming into force far enough in the future to allow 'the full implications to be further discussed'.[135]

MacBride was warned by Evatt that the British would offer another conference, this time in Dublin. 'He warned me not to agree, since he and Fraser could not leave Paris. I had hardly put the phone down when Rugby came trotting in. He said the Prime Minister was worried – we must reach some conclusion. I could have fallen for the Dublin proposal quite easily if I had not been warned by Evatt. I said I had better find out if the Commonwealth Prime Ministers were free to come to Dublin . . . The British very reluctantly agreed to meet in Paris.'[136]

MacBride, McGilligan and Lavery began their talks with the British and Commonwealth representatives in the British embassy in Paris on Monday, 15 November. The British argued that repeal meant that Ireland would become a foreign country; the Irish said there had been no constitutional change since 1937. Fraser said he favoured Ireland staying in the Commonwealth, but the Irish said this was not going to happen, as Ireland was not, and would not become, a member. In the end, Evatt suggested a form of words that proved acceptable to the Irish and Commonwealth members. Under his proposal, the Commonwealth and Ireland would agree not to regard each other's citizens as foreign because of 'the fact of a special association', with the eventual granting of reciprocal citizenship rights to be announced in the Dáil during the debate on the Republic of Ireland Bill. Faced with isolation, the British agreed to go back to their government with the Evatt formula.[137]

One important issue in turning the Commonwealth leaders against the British was their fury over leaks after the previous meeting. Commonwealth Secretary Noel-Baker had briefed the lobby correspondents on the afternoon of the Chequers meeting about the 'serious consequences' for trade and nationality that would be caused by the repeal of the External Relations Act.[138] When challenged in Paris, Lord Chancellor Jowitt and Noel-Baker began talking about the free press. MacBride then produced an official Commonwealth Relations Office press release about the Chequers talks, indicating exactly where the leaks had come from. 'Jowitt said he was shocked. Noel-Baker was silent. Then a most dramatic incident occurred. Fraser put his hand in his pocket, pulled out a handful of coins and threw them on the table. He called an official and told him to go out and buy all the papers and see if there was any leaks in them. That ended the conference save for a few perfunctory politenesses. That was the end of it. That was how Ireland left the Commonwealth.'[139]

Noel-Baker told the British Cabinet on 18 November that they could not treat Ireland as a foreign country, despite repeal: 'The practical difficulties would be greater for the UK than for Éire; and, furthermore, that they would thereby forfeit the sympathy and support of Canada, Australia and New Zealand.'[140]

The Irish side agreed in Paris that they would not say anything during the debate on the Republic of Ireland Bill which would increase the legal and political difficulties for the British and Commonwealth governments; for their part, the Commonwealth countries agreed not to say anything which would make it more difficult to maintain that Ireland was not a foreign country. The Irish also agreed to say during the Dáil debate that, in the light of the British Nationality Act, British and Commonwealth citizens would enjoy similar rights in Ireland, and that these rights would be put on a statutory footing. The Irish and British undertook to co-operate to fight off any most favoured nation claims.[141]

In an effort to ensure the maximum effect, Costello instructed Moynihan not to give the long and short titles of the Bill to the evening papers on the day before it was to be introduced; they were to be given to broadcasting organisations at 6 p.m., so as to miss the BBC's 6 p.m. bulletin but catch Radio Éireann's 6.30 news. The Department of the Taoiseach only found out on Saturday, 13 November that Costello intended to introduce the Bill and pilot it through the Oireachtas; they had thought up to then that MacBride would do this.[142] Noël Browne suggested that this decision 'to deprive Seán MacBride of his rights, as the relevant Minister, to introduce the Bill . . . was surely both ill-mannered and ungracious'. He claimed that MacBride did not appear at the following year's Easter celebrations to mark the coming into force of the Act in 'a pitiful protest' at this.[143] But according to Patrick Lynch, Costello decided to introduce the Bill himself in order 'to demonstrate his proprietorial role in the decision'.[144]

Costello moved the first reading of the Republic of Ireland Bill on 17 November.[145] One of the Independents supporting the government, Alfred Byrne jun., proposed a motion on 24 November to refuse a second reading, on the grounds that it would impair the prospects of ending partition. His motion was seconded by his father.

The most important part of Costello's speech moving the second stage dealt with citizenship: 'The position of the Irish government is that while Ireland is not a member of the Commonwealth, it recognises and confirms the existence of a specially close relationship arising not only from ties of friendship and kinship but from traditional and long established economic, social and trade relations based on common interest with the nations that form the Commonwealth of Nations. This exchange of rights and privileges, which it is our firm desire and intention to maintain and strengthen, in our view constitutes a special relationship which negatives the view that other countries could raise valid objections on the ground that Ireland should be treated as a "foreign" country by Britain and Commonwealth countries for the purpose of this exchange of rights and privileges.'

Other points made by Costello included the assertion that repeal was not anti-British; it did not involve leaving the Commonwealth because Ireland had left long ago; the Cabinet had decided on repeal before he left for Canada; the move would end the bitterness and animosity of the past quarter-century; Fine Gael was no longer bound to the Anglo-Irish Treaty, as it no longer existed; it would not reinforce partition, because the External Relations Act had been on the statute books for eleven years without generating any friendly gesture from Stormont; and now everyone could concentrate on partition without the distraction of constitutional issues.[146]

According to Rugby, officials from External Affairs were keeping a close eye on the Taoiseach, whose 'incautious oratory' made them uneasy, to make sure he kept to the text agreed with the British. Not surprisingly, the British representative was unimpressed with Costello's performance, claiming that 'there was too much humbug about it all for supporters as well as opponents . . . the Belgian Minister somewhat naively whispered to me "Why do the Opposition not applaud?" . . . Later in the debate Mr Lemass duly provided the answer to that question and . . . all the animosities of the Civil War were unloosed . . .'[147]

De Valera said he rejoiced to see this day, his only regret being that he was not introducing it as Taoiseach. Independent deputy William Sheldon opposed the Bill because it took Ireland out of the Commonwealth, as did Maurice Dockrell of Fine Gael, because he regarded the Commonwealth, along with the United States, as the group of nations in which lay the hope of the world.[148] In an editorial, the *Irish Times* claimed that 'nothing that the Taoiseach said yesterday can justify what appears to have been a flagrant breach of political faith' by Fine Gael as the Commonwealth party.[149]

On the following day, Prime Minister Clement Attlee told the Commons that Britain would not regard Éire as a foreign country, or its citizens as foreigners. Winston Churchill complained that Éire was being given the rights of Commonwealth membership without giving anything in return.[150] When MacBride announced Attlee's comments to the Dáil, Byrne withdrew his motion. In the continuing debate, Peadar Cowan said the only way to solve partition was to march across the border, using force. Lemass said Fine Gael were within their rights to change their minds, but they should admit having done so. He also advised the *Irish Times* to 'stop bleating', claiming that the turn of events was the result of their efforts to get rid of Fianna Fáil and install the inter-party government.[151]

The second reading was passed unanimously after a seven and a half hour sitting on the 26th. MacBride, closing the debate for the government, outlined three aims for the Bill: to clear up anomalies; to get rid of acrimony; and to improve relations with Britain. He told the Dáil that there had been no talk of defence arrangements during the Chequers or Paris talks, nor 'was there the slightest disposition to question the right of the Irish government to repeal the act'.[152]

The Bill passed all remaining stages in the Dáil on 2 December 1948,[153] and was passed by the Seanad a fortnight later.[154] President O'Kelly signed the Bill into law on 21 December.[155]

Writing to London about the debate, Rugby noted that no deputy objected to the statement that the Commonwealth countries would not be treated as foreign; he also observed that 'no leading politician dare to appear unwilling to join the anti-partition bandwagon or to seem doubtful about giving it a hearty shove. And yet it should be evident that there is a stiff ditch in front of them, dug deep by Éire's neutrality in the war, and now deeper still by the formal declaration of a republic – a move away from crown and Commonwealth which has still further outraged the feelings of the loyalists of Northern Ireland.'[156]

MacBride suggested Easter Monday, 18 April 1949, as the date for the coming into force of the Act, 'in order to obviate the possibility of speculation as to the reasons for the delay', and because the 'British Government will have completed any legislative or other changes necessitated on their side by the enactment of the Republic of Ireland Act before the 18th April'. He also noted that 'Easter Monday, and not the 18th April, will be observed in future years as Independence Day',[157] a fond hope that was not realised.

The British had not been kept informed of these developments, not knowing until 20 January that the date for the Act to come into force was to be deferred from the following day, the planned date. Despite MacBride's hope that the Easter date would allow the British to bring in consequential legislation, Attlee decided to delay until after the Easter recess so that 'it should be abundantly clear that it is the Éire government themselves who, by their own action, have taken Éire out of the Commonwealth'.[158]

MacBride's proposals for celebrations to mark the coming into force of the Republic of Ireland Act were approved by Cabinet on 5 April,[159] although in the event he wasn't there to enjoy them, as noted above. Fianna Fáil were also absent – party members on Dublin Corporation voted against putting up bunting, while de Valera refused to go on Radio Éireann to mark the occasion. Even the *Irish Times* referred to Fianna Fáil's refusal to take part in the celebrations as a 'persistent attitude of silly aloofness'.[160]

But the celebrations went ahead, with a twenty-one-gun salute on O'Connell Bridge as Ireland officially became a republic at midnight (the salute was three minutes late as crowds broke through the protective cordon, showing either a rush of enthusiasm or some late-night overindulgence). Radio Éireann at one minute past midnight noted the historic nature of the occasion, before stating: 'Our listeners will join us in seeking God's blessing on the Republic, and in praying that it will not be long until the sovereignty of the Republic extends over the whole of our national territory.' Goodwill messages were requested, and received, from President Harry Truman, King George VI, Attlee, and the Commonwealth Prime Ministers.[161] There was a major military parade before the GPO in Dublin on Easter Monday, as well as speakers on Radio Éireann and church services.[162] Military ceremonies were also held in Dún Laoghaire,

Cork, Athlone and Spike Island.[163] But despite the celebrations, the British soon indicated that little had changed – Irish affairs were still to be dealt with by the Commonwealth Relations Office rather than the Foreign Office.[164]

Ironically, just as the Republic of Ireland was leaving the Commonwealth, different arrangements were being made for India. The British Cabinet in October 1948 'tactfully agreed' a convention of referring to the 'Commonwealth of Nations', rather than the 'British Commonwealth of Nations'.[165] In April of the following year, after a meeting of Commonwealth Prime Ministers in London, it was announced that India was to remain a full member of the Commonwealth, despite its republican status. The King was to be recognised as 'head of the Commonwealth',[166] a suggestion made by Sir Stafford Cripps[167] which clearly owed something to Irish ideas of how the Commonwealth could operate. Even Churchill now accepted that 'it should be possible to retain a republican India in the Commonwealth'.[168] Attlee felt that Indian Prime Minister Jawaharlal Nehru showed 'high statesmanship' in accepting the new relationship, despite the criticism of doctrinaire republicans in his own country.[169] He also felt that if the Indian precedent had been set earlier, both Burma and Ireland might have remained within the Commonwealth.[170] But, as Nicholas Mansergh put it, 'by the time the British found the answer, the Irish had lost interest in the question'.[171]

In order to consolidate the state's new status, Irish diplomats now concentrated on two issues: citizenship rights and the exchange of ambassadors. A series of measures extended reciprocal citizenship rights to British, New Zealand, Australian, South African, Southern Rhodesian, and Canadian citizens. At the same time, despite initial opposition from the British, ambassadors were exchanged with the Commonwealth countries. The first was India, in May 1949,[172] followed by Canada in December. The British tried to stall on the issue, claiming it should be decided by the forthcoming Commonwealth conference in Colombo, but the Canadians replied that 'as Ireland is no longer a member of the Commonwealth, the designation of representatives exchanged with Ireland is not and should not be related to the question of the designation of representatives exchanged between Commonwealth countries'.[173]

In January 1950 it was announced that the legations of Ireland in Washington and of the US in Dublin were to become embassies,[174] which they did in April. The following month, MacBride began his attempts to have the Irish representative in Britain raised to the rank of ambassador, noting that the British would probably be prepared to agree to the change following the Canadian precedent.[175] On 24 July, it was simultaneously announced in London and Dublin that the Irish and British representatives in the respective capitals were to become ambassadors.[176] Finally, when embassies were exchanged with Australia in September, the term high commissioner disappeared from Ireland.[177]

The most immediate effect of the repeal of the External Relations Act, though, was on the North. Following the Chequers conference in October 1948, Attlee told the House of Commons that the North had not been discussed, and that the government believed that no change should be made in the constitution of Northern Ireland without Northern Ireland's approval.[178]

Attlee received the Northern Ireland Prime Minister, Sir Basil Brooke, in Chequers on 20 November. Brooke raised a number of matters which he felt would strengthen the position of Northern Ireland, including a declaration about its constitutional status, a more stringent residency qualification for Westminster elections, and a change in the name of the state to Ulster (to highlight that while it shared the island of Ireland, it was not part of the Irish state). A special working party was set up by the British to examine the proposals.[179]

It seemed to Stormont officials that the only change that was likely to be examined seriously by the British was the name change – as the British wanted to introduce the minimal legislation and the Ireland Bill would deal with changed names and titles. A report suggested that 'some difficulty . . . is to be anticipated in securing the acceptance of the declaratory clause safeguarding Ulster's position'.[180] Brooke stressed that he regarded some form of declaration as the most important guarantee, telling the Cabinet that they 'ought to concentrate . . . efforts on strengthening Northern Ireland's constitutional position so as to eliminate the possibility of interference by any government in Whitehall now or in the future and on anticipating any pressure which might be exercised by the government of Éire to force Northern Ireland to make concessions on the partition issue'.[181]

The order in which Brooke ranked the dangers is interesting – he appeared to fear London more than Dublin. This is understandable in view of a controversy earlier in 1948, when Unionist MP W.F. McCoy advocated that Northern Ireland should become a self-governing dominion, independent from Westminster, because of his dislike of the Labour government and the fear that 'the British Government could pass an Act in one session putting Northern Ireland into Éire without asking the people of Northern Ireland or the Northern Ireland Parliament one word about it'.[182] Such concern was especially understandable while a Labour government was in power, with a Prime Minister who was the son of a Gladstonian Liberal Home Ruler and whose own constituency in London's East End contained a large Irish population.[183] While Brooke dismissed the McCoy agitation at the time,[184] the aftermath of the repeal of the External Relations Act gave him an opportunity to put the agitation on this issue to rest for good. The irony was that Attlee, far from being sympathetic to anti-partitionists, gave 'his strong personal support' to what became the Ireland Act, and particularly the guarantee clause.[185]

Another meeting between Brooke and Attlee in January 1949 prompted Dublin to express concern. An Irish *aide-mémoire* hoped that the British would take no action, legislative or otherwise, which could strengthen 'the undemocratic anomaly whereby our country has been partitioned against the will of the overwhelming majority of the Irish people'; it also hoped that nothing would be done to encourage 'further denials of elementary democratic rights in the six north-eastern counties of Ireland'.[186]

At a meeting with Attlee and Home Secretary James Chuter Ede in London later in January, Brooke expressed concern that the use of the title 'Republic of Ireland' would lend credence to the nationalist claim to jurisdiction over the entire island, noting that it had taken a great deal of work since 1937 to ensure that 'Éire' was used rather than 'Ireland' in official circles, as well as on the BBC and in the press. Attlee confirmed that the term 'Irish Republic' would be used by government officials.[187] Brooke expressed satisfaction to his Cabinet in Belfast – it now seemed that a three-month residency qualification would be introduced for Westminster elections, which would disenfranchise migrant workers from the South.[188]

The intervention of Dublin politicians in the Northern elections in February, discussed in more detail in the next chapter, was skilfully exploited by Brooke to extract concessions from Attlee. The British position was outlined by Attlee in the House of Commons early in February 1949 – no useful purpose would be served by making a protest against Dublin's anti-partition campaign.[189] The question had been asked in order to secure just such an answer for use against the Northern Ireland Labour Party in the course of the election.[190] Brooke saw an opportunity for further advantage. He asked the Unionist MPs at Westminster not to follow up on the issue,[191] while writing to Attlee demanding an assurance that his government 'will not tolerate a continuance of the policy of threats and incitement directed against this part of the United Kingdom'.[192]

Attlee's response pointed out that any protest would be ineffective, as it 'would only encourage Éire Ministers to make further statements in support of the campaign'. As regards an assurance, he referred to the affirmation of the 'constitutional position and territorial integrity of Northern Ireland' in the draft Ireland Bill, and promised to make 'a clear and firm statement on the subject of Partition in the proceedings on this Bill'. Attlee was also able to tell Brooke that his Cabinet had agreed to a three-month residency qualification for Westminster elections in the North, but he insisted that despite Stormont's objections the term 'Republic of Ireland' would have to be used in the Bill.[193]

Brooke replied expressing agreement with the proposed statement during the debate on the Ireland Bill, and gratitude on the proposed change to the franchise. But he was still unhappy about the term 'Republic of Ireland', claiming that its use 'will be held to connote a tacit recognition by the British government of the claim of Southern Ireland to sovereignty over the whole island'.[194]

The British had gone to considerable trouble to ensure that 'Éire' was used whenever possible – even in the 1948 Olympic Games in

London. On that occasion, members of the Irish contingent objected to being called 'Éire' and tried to take their place in the opening parade between Iraq and Italy, but were removed.[195] The Commonwealth Relations Office advised the Olympic Organising Committee that they were within their rights in this case, as the rules of the Games stipulated that the terms used to describe participating countries were those given to them by the host nation, and as Éire was 'the recognised style of the territory formerly known as the Irish Free State'.[196]

There was some confusion on the Irish side as to the exact description of the state. In November 1948, Frederick Boland had advised Neil Pritchard of Lord Rugby's office that the government would want the state to be known as 'the Republic of Ireland', and hoped that the British would use this description *or* 'the Irish Republic' in place of 'Éire'.[197] But the following month, Costello told the Seanad: 'We wanted to get rid of the jeering use of the word "Éire" which has become current in the last few years. That is the practical reason why we have adopted the expression the Republic of Ireland [as opposed to the Irish Republic] and the practical reason coincides with the Constitutional necessity of using the word "Ireland".'[198] Rugby advised his superiors that they should emphasise the republican status of the state by referring to it as 'the Irish Republic', and that 'seen in its proper light, this should be welcome to the North'.[199]

In September 1949, the Department of External Affairs circulated a memorandum advising the use of Ireland, Irish Republic and the Republic of Ireland alternately, 'giving at all times a preference to the term Ireland'.[200] The memo drew a rapid response from Maurice Moynihan, who pointed out that the term 'Irish Republic' had no constitutional or statutory basis, and that since the British wanted it to be used, 'this Department has held quite definitely the view that, far from being encouraged to use the expression themselves, Irish officials should oppose its use in any circumstances by others'.[201]

At the beginning of May, de Valera told a demonstration in Earls Court that if the British copper-fastened partition, it would resow the seeds of enmity between the two peoples. 'We are compelled to be enemies while you are doing us an injustice.' De Valera added that if the British went ahead, he would be 'back again' to his position of 1919.[202] At around the same time, in a telephone conversation with Rugby, now retired, de Valera conceded that the actions of the Costello government had created a difficulty for the British, but insisted that two wrongs did not make a right.[203]

The Ireland Bill was published in London on 3 May. It recognised the Republic, and stated that neither in past nor in future legislation would the word 'foreign' be taken to refer to the Republic or its citizens. But the Bill also said that 'in no event will Northern Ireland or any part thereof cease to be part of His Majesty's dominions and of the United Kingdom without the consent of the Parliament of Northern Ireland'. MacBride said this clause would add enormously to existing difficulties, while de Valera said it was 'the worst thing that has happened for the relations between our two countries since 1920'.[204] The *Irish Times* commented in an editorial that 'the guns of last Easter Monday morning were loaded with blanks, but they may prove to have blasted the chief hope of every true nationalist'.[205]

MacBride condemned 'this new attempt by Britain to legislate concerning a portion of Ireland' as 'a clear usurpation of the fundamental right of the Irish people to determine their own affairs without outside interference'. He compared the British action to those of Germany before the war and of Russia since, adding that the Bill would further damage Anglo-Irish relations and 'inflame the already highly dangerous situation'.[206] An *aide-mémoire* to the British, approved by Cabinet on 7 May, stressed the government's 'emphatic and solemn protest against the re-enactment by the British Parliament of legislation purporting to confirm the unjust partition of Ireland . . . The government of Ireland deplores such a destructive and unfriendly attitude . . .'[207]

When the government announced its intention of moving a motion in the Dáil calling on Britain not to put through the Bill, de Valera promised full support.[208] Following a suggestion by de Valera in a letter to Costello,[209] the all-party Mansion House conference met to draw up a plan of action in opposition to the Bill. A public meeting was planned for O'Connell Street, while a propaganda campaign in the US was also considered.[210] On Friday, 13 May, Costello, Norton, MacBride, de Valera and Frank Aiken, Fianna Fáil spokesperson on External Affairs, addressed a mass meeting in O'Connell Street from a platform by the Parnell Monument.[211] The event was marked by the publication of a special supplement by the *Irish Press*, which the British noted 'is a comment on Irish propaganda methods since the photographs of [British] soldiers and armoured cars must have been taken in the early 20s!'[212] Meanwhile, the Dáil had unanimously passed the motion against the Ireland Bill on 10 May. Costello threatened to 'hurt the British in their pride, pocket and prestige, and every effort we can make we will make if they present us with that horrible alternative'.[213] The new British representative in Dublin, Sir Gilbert Laithwaite, noted that this comment drew applause from the House.[214]

One of those closest to Costello at the time felt his Dáil speech was an example of the 'dangerous rhetoric' of which the Taoiseach was often guilty – in later life Costello was prepared to admit that some of his phrases were unfortunate.[215] Laithwaite was very critical of Costello's performance, complaining of 'his petulance, his refusal to see the arguments for the other side, his readiness to appeal to prejudice'. He added that 'Mr Costello fails to recognise the difference between the tactics and phrases that can properly be adopted by an advocate anxious to move the feelings of a jury, and those appropriate to a Prime Minister . . .'[216]

In the House of Commons, Attlee assumed an air of injured innocence, claiming to have pointed out at the Chequers talks that declaring a republic would make the ending of partition more difficult. He said he had concluded that leaving the Commonwealth was more important to the Irish government than ending partition, and that the guarantee was not new and had been made inevitable by the actions of the Irish government.[217]

On 22 May, MacBride issued a statement complaining that the British had broken the agreement reached after the Chequers and Paris talks for the two governments to consult on actions to be taken over the repeal of the External Relations Act. He pointed out that the governments had been in close consultation over a variety of matters, including Costello's speech introducing the Republic of Ireland Bill and Attlee's reply. However, he said, despite repeated requests, no copy of the Ireland Bill had been given to the Irish high commissioner in London. He finished his statement with the observation that 'the unilateral and unnecessary action of the British government . . . was not in conformity with a policy of friendship and co-operation'.[218] In the Dáil a few days later, MacBride again claimed that the government had kept the British informed of the proposal to repeal the External Relations Act, and that he had told Rugby 'in informal conversation that most of my colleagues in government had opposed the passing of the External Relations Act or had criticised it since, and that the act was likely to be repealed'.[219] While, as we have seen, this was quite true, there was no formal warning, and so Attlee was able to tell the Commons with a clear conscience that 'no notification was received' from the Irish before the announcement was made.[220]

The repeal of the External Relations Act, then, while it may have given Ireland a new status in international affairs, had also managed to strengthen partition. It was the most important development in external affairs during Costello's first term as Taoiseach, and was also one of the most controversial decisions ever taken by an Irish government in foreign policy. The question of whether Costello had prior Cabinet approval for what he said in Canada will no doubt remain a subject of controversy. However, this author thinks it is clear that he, along with most of the Cabinet, believed that he was merely confirming the truth of a story that had appeared in the *Sunday Independent*, probably at MacBride's instigation. It is also clear from the British records that London was expecting repeal, although the timing of Costello's statement came as a surprise.

Finally, we must ask if repeal was indeed the price for Clann na Poblachta's involvement in the government. The answer to this is an emphatic negative. MacBride had accepted that his party could not dictate policy on this issue; it was only when other members of the Cabinet indicated that he was pushing an open door that he began the manoeuvring that led to repeal. If the Cabinet, or even the Fine Gael members of it, had been united in opposition to repeal, there was no way that Seán MacBride could have forced it through.

FOUR

A SUPERFICIAL SUAVITY

There is only one prime minister here, and his name is not John Costello.
Sir Basil Brooke[1]

For the first time in many years, we have succeeded in making Partition a live issue once again.
Department of External Affairs[2]

There were two facets to the inter-party government's policy on the North: propaganda against partition, at home and abroad, and attempts to engender co-operation. The first was more or less forced on them by the activities of Eamon de Valera, who, free of the constraints of office, toured America, Australia and Britain speaking out against the perceived evils of the division of the nation. De Valera's successful visit to his native country in March 1948 included being made an honorary citizen of New York City[3] and paying a fifteen-minute courtesy call on President Harry Truman.[4] Possibly in reaction to de Valera's visit, MacBride told the Dáil that the government regarded partition as 'the most serious obstacle to the political and economic welfare of our people'.[5]

In similar vein, Taoiseach John A. Costello said in a St Patrick's Day broadcast to the United States that the government would 'bend our energies to the restoration of the territorial integrity of our native land . . . In pursuit of these great aims on behalf of our motherland we invoke the blessings of St Patrick.'[6] He claimed that while partition lasted 'the sympathy of our race in the USA and in the other great countries to which I speak can not be expected to be fully directed towards the task of helping European recovery. While partition persists, therefore, the defences of western civilisation are weakened. The world cannot afford to let the unnatural partition of

our country distract the generous sympathies of the Irish race . . .
We hope that before next St Patrick's Day the Dove of Peace may
hover over the world with warm breast and bright wings; and that
our Mother Ireland will be able to walk through four of her beau-
tiful green fields, and that she will walk with the walk of a Queen.'[7]

This concentration by the new government on 'the bones of the
old partition controversy' was most unwelcome to the *Irish Times*,
which blamed the whole debate on de Valera's 'cleverly timed' visit
to the US.[8] When the Fianna Fáil leader returned from America
early in April, he was welcomed by several thousand people on
College Green. He urged them to mention partition in every letter
sent to friends abroad; an *Irish Times* editorial acknowledged de
Valera's 'remarkable flair for publicity', but judged the campaign to
be ill-advised. 'Mr de Valera's self-appointed mission may not have
been meant to embarrass the new government; but it certainly has
done nothing to lighten its difficult task.'[9] At the end of April, de
Valera visited Australia at the invitation of his old friend Archbishop
Daniel Mannix.[10] The next month, he and Frank Aiken left Australia
for New Zealand,[11] and early in June spent two days in India with
Prime Minister Jawaharlal Nehru.[12]

While de Valera's activities were causing problems for the government in Dublin, they were having little effect in Belfast. Prime
Minister Sir Basil Brooke told the Unionist Party's publicity subcommittee that he was confident the tour 'would not influence the
course of events in the slightest degree' as the US administration 'was
opposed to any step which would whip up – as Mr de Valera's tour
was intended to do – anti-British feeling, particularly at a time when
the UK was so much dependent upon Marshall Aid'. However, the
Northern Premier expressed his determination to put the whole
weight of his government behind any publicity upholding the position
of the state. 'The whole constitutional structure of Northern Ireland
was being assailed from every angle and it was an elementary duty
of the government to answer any attacks which may be made upon
its structure.'[13]

Costello stated in the Dáil in July 1948 that 'for the first time
since 1922, this Cabinet will . . . give some hope of bringing back to
this country the six northeastern counties'.[14] A possible explanation
for this optimism was the arrival of British Prime Minister Clement

Attlee in Dublin for a three-week holiday and the signing of the Anglo-Irish Trade Agreement, and also Costello's belief that Irish participation in NATO was a major concern for Britain. On the day of Attlee's arrival, Sir Basil Brooke issued a statement commenting on the change of attitude since the inter-party government assumed office, with the new ministers displaying 'a superficial suavity which fails to conceal the same old separatist policy'. While he welcomed co-operation on security and trade, he warned against trying to bargain on partition: 'Do they think our constitutional status is up for auction? They may bid as high as they please, but our answer remains the same – Ulster is not for sale.'[15]

Attlee wasn't the only distinguished British visitor: the Lord Chancellor, Benjamin Jowitt, arrived on 10 August for a three-week stay.[16] On 14 August, Attlee, Commonwealth Secretary Philip Noel-Baker, Seán MacBride and Noël Browne met informally in Mayo, where Noel-Baker ruled out any movement on partition, while Attlee even rejected the idea of changing the status of high commissioners to that of ambassadors.[17] Browne later said he didn't think MacBride 'could have come back from Mayo without knowing for certain that there was no question of concessions on Partition from the Attlee government'.[18]

Ironically, the next day the *Observer* reported that a new Anglo-Irish Treaty was being discussed by Attlee in Ireland, involving unification with safeguards for religious minorities, and Ireland joining the Brussels Treaty, a military alliance of Britian, France and the Benelux countries signed the previous March. The report was quickly denied in London, Dublin and Belfast,[19] while Attlee, questioned by reporters at the Border as he drove to stay with Brooke in Fermanagh, 'proceeded to dictate a statement of about four hundred words, without hesitation or amendment, contradicting the *Observer* story point by point'.[20] The *Observer*'s correspondent in Belfast had tried to convince 'those clever young men in London that they had got hold of a ringer, but it was no use'.[21]

Leaving the country after a 'great holiday', Attlee was questioned about his visit's significance for partition: 'People who talk like that underestimate the attractiveness of this country; perhaps [British politicians] are coming here to avoid political discussion.'[22] In his memoirs, Attlee merely noted that he had 'the rather unusual experience of being cheered on both sides of the border'.[23] The only tangible product of his visit was a suit he had made out of a length of Donegal tweed presented to him by MacBride.[24]

De Valera continued his anti-partition campaign with a series of engagements in Britain in October and November 1948. Elaborate arrangements were made by the Stormont government to counter any publicity that might be generated by the campaign, with local supporters keeping an eye on his meetings and the government press officer monitoring wire service coverage of his speeches in order to issue instant responses.[25] While Stormont's agent in Britain, E.P. Northwood, sneered at the supporters de Valera could expect at his meetings ('Southern Irish elements of poor type'), he had to admit that any counterdemonstrations organised by unionists would fail due to lack of support.[26]

In May 1949, at the height of the controversy over the Ireland Bill,[27] the Cabinet approved outline proposals from MacBride relating to publicity abroad and the establishment of an Irish News Agency.[28] The government announced on 16 June that the agency was 'to supply Irish news to newspapers throughout the world, to give Ireland's viewpoint and to counteract anti-Irish propaganda'. The government also announced plans to appoint press attachés in Irish legations around the world.[29] MacBride claimed that the Irish News Agency would 'not be a political propaganda medium', but would represent Ireland's point of view objectively, with a supply of truthful information to counteract hostile propaganda.[30] The establishment of the agency had little impact on newspapers in Ireland. 'It caused suspicion among journalists whose sideline earnings on correspondence for English or American newspapers seemed to be threatened and it was entirely government-funded, so that it was easily labelled a mere propaganda machine.'[31] In the words of one observer, it was 'an all-star cast, putting on a pantomime'.[32]

The campaign of vilification of Britain raised the temperature of political debate on both sides of the Border; in January 1951 a home-made bomb was thrown at the British embassy in Merrion Square. A window was broken and a car damaged, and it was believed a controversy over Dutch pilots training in the North was the immediate cause.[33] The agitation against the Dutch airmen was once again turned to Stormont's advantage by Brooke, who complained to Attlee that London had not defended its right to have allied troops 'in any part of the country they chose'.[34] A handwritten note from Attlee to 'My dear Brooke' apologised fulsomely and promised to make the position clear should an opportunity arise.[35]

Another issue which caused concern was a visit to the North by Princess Elizabeth and the Duke of Edinburgh to receive the freedom of Belfast in May 1949. Con Lehane of Clann na Poblachta objected to the proposed visit in February, demanding for the people of Belfast and the rest of the North 'freedom from British interference and aggression'.[36] Independent TD Captain Peadar Cowan put down a Dáil question to Costello about the visit; at the request of the Dáil office, he added the phrase 'Her Royal Highness' to his description of the Princess![37] Costello's reply was that 'it would not be helpful towards the solution of the problem to make the visit the subject of a protest to the British Government'.[38] However, MacBride did complain to the British representative in Dublin, Sir Gilbert Laithwaite, about this; British Cabinet papers show London's response – that 'this was a piece of impertinence which was deeply resented in Whitehall'. MacBride didn't appear to be chastened by this: he later claimed that Laithwaite was known as 'Ambassador Lightweight' and was not taken very seriously in either London or Dublin.[39]

Interestingly, MacBride later revealed that King George VI had expressed a desire to visit Ireland, in an informal conversation at a reception held in Buckingham Palace in May 1949 during preparations for a Council of Europe meeting. Hugh Dalton recalled in his memoirs that the two 'had a very animated and friendly conversation full of jokes and laughter'.[40] MacBride also recalled a dinner arranged by Attlee with Winston Churchill late in 1948, following Attlee's visit to Ireland, during which Attlee told MacBride that he couldn't do anything on partition without the support of the Conservative leader. Churchill said he and MacBride's father had fought in South Africa, although on different sides, and that he and MacBride were at the Anglo-Irish Conference in 1921, again on different sides. Churchill then said: 'So much the better, because on the Irish question, I have my loyalties. I cannot let down my Unionist friends in Ulster.'[41]

While the government's attempts to influence London on the partition question could be characterised as ineffective, their impact on electoral behaviour in the North itself was entirely counter-productive. In October 1948, J.E. Warnock, the Northern Minister for Home Affairs, said that the choice before the people of the North was to restore a solid Unionist government after the next election, or perish. He added that if ten or twelve more Labour members were elected, it would be the end of Northern Ireland. He also compared Costello's claim that, constitutionally, he was the real Prime Minister of Northern Ireland to that of a man in Purdy's Burn mental hospital 'who thinks he is the Emperor Napoleon'![42]

The 1949 Northern elections were called for 10 February.[43] Launching his manifesto, Brooke claimed that the country was in danger, calling on loyalists to rally round to 'give an answer to our opponents at the polls that will resound around the world – "No surrender! We are King's men!"'[44]

In response, Costello invited the leaders of all parties in the Dáil to a meeting in the Mansion House to consider how to help anti-partition candidates in the election.[45] MacBride had proposed as early as April 1948 that an all-party committee should be set up to deal with partition, to avoid the issue being used 'for party purposes, which is manifestly undesirable'.[46] The conference agreed to make a collection to fund anti-partition candidates on the Sunday after their meeting. MacBride said the all-party meeting was 'the first real sign of unity in the national sense since 1921'.[47] Perhaps – but only south of the Border. Unionists were reported to be delighted, feeling the move would bring thousands of apathetic unionists to the polls, while nationalists said the money raised would arrive too late to be effective.[48] The church-gate collection was duly held on 30 January, and was reported to have raised over £20,000.[49]

A few days later Brooke attacked the 'unwarrantable and impudent attempt by Éire' to interfere in Northern affairs, especially when the inter-party government 'appear to be holding out to us the hand of friendship and . . . have . . . the effrontery to complain that we do not respond . . .'[50] The next day the Mansion House fund was reported to be at £42,500.[51]

But as Cornelius O'Leary has pointed out, the church-gate collection was of little use to the anti-partitionists, none of whom sat for a marginal constituency. However, it did lead to electoral wipe-out for the Northern Ireland Labour Party (NILP). The

Unionist share of the vote in contested constituencies rose from 50 per cent in 1945 to 63 per cent, and they made a net gain of four seats.[52] The left as a whole got just a quarter of its 1945 vote, and shortly afterwards, the NILP split on the 'constitutional' question.[53]

Despite this disastrous intervention in the Northern elections, the Mansion House Committee kept up its work. In March, the Cabinet seconded two officials – Frank Gallagher, publicity officer in the Department of Health, and Thomas O'Neill of the National Library – to help its work.[54] Gallagher was to head a committee charged with presenting historical, economic and political information about partition 'with a view to presenting them in the clearest light'.[55]

The Mansion House Committee met in October 1949 to discuss the forthcoming British general election. Costello, de Valera, Norton, MacBride and Aiken attended, along with 'several representatives from the UK'.[56] They decided not to intervene in the Westminster election, because the campaign in the Northern election had been counterproductive.[57] However, the information division of the Department of External Affairs devised posters for the election campaign, and twenty thousand were printed and sent North, along with large quantities of the pamphlet *Ireland's Right to Unity*.[58]

At the end of the month, the British section of the Anti-Partition League (a nationalist organisation which campaigned on both sides of the Irish Sea) decided to advise Irish voters to oppose Labour, as well as putting up candidates in three Labour-held constituencies with strong Irish populations – Bootle in Liverpool, Gorbals in Glasgow, and Coalbridge in Lanarkshire.[59] In February 1950, MacBride intervened personally in the Fermanagh/South Tyrone constituency on behalf of the anti-partitionist candidate, Cahir Healy. MacBride was nearly involved in a scuffle when police seized two tricolours during a march in Enniskillen[60] – the tricolour was, of course, illegal in the North, and in March the government protested to the British over the arrest and conviction of a man for displaying it in Armagh.[61] During his visit to the constituency, MacBride also suggested a federal Ireland with a parliament in Stormont.[62] He was later criticised for this at the Clann na Poblachta ard fheis, as federalism was not Clann policy.[63] Attlee won a narrow majority, while in the North the Unionists took West Belfast from Jack Beattie, and Cahir Healy won Fermanagh/South Tyrone.[64]

At the Fianna Fáil ard fheis at the end of October 1950, there were criticisms of the Mansion House Committee, as well as of the government's policy on partition. De Valera insisted that the party's only role on the committee was to oversee the spending of the funds, and that refusal to join would be misrepresented. He also insisted that 'the total responsibility for national action on partition must necessarily remain the responsibility of the government, no matter what government is in office'.[65] This ignored de Valera's own role in fulfilling a number of speaking engagements in Britain as part of the committee's campaign.[66] The extent of the bipartisan approach to the North was demonstrated when de Valera told his parliamentary party in May 1949 to tone down attacks on Costello and concentrate on partition instead.[67]

Propaganda and electoral intervention were not the only policies adopted towards Belfast. Early in March 1948, MacBride set out the other side of his approach to the North, advocating an economic union of the island, or a customs union. 'We should have closer contact with our brothers and sisters in the North, whether Protestant or Catholic, Unionists or Nationalists. There should be as much economic and cultural relations as possible. It is strange that, at a time like this, when there is a great necessity for co-operation among the nations of Western Europe and America, that we should find our country divided and unable to act as one economic and political entity.'[68]

Later in the month MacBride was reported to have said that the government planned to develop economic relations with the North along the lines of the proposed Benelux union.[69] But although such grandiose schemes were certain to come to nothing, significant co-operation was attained on a number of other issues – notably the Great Northern Railway (GNR), the Erne scheme, and the Foyle fisheries.

The GNR system linked North and South as well as operating rail services on a reasonably extensive network on both sides of the

Border. Its main problem was that, in an era of state-owned transportation, it was a private company. The Ulster Transport Authority
(UTA) set up by Stormont in 1946 took over all the GNR's road
services in the North, which put further financial pressure on the
company. In April 1949, GNR chairman Lord Glenavy warned the
Northern Minister for Commerce, Brian Maginess, that the company would make a loss in that year, and that 'immediate action' was
needed if services were to be maintained.[70] The Northern Cabinet
declined to make any proposals to deal with the situation, preferring to let CIÉ and the GNR make suggestions.[71] The company
made a similar approach to Dublin, and in July Ted Courtney of
CIÉ and Frank Pope of the UTA began an investigation into the
GNR's financial condition.

In October, Maginess told Socialist Republican MP Harry
Diamond that 'political considerations do not enter into this question
at all. It is a matter of economics.'[72] In fact, there were worries in
Belfast that Dublin might use the crisis for political purposes. As
the GNR was a Southern company, the Northern government had
no power of compulsory purchase – it could only acquire by agreement. But it was believed in Stormont that Dublin could buy out
the entire company. While it was felt that the Southern government
would only do so in co-operation with the North, the possibility of
a politically motivated attempt to embarrass Stormont was raised,
with 'the operation of the GNR system in Northern Ireland by CIÉ
as a political demonstration'.[73] This fear delayed the start of talks
between the two governments.

The Courtney–Pope report was finally presented to the two
governments in April 1950.[74] It recommended purchase of the
company for a price of £5.3 million, representing the average stock
exchange valuation of the company over the three years between
1946 and 1948 (compared to a valuation of just £3.8 million in
February 1950).[75] However, William McCleery, the new Northern
Minister for Commerce, was just as reluctant as his predecessor to
enter into any open-ended commitment. Losses in the North were
likely to continue, and if the UTA took over the company, higher
wage levels would cost an extra £50,000 a year. The UTA was
already making a loss, and the only way to carry the GNR as well
would be to cut services (leading to intense political opposition) or

to pay for transport losses out of public funds (a reversal of Stormont policy). McCleery recommended that the UTA should co-operate with the GNR to replace rail lines with road links.[76]

The Northern Cabinet decided against direct contacts between McCleery and the Southern Minister for Industry and Commerce, Dan Morrissey, because, in the words of the Deputy Prime Minister, Maynard Sinclair, 'correspondence had not previously taken place between Ministers of the two governments'.[77] In fact, one meeting had been held, two decades previously, when Patrick Hogan of Cumann na nGaedheal met his counterpart, Northern Minister for Agriculture Sir Edward Archdale.[78] So, on 30 May, the permanent secretary of the Ministry of Commerce, J.A. McKeown, met his counterpart at the Department of Industry and Commerce, John Leydon, in Dublin.[79]

In mid-August, the Northern Cabinet, on the recommendation of Brooke, agreed to change its view on contacts with Dublin, and McCleery was authorised to seek a meeting with Morrissey. It is clear from the minutes that the decision was taken for political, rather than economic, reasons – 'in view of the serious political repercussions which might be expected in Northern Ireland if the Republican government or . . . CIÉ acquired the whole railway'.[80] In the event, at their meeting in Dublin,[81] McCleery was 'very agreeably surprised to find that Mr Morrissey's attitude and views about the GNR are practically identical to his own. Apparently, the Republican government are just as unwilling to have to buy out the railway . . . The Minister is quite satisfied that there is no likelihood of Dublin trying any "quick ones", and that none of the unpleasant possibilities which were recently under consideration is likely to arise.'[82]

McCleery later met Liam Cosgrave, acting as Minister for Industry and Commerce, in Dublin to discuss the situation. Cosgrave estimated that the company would cost around £4 million to purchase, and suggested instead the payment of a subsidy, to which Dublin would contribute, despite the fact that no losses were made on that side of the Border. McCleery suggested a third alternative, involving the leasing of the railway line from the GNR for a number of years. Cosgrave also 'tentatively mooted the idea of a joint transport system for the whole of Ireland. This, of course, was not followed up.'[83]

On 23 November, the Northern Cabinet decided that little progress was likely to be made through the subsidy or the leasing proposals, and that the only practical way out of the difficulty was compulsory purchase.[84] However, Dublin was now moving in a different direction, with the Cabinet authorising Cosgrave to write to Belfast 'suggesting the establishment of an all-Ireland Transport Board to control all forms of rail and road transport in both areas'.[85] This was a politicisation of the crisis, although not in the form expected by Belfast. A brusque reply to Cosgrave's letter said Belfast could not entertain his suggestion, and again urged the purchase of the company as a matter of urgency.[86] Cosgrave responded, demanding detailed objections to the plan for a transport authority and repeating his opposition to purchase of the company in its existing form, saying that, because 'the road services of the Six County Area [had] . . . been separated from it', it was now 'a cripple rail system'.[87]

A further meeting in Belfast on 11 December and renewed correspondence failed to bridge the gap between the two governments. Cosgrave still advocated either a subsidy or an all-Ireland authority, while McCleery insisted that purchase was the only way out.[88] The Southern government even tried to bring British pressure to bear, with the ambassador in London, Frederick Boland, making an approach to the Home Secretary which was rebuffed.[89]

Early in January 1951, the GNR announced in the official Belfast *Gazette* that it would close on or after 14 February in the North. No indication was given about what would happen in the Republic.[90] The sense of crisis was heightened when the company warned it would have to give one week's notice to over a thousand staff by 12 January. McCleery and Maynard Sinclair travelled to Dublin for talks with Cosgrave and the Minister for Finance, Patrick McGilligan.[91] The Southern ministers made another attempt to secure agreement to an all-Ireland authority, suggesting at one stage that they would only agree to a subsidy if it was a step towards such an authority. The Northern ministers refused to discuss this.[92] After two days of talks the two governments finally agreed to purchase the GNR at a price of £3.9 million. The Dublin Cabinet approved the purchase on the afternoon of 9 January.[93]

However, the purchase could not be finalised, mainly due to political considerations. Dublin wanted the company run as a joint venture; Stormont insisted on the UTA taking over the Northern parts of the company, leaving only the cross-Border service to be operated by a joint board. 'While, from a purely operational stand-point, there might be advantages in joint control over the whole system, such a step would be wholly undesirable from a political point of view.'[94] It was left to the new Fianna Fáil government to finally agree the structure of the company's operations.

While the GNR discussions dragged on, a major agreement on draining and developing the Erne was agreed. The proposal was instigated by the Electricity Supply Board (ESB); it was anxious to establish a hydroelectric scheme, which would require the deep-ening and widening of the River Erne at a cost of half a million pounds. This, in turn, would allow the Stormont government to control flooding on Lough Erne which had previously been seen as too expensive. Brooke was keen on the idea, as his constituents in Fermanagh were affected by flooding of the lough, although the details of the scheme came in for some criticism from locals.[95] The Erne Drainage and Development Bill was published on 8 May 1950 and came before the Dáil and Stormont the following day. It was an agreement between the Northern Ireland Ministry of Finance and the ESB, rather than the two governments.[96] The only speaker against it in either parliament was Captain Cowan, who claimed it recognised the six-county government for the first time.[97]

A further area of co-operation concerned the River Foyle. The fishing rights on the river had been held for many years by the London-based organisation, the Honourable Irish Society, which had once held the charter for Derry city. Its fishing rights had been challenged by Donegal fishermen, leading to a 48-day High Court hearing in 1948, which the society lost. The society was due to appeal the decision to the Supreme Court.[98] However, in April 1949, the Northern Attorney General, Major Lancelot Curran, wrote to his Southern counterpart, Cecil Lavery, suggesting 'that the Authorities of both countries should get together with a view to the adequate regulation of the fishing in the River Foyle . . . I hope that you and those concerned in your government will regard this in its true light, namely, as an attempt to arrive at a practical solution of the problem in a friendly spirit. You will appreciate that my approach to you is informal.'[99] Curran had to ask Lavery several times whether there was any progress in this matter, and finally, in December 1949, Lavery was authorised to enter into discussions with the Northern government.[100] In June 1950 the Northern government dropped its demand to sole control of fishing rights on those parts of the river which ran through Derry only,[101] and in the following month, the two governments agreed to buy the fishing rights of the Foyle and set up a joint authority to manage them[102] – the first such initiative to be agreed between Dublin and Belfast.

The question of the Foyle had been debated by the British Cabinet in January 1949, during the discussions on the Ireland Bill. A memorandum by Attlee proposed that the Northern government and parliament should be given 'extraterritorial powers' to act in conjunction with the South 'athwart the boundary' for certain specific schemes, including the 'conservation of fish'. This allowed the two governments to set up the Foyle Fisheries Commission without dealing with their respective claims over Lough Foyle.[103] The British also decided that they needed to ensure access to the strategically important Lough Foyle, and to Carlingford Lough. The Admiralty believed that Derry was 'a naval base vital to the defence of the UK because of its importance to North Atlantic convoys in war. The usefulness of the port as a base depends upon our having continued unrestricted use of the navigable channel in Lough Foyle. This channel hugs the Irish Republic shore . . . My Lords . . . hope that there will be no question of establishing a dividing line in the Lough . . . [and] that a careful watch should be kept to ensure that the responsibilities of the joint conservancy board . . . permit of our having access to the waters of the Lough adjacent to the Irish Republic side.'[104]

The result was the phrase 'or any part thereof' in the guarantee clause to the North in the Ireland Act. It was interpreted in the South as a refusal to consider relinquishing areas with nationalist majorities, but under another interpretation, it simply provided additional protection for the British claim to jurisdiction over Northern waters, especially Lough Foyle.[105]

The significance of these three major initiatives by the two governments – on the Erne, the Foyle and the GNR – was summed up at the Fine Gael ard fheis in February 1951 by Costello, who said they 'have given some grounds for the belief that friendly relations can do much to achieve eventual unity more certainly than threats of bloody warfare'.[106] During the 1951 election campaign, his party colleague Seán MacEoin said that the three agreements 'show that both governments today can sit around a table and come to arrangements in the interests of all the people'.[107] However, it was clear from the reaction to the suggestion of an all-Ireland transport authority that while economic co-operation was welcome, Brooke's government would not make political concessions in return.

As well as strengthening economic links with the North, MacBride was also keen to give Northern nationalists a voice in the Oireachtas. Shortly before the 1948 election, Cecil Lavery prepared a memo for the Clann leader on this question. He said that, because the constitution was enacted by the people of the twenty-six counties, it was difficult to see how it could be binding of the people of the North, although there was a claim in the constitution that it covered the entire nation. Lavery concluded that, because of the lack of citizenship and the fact that Northern elections were not carried out by proportional representation, there could be no Northern representatives in the Dáil, but that the power of nomination to the Seanad could be used to appoint Northerners, and that 'a right of audience can be accorded in either House, possibly under rules of procedure and certainly by legislation'.[108]

Clann na Poblachta lived up to its ideals on Northern representation with the nomination of Denis Ireland, a nationalist Protestant, to contest the Seanad election. He said that if elected he would interpret legislation as it affected Ireland as a whole, but would not interfere in purely twenty-six-county legislation.[109] Although he failed to be elected, he was appointed as one of the Taoiseach's eleven nominees on MacBride's nomination, a concession to Northern opinion which began the estrangement with Noel Hartnett, who had been expecting the appointment.[110]

Following his election to Stormont in February 1949, Eddie McAteer of the Nationalist Party sent a telegram to MacBride, saying that the electors of Mid-Derry instructed him to claim his seat in the Dáil. 'Please prepare the way.'[111] In a letter to the *Irish Times* the next day, Con Lehane made it clear that his party 'would welcome the attendance, not alone of Mr McAteer, but of all elected parliamentary representatives prepared to give allegiance to the Republic'.[112] Peadar Cowan put down a question on the matter to Costello, who consulted MacBride before replying. He told Cowan that the matter was under examination by the government, and that Cowan should put the question down again in a couple of weeks.[113]

Costello put the matter on the government agenda for 4 March, but postponed it to 15 March, and then dropped it from the agenda of the following meeting, apparently to MacBride's surprise, as his private secretary wrote to the Department of the Taoiseach seeking an explanation. No action was taken on this request.[114] In the meantime, de Valera made public his disapproval of the idea, saying it 'would be a demonstration without any value, and would have a lot of evil consequences'.[115] McAteer kept up a correspondence with MacBride, telling him in a letter of 5 March that he was concerned 'to find a good deal of misapprehension concerning my recent telegram . . . I fully recognize the many practical obstacles to full Dáil membership. Equally, I recognize the desirability of keeping clear of any controversial "domestic" issues on your side of the Border. All that I want is a token attendance – right of audience or something of the sort which gives little administrative difficulty. I am concerned only with the symbolism of the thing.' He added that the other Nationalist MPs agreed with this approach.[116] However, a letter to Costello from Malachy Conlon MP, secretary of the Anti-Partition League, while stressing the Northerners' wish to avoid domestic issues and their intention not to seek a vote, added that 'we would expect the right to speak in any discussion in which the question of partition was a relevant issue'.[117] And, as members of the Council of Europe's Consultative Assembly in Strasbourg – discussed below – were to find out, partitition could be found to be a relevant issue in practically any discussion.

On 5 July 1949, the government approved a reply to a question from Lehane about the issue of Northern representation: 'The government have given very full and careful consideration to this matter. Having regard to the constitutional, legal and other difficulties involved, the government do not intend to make any proposals for the admission to Dáil Éireann of the representatives referred to in the Deputy's question. The Government, however, have been considering whether Seanad Éireann should not be consulted with a view to making a provision for giving them a right of audience in the Seanad.'[118]

The matter came before government again in May 1950, after the Irish Anti-Partition League wrote to Costello asking for a meeting to discuss six-county representation. MacBride submitted a memo to the government on the issue, which concluded: 'It will be recalled that the government were in agreement in principle to the giving of a right of audience in the Seanad to the elected representatives of the Six County Parliament. While the Minister for External Affairs would have preferred that they should be admitted to An Dáil, it being the more important of the two Houses of the Oireachtas, he considers it desirable that, as an alternative, they should now be admitted to An Seanad.'[119] The matter was on the agenda for a government meeting on 23 May, but it was postponed from then until 4 July, when it was finally withdrawn.[120]

On 4 July, Lehane asked Costello if he had received a letter from the Anti-Partition League. The draft reply from the assistant secretary at the Department of the Taoiseach said that the honorary secretary of the league, Seán McNally, had been informed that the matter was under consideration. Costello changed the answer to: 'A reply will be sent in the course of the next few days.' When Lehane then asked what the reply would be, Costello was able to avoid answering on the grounds that the league should get their reply first[121] – thus managing to look as if he was doing something without having to go into details.

Costello and Labour leader William Norton met the delegation from the Anti-Partition League on 31 July. Costello said he had discussed the matter with the Mansion House Committee, and it was clear that 'it would not be possible to get the general agreement of the Deputies in Dáil Éireann to the League's proposal', and that he therefore did not feel able to pursue it. McAteer pointed out that the government were treating the matter differently from proposals such as the social security legislation, which didn't need 'substantial agreement', and wondered if it was a fair inference that some of the government parties were against the proposal.

Costello then said he had an alternative which would allow the government to keep in closer contact with Northern nationalists, but would only reveal it if they promised not to tell the press. The members of the delegation felt unable to make such a promise, and the meeting broke up.[122] In a further exchange of letters with McNally, Costello revealed that his alternative would involve 'the establishment of a small committee representative of Six County Anti-Partition groups which would maintain liaison and close contact with a small group of members of the Government'.[123] This was a far cry from the 'symbolism' of an audience in the Dáil sought by McAteer.

With a sense of closing the issue, Costello told Cowan during Dáil question time in October that the government would not sponsor a scheme to give Northern MPs seats in the Dáil or Seanad.[124] But the matter would not remain closed for long. Charles McGleenan, the anti-partition candidate, won the South Armagh by-election early in December 1950, and promised to take a seat in the Dáil.[125] Speaking in Clones a week later, MacBride urged all parties to consider 'objectively' audiences in the Dáil for Northern MPs.[126]

On 9 February 1951, Lehane put down a motion proposing that McGleenan be given a right of audience, pending legislation allowing him to take a seat. On 26 February, McNally wrote to Costello, informing him that McGleenan would turn up on 1 March to claim his seat.[127] The Ceann Comhairle, Frank Fahy, sought directions from the government on what he should do. The normal procedure would be to admit McGleenan, as a member of another parliament, to the distinguished visitors' gallery, but it was felt that he would try to make a speech, in which case he would have to be ejected. Norton was left to deal with the matter, as Costello was away due to a family bereavement. The Tánaiste suggested that Fahy should ask McGleenan to defer his action until Lehane's motion was debated, but secretary of the Department of the Taoiseach Maurice Moynihan warned that he would simply turn up, enter one of the visitors' galleries, and 'take steps to assert his claim'. Norton then instructed Moynihan to see if MacBride could contact McGleenan through Lehane. The Minister for External

Affairs said this wouldn't be possible, but proposed that McGleenan could be admitted to the floor of the House, as Nehru had been. Norton vetoed this.[128]

However, much to the relief of the near-hysterical officials, there was no unseemly behaviour when the delegation of Northern senators and MPs handed in a letter to Fahy requesting admission to the Oireachtas, particularly for McGleenan. Some of the sting was taken out of the issue when Costello promised Con Lehane at question time that time would be allotted for a debate on this issue.[129] But still nothing was done; McGleenan wrote to the Taoiseach in May, urging him to take immediate action on his admission to the Dáil, so that his constituents would know 'that everything possible had been done to give effect to their verdict at the polls'. For once, Costello's reply was prompt – he wrote back on the same day to say that 'in the circumstances existing in the past few weeks it was not possible to find time for a discussion of the matter . . .'[130] Ironically, the Mother and Child crisis, which had done so much to provide propaganda for unionism (the Ulster Unionist Council having printed the Dáil debates on the matter as a pamphlet demonstrating 'Rome Rule'), saved the inter-party government the embarrassment of finally making public its views on this thorny issue.

The danger for Clann na Poblachta was that the lack of progress on issues such as Northern representation would unleash more sinister currents within the party – particularly a certain ambivalence towards the use of violence. At the party's 1949 ard fheis, four branches proposed a motion that force should be used to reunite the country. Although MacBride managed to avoid such an embarrassing motion being adopted, the speeches in support of it indicated that there was strong support for a harder line on partition.[131] A former party member, Captain Peadar Cowan, tried to tap into this support early in 1950, when he started to organise his own private army to take back the North.

Advertisements were put in the morning papers in February 1950 stressing that 'Talk has never achieved anything, and will never achieve anything. Action, not talk, will end Partition. A strong Volunteer movement determined to end Partition is needed and must be organised now. Further delay is dangerous . . .'[132] At a meeting in Fairview in Dublin in May 1950 Cowan said the aim was not piecemeal occupations of territory or acts of sabotage (as in the IRA's Border Campaign of the later 1950s): 'The force will be so organised that it will move across the border and take possession of the Six Counties within a day . . . every man in the 26 Counties will be fit for active service.' About eight hundred people attended this particular meeting, at which fifty men marched in military formation.[133]

De Valera was so concerned by this that he asked a Dáil question – his first since losing office.[134] He asked what steps the government were taking to vindicate the constitution, which gave the Oireachtas the sole right to raise or maintain military or armed forces.[135] The matter was discussed at the government meeting on 23 June, and three days later Costello approved a draft reply, stressing that if a situation demanding government action arose, 'all proper and necessary steps' would be taken, but warning against untimely action which could be counterproductive, giving persons or groups undue importance.[136] However, the following day, after informal consultations with his colleagues carried out by Liam Cosgrave, Costello settled on a much shorter answer: 'The Deputy may rest assured that the provisions of the Article of the Constitution referred to have been and will continue to be vindicated by the government.'[137] In response to supplementary questions, Costello insisted that nothing had occurred which 'is in any way as serious as the Deputy suggests'; all that was in question was a group of 'volunteers', who hadn't engaged in military activities and who didn't threaten the authority of the Dáil.[138]

During the debate on the Justice Estimates, Fianna Fáil's Gerald Boland called on the Minister for Justice, Seán MacEoin, to ban Cowan's volunteers, on the grounds that although Cowan was 'more or less play-acting', others might be more serious, and that the government should not wait until shooting started. Cowan said that his movement was growing – especially since being criticised by Boland.[139] When the debate resumed, Seán MacEntee claimed that the volunteers were a communist plot. MacEoin responded that the previous government had dealt with Cowan in the same way he was – by doing nothing. He added that the *Irish Press* was the only paper advertising the volunteers.[140]

However, Cowan's activities were having consequences north of the Border – although not ones he would have welcomed. Sir Basil Brooke said in Stormont in November 1950 that a reserve of B Specials had been formed at Ballykinlar Military Camp, Co. Down, 'in consequence of threats made by a gentleman in the South', who had threatened to come and cut the throats of all loyalists.[141] It was, in a way, a fitting comment on the inter-party government's Northern policy as a whole. Attempts to intervene in affairs in the North had played into unionist hands, particularly during elections, by creating the illusion that the Border was in danger. The other policy pursued by Costello's government, co-operation on mutually beneficial projects, worked, but only up to a point. When both governments were benefiting, Stormont was happy to play along. But any attempts to make political capital out of such arrangements were quickly brushed aside. North–South co-operation was quite acceptable to Belfast, as long as it did not look like giving any encouragement to Dublin's fundamental hope of unity.

The obsession with partition also had an adverse effect on foreign policy in the period. In February 1949, Costello told the Fine Gael ard fheis that 'we have brought the partition question up to the international plane, as we intended to bring it, and on that plane we will succeed in ending partition'.[142] Even the Korean War, which broke out in June 1950, was seen in Ireland in relation to domestic issues; MacBride told the Dáil on 12 July that the Korean War was the product of an unfinished peace, as was the situation in Ireland. He expressed the hope that the world would take another look at partition before there was trouble in Ireland too.[143]

Ireland made three attempts in these years to participate in international organisations – the Organisation for European Economic Co-operation, the United Nations, and the Council of Europe – and set conditions for taking part in a fourth, the North Atlantic Treaty Organisation, which were certain to be rejected. In this, as in other areas of foreign policy, the dominant issue was partition. The increasing importance of foreign affairs was matched by increased activity in Iveagh House – home to the Department of External Affairs – with the establishment of the Cultural Relations Advisory Committee,[144] the setting up of political and information divisions,[145] and the increased distribution worldwide of the department's *Weekly Bulletin*, rising from 2,000 copies in November 1949 to 4,300 copies in March 1951.[146] Spending on the Department of External Affairs reached 0.41 per cent of total government expenditure in 1950, the highest proportion in the first half-century of the state's existence.[147] Unusually for an Irish minister, of course, Seán MacBride was fluent in French, which added to his enjoyment of the External Affairs portfolio,[148] although not everyone was convinced of his complete mastery of the language.[149]

In February 1949, following a query from the French minister in Dublin, MacBride was authorised to tell him that Ireland would accept membership of the Council of Europe if asked.[150] In May 1949, the ten founding members of the Council of Europe, including Ireland, met in London.[151] The Consultative Assembly of the Council met for the first time in Strasbourg the following August. MacBride's attempt to have 'the study of the best means for pacific settlement of disputes between member nations' put on the agenda for the Assembly meeting was defeated – his was the only vote in favour.[152] Despite this setback, the Irish delegation were determined to raise partition, with MacBride claiming that it was one of the points of friction which the Council of Europe was set up to remove, and de Valera stressing that partition was an international question rather than a domestic one.[153]

The next day, the Irish delegation put forward an item for the agenda which would allow partition to be raised – 'the consideration of the best methods for eliminating causes of disputes between member states'. Norton claimed that in its dealings with Ireland, Britain 'had tried persecution, military domination, violence and other distinguishing acts of an invader. The one method which Britain has refused to adopt is that of friendship and co-operation . . .' The Irish expected support from Turkey, Sweden, Denmark, and Norway,[154] but the motion was turned down on a technicality – it was only signed by the four Irish delegates, rather than the ten specified in the rules of procedure. An appeal for time to gather six signatures from amongst other delegates was turned down, and the Irish announced their intention of raising partition during a discussion of a human rights clause, proposed by Winston Churchill.[155]

Norton launched a bitter attack on Britain on 16 August. 'It is Britain's moral responsibility to undo the wrong she has inflicted on Ireland . . . I urge the Assembly to endorse Ireland's claim to complete freedom of her entire territory . . .'[156] While the Irish papers reported the Consultative Assembly as being 'stunned . . . into an uneasy silence' by Norton's speech, the British, naturally, had a different interpretation – the London *Times* simply reported that there had been no applause after the Tánaiste finished. The British representative in Dublin, Sir Gilbert Laithwaite, told MacBride that he 'did not attach any serious importance to this alleged Irish ill-will'.[157]

Norton later used even more intemperate language, referring to 'the intolerable dictatorship in the Six Counties [with a] . . . veto as strong as Molotov often wielded over the right of the Irish people to national self-determination'.[158] De Valera said that Ireland would not join any European federation as long as partition remained,[159] while MacBride said that the Irish had succeeded in educating Europe about partition.[160] According to an *Irish Times* editorial, Norton had beaten de Valera in the anti-partition stakes 'by a short head' by getting in first with an attack on Britain.[161] The effect this was having on the other delegates may be judged from the response of the Assembly President to an attack by Seán MacEntee on Derry MP Sir Ronald Ross: 'I beg of you, please, keep to the subject. We must not make every debate an exchange between the Irish representatives.'[162] Perhaps the rhetoric was having an effect – Ross would not have been happy at his inclusion among 'the Irish representatives'.

The Irish delegation to the Assembly in 1950 proved equally disruptive, causing uproar when all four spoke in quick succession against Churchill's proposal to set up a European army, on the familiar grounds of partition.[163] According to 'Observer' in the *Sunday Press*, 'there was the blessed quality of high courage in that scene . . . our delegates were boohed and attempts were made to silence them'.[164] However, it appears that the shouts of other delegates at de Valera were not caused by the content of his speech – he had taken his earphones off, and so could not understand the President of the Assembly, who was trying to tell him he had exceeded the permitted three minutes speaking time![165]

The Irish also caused a stir in the other major body with which they were involved, the OEEC. In one of his first appearances on the world stage, MacBride told journalists in Paris that the enemies facing Western Europe were 'hunger, poverty and economic insecurity. If the nations of Western Europe are willing to fight these enemies with the same . . . unity of effort as they would fight a war of destruction, with the help of the United States, I believe that Western Europe can be saved from the ravages of another cataclysm.'[166] In the course of his speech, MacBride said that 'in order to achieve the best results, the economic unity of Ireland will have to be achieved. Thus we will be enabled to face the task not merely competently but with enthusiasm.'[167] Once again, partition was being raised at a wider international level.

Ireland's application to join the United Nations was vetoed by Russia, along with those of Portugal, Italy, Austria, Finland, Jordan and Greece, in September 1949.[168] The reason for this was clear – the government made no secret of its pro-American stance, although the anti-partition campaign was to keep Ireland out of the other new international organisation, NATO, which would have given a natural home for such sentiments. There is a possibility that if de Valera had still been in power, the situation could have been handled differently. In November 1947 he told Commonwealth Secretary Philip Noel-Baker 'that he hoped that Éire would soon be admitted to the UN; that she would then take part in a West European Regional Defence System . . .'[169] In the light of subsequent statements by the Fianna Fáil leader, this interpretation may have been wishful thinking on the part of the British.

Opening the debate on the Estimates for the Department of External Affairs in 1948, MacBride stated that 'our sympathies lie clearly with Western Europe', but that the continuation of partition prevented Ireland from playing its full role.[170] There can be no doubt about where the Irish people's loyalties lay in the Cold War. In May 1949, forty thousand protested in Dublin's O'Connell Street against the imprisonment of Hungary's Cardinal Jozsef Mindszenty by the Communist government.[171] In July 1950, at a dinner for the officers of a visiting Spanish ship at McKee Barracks, Costello paid tribute to the part Spain and Ireland were playing in the world against 'materialistic and pagan ideologies'.[172] Obviously, Franco's fascist regime was preferable to any tinged with anti-clericalism. In September 1950, a protest meeting was held in Abbey Street in Dublin to protest against the participation of Yugoslavian and Spanish Republican delegates in an Inter-Parliamentary Union meeting in Dublin. The extreme Catholic organisation Maria Duce also sent telegrams of protest to President Seán T. O'Kelly and the Ceann Comhairle, Frank Fahy.[173]

Costello was virulently anti-communist, and particularly anti-Soviet. In 1946 he had told the Dáil 'it should above all be clear that, whether or not we were neutral in the last war, there can never be any question again of this country being neutral in any future war'.[174] Ireland's position on the ideological spectrum was recognised by an unofficial Spanish approach in April 1948 asking if the government was interested in participation in a neutral bloc including Spain, Portugal, and Argentina, based on 'the defence of the Catholic religion and resistance to Communism'.[175] The government declined this opportunity to get involved with Franco, Salazar and Peron.

As early as May 1948, the US State Department director of European affairs, John Hickerson, wrote to the American minister in Dublin, George Garrett, pointing out that 'if the Dublin government were to gain control of Northern Ireland, facilities in that area might be denied us in the future . . . With the United Kingdom in control of Northern Ireland we have . . . every reason to count on the use of bases in that area in the event of need. I am sure you will agree that this is a powerful argument for this government favouring the continued control of Northern Ireland by the United Kingdom.'[176] This conclusion undermined the entire basis of the Irish handling of the invitation to join NATO.

In July 1948, security talks in Washington decided that 'it would be desirable' for Ireland to be included in NATO; on 9 September (two days after Costello's announcement in Ottawa) this was downgraded to 'it might well be desirable' to have Ireland as a full member of the pact.[177]

According to Frederick Boland, Costello had expected to be approached in Canada by 'generals', presumably with inducements to join NATO. In Ian McCabe's opinion, the fact that these approaches never happened would have alerted Costello 'that Éire no longer had a strategic bargaining position'.[178] Whether Costello did realise this is open to question – it certainly seemed to make no difference to the handling of a US *aide-mémoire* of 7 January 1949, which asked for the Irish attitude to possible NATO membership, set out the objectives of the draft treaty, and outlined the obligations on members.

While the Irish government was considering its response to this *démarche*, the chances of its strategy of trading neutrality for an end to partition were being reduced by the British Cabinet. In October 1948, Clement Attlee's government decided that while they had always held that 'partition was an issue for settlement by the Irish themselves . . . for defence reasons it was not possible any longer to maintain that position'.[179] This position was strengthened in January 1949, when the Cabinet concluded that Northern Ireland's presence in the UK was 'essential for her defence', and that the Irish government would not be prepared to trade unity for neutrality. 'Her recent legislation has shown that she laid more store on formal independence than on the union of Ireland.'[180]

Boland later wrote that the legation in Washington had taken soundings on Capitol Hill about the idea of trading neutrality for an end to partition, and had been told in no uncertain terms that this was not on. MacBride subsequently got a rough ride in Cabinet about this, according to Boland, when 'the cabinet made it perfectly clear that they thought the people in America were right, that we were foolish to go on with the business of asking them to end partition as our price of going in . . .' MacBride was particularly annoyed because James Dillon had been tipped off about the response of the Irish-Americans, by Garrett according to Boland.[181]

A fortnight after the delivery of the American *aide-mémoire*, Garrett reported that while MacBride was opposed to entering NATO while partition remained, 'I have a feeling that he may find himself in a minority and that this country will join . . .'[182] Garrett's assurance was badly shaken a few days later, when he had to report that Dillon, a pro-American who had opposed neutrality during the Second World War, shared the views of the Minister for External Affairs.[183] MacBride told Garrett on 2 February that his reply to the US *aide-mémoire* would 'keep the door open so as not to make the answer entirely negative'.[184]

On 8 February, the Cabinet approved a reply to the American communication of 7 January. It stressed that Ireland was in agreement with the general aim of the proposed treaty, particularly as the country was attached to democracy and Christianity, and had been more immune from communism than any European country, but added that 'any military alliance with . . . the state that is responsible for the unnatural division of Ireland . . . would be entirely repugnant and unacceptable to the Irish people'. The *aide-mémoire* also suggested that no Irish government, no matter what its political complexion, could afford to join a military alliance with Britain, and that if it did it could face, in a crisis, 'the likelihood of civil conflict within its own jurisdiction . . .'[185] According to Dermot Keogh, this reply 'was a victory for MacBride over many in government like Dillon who favoured participation in NATO. It was vintage old-guard nationalism . . .'[186]

However, it can also be seen as a move away from neutrality – Ireland was prepared to take part in the Atlantic Alliance, but was setting conditions for entry. During the Second World War, de Valera had refused to abandon neutrality when approached by the British with an offer of a declaration in favour of unity. De Valera would only promise that he 'might' consider entering the war if a constitution for a united Ireland was fixed first; the British clearly couldn't concede a united Ireland in return for a 'might'.[187] The British were not prepared to pay the price demanded in 1949 either, but it seems the price had been lowered somewhat.

A decade later, the Department of External Affairs was still expressing surprise that 'this document was presumably interpreted as a refusal on our part to participate in the proceedings . . . and we did not in fact receive an invitation to attend the conference that drew up the Treaty'.[188] However, the American view had been set out clearly to Garrett: if the Irish raised partition in relation to the North Atlantic Treaty, they were to be told that 'we take their action in raising partition to mean they are not seriously interested in the Atlantic Pact and will accordingly not consult them further'.[189]

At the Washington exploratory talks on security on 4 March 1949, the Canadian ambassador to the US said that the Irish had made 'unacceptable conditions' for participation. A week later the US Secretary of State, Dean Acheson, said he assumed that 'all agreed that the question should not be pursued further with Ireland', and on the suggestion of the Dutch ambassador, the US agreed to make an informal approach saying that in view of the Irish government's position, the question of Irish participation could not be discussed.[190] Patrick Keatinge has argued that the attempt to offer 'defence co-operation as a lever to extract British concessions on Northern Ireland . . . was to be made impossible by de Valera's linking of the partition and neutrality issues'.[191] In fact, it was made impossible by the British and American assessment that they could not afford to lose bases in the North for the possibility of getting the South into the alliance.

A CIA assessment of the importance of Ireland accepted that Irish neutrality was probably 'tolerable', but concluded that in view of the dangers to Britain of enemy bases behind their defences and the possibility of Ireland being used as a base for bombing North America, 'the denial of Ireland to an enemy is an unavoidable principle of US security . . .' Had MacBride known of this assessment, he would have felt confirmed in his belief that the Atlantic Alliance needed Ireland. His mistake was in believing that the Americans and the British would be prepared to trade movement on partition in return for Irish involvement. In fact, without Irish involvement, both countries would actively oppose the unification of the country, as the CIA report made clear. 'The end of partition is conceivable only in connection with Ireland's adhering to an alliance such as the suggested North Atlantic Pact, in which case bases would presumably be available under the terms of the alliance.'[192]

On 29 March 1949, MacBride told Con Lehane in the Dáil that an *aide-mémoire* on NATO had been delivered to the US government on 8 February, and that no response had been received.[193] As the question came from one of his own backbenchers, MacBride had almost certainly planted it – possibly as a way of putting pressure on the Americans to reply. But the NATO pact was signed in Washington on 4 April, while MacBride was in the country for celebrations in connection with the Republic,[194] without any response to the Irish *aide-mémoire*.

The Dublin government were not the only ones to recognise the importance of opinion across the Atlantic. In March 1950, Stormont voted £6,500 to pay for the Prime Minister, Sir Basil Brooke, to visit the US and Canada.[195] Such a visit had been mooted in June 1949 by the president of the Ulster-Irish Society, who felt that it 'would be very timely, due to the adverse publicity granted to . . . Éire officials'.[196] After being booed on arrival, Brooke met Acheson for a private meeting.[197] One Stormont official expressed his distress that President Truman 'finds it impossible to meet Sir Basil when in Washington . . . There is, however, nothing we can do about it.'[198] Because of the level of opposition from Irish-Americans, Brooke was forced to redraft his speeches – which had concentrated on appeals for investment – to address the political situation. This was made even more pertinent by the fact that he was being followed around by the eccentric Brigadier Dorman O'Gowan, an Anglo-Irish landlord who had served with Montgomery but became converted to the nationalist cause.[199] While Brooke was avoiding the subject of partition in the National Press Club in Washington, O'Gowan was claiming that he was 'the most complete puppet dictator this side of the Iron Curtain'.[200] Brooke had to be escorted around Toronto by more than forty policemen after a smoke bomb was thrown at him.[201] But on his return to Belfast, he was welcomed by a crowd of fifty thousand.[202]

George Garrett wrote to Truman on 10 July 1950 recommending the provision of some military aid to Ireland. He said MacBride had volunteered, in the event of such aid being provided, to 'make an all-out effort to secure bipartisan support for a bilateral treaty of defence . . . [A] bilateral treaty . . . although in the nature of a side-door entrance, would . . . bring Ireland into the defence picture against any aggression on the part of the USSR.'[203] This approach to the Americans was, according to Jack McQuillan, made without the knowledge of anyone in Clann na Poblachta, and indeed was contrary to party policy.[204]

MacBride's approach to Garrett led to a National Security Council review of Irish participation in NATO, NSC 83/1, which concluded that 'without question, Ireland would make a valuable contribution to the collective defense of the North Atlantic community'. However, the Americans felt that a new US approach would only encourage the Irish to believe that they could secure bilateral arrangements, rather than joining NATO, and that the Irish would still refuse to sign the North Atlantic Treaty unless there was movement on partition, on which the US view had not changed: 'reopening the question would be desirable only under the stress of military necessity. This necessity does not exist.'[205] On 3 November 1950, President Truman approved a policy document on the matter: 'The US should (a) continue its present policy of maintaining an attitude of readiness to welcome Ireland as a member of the North Atlantic Treaty Organisation, at this time leaving the initiative to Ireland; (b) avoid discussion of bilateral arrangements for a military assistance program outside NATO.'[206]

In October, James Dillon warned that every free country in Europe would 'be conquered one after another by the Cominform' unless a new Anglo-American Commonwealth was formed, open to 'any bona fide democratic nation that wants to join it'. Naturally, Dillon was keen for Ireland to be a member.[207] Costello picked up on this idea in his St Patrick's Day broadcast in 1951; he proposed a new international organisation of all the non-communist countries for economic and political (but not military) co-operation. The organisation would include India, Pakistan, Burma, and Ceylon, as well as the older members of the British Commonwealth, along with Europe, the United States and Latin America. Interestingly, Costello forecast a key role for Ireland within the organisation, because 'as one of the very few European countries which have experienced protracted foreign domination, Ireland would understand not only the viewpoint of her European sister nations, but could also interpret and appreciate the views of the Asiatic states'.[208]

After MacBride met Dean Acheson for thirty-five minutes in Washington in March 1951 he addressed the National Press Club, where he blamed Britain and Russia for preventing Ireland from playing her part in world affairs; the latter by vetoing UN membership, the former by making NATO membership impossible due to partition. He added that he could see no difference between the two countries as far as 'orderly democracy' was concerned.[209]

There was a quick response to this speech, with Liam Cosgrave telling a Fine Gael meeting that the cause of unity was not helped by such 'extravagant statements . . . To suggest that there is no difference between the Communist system in Soviet Russia and the democratic form of government in Britain is to refuse to face facts and does not help the cause of Irish unity. I do not assent to that view and I do not think it represents the views of the people of this country.'[210]

MacBride sent a message to Costello through Maurice Moynihan, pointing out that he was to meet Truman by special appointment, and noting 'newspapers here report that Liam "rebukes me", inferred on your behalf. Effect of this here unfortunate and if opportunity arises of correcting false impression created here by this report before I see Truman it would be helpful.'[211] In fact, Cosgrave had made the speech on his own initiative, without Costello's prior knowledge – but no attempt was made to repudiate it, and no disagreement was expressed with its contents.[212]

MacBride's comment about the similarities between Britain and Russia also drew hostile comments from American officials in the Dublin embassy, one of whom was reported as telling his British counterpart that 'Irish influence in America was steadily declining and . . . MacBride's ridiculous statement . . . had brought it to a "new low". He could not understand the idiocy of such a statement. The American people knew very well that Great Britain had supported them in recent years far and away above other nations.'[213]

MacBride's meeting with Truman was arranged by the US Attorney General, J. Howard McGrath, and the Irish ambassador, John Hearne, during a golfing weekend in Rhode Island. The State Department was furious at the Irish practice of going outside official channels, and also because MacBride would probably say he had discussed partition with the President, thereby upsetting the British. In the event, Truman avoided the issue by telling MacBride that 'outsiders intervening in family issues always suffered and the issue was rarely settled'.[214] After the meeting, MacBride refused to indicate what had been discussed, but said that relations between the two countries were 'probably closer than ever before'.[215] But not close enough for Truman to play a role similar to that he adopted towards Israel, where he decided to upset the British in a bid to secure Jewish votes. It was to be many years before the Irish lobby in America was organised enough to have similar political clout.

It has been argued that de Valera's anti-partition crusade was forced on him by fear that Clann na Poblachta would usurp his leadership of the republican cause.[216] Whether or not this was the true cause of his propaganda trips, it left MacBride and Costello little choice but to follow his example. The results were not impressive. Although MacBride played a largely constructive role in the OEEC, the overall impression left by Irish foreign policy during this period is of a spoiled adolescent, with an inflated idea of its own importance and no understanding of the realities of power politics. The 'sore thumb' raised by Ireland after the war was a sad contrast to the more statesmanlike performance of the Cosgrave government in the Commonwealth and of de Valera in the League of Nations. It also did absolutely nothing to end the division between North and South. Like other aspects of inter-party policy, it actually deepened those divisions, much to the satisfaction of unionists.

FIVE

THE COURSE OF LEAST DISADVANTAGE

Beware of the Department of Finance. It has always been restrictive of development.

Sean Lemass[1]

So far as I was concerned, I was in Easy Street for money . . . I had the savings of the community given to me. I had departmental funds. I had the American money . . .

Patrick McGilligan[2]

The parties that coalesced in 1948 were deeply divided on economic policy. Fine Gael was obsessed with lowering taxation, Labour with the cost of living, Clann na Poblachta with the need for more state investment. At any other time, these contradictions might have destroyed government cohesion. But 1948 marked an auspicious year to take power, because the flow of money from Marshall Aid allowed the government to adopt an expansionary investment policy, while at the same time cutting tax rates.

Patrick Lynch, one of the key figures in the new economic thinking, later suggested that the difference between Fianna Fáil and inter-party policies lay in the belief 'that capital investment by the state . . . could best solve the basic Irish economic problem of providing jobs for the thousands who were unemployed or who emigrated . . . This new economic faith composed differences of doctrine between right and left, between advocates of state intervention and devotees of private enterprise. Keynes had come to Kinnegad.'[3] As we shall see below, however, the Capital Budget which put the new thinking into practice was far from a full-blown Keynesian device.

140

Some believed the Minister for Finance, Patrick McGilligan, was simply using the latest economic theory to justify policies which pleased his coalition partners. As Seán Lemass put it: 'On every occasion when he had to decide between the principles of financial policy that he himself enunciated in the past and the maintenance of cordiality between the coalition sections he sacrificed his principles for the political advantage to himself of keeping the Coalition together.'[4]

Marshall Aid also caused Ireland, for the first time, to think seriously about its position in the wider European economy. This new thought, forced on policy makers by involvement in the Organisation for European Economic Co-operation, was powerfully backed by the Minister for External Affairs, Seán MacBride, who wanted to move the economy away from its dependence on British markets. But MacBride's thinking, in this area as in many others, was far in advance of his colleagues, and was probably unrealistic in the circumstances of the time, with the economy so dependent on agriculture and on the British market. This was marked by the Anglo-Irish Trade Agreement (which effectively cut off European markets) and by the debate over sterling devaluation.

For the civil servants charged with the protection of the state's finances – secretary of the Department of Finance James McElligott and governor of the Central Bank Joseph Brennan – the new government had pros and cons. Chief of the cons was of course MacBride, who had already displayed his radical approach to economics in the election campaign and was later to try to have McElligott sacked[5] and to oppose Brennan's reappointment. However, with the coalition dominated by Fine Gael and McGilligan as Minister for Finance, the two men must have been somewhat reassured. Although both were life-long nationalists (McElligott fought in the Easter Rising, while Brennan helped Michael Collins during the Treaty negotiations when working in Dublin Castle),[6] their main shared characteristic was the financial orthodoxy and conservatism instilled by the British Treasury.

An indication that their conservative approach was shared by the new administration was given soon after it assumed office, when the seriousness of the financial situation was stressed by the Taoiseach, John A. Costello, in a letter to each minister. He called for economies, requesting that even expenditure already approved by the Department of Finance be reviewed to see if it was really necessary. 'It is not too much to say that the fate of our government depends on the success or failure of the economy drive by individual Ministers.'[7]

One of the first decisions taken by the new government, in line with election promises made by all the parties involved, was to remove the Supplementary Budget taxes on beer, tobacco, and cinema tickets. The second meeting of the Cabinet agreed to remove them 'at an early date' subject 'to the consequential loss of revenue being made good by economy and retrenchment in the public services'.[8] However, while all parties were happy to see the taxes removed, McGilligan's efforts to make up the shortfall proved more contentious.

In his first Budget in May 1948, McGilligan took an axe to the Estimates prepared by Fianna Fáil, which planned a £6 million increase in spending, largely on food subsidies, rural electrification, and the treatment of tuberculosis.[9] He planned to save £6.7 million and borrow £600,000, while the 6d in the pound hike in income tax signalled in the October 1947 Supplementary Budget would bring in an extra £1.9 million;[10] £0.75 million was cut from Defence, while £2.5 million was saved by anticipating cheaper wheat imports under the Marshall Plan. Subsidies for sugar, margarine, oatmeal, and other agricultural products were all severely reduced.[11]

In mid-May, McGilligan asked Cabinet to approve spending cuts in order to secure the savings he had promised in his Budget. But his plans to shave £4.4 million off expenditure were fiercely resisted by his fellow ministers. Among the relatively painless decisions approved were the non-payment of £450,000 to the Pensions Investment Account; £315,000 saved by dropping the transatlantic air service; and a cut of over £600,000 by transferring the cost of 'cash supplements' under various social welfare schemes from the state to contributors.

But the Cabinet decided against a number of other measures, including less frequent rural post deliveries; monthly rather than weekly children's allowances; taxation of TDs' and senators' allowances; and an increase in the radio licence. Although ministers promised to find extra savings rather than see their favourite schemes dropped,[12] the savings realised fell far short of what the Department of Finance considered necessary.

In June Costello wrote to each minister again, complaining that his earlier appeal for retrenchment had achieved disappointing results, and that 'it is incumbent on each of us to do all in his power to ensure that further substantial economies are made with the minimum of delay'.[13] The Department of Finance went further the following month, threatening extra taxation in an autumn Budget unless economies were achieved. Of particular concern was the fact that while the Budget had allowed for an increase of 10 per cent in spending, issues in the first quarter of the year had risen by no less than 52 per cent.[14]

This, however, was a rather misleading statistic, because advances did not equal expenditure, especially in the first quarter, when the paymaster general would in some years have unspent departmental balances, and therefore would not draw down Exchequer advances until those balances were exhausted. In the case of Defence, while Exchequer issues in the first quarter of 1948 were £80,000 higher than in 1947, actual expenditure was down by £20,000.[15]

Despite having this piece of financial sophistry exposed, McElligott continued to put pressure on his minister to secure cuts, complaining in November 1948 that Finance was 'not only finding it difficult to secure from Departments the economies which they promised us at Budget time, but we are inundated with demands for additional expenditure . . . The obvious line of approach would be to restore the taxes remitted earlier this year on beer and tobacco.'[16] McGilligan responded with a memorandum to government, complaining that the Budget had become 'an instrument of socialisation . . . Some redistribution of incomes is necessary in the interests of social justice but the disparity of incomes was never so marked in this country as, for instance, in Britain, and the redistribution of incomes has already proceeded so far that Ireland is probably one of the most egalitarian countries in the world . . . if crippling increases in taxation are to be avoided, a drastic pruning of expenditure must be effected without delay.'[17]

In his Estimates for 1949/50, McGilligan proposed cuts of £5.2 million in spending on supply services, again reducing subsidies on food (£3.6 million) and fuel (£1 million). On the expenditure side, he proposed increases in pensions (£1.9 million) and unemployment assistance (£0.7 million).[18] But the measure closest to his heart was a cut of 6d in income tax, bringing it to 6s 6d in the pound at a full-year cost of £1 million. This had been an election pledge of Fine

Gael's, but the minister faced stiff opposition from the secretary of his department to the idea. In a handwritten note just three days before the Budget, McElligott suggested the cut was 'going too far in the way of remission' and that 'it seems somewhat illogical in the same Budget to be taking on heavy additional expenditure and at the same time to remit taxation'. He also put forward the extraordinary argument that income tax concessions 'will not please Labour. There is nothing, it will be said, in the Budget for the working man – nothing off beer and 'baccy . . .'[19] McGilligan seemed to have little trouble in ignoring McElligott's new-found concern for the 'working man'.

In the run-up to the preparation of the 1950/1 Estimates, yet another Department of Finance circular stressed that 'the risk of inflationary developments which has been increased by the depreciation of Sterling must be counteracted by all means at the disposal of the Government and, in particular, by achieving substantial economies in public outlay. Despite the special appeal last year and the year before for economies, state expenditure – and, consequently, taxation – continues to be inordinately heavy . . . Government policy will be thwarted and serious economic consequences may arise unless the Budget for 1950/1 is considerably less than that for 1949/50.'[20]

This concern was also expressed in private by McElligott, whose warnings to McGilligan about increased spending grew almost hysterical. In February 1949 he made a veiled criticism of his minister: 'Public announcements are made by Ministers on schemes which have a most important financial bearing without any prior consultation with the Department or, *as far as we know*, with the Minister for Finance . . .'[21] Seven months later, he claimed that 'the Department of Finance has lost its power to control the situation',[22] and during the preparation of the 1950/1 Estimates, he said it was impossible for officials to agree reductions – 'it seems to me that the matter must be taken in hands by Ministers . . . I suggest, therefore, that *your personal intervention is required now* . . .'[23] The increasing stridency of his complaints reflected departmental concern that McGilligan was not active enough in pushing the Finance line in Cabinet.[24] As was noted in Chapter Two, McGilligan preferred to avoid direct confrontation, especially with MacBride, and his officials often couldn't contact him.

Frustrated in his attempts to trim spending, McGilligan turned to the easier option of borrowing. In March 1948, he announced the largest national loan in the history of the state, and the first since 1941, for £12 million.[25] A year later, he announced another loan of the same size,[26] and yet another in September 1950, this time for £15 million, again breaking the record for loan size, and bringing the total of all national loans to £65 million.[27] At the same time, Marshall Aid monies were also being used to fund state investment in a wide range of projects, paying for just under half of all government capital spending between 1949 and 1952.[28] The government's need for this extra money was partly due to the need to invest in pet projects of each of the parties involved. But it was also due to a change in thinking in official circles, with the adoption of Keynesian ideas which advocated government borrowing to inject money when demand was deficient.

This was partly due to the influence of Patrick Lynch, a Finance official who became special economic adviser to the new Taoiseach. Lynch wanted to introduce more up-to-date economic theory into policy, and Costello proved receptive. Within two years of entering office, the Taoiseach had moved away from traditional Fine Gael economic thinking, thanks to long discussions with Lynch and with Alexis Fitzgerald, his son-in-law. Costello insisted on talking through economic questions in some detail, ensuring that he fully understood the issues involved.[29] At the same time, another young economist, T.K. Whitaker, was pushing a broadly similar policy within the Department of Finance, eventually writing the 1950 Budget speech 'to clothe with respectability the more dynamic policy which Paddy Lynch had been advocating through the Taoiseach'.[30] McGilligan too was imbibing the new economic theories, becoming 'an intellectual as well as a political convert to the potential of moderate Keynesianism in Irish circumstances'.[31]

Not surprisingly, such ideas were resisted by Central Bank governor, Joseph Brennan, who was particularly concerned at the inflationary aspects of the government's capital investment programme. In the Central Bank's report for 1948/9, he hoped that 'measures of restraint will be accepted as a matter of urgency. In particular the scope and scale of State capital projects raised questions which have a vital bearing on Irish monetary stability. The avoidance of inflation in the methods adopted to finance these projects is a consideration of high importance.'[32]

This report was not released without difficulty. Following a meeting with Costello, McGilligan, Richard Mulcahy, and McElligott, Brennan was forced to abbreviate one passage to which the politicians took particular exception – although the substance of the criticism remained unchanged.[33] Maurice Moynihan, who later served as governor of the Central Bank, noted that its advice was not popular with political leaders at the time. 'There was . . . a growing sense of irritation at the Bank's warnings against financial imprudence, with a tendency in some cases to evade their serious import by treating them with derision. It became fashionable to refer to the Central Bank as "the banshee of Foster Place".'[34]

In January 1950, the government agreed to reappoint Brennan as the governor of the Central Bank.[35] MacBride took the strongest possible exception to this, on the grounds that Brennan's 'views, policies and acts . . . are in direct conflict with the policy of the government'. He added that this sort of office, in an inter-party government, 'should be filled by an agreed nominee'.[36] Indeed, Brennan himself had been reluctant to let his name go forward, but was told by Costello that he had been reappointed.[37]

The Central Bank's annual report again criticised the government's expansionary policy in 1950, noting that 'the incurring of a large volume of expenditure over a short period by executing the extensive programme of capital works on which the state is engaged must contribute towards weakness in the position of the Irish pound, even if the financing of such a programme could be met by current savings by the community . . . steps to curb inflation, especially in the field of investment, are now urgently needed . . .'[38]

In private, Brennan suggested to McGilligan that 'realism requires a drastic slashing of many existing services which the country on a broad view of its economic difficulties cannot now afford'.[39] McGilligan replied that he had 'to be as realistic as possible . . . there is no use urging the Government to adopt courses which I know to be unacceptable'.[40] The political problems involved in pressing the case for retrenchment were underlined by a memorandum from the Minister for Agriculture, James Dillon, who condemned 'the ball and chain' of Finance's attitude. 'Do we mean to house the people, provide hospital beds for the sick, or do we not? I think we do, and prophesying woe and destruction as a result . . . cuts no ice at all, because whatever economic consequences may transpire . . . they cannot be worse than letting TB patients cough their lungs out in the family kitchen, or letting the rats of Ringsend eat the second ear off the child who has already lost one . . .'[41]

The change in government policy was signalled by Costello in November 1949 in a speech to the Institute of Bankers at the Royal Hibernian Hotel in Dublin. Costello said the government accepted its responsibility 'to abate poverty and reduce unemployment, and we shall regard our ability in discharging this responsibility as a criterion of our success or of our failure'. He blamed the low level of national wealth and the lack of jobs on the lack of capital investment, especially in agriculture. Capital investment had risen from £2 million in 1946/7 to about £16 million in 1949/50, apart from Marshall Aid money to be spent on land drainage and reclamation. But the government wanted to invest more.

He said 'recent experience has taught us that a particular level of foreign assets is no longer as sacrosanct as many were inclined to believe in the years before the war', and referred to plans to repatriate some assets to invest at home, although the investments must be as secure as those available abroad.

Costello said the government viewed infertile land, lack of housing and shortage of hospital accommodation as far worse evils than a temporary disequilibrium in the balance of payments, and that short-term economic loss would be justified for the sake of social and long-term economic gain – as long as a deficit on the balance of payments was for investment rather than consumer spending. While some investment – such as in the telephone system – would earn enough revenue to pay interest, other projects would not earn revenue, but would improve the level of employment and living standards. Costello called for more savings to pay for this investment programme.

'A new Jerusalem cannot be built overnight. If we attempt to do too much at any one time, our schemes may jam each other and all may fail . . . It would be useful if this policy of capital investment for productive and social purposes by means of repatriating part of the sterling assets were clearly indicated to the public by making a distinction between the annual revenue budget, or the national housekeeping budget as it may be called, and the capital budget . . . In his last budget, the Minister for Finance did, in fact, underline the importance of that distinction . . . in view of their separate but equal importance it is desirable to consider carefully whether the advantages of bringing the capital budget and the revenue budget separately to the attention of the Dáil and the public would justify a departure from the traditional practice.'[42]

The speech was written by Patrick Lynch with the help of Alexis Fitzgerald. He showed the draft to McGilligan before delivery, but the minister 'made no changes of substance'[43] – effectively cutting the ground from under the feet of Finance officials who wished to object. Lynch wanted to put across the point that 'Ireland's need was to eliminate the causes of the chronic under-investment that had plagued the country while sterling assets were accumulating in Britain to an extent far beyond the liquidity requirements of the Irish banking system and continuously declining in real value'. He felt that sterling disinvestment could be achieved through deficits in the balance of payments, although the text emphasised that inflation must be avoided.[44]

The historian of the Department of Finance wrote that 'it is difficult to exaggerate the significance of Costello's speech . . . never before in the history of the state had the head of government delivered a major speech devoted exclusively to the principles underlying his government's economic policy'.[45] While the change in policy has been seen as positive by most historians, Brian Girvin has strongly argued that it did not represent a commitment to Keynesian demand management, or if it did, 'it was remarkably short lived. Subsequent budgets were deflationary, emphasising a continuing commitment to the balanced budget and the fear of balance of payments crises.'[46]

There is some truth in this view. The massive state investment programme signalled in the speech was only possible because of Marshall Aid. Once that source of funding ran out, governments simply didn't have access to independent sources of capital. It was only from 1957, when Ireland joined the International Monetary Fund and the World Bank, that such sources became available.[47] It is also true that the idea of designating some spending as 'proper to be met from borrowing' was not new[48] – Frank Aiken's postwar Transition Development Fund was one example. According to T.K. Whitaker, the Capital Budget derived from accounting principles in defining expenditure to be met from borrowing. Keynesian theory had a different basis, and was only used to provide a certain amount of respectability for this borrowing.[49]

However, Whitaker was to refer later to 1950 as a 'financial turning point' because 'accounting convention, political advantage and practical economic justification joined hands'[50] to produce a significant policy advance. Despite the fact that the use of Keynes was extremely convenient for the government, the Capital Budget still represented an attempt to think seriously about economics, to find ways out of chronic problems, and to put in place a strategy to best use the available resources. While the attempt was short-lived, lessons were learned which would prove extremely useful at the end of the decade.

Not surprisingly, McElligott, who was 'more in sympathy with Adam Smith and Gladstone than with Keynes or Dalton',[51] was less than impressed with the new departure. He met Lynch on the steps of Government Buildings on the day after the speech. 'You are a very young man, I want to give you one piece of advice. The more politicians know, the more dangerous they are.'[52]

The 1950 Budget was the largest ever, at £106.8 million. Just over £31 million of this was for capital purposes, with the largest chunk, £14 million, to go on housing, compared to just £360,000 devoted to MacBride's pet project, afforestation.[53] McGilligan said the sources for capital spending included the Marshall Aid counterpart fund, of which £13 million was uninvested at the end of March. Another £5 million was expected to come from the Post Office Savings Bank during the course of the year, and a new national loan would also fund capital investment.[54]

While the Capital Budget could be seen as a success for McGilligan, there were grounds for criticism of his tenure in Finance. Although he had delivered tax cuts, he had not done so through the retrenchment he had promised, but through dramatic increases in borrowing, which rose from 3.7 per cent of gross national product (GNP) in 1948 to 13 per cent in 1951.[55] And public sector spending as a percentage of GNP rose from 28.8 per cent (£86.4 million) in 1947/8 to 41.3 per cent (£157.9 million) in 1950/1. Seán MacEntee, the new Minister for Finance, cut public sector spending back to 38 per cent of GNP the following year (although its absolute value rose slightly to £160.8 million).[56]

This massive rise in the ratio of public expenditure to GNP, funded both by Marshall Aid and by borrowing,[57] was used to greatly expand the scope of investment. Between February 1948 and March 1951, a total of 19,886 phones were installed – an annual average of over 6,600, compared to the previous high point of 2,300 in a single year.[58] The limit on borrowing by the ESB was raised to £12 million in July 1948,[59] and to £16 million seven months later.[60] The limit on advances from the Local Loans Fund to local authorities for vocational education, public health and, most significantly, housing was raised a number of times – to £25 million in February 1949, £35 million in April 1950, and £50 million in June 1951.[61] The forestry plantation rate was stepped up, to 8,310 acres in 1949, 7,444 in 1950 and 9,160 in 1951.[62] And a £10.75 million expansion plan for the turf industry was launched in March 1949.[63]

But the most dramatic growth was in housing. In 1947, 744 local authority houses had been completed. By 1950, the annual figure had risen to 8,117.[64] Building and construction rose as a proportion of investment from 34.5 per cent in 1947 to 65.3 per cent in 1951.[65] This massive increase in housing construction was pursued by successive Labour Ministers for Local Government, Tim Murphy and Michael Keyes, against the opposition of Finance, which complained that 'unnecessary risks are being run by trying within one decade to dispose of a problem that has been accumulating for generations'.[66] While the housing drive stands as one of the most outstanding successes of the first inter-party government in human terms, Finance seemed to be vindicated by the report of American economic consultants in 1952, which suggested that the amount of investment in public housing was too great in relation to overall national production.[67]

The effects of all this investment could be seen in the unemployment rate, which fell from 9.3 per cent in 1947 to 7.3 per cent in 1951, while industrial production increased by an annual average of 10.7 per cent between 1946 and 1951[68] – although this was partly due to the availability of supplies again after the war. Some economists have claimed that, despite the increase in the overall borrowing requirement, 'a strong case existed for the continuation of expansionist policies. The domestic economy was by no means overheated in 1950 and 1951 – quite the reverse . . . Fiscal policy undoubtedly served to arrest a more serious depression.'[69] Whitaker's view that there were 'practical constraints to expansionary policies in an era when . . . foreign borrowing possibilities were virtually non-existent'[70] has already been noted.

Also interesting is the effect of the new policy on Fianna Fáil. At the time, capital spending on housing, schools, and hospitals was referred to by Fianna Fáil's Erskine Childers as 'slush',[71] and Seán Lemass claimed the government was leading the country 'into a lunatic sort of socialism'.[72] But the party was later to change its tune. Within Fianna Fáil governments, Lemass had been advocating Keynesian, expansionary policies as early as 1944, when he proposed spending £100 million on housing, electrification, roads, afforestation, etc.,[73] but got nowhere. His most recent biographer suggests that the electoral volatility after the war 'substantially impeded his attempts to secure a broader base within the party for the review of . . . key policies'.[74] The balance of payments difficulties caused by the expansionary policies of the first inter-party government may well have weakened Lemass's hand against MacEntee in the early 1950s, but at least they put expansion on the political agenda.

By 1955, Lemass was publicly outlining a plan to create 100,000 jobs by investing £67 million worth of repatriated sterling assets. Lemass himself believed the speech in which he made this suggestion 'promoted public acceptance of the idea of programming, planning and active government intervention to eventually produce a pre-defined economic plan'.[75] It had taken a decade to bring these arguments from the Cabinet table to the public. It is likely that the influence of Costello's speech and the first Capital Budget helped in this process.

The inter-party government's expansionary policy was intimately bound up with Marshall Aid, the area where the conflict between MacBride and McGilligan was most pronounced. De Valera had already entrusted the Department of External Affairs with control of Ireland's participation in the European Recovery Programme (ERP), and in May 1948 the new government confirmed this decision.[76] But while this represented a victory for MacBride, he was to be disappointed by the amount of aid, which never lived up to his expectations. Ireland's total allocation under Marshall Aid between 3 February 1948 and 2 May 1951 was $18 million in grants and $128.2 million in loans,[77] worth £6.4 million and £45.8 million respectively (at rates of exchange applicable after the devaluation of the pound in September 1949, which is discussed below). This compared to MacBride's prediction in May 1948 that Ireland could expect between £100 and £150 million in aid over the four years of Marshall Aid (although he stressed that 'this is a maximum which may not materialise . . . there should be no undue optimism and . . . no public reference should be made by members of the Government'). He urged his colleagues to draw up plans to spend the money, in order 'to lift ourselves out of our present rut . . . We must plan on the most optimistic basis and we must be dynamic in our approach.' MacBride wanted to spend money on developing hydroelectric and turf-fired power stations; field drainage and fertilisers; afforestation; development of the deep-sea fishing fleet; and mineral and turf development.[78] James Dillon was also keen to spend money on land reclamation, as well as agricultural training, improvements to farm buildings and equipment, and the importation of maize to allow more poultry, eggs, and pigs to be produced.[79]

The main categories of goods imported using Marshall Aid credits were bread grains (12 per cent), corn (30 per cent), tobacco (24 per cent), industrial raw materials (12 per cent), machinery, vehicles and equipment (9 per cent), and petroleum products (9 per cent)[80] – all vital to the Irish economy, and unobtainable without dollars. The theory was that Ireland's contribution to the ERP would lie in increased food production, particularly protein foods and fats. The Economic Co-operation Administration (ECA), which ran Marshall Aid from the US side, projected that Ireland's exports to participating countries would rise from £25 million in 1947 to £30 million in 1948/9 and to approximately £50 million in 1951/2.[81]

MacBride made it clear that he favoured a grant rather than a loan, telling the State Department in May 1948 that a loan would not be accepted, 'as we would be unable to repay it'.[82] But a few days after he wrote his memo, Ireland's Marshall Aid allocation was announced – £2.5 million on loan to cover the period April to June. Not only was the method of payment unwelcome, the amount involved was far less than MacBride had hoped. MacBride flew to New York a few days later, warning that Ireland might not accept loans under Marshall Aid, because 'we . . . do not like entering into obligations that we see no prospect of being able to meet'.[83] The following day, in New York, he added that 'the more food we can send to Europe, the less dollars Europe will need for food. But we need fertilisers, livestock feed and agricultural machinery to do it.'[84]

However, the basis for MacBride's demands was undermined in a memo prepared for the Secretary of State, Dean Acheson, during the Irishman's visit, which advised that 'there are no overriding international political considerations which would warrant preferential treatment towards the Irish'.[85] ECA boss Paul Hoffman remarked privately that it would be Ireland's 'funeral' if it refused the loan, as there were plenty of other countries who would gladly accept.[86] This American indifference, strengthend by irritation at MacBride's tactics,[87] undermined his attempts to secure movement on partition as well as his efforts to secure Marshall Aid by grant. Despite this, MacBride was never to stop believing that Irish friendship was valuable to the Americans.

A Cabinet meeting in June considered the views of MacBride and McGilligan on the ERP. The Department of Finance had originally believed that Marshall Aid should only be accepted as a grant – the acceptance of loans 'could not be justified by anything in our present outlook without some form of British assurance that we would get dollars for the purpose of conversion of sterling' at the time of repayment.[88] But by June, Finance had agreed with the

British Treasury not to draw on the sterling pool – the dollars held by currencies linked to sterling – during Marshall Aid. The Treasury was now urging Finance to accept a loan rather than break that agreement. McGilligan recommended that Ireland 'should proceed on the basis of full participation in the recovery plan and should take the best terms that are offered to us . . . The vital factor is the impossibility, without dollar aid, of our importing the goods necessary . . .' He added that future convertibility problems might mean that loans would never have to be repaid.[89]

MacBride replied that if a loan was accepted, a tactical advantage in the attempt to win grant aid would be lost, without any guarantee that the sterling pool wouldn't have to pay for goods that the ECA might not agree to cover. He also made a decision which lost the state a chance to save a great deal of money. An ECA official had suggested that the Irish debt should be in Irish currency rather than dollars. In the light of McGilligan's optimism that the loan might never be repaid, MacBride said he would not follow up on this suggestion.[90] A total of $47 million of Marshall Aid was converted into Irish currency before devaluation,[91] at a value of £11.7 million. When it was paid back after devaluation, the dollar equivalent was £16.8 million – a loss of £5.1 million that could have been avoided if the debt was in pounds rather than dollars.

The Cabinet initially backed MacBride and decided not to seek a loan for that quarter, although it did not rule out the acceptance of a loan in the future. MacBride was authorised to take active steps to secure aid in the next quarter, either by grant or by loan.[92] A fortnight later, the Cabinet reversed its decision, deciding to accept a loan for the current quarter if it was still available. Loans were to be accepted as necessary in future.[93] It appears that this reversal of the earlier decision was related to the Anglo-Irish talks of June 1948, at which British Chancellor Sir Stafford Cripps told the Irish that from 30 June they would no longer be able to draw dollars from the sterling pool.[94] Bernadette Whelan cites this incident as a demonstration of Ireland's lack of economic independence. 'The hope of reducing dependence on Britain was a factor in Ireland's decision to participate in ERP but Ireland's future was still decided outside Dublin . . .'[95]

When Hoffman announced tentative allocations for the period July to September, Ireland was offered £5.25 million in loans, but nothing in grants.[96] External Affairs had to cut back the ambitious programme of imports for that quarter from £10.75 million (with £1.75 million paid for by the earnings of Irish exports and the rest from Marshall Aid) to £6.4 million (with just over £1 million paid for by earnings).[97]

In September, Finance recommended that, where possible, imports from the dollar area should be kept to a minimum. Even if the ECA authorised certain imports, they should come from non-dollar countries if at all possible: 'the making of a loan agreement . . . does not involve necessarily a level of dollar expenditure up to [the] maximum [agreed] . . . the loan should be used only to meet essential requirements and should not be applied to unnecessary goods or services'.[98] At a meeting the following month the Cabinet agreed with the Finance line, excluding luxuries from dollar allocations and deciding that only half of the dollars spent in the first half of 1948 would be spent in the same period in 1949.[99]

When the US minister in Dublin, George Garrett, asked MacBride how the ERP funds were to be spent, he was told, unofficially, that the government planned 'to use these funds for development purposes, to increase the productivity of the nation. The degree and extent to which this can be done will depend largely on whether repayment arrangements have to be made or not. If the funds are available by way of a loan, all schemes will necessarily have to be conditioned by the repayment prospects.' This was the first of four main considerations underlying the government's plans, the others being the avoidance of inflation, a ban on competition with private enterprise, and a concentration on developing primary rather than secondary industries. MacBride envisaged seven areas likely to benefit from the funds, the first four from loans and the last three only from grants (as returns would be negligible): land reclamation and drainage; afforestation; fisheries; electricity development; agricultural training; provision of fertilisers; and harbour development.[100]

At the end of 1948, a White Paper outlining a four-year plan under the ERP was published. It provided for the improvement and intensification of agricultural production; the development of industry; a programme of natural capital development including reafforestation, land drainage and reclamation, mineral development, and electrification; and measures to tackle balance of payments problems, particularly with regard to the dollar area.[101]

However impressive this may have sounded, T.K. Whitaker, who was involved in preparing it, later admitted that 'it was never conceived of as a programme for policy. It was conceived as something to satisfy the Americans so that we could get Marshall Aid . . . We were told that, in order to get aid, you have to show that you will be viable in four years' time. So you worked to that schedule. But what you were saying had a very limited influence on government policy.'[102] One historian has asserted that the White Paper bore 'no relation to a programme, much less a plan. It was a jumble of statements thrown together in order to extract as much as possible from the Americans.'[103] While this is true, it is also true that the document 'did represent Ireland's first attempt to set forth and to publicise targets of growth'.[104] And it is interesting to note that while Whitaker and Sarsfield Hogan, the head of the exchange control division in Finance, drew up the predictions for the balance of payments consequences of the programme 'tongue in cheek', they were surprised to find four years later that the targets had actually been met.[105]

In February 1949, fearing that unspent dollar allocations would be forfeited, the government adopted a policy of making maximum use of available ECA funds. The decision was initially taken by Costello, MacBride, and McGilligan, and later confirmed by the full Cabinet. In particular, it was agreed that 'available ECA allotments would be firmly committed to the maximum extent' before the end of March.[106] As a result of this decision, dollar applicants who had recently been rejected were invited to resubmit their proposals.[107] This reversal of the Cabinet's decision the previous October to strictly curtail the use of dollars once again demonstrated the Department of Finance's lack of control in this area.

In December 1949, the Americans offered the first grant, of up to $3 million.[108] By the following June, various departments had suggested schemes costing £100 million to be paid for with grant aid – at a time when Finance was estimating that the maximum grant *and* loan aid under the ERP was likely to be around £55 million![109] The head of the ECA in Ireland, Joseph Carrigan, had suggested to MacBride that up to 10 per cent of the grant aid should be used to develop tourism, with the rest covering the capital cost of setting up an agricultural institute to improve farming techniques,[110] and Cabinet approved this suggestion in the middle of July.[111] At the end of November 1950, Paul E. Miller, who had taken over from Carrigan,[112] informed Costello that $13 million in grant aid would be paid during 1950/1.[113]

In December, it was announced that Marshall Aid to Britain was to end eighteen months early, on 1 January 1951, because the dollar deficit had been wiped out.[114] In an attempt to avoid a similar fate, MacBride submitted proposals to the ECA for a major Technical Assistance Programme,[115] and also wrote to Miller expressing concern that the deteriorating international situation would prevent Ireland importing vital raw materials.[116] However, on 16 February 1951, MacBride was handed an *aide-mémoire* by the US ambassador indicating that his government was considering the suspension of aid to Ireland.[117] On 2 May, aid was suspended, on the grounds that Ireland 'no longer needs outside dollar assistance to maintain a healthy economy'.[118]

Finance noted that 'for the future, in so far as our own dollar earnings are insufficient, we shall procure the foreign exchange necessary to pay for our essential imports from the dollar area by converting Sterling through the mechanism of the Sterling area dollar pool. In this connection, the British Treasury has already requested an estimate of our dollar requirements for 1951/2 and of our dollar deficit.'[119] This marked a return to the reliance on London of which MacBride so disapproved, but which Finance officials believed to be the primary economic relationship for the state.

The Irish and American governments have been criticised for concentrating Marshall Aid on agriculture.[120] But this was hardly surprising at the time, as agriculture was still Ireland's main industry and most exports were agricultural products. The OEEC recognised this early in 1949, saying that 'the solution of Ireland's problems depends on its chances of using a surplus from trade with Britain to offset a deficit with the Western hemisphere . . . The preparation of the country for the ultimate task of becoming a major meat and dairy producer will be marked by a return to animal husbandry based on imported needs, as against the present government-sponsored plans for the raising of home-grown cereal crops.'[121]

This concentration on cattle was timely, as James Dillon had three main aims in agriculture, all of which encouraged the Fine Gael preference for grass over grain: his reliance on the British market to the exclusion of others was buttressed by the Anglo-Irish Trade Agreement; his opposition to government regulation caused the end of compulsory tillage; and his enthusiasm for investment led to the Land Project. A government committed to self-sufficiency in wheat would not have played as obvious a part in Marshall Aid.

One of Dillon's first actions as Minister for Agriculture was to announce that compulsory tillage, which had been introduced by the Fianna Fáil government during the Emergency, would stop from 1949 (although he stressed that the law still applied for the current year).[122] He later outlined the philosophy behind this decision, saying the best way to increase the production and export of agricultural products was to encourage farmers 'to develop production on the lines that time and experience have proved most economic, namely livestock and livestock products'.[123]

This reliance on traditional production implied also a reliance on traditional markets – and Dillon was prepared to forgo other opportunities in order to cement the relationship with Britain. 'We would be glad, by restricting shipments elsewhere, to give our old customers preference, provided they do not actually discriminate against us.'[124] This outlook was repeated in June 1948 as he arrived in London for the opening of talks on a new Anglo-Irish Trade Agreement, promising to 'drown you with eggs' and saying that Ireland was 'relying on the expanding capacity of the British stomach'.[125]

In the agreement, the British agreed to remove the price differential between Irish fat cattle and animals fattened in Britain. The Irish promised increased exports of agricultural products, agreeing at the same time to limit such exports to other countries.[126] Although Seán Lemass noted that there was no particular achievement in selling agricultural products in a world that was short of food,[127] Dillon regarded the agreement as his greatest single achievement, because it 'poured countless millions into the pockets of the small farmers'.[128] Its usefulness was demonstrated in April 1949, when British farmers demanded a 4s 6d per hundredweight price increase for beef, which was passed on to Irish farmers a week later.[129] On the other hand, the British failed to live up to part of the bargain in 1951, when coal supplies fell far short of what was promised in the agreement, provoking a fuel crisis in Ireland.[130]

Perhaps Dillon's most dramatic innovation was the Land Project, announced in February 1949, which aimed to reclaim four million acres through drainage and fertilisation, over eight to ten years. The scheme envisaged the use of two million tons of ground limestone and a quarter of a million tons of rock phosphate, the employment of fifty thousand men, and a total cost of £40 to £50 million.[131] The day after his announcement, Dillon got Cabinet approval for 'the principles underlying the scheme' and was authorised to 'proceed with the further consideration, in detail, of the proposals . . . in consultation with the Minister for Finance and the other Ministers concerned'.[132]

Improvements in the land were clearly needed after the war years, when compulsory tillage was 'superimposed upon a desperate famine for fertilisers'.[133] The scheme was backed by Carrigan of the ECA, who felt that 'agriculture is the goose that lays the golden egg . . . [but] the goose has not been receiving the proper amount of attention'. Carrigan believed that agriculture would provide 97 per cent of the expected increase in Irish exports following Marshall Aid.[134]

The results of Dillon's term – particularly the removal of compulsory tillage and the recovery from wartime shortages – were clear to see in the statistics. In 1948, more than one and a half million acres were devoted to growing corn crops. By 1951, this had been reduced by a third. In the same period, the total number of cattle in the country rose from 3.9 to 4.3 million – despite the concurrent dramatic rise in exports. The value of egg exports rose from £0.7 million in the first quarter of 1947 to £2.6 million in 1950. In the same period, the value of cattle exports rose from £3.1 million to £5.7 million, with the numbers involved increasing from 107,282 to 132,873 – in other words, an 84 per cent increase in total value compared to a 24 per cent increase in volume. Creamery butter production increased from 35,827 hundredweight in 1947 to 88,827 in 1950, while the number of pigs delivered to bacon factories in a nineteen-week period rose from 92,007 in 1947 to 254,915 in 1950.[135]

The overall public perception of Dillon seemed positive. Although an Independent himself, his former association with Fine Gael led many to identify him with that party, and this was credited by some observers with part at least of its revival at the polls in 1951.[136] Perhaps the best tribute came from the Gaeltacht areas, where his work and commitment were long remembered, with day-old chicks known as 'Dillons bheaga' (little Dillons) for years afterwards.[137]

But while his aims had been achieved – compulsory tillage was gone, the relationship with the British market had been underpinned by the 1948 Trade Agreement, and a major investment programme in the land had been started – it is open to question whether these were the best options for the country. In the deteriorating international situation in the early 1950s, a new war and therefore difficulty in importing grain was a distinct possibility. The Land Project was viewed by many (including the Department of Finance) as an inefficient use of Marshall Aid funds. And the agreement with Britain precluded attempts to sell cattle to Europe, while at the same time it 'tied Ireland to one of the slowest growing economies in post-war Europe'.[138]

In fact, several promising trade agreements had been agreed with other Western European countries, trading shellfish and tweeds for French fertilisers and cement,[139] cattle for Dutch superphospate and machinery,[140] and various agricultural products for West German chemicals.[141] But the chances of expanding trade to the continent were severely reduced by the decision to limit exports of cattle under the terms of the Anglo-Irish Trade Agreement, a point continually made by MacBride.

The question of increasing exports, especially to the dollar area, was closely linked to the Marshall Plan. It also provided another point where the interests of External Affairs and Finance collided. Seán MacBride put forward many ideas, most of which were dismissed as half-baked by his Cabinet colleagues. Rereading the memoranda, it is difficult to argue with many of his suggestions.

There was constant pressure from the Americans for Ireland to increase dollar exports – if Europe sold more, Marshall Aid would not be needed. Practically speaking, there were two main ways of increasing dollar exports: attracting more American tourists and identifying export possibilities in the American market for goods that could be transported the distances involved. The ECA was not slow to offer advice – in August 1949, the organisation's boss, Paul Hoffman, claimed during a visit to Dublin that Ireland could solve its dollar problems if it earned $75 million a year. He observed that US tourists spent $500 million in Europe in 1948. 'If Americans, and particularly Irish-Americans, knew more about the beauties of this country, you would, perhaps, be overrun by tourists.'[142]

His comments followed a visit to Dublin by the head of the ECA's travel development section, Colonel Theodore Pozzy, who recommended the abolition of visa restrictions and frontier formalities, an advertising campaign in the US, more hotel rooms during the summer, and more off-season events.[143] He also described many Irish hotels as 'below par'.[144] Taking the heavy American hints about tourism, in October 1949 the government discussed an off-season publicity campaign in the US being organised by the OEEC. Patrick McGilligan felt that the campaign would do little for Ireland 'as weather conditions here in Winter and Spring are discouraging and there are no special attractions'. But the Minister for Industry and Commerce, Dan Morrissey, warned that non-participation might 'give cause for adverse comment by the ECA and might react adversely on the value of assistance received in this country under the ERP',[145] and it was agreed to take part.[146]

The American complaints appeared reasonable – it was reported from Washington that 'you could not get Scotch whisky in Britain because they were exporting it for dollars but . . . in Ireland you were told that they could not export whiskey for dollars because they needed it for consumption at home'.[147] In December 1949, Joseph Carrigan, head of ECA operations in Ireland, wrote to MacBride expressing 'deep concern' about Ireland's dollar earnings and urging the government to be 'more active in connection with it'.[148]

In May 1950, MacBride proposed a number of initiatives to tackle the problem of dollar exports, including the establishment of an Exports Corporation and a Dollar Earnings Board, and the provision of more tourist accommodation.[149] Cabinet approved the establishment of a Dollar Exports Advisory Committee,[150] chaired by the secretary of the Department of Industry and Commerce, John Leydon.[151] McElligott had pointed out that apart from the obvious practical advantages of such a committee, it would also appeal to the ECA. 'If ECA had reason to think that we were being unduly inactive it might well react on the total amount of aid to be received by us and almost certainly would reduce the amount we might receive by grant.'[152] More importantly, the Dollar Exports Advisory Committee led in turn to the establishment of Córas Tráchtála the following year, an organisation 'which rivalled the IDA in significance'.[153]

MacBride also submitted proposals for cutting down on dollar imports, suggesting increased production of barley, wheat, and sugar, and the use by the ESB of turf rather than oil.[154] In an acidic response, Dillon suggested that such minor adjustments were of little real use. If convertibility was not restored by the time Marshall Aid ran out, 'the principal concern of any man or woman in Western Europe will be to furnish himself or herself with some kind of transport in which he can proceed in the general direction of the setting sun . . . with the certainty that should he fail he is destined for a trip to the Siberian salt-mines, where the questions of maize, wheaten flour, sugar or canned fish are not likely greatly to trouble his mind'. Dillon also suggested that turf was about as efficient a source of energy as camel dung, 'and I find it hard to persuade myself that Egypt would be wise to exclude oil . . . purely for the purpose of saving dollars . . .'[155]

But while efforts to increase dollar exports and cut down on imports were laudable, in the view of the Americans the greatest progress could be made in tourism. In July, Colonel Pozzy told MacBride that the patience of the ECA 'was exhausted and . . . effective government action in this field . . . was essential . . . If Ireland did not show some real interest in increasing her dollar earnings in the line which seemed most feasible, the ECA could hardly be expected to continue their aid at the forecast level.'[156] A month later, Pozzy made his criticism public, pointing out that only 10 per cent of the $3 million grant to Ireland was being spent in this area, while 40 per cent of Ireland's dollar earnings in 1949 came from tourism[157] – an ironic criticism in view of the fact that Carrigan had suggested this proportion.

The Americans also put pressure on the government to drop the Shannon stopover rule. Under the terms of the 1945 bilateral agreement on civil aviation, American flights were obliged to land at Shannon. In discussions between a US delegation and government representatives in September 1949, the Americans claimed that direct flights to Dublin would increase tourism, and therefore dollar earnings. The Irish representatives made the point that if there was no mandatory stopover, US planes would be able to use navigation facilities at Shannon without paying for them by way of landing charges.[158] Naturally, McGilligan was opposed to the idea of investing in improving Dublin airport so it could cater for transatlantic flights when Shannon was unable to pay its own way, while Morrissey, a Tipperary man, was conscious of the benefits of the latter airport to the mid-west.[159]

MacBride suggested that American airlines should make a contribution towards the costs at Shannon, and that Shannon should be used as a distribution centre for air-freight from the US to Europe.[160] US ambassador George Garrett replied that the first suggestion would create an unwelcome precedent, while his government couldn't force airlines to agree to the second.[161] The Department of Industry and Commerce recommended a rejection of requests for amendment of the 1945 agreement.[162] MacBride, realising the need to placate the Americans, wanted to agree to a new request from Garrett, for just one American flight to be allowed fly to Dublin, after landing at Shannon.[163] Morrissey said this would be the 'thin end of the wedge' and again urged rejection, supported by McGilligan.[164] There the matter was allowed to rest, although no formal rejection of the American request was noted on the file.

In October 1950, MacBride appointed trade officers in Chicago, New York, and Paris to promote the sale of Irish goods, particularly for dollars.[165] Before they took up their posts, the new officers visited factories to ascertain what was available for export, in what was apparently 'the first physical survey of this kind'. Their report should have punctured some illusions – 'the surplus of manufactured goods available for export was very small . . . most firms are interested almost entirely in the home market and are not prepared to make a special effort to meet the export market'.[166] With such a lack of interest on the part of private enterprise, it appeared there was little the government could do to improve Ireland's dollar export position.

In such a situation, Irish economic dependence on Britain continued, as was demonstrated in no uncertain terms by the sterling devaluation of September 1949. This crisis once more pointed up the differences between Seán MacBride and the Department of Finance; and again, the government opted to follow the orthodox approach rather than the radical solution canvassed by the Clann leader.

The problem for sterling was that it had been artificially fixed at the 1939 rate of $4 to £1. That this was unrealistic was shown by the continuing adverse balance with the dollar zone. The British Chancellor of the Exchequer, Sir Stafford Cripps, was reluctant to devalue, but by 1949 the pressure was too great. Ironically, the gains were to be almost immediately wiped out by the Korean War, both in its effects on prices and in the increase in defence spending which diverted resources away from productive ends, reduced exports, raised taxes, and sealed the fate of the Labour government in the 1951 election.[167]

A Department of Finance memo dated 13 June 1949 said 'it seems unlikely . . . that there will be devaluation of sterling in the immediate future; on the contrary, Britain is not likely to devalue until every other alternative has been tried and, even then, only when the ultimate monetary reserves of the sterling area have been seriously reduced'. The memo went on to warn that Ireland would lose by devaluation, unless imports from hard currency areas were reduced, or exports greatly increased. 'There is no evidence that such a change in trade would be possible and to the large loss on capital account a considerable loss on current trading account would have to be added, thus making for balance of payments difficulties. As our existing balance of payments is already in grave disequilibrium, this would be a serious matter.'[168]

MacBride replied with a memo of his own, claiming that Ireland had already lost out through depreciation of sterling, because of 'the disastrous financial policy of under-investment and under-capitalisation of our own resources, coupled with dependence on the "sterling assets" invested in Britain'. He called for urgent repatriation of 'sterling assets' to safeguard them against devaluation, with the money to be invested in forestry, arterial drainage and land reclamation, building factories and industrial plant, mineral development, electricity production, and harbour development.[169] Unusually, McGilligan didn't object to this memo intruding on his area of responsibility, and it was put on the Cabinet agenda for 28 June 1949 – and was thereafter postponed on no less than fourteen occasions, until it was overtaken by events.[170] The secretary of the Department of Finance, James McElligott, meanwhile, met in London with British Treasury officials who 'explained the seriousness of the position and . . . asked for the co-operation of the Irish Government in avoiding further encroachment on the reserves of the sterling area'.[171]

Costello was handed a note from Clement Attlee by the British representative in Dublin, Sir Gilbert Laithwaite, at 10.15 a.m. on Saturday, 17 September, telling him of the British decision to devalue. 'I need hardly emphasise the importance of preserving the utmost secrecy about the contents of this message until the time of the announcement. I regret the very short notice which I have been able to give you, but, as you will appreciate, it was essential to make the interval between the final decision and the announcement as short as possible.'[172]

The Cabinet met in the Taoiseach's rooms in Government Buildings for almost two hours on Saturday evening, before ministers had to go to Iveagh House for a dinner in honour of Archbishop Cushing of Boston. At eleven o'clock the dinner finished and the Cabinet meeting resumed in Iveagh House until 4.45 a.m. The Cabinet met again on the Sunday evening from 6.30 to 8.15.[173] Under consideration was a Department of Finance memo, dated 3 September, which had apparently been circulated by McGilligan to some ministers in the previous two weeks.[174] All ministers were now given a copy. It was broadly similar to the 13 June memo, except that it put the chances of devaluation higher,[175] and was even more insistent on the undesirability of breaking the link with sterling.

The new memo pointed out that gold and dollar reserves in London had fallen to around £350 million, or about two-thirds of the figure considered the minimum for safety. It warned that 'a continuance of the drain at recent rates would result in devaluation before the end of the year unless a decision were taken that the reserves should be allowed to fall to a very low level in the hope of an alteration in the British trading position before they were approaching exhaustion'. It went on to state that the professed British policy of reducing dollar imports by £100 million compared to 1948 would be difficult because many of the imports were of food and essential raw materials, finishing with the observation that 'recently, financial editors of British papers have been canvassing the possibility of devaluation and the actual date has been openly considered, thus indicating that they regard postponement as impossible. The 18th of September, being the Sunday following the meeting of the IMF, has been suggested as a likely date.'

The June memo had said that 'in view of the closeness of our economic relation with Britain, and the settled tendency towards a parallel structure of wages and prices, any exchange value between the Irish pound and sterling other than parity would be unreal'. By September, a much stronger warning was in place: 'in view of the weakness of our balance of payments position and in our domestic position – high imports, low exports, high levels of taxation and of government expenditure on both capital and current account – we are in no position to sustain a higher value for our pound as compared with the British pound'.[176]

The Cabinet on Sunday evening finally approved a draft statement submitted by McGilligan, stating that 'the course of least disadvantage' was to follow the British devaluation.[177] This phrase was regarded by McGilligan as having saved the day, as the Cabinet could accept that while devaluation was disagreeable, there was no alternative. The phrase had been part of the statement drafted by T.K. Whitaker on the Sunday, after a few hours' sleep following the Iveagh House meeting.[178] The decision to devalue the Irish pound from $4.03 to $2.80 was announced on the Sunday evening.

Ronan Fanning, after interviews with MacBride, Whitaker, Patrick Lynch, and Sarsfield Hogan, constructed a detailed account of the 'prolonged and bitter discussions' at Iveagh House. MacBride, with Noël Browne in a supporting role, and McGilligan and Dillon opposed, argued against an Irish devaluation.[179] The Cabinet's decision remained in doubt until 'Norton threw his weight behind Finance's advice'.[180] Whitaker recalled MacBride sitting in the middle of the room in Iveagh House, using his senior counsel skills as he adopted the role of prosecutor. McElligott insisted that devaluation would have a minimal effect on prices, a statement Whitaker considered 'improbable and unsound'. As a result, Whitaker was concerned about how he 'could reconcile my concern for the truth with my loyalty to my superiors. Fortunately, the dawn broke and I wasn't put before the bar.'[181]

But MacBride was still determined to have a full discussion of the issue. On 20 September, a government meeting commissioned memoranda from McGilligan, Morrissey, and MacBride on the effects of devaluation. Morrissey concluded that while there would be some increase in domestic prices as a result of devaluation, 'these increases are not likely to be serious in the immediate future'. A price freeze or a standstill order on wages, salaries, and profits was unnecessary, and potentially inflationary.[182] McGilligan felt that current revenue and expenditure would not be affected, but that capital spending would be more difficult, because materials would be dearer. 'To curb the forces of inflation . . . substantial economies in public expenditure, both current and capital, must be achieved and a firm stand must be taken against increases in wages, salaries and profits. Whatever increase there may be in the cost of living owing to devaluation must be accepted.'[183] Dillon argued, in an unsolicited contribution, that for the moment every effort should be made to hold down domestic prices, and that a revision of the Anglo-Irish Trade Agreement should not be sought unless the British tried to charge more for raw materials exported to Ireland than was charged to British farmers.[184]

It was MacBride, as usual, who wanted radical action. He called for a price freeze to stop profiteering; a major effort to increase dollar earnings through providing extra tourist accommodation with prefabricated 'road-houses'; the appointment of more trade attachés; the use of existing legislation to allow the government to amend parity between the Irish pound and sterling; repatriation of government and Central Bank investments in Britain for investment at home; and revision of the Anglo-Irish Trade Agreement to increase prices and allow Ireland to export cattle and meat to countries other than Britain. MacBride urged 'in this situation the trade policy of the government should be to purchase our imports in the cheapest markets and to sell our exports where we will get the best prices possible'.[185] In a separate memo he warned of the 'possible disintegration of the sterling area', and said the very least that could be done was to invest money in other countries of the area, before it collapsed, trapping the money in the UK.[186]

These memoranda were discussed on 28 September, when it was decided that McGilligan, Morrissey, Dillon, and MacBride should independently examine the questions raised and report back to the government on the effects of devaluation on prices. Morrissey was to look into the advisability of a standstill order on prices and to submit proposals on the tourist industry, while the Attorney General, Cecil Lavery, was to consider whether the government had the authority to amend parity between the Irish pound and sterling.[187] This was all, of course, the result of MacBride's urging.

Lavery informed Costello on 4 October that MacBride's claim that there was power to amend parity in existing legislation was incorrect.[188] Morrissey reported back on 12 October that the increase in the price level of imports might be around £19.5 million, or 16 per cent, while the increase in the cost of all goods and services would be 3.8 per cent, equal to £6 10s per head, or £39 per annum for a family of six. The effect of these predictions was somewhat lessened by the observation that they were the result of guess-work and almost certainly wrong![189] MacBride estimated that goods would increase in price by about £29 million, or 10 per cent,[190] while Dillon said that 'reasonable prudence' could avoid a rise, and that 'therefore any attempt to adjust the economic pattern of our community ... would be premature'.[191] A further memo from Morrissey advised that existing arrangements could deal with the effects of devaluation at least as well as a standstill order on prices, and that such an order would lead to strong pressure for a similar measure to control wages.[192]

Devaluation had been withdrawn from the Cabinet agenda on 18 October, on the understanding that when all the memoranda sought had been submitted, Costello was to be consulted about putting it back on.[193] Maurice Moynihan noted in February 1950 that memos were still outstanding from McGilligan and Dillon, adding: 'I have spoken to the Taoiseach. There is no need to remind the Ministers for Finance and Agriculture further in this matter.'[194] This ensured that the divisive issue of devaluation, and the awkward questions posed by MacBride, would be kept off the Cabinet agenda indefinitely.

A further delaying tactic was the establishment of a committee to consider the situation created by devaluation. As well as Costello, McGilligan, Morrissey, Dillon, and MacBride, it was to include the secretaries of the Departments of Finance and External Affairs, the director of the Central Statistics Office, several other civil servants, a number of prominent economists, and representatives of the Irish Banks Standing Committee.[195] A note by Whitaker a decade later indicates that it never met.[196] This was just as well, because in reality the government had little choice, given the extent of Ireland's trade with Britain, but to devalue. However, it is at least arguable that MacBride's radical approach deserved further study, if only to generate new thinking about Irish economic affairs.

Thus outmanoeuvred in Cabinet, MacBride showed his displeasure in public. Speaking in the Catholic Commercial Club in October 1949 on 'the link with sterling', he attacked the banks. 'The time has come when our banking system and our financial authorities should cease to look upon themselves as mere money lenders who treat money and credit as a commodity to be exploited, irrespective of the needs of the community as a whole.' The immediate cause of his comments was the refusal by the banks to lend Dublin Corporation £5 million for housing, but he also criticised them for investing the nation's savings abroad, leading to 'chronic under-investment at home'.[197] He predicted that 'a further and more substantial fall in the purchasing power of the pound may be expected'.[198] The governor of the Central Bank, Joseph Brennan, complained to Costello and McGilligan about these remarks, on the basis that they amounted to 'a public censure of the Central

Bank', while he considered the remarks about the future purchasing power of the pound 'injudicious'.[199]

In retrospect, MacBride felt that the devaluation crisis adversely affected the standing of the Department of Finance within the government; according to Fanning, 'the devaluation crisis accelerated the polarisation of opinion in government circles on financial policy and this meant that the Department of Finance's advice was increasingly questioned, and sometimes rejected, by the government'.[200] However, at the time the Minister for External Affairs was deeply disillusioned, even considering resignation if the government's performance did not improve.[201] Certainly, from the course of events after devaluation, when Costello ducked the questions posed by the Clann leader, it would seem that although MacBride had been right about the implications of devaluation, it was his prestige that was on the wane, not the Department of Finance's.

As the crisis over devaluation faded, another with the balance of payments loomed. The state's very serious and protracted problems with the balance of payments reached crisis proportions in the latter half of the inter-party government's term of office – there were deficits in the current balance of payments of 7.6 per cent of GNP in 1950, and 14.7 per cent in 1951.[202] Rapid domestic expansion fuelled by the state investment programme, the devaluation of sterling (which increased import prices but left the price of agricultural exports unchanged), and rising raw material prices caused by the Korean War all played a part in the unfolding problem.[203]

Whether these deficits were really as serious as was believed at the time is open to question. Patrick Lynch pointed out that despite deficits of around £160 million in the balance of payments between 1947 and 1952, Irish sterling assets were still at a very healthy £400 million or so in the early 1950s, the deficits having been largely met by Marshall Aid and capital imports, with just £35 million of sterling assets being liquidated.[204] It is only when looking at the longer term that one appreciates the panic felt in government circles at the time. The average deficit from the end of the war to 1968 was just £16.8 million[205] – which amounted to a quarter of the deficit in 1951.

With imports outstripping exports in the early postwar years, partly due to the rebuilding of stocks, Ireland's sterling holdings had to be drawn down. These had increased by £125 million during the war because of the difficulty of importing goods, leaving total Irish sterling assets at £400 million in 1945. MacBride was obsessed with the 'repatriation' of these holdings for investment at home. More conservative figures, including Brennan, McElligott, and the commercial banks, insisted that the money should be held in London, as it was more secure and more liquid in the much larger financial market there.[206] Another point was that the government only owned 13 per cent of these assets, mainly in the form of investments of the Post Office Savings Bank. The state, along with the Central Bank (12 per cent of the assets) and the commercial banks (34 per cent), 'are less owners than trustees. They hold sterling primarily as cover against their liabilities to private persons.'[207] The government could not simply order the owners of these assets to invest them at home. However, a deficit on the balance of payments would effectively do the same thing, as Costello pointed out in the speech which led to the 1950 Capital Budget. The danger was that if the deficit was too large, Ireland's external reserves would be completely wiped out.

The balance of payments situation caused some anxiety at the start of the government's term, with Morrissey warning in April 1948 that if people continued to spend sterling on luxuries without increasing exports, the government would have to consider import restrictions.[208] McGilligan wanted to cut spending and limit imports to adjust the balance of payments. Finance blamed the disequilibrium in external finances on domestic inflation, which was fuelling a consumer boom – the department claimed that 90 per cent of imports were consumption goods.[209] The Cabinet approved import restrictions in principle at the end of August.[210] A month later, Morrissey asked the government to reconsider its decision. He claimed that on a broader interpretation, 31 per cent of imports in 1947, or £41 million, were capital goods, compared to a £30 million decrease in sterling holdings. Morrissey pointed out that the situation was improving, with exports increasing while imports decreased, and that 'the introduction of a regime of restriction and austerity would involve unemployment and emigration'.[211] In fact, the adverse balance of trade for August was the lowest on record since goods began to flow more freely after the war.[212]

Not surprisingly, McGilligan objected to Morrissey's arguments, insisting that 'a loss arises if external assets are realised to pay for imports (even if these are regarded as "capital" goods) which do not yield greater assistance to the balance of payments than the income of the surrendered external assets'. He also suggested that the best way of controlling the situation was to decrease domestic inflation, and to this end proposed a 10 per cent cut in each department's Estimates for the coming financial year![213] The matter was referred to the Cabinet Economic Committee,[214] but the improved balance of trade in the latter half of the year removed the need to impose such restrictions.[215] In the event, the adverse balance of trade actually decreased by £2 million during 1948.[216] Morrissey claimed that the increase in imports in 1947 and 1948 was largely the result of stocking up after 'seven lean years', and he predicted that the adverse balance would be 'considerably lessened' during 1949.[217]

He was correct in this, with the deficit falling to £9.6 million in 1949 from £19.9 million the previous year; but the balance of payments deficit for 1950 was £30 million, to be followed the next year by a deficit of £61.6 million, which, at 14.7 per cent of GNP, was 'relatively, the highest ever recorded in Ireland'.[218] However, increasing prices, rather than an increasing volume of imports, were largely responsible for the problem. An analysis of the £53.8 million increase in the deficit between 1949 and 1951 shows that £30.6 million of it was due to price increases; £16.8 million due to a faster rise in the volume of imports than the volume of exports; and the remaining £6.4 million 'to the joint effects of price and volume'.[219]

Although, as we have noted above, the increase in import prices was largely due to factors outside the government's control (devaluation and the Korean War), the blame was put squarely on the capital investment programme, which was sharply cut back in Seán MacEntee's deflationary Budget of 1952. Kennedy and Dowling noted that even before that Budget had taken effect, both the price and volume of imports were falling, leading to a balance of trade deficit of £16.4 million in the second quarter of 1951, only £1 million more than that of the second quarter of 1949, before the crisis started. 'This would seem to confirm the wisdom of the government's action in 1951 in holding back on deflationary measures.'[220]

Costello condemned the 1952 Budget as 'cruel, unjust and unnecessary', but without Marshall Aid and with no alternative source of foreign borrowing, his own government would have had little option but to follow a similar course,[221] although it might have shown less enthusiasm for cuts than MacEntee.

Even before the government's policy of expansion led to trouble with the balance of payments, a more fundamental problem was evident – the failure to create jobs. Between 1946 and 1951, only eight hundred new jobs were created every year, or one job for every thirty people seeking employment.[222] The solution put forward by the inter-party government as part of its state-led expansion strategy was the establishment of the Industrial Development Authority (IDA). Not surprisingly, the Department of Finance reacted with suspicion to suggestions for such a body. A departmental memorandum in December 1948 suggested that if such a board had to be established, it should have no independent powers and should have to submit all proposals to Cabinet 'insofar as Cabinet is protection against foolish or corrupt ministers'. The IDA would have to win acceptance from the business community, 'who must feel from the start that they will get a fair crack of the whip and that the Board is not a gang of crack-pot socialist planners'. The memo concluded that such a board should bring possibilities of industrial development to the attention of entrepreneurs; it 'should definitely *not* be within their scope or function to themselves . . . plan industry or any branch thereof. They should be purely an industrial development advisory board and it might be as well to title them as such.'[223]

The Cabinet agreed to the establishment of the IDA in February 1949.[224] The five members of the authority were to initiate proposals and schemes for the creation and development of Irish industries; survey possibilities of further industrial development; advise government and entrepreneurs on steps necessary for establishing new industries and for expanding and modernising existing ones; investigate the effects of protective measures, especially on employment, prices, and wage levels; and examine government proposals for tariffs, quotas, and other protective measures.[225]

The authority, chaired by J.P. Beddy of the Industrial Credit Corporation, was named in March. The other members were Senator Luke Duffy, secretary of the Labour Party, K.C. McCourt of the Federation of Irish Manufacturers, J. O'Brien of the Federated Union of Employers, and J.J. Walsh, a director of Easons.[226] Although the IDA began work at the end of May,[227] and had submitted its first proposals to government by September,[228] the members' contracts were not approved by Cabinet until March 1951,[229] while the Bill establishing it had a tortuous passage through government and the Dáil.[230]

When the government held a special joint meeting with the IDA in October 1950, Beddy complained that, without proper staff and funding for capital investment, the authority wouldn't be able to carry out its functions. The authority felt that the Department of Finance was too restrictive in considering applications for trade loans, apparently applying the same criteria as applied by commercial banks. According to the authority, the Industrial Credit Corporation was inadequately capitalised. The IDA wanted finance to be made available to build factories, either by the authority itself or with capital supplied by it. They pointed out that the buildings themselves would provide good security for the investment. MacBride strongly supported the IDA's requests, pointing out that the Industrial Credit Corporation earned profits of between 10 and 12 per cent, indicating that if more of the sterling assets held by the government and the Central Bank were reinvested in such development, they would be safer and more profitable than in Britain.[231] McGilligan and Morrissey opposed the circulation of the memorandum in which MacBride set out his views, and as the matter lay outside the External Affairs brief, Costello decided not to distribute it.[232]

The establishment of the IDA was to lead to the start of many important new industrial projects, but the problems it faced in 1951 were serious, including overprotection, mediocre managerial competence, and little progress in developing exports.[233] In 1952, grant aid began to help the establishment of new industries, a development described as 'the significant innovation in the 1950s', and one that was largely made possible by the creation of the IDA.[234]

But such achievements were far in the future, and the inter-party government had more pressing concerns. By mid-1950, inflationary pressures driving up prices were becoming increasingly obvious, a development which the Central Bank report for 1951 was to blame on 'the constantly increasing scale of the expenditure of the State and local authorities and the continuing rise in general levels of remuneration'.[235] We have seen that the Korean War and devaluation were also culprits, but it was unfortunate indeed for the popularity of the parties making up the government, and more particularly for Labour, that the cost of living should once more be on the rise.

Because of the widespread belief that prices were rising, the government ran into serious trouble on the industrial front, particularly with the repudiation of the 1948 wage agreement by both the Irish Trade Union Congress and the Congress of Irish Unions after the employers refused to amend it[236] and the Labour Court rejected a request for a general increase in wages to make up for the rise in the cost of living since 1948.[237] The agreement, the first recognisable negotiated pay round,[238] had been signed after the change of government, but on the initiative of de Valera. It specified wage increases of 11 shillings a week all round, with no further demand for increases except in 'exceptional circumstances',[239] but had been agreed in the belief that prices would fall, just after the inter-party government came into office promising to lower the cost of living.[240]

Faced with pressure from the unions, the government announced a new Household Budget Survey in October 1950 to see if the weights for the cost-of-living index were correct.[241] The suggestion for this came from Costello, after consultation with McGilligan, Morrissey, and Norton.[242] However, the survey, covering five thousand randomly selected families, would not be complete until the middle of 1952,[243] which was to prove too late to help the government.

A Labour Party delegation met Costello, Morrissey, McGilligan, and Dillon in November 1950 to urge a review of the government's control of prices, the reimposition of the Excess Profits Tax, and a commitment that workers should not have to pay for increased prices.[244] Similar demands were made to ministers by delegations from the ITUC[245] and the CIU.[246] At the end of November, the

Parliamentary Labour Party insisted to Costello that attempts to enforce price control 'will be ineffective unless an immediate decision is made to "freeze" prices as from a fixed date'.[247]

Earlier in the year, at the Fine Gael ard fheis, Richard Mulcahy had stressed his party's commitment to private enterprise and the profit motive, adding that 'it is all the more necessary to emphasise it in case it should become necessary for the government to interfere to prevent unreasonable profit making or the obstruction of urgently necessary public policy by monopoly'.[248] However, in November, his party colleague Liam Cosgrave made a rather incautious speech in the Dáil, during which he claimed that the government had kept prices steady for two and a half years, until the outbreak of the Korean War, and that the situation was still better than in Britain and elsewhere.[249]

This was not a suggestion likely to calm the prices agitation, and a fortnight later Labour leader William Norton assured the Dáil that the government planned to introduce 'without delay . . . the most extensive and practical prices freeze that we can devise'. He also claimed that, under Fianna Fáil, 'the wealthy elements of the community were allowed to get away with a bundle of swag that astonished even themselves'.[250] Lemass later claimed the government was forced into the freeze by 'the rushing tactics' of Norton, 'who knows nothing . . . about the problems of business management and who is concerned only with the political reaction to a very foolish speech' by Cosgrave, adding: 'The adverse public reaction to that speech threw the government into a panic.'[251] Another view of the situation was that while the freeze was unlikely to be effective, 'to Norton's way of looking at it, this was immaterial. The question was, would it appease public wrath for a while? If it would, then why hesitate?'[252]

Proof that prices were rising came with the publication of the cost-of-living index. The base figure for the index was 100 in August 1947. It was still at 100 in mid-November 1949 and mid-August 1950, but by mid-November 1950 it had risen to 102.[253] On 2 January 1951, the government announced a 'price freeze' over a comprehensive list of goods, backdated to 2 December. All prices which had been increased since that date had to be reduced to their original level. A Prices Advisory Council was set up to adjudicate on all applications for price increases, under the chairmanship of the former Attorney General and now member of the Supreme Court, Mr Justice Lavery, with a barrister, an accountant, a businessman, and two trade unionists as members.[254]

Seán Ó Broin, the secretary of the Department of Agriculture, wrote to Maurice Moynihan at the Department of the Taoiseach on 3 January with a departmental note objecting to the order in the strongest terms. (Dillon was away and so could not present the objections.) 'There seems no possibility of giving real effect to the Order . . . If, however, effective control could in some manner be achieved, the result generally would be to depress supplies and to provoke black market practices.' The department felt that the prices for some goods – for instance wool – were based on export prices; freezing the price would simply hand a large profit to the exporter at the expense of the producer. Other goods, such as potatoes, were affected by seasonality; if the price fixed was that of the main crop, no early potatoes would be grown.[255]

The Federation of Irish Manufacturers claimed that international shortages had driven up the price of raw materials; now, thanks to the 'freeze', Irish manufacturers would be unable to bid for them.[256] The federation also objected to showing accounts to the Prices Advisory Council in public session, calling the order 'a little outburst of totalitarianism' by the government.[257]

The Prices Advisory Council confounded their friends and delighted their enemies with a statement at the end of January insisting that a reasonable profit must be given to manufacturers, adding that 'the public will have to recognise that, in existing world conditions, price increases in many goods are unavoidable, and that no control can maintain present prices generally'.[258]

Despite this, the Association of Chambers of Commerce of Ireland urged the government to withdraw the standstill order.[259] Costello told their delegation that 'a serious position had arisen before Christmas and a campaign in connection with the cost of living had been directed against the government in the newspapers and throughout the country . . . The agitation was, however, calmed immediately on the coming into operation of the Standstill Order.' Costello added, presumably in response to comments made by the delegation, that 'he would like to pay tribute to the Tánaiste, Mr

Norton, who had been a tower of strength to him and his colleagues in the difficult time that had been passed'.[260]

On the first Saturday in March, a newspaper notice advised that the number of items covered by the freeze was being reduced to just thirty-seven.[261] Lemass pointed out that this removed three-quarters of the goods originally 'frozen', adding that 'only a Government of lawyers could have done what they have done and I will say this about lawyers, that outside the law courts and matters concerning the law, they are the most ignorant tribe of people . . .'[262] The interim cost-of-living index for essential items rose six points from 103 in February 1951 to 109 in May (based on August 1947 = 100),[263] and this fact may go far to explain the government's election defeat.

The economic policy of the first inter-party government, then, had pluses and minuses. Its adoption of a Keynesian (or, at least, a quasi-Keynesian) policy allowed it to submerge differences between left and right, and to introduce a programme of state capital investment with many beneficial results, particularly in housing. But the policy also contained the seeds of its own destruction. An economy dependent on agricultural exports to Britain, which adopted a cheap food policy and which was also one of the worst performing economies in Western Europe, could never on its own generate enough capital to continue this investment programme. Once Marshall Aid ran out, the state simply had no access to alternative sources of capital. The inter-party government was unlucky in that the Korean War, on top of the effects of devaluation, made a balance of payments crisis inevitable. This led to an increase in the cost of living, and also to the deflationary Budget of 1952 and the discrediting of expansionary policies for almost a decade.

At the same time, ideas generated during this period were of key importance in developing the policies which eventually lifted Ireland out of its rut: state-led investment, borrowing for productive purposes, the IDA, Córas Tráchtála, the export drive. All were to become important components in a changed economic environment

– although, despite their earlier opposition, Seán Lemass and Fianna Fáil were to pursue these policies and reap the political benefits.

Finally, it is important to ask whose economic policies were followed by the inter-party government. It is clear that officials in the Department of Finance were unhappy with their minister's unwillingness to confront the demands of the minor parties for increased spending, particularly those of Seán MacBride. But it is also true that MacBride's ideas were only accepted if leading members of Fine Gael agreed with them. Patrick McGilligan and John A. Costello both became convinced of the advantages of a state-led investment programme, thanks to the influence of economists like Patrick Lynch, Alexis Fitzgerald, and T.K. Whitaker. But they never accepted MacBride's proposals for a break with sterling, or the wholesale repatriation of investments in London. This indicates once again that the minor parties needed support in the ranks of their senior partner in order to change government policy.

SIX

A DEFINITE CLEAVAGE OF OPINION

Mr MacBride and Mr Norton may want one thing, but Mr McGilligan may want quite another, and nobody knows, with a Coalition regime in existence, which party is going to prevail. The difficulty is, in short, under which thimble, if any, one is likely to find the pea.

Irish Press editorial[1]

While Fine Gael was rebuilding its appeal as a party of government, and Clann na Poblachta was making progress on the Republic and in Health, a number of issues were closely identified with the fortunes of Labour, among them the nationalisation of Córas Iompair Éireann and the housing programme, both of them policy successes for the party.

Nationalisation of CIÉ had been a key Labour pledge in the 1948 general election. The company was a strange hybrid of private enterprise and state control, and in the climate of the times clearly had no future. In June 1948, the government decided to appoint a Dublin-born transport expert based in Britain, Sir James Milne, to carry out an enquiry into the transport system.[2] His report, which was released on 23 December (thus leaving coverage to the Christmas Eve newspapers) went against nationalisation, instead recommending two more government nominees on the board of the company, but with a reduced power of veto, thereby effectively strengthening the position of the shareholders' representatives. Among his other suggestions were a 5 per cent reduction in the wage bill and the withdrawal of long-distance bus services parallel to the railways.[3] The Milne Report might have offered CIÉ a chance of a viable future, but it was politically unacceptable, and on 4 February 1949

Cabinet approved a buy-out of CIÉ, with no redundancies.[4] The new, nationalised company, also called CIÉ, came into being on the first day of June 1950,[5] a victory for Labour.

As was mentioned in the previous chapter, housing was one of the most outstanding success stories of the first inter-party government, and here again Labour could claim much of the credit, thanks to Tim Murphy and Michael Keyes. While construction could have been expected to pick up after wartime shortages, the more than tenfold increase in the number of local authority houses built annually between 1947 and 1950 showed a real commitment to the issue. Fianna Fáil speakers were quick to point to the White Paper published by the previous government during the 1948 election campaign, which called for the building of 100,000 houses in ten years.[6] However, without the extensive use of Marshall Aid funds outlined in Chapter Five, the progress made under Murphy and Keyes would not have been possible. Also significant was the successful effort by the government (particularly Patrick McGilligan and John A. Costello) in November 1949 to persuade the main banks to provide a loan of £5 million to Dublin Corporation for housing purposes at an acceptable rate of interest.[7] The banks finally agreed in December.[8] The Department of Local Government, along with the Department of Social Welfare, also sponsored a scheme to attract building workers home from Britain, with the promise of jobs for years to come[9] – a promise that was to prove hollow as depression gripped the construction industry in the mid-1950s. Quite apart from the obvious social need which the scheme met, as well as its electoral appeal, it was an important source of employment in a labour-intensive industry, and association with it certainly helped to improve Labour's image.

But Labour's main priority in government was the introduction of a comprehensive social welfare scheme. Unless it could make progress on the issue, the coalition experiment would prove of doubtful value to the party.

The difficulties faced by the Minister for Social Welfare, William Norton, in bringing in a comprehensive social insurance measure to make a coherent system out of the maze of different schemes available should not be underestimated. Chief among them was the opposition of some members of Fine Gael, and particularly McGilligan. In notes apparently written while preparing the 1948

Budget, McGilligan's views are made clear, albeit in outline form: 'Social services – levelling down – . . . Servile State . . . all taken by State – pay out pocket money.'[10]

Even before the change of government, Norton expressed interest in a comprehensive social security service, asking the then minister, Jim Ryan, in October 1947 when he would be in a position to introduce his legislative proposals on this matter; Ryan indicated that this could happen by the end of the financial year.[11] However, the general election intervened and Norton's more ambitious plans took much longer to prepare – as well as generating considerable opposition from his Cabinet colleagues.

In June 1948, the new minister told the Post Office Workers' Union annual conference in Cork that he hoped that in five years' time, if the government lasted long enough, 'that unfortunate section of humanity for whose economic conditions I am . . . responsible, will find their conditions better and their lives brighter than they are today', adding that all the hazards of life must be covered in a comprehensive scheme of social security.[12]

The first move in Norton's plan to overhaul the social services involved the National Health Insurance Society, which insured one-fifth of the population against loss of earnings through illness. Norton wanted to dissolve the society and absorb its functions within his department, on the grounds of efficiency. Two-thirds of the society's clients were also insured against unemployment, through the Department of Social Welfare, and this involved the stamping of two contribution cards every week. Norton submitted a memorandum to government in June 1948 seeking approval in principle for the abolition of the society, in order to facilitate the planning he was undertaking for a comprehensive scheme.[13] McGilligan objected, on the grounds that the society carried out its work efficiently – and that it might with more profit absorb the Department of Social Welfare! He also predicted 'considerable public opposition . . . to the abolition . . . as an example of the insatiable appetite of bureaucracy for swallowing up organisations which are perfectly capable of fulfilling their functions . . .'[14] It was the first set-piece battle between Norton and his Fine Gael opponents, and the Labour leader won.[15]

That is not to say that Norton's plan to dissolve the society and transfer its functions to himself enjoyed an easy passage. The progress of the proposal, finally embodied in the Social Welfare Bill 1949, was tortuous. The Cabinet gave leave to introduce the Bill in the Dáil in December 1949,[16] the general scheme was approved a month later,[17] the text was approved in March 1950,[18] and it passed all stages in the Dáil without a division at the end of May.[19] In June it was decided to invoke Article 25.2.2 of the constitution (which facilitated a speedy signing of a Bill by the President) because elections to the society's committee which were due had been cancelled because of the Bill.[20] It thus took nearly two years for the proposal to become law after being approved by the Cabinet.

On the broader social welfare front, Norton introduced a Bill in July 1948 giving a £2.5 million pension increase to widows, orphans, and the elderly.[21] Old age and blind pensions increased to 17s 6d (87.5 pence)[22] in all areas, from 15s 0d (75 pence) in urban areas and 12s 6d (62.5 pence) in the country.[23] The measure also allowed blind pensions to be paid at the age of twenty-one instead of thirty, and relaxed the means test for all pensions.[24] Speaking on the Bill in the Dáil, Norton claimed that Irish workers 'would gladly increase their contributions to build up better widows and orphans and old age pensions instead of their money being utilised in the ghastly tragedy of trying to establish transatlantic air services when every air service in the world was losing millions of money'.[25] On the committee stage, Fianna Fáil's Seán MacEntee said the increase in insurance contributions would cost workers 6d (2.5 pence) a week without any benefit, while Norton claimed the increased contributions would assure them of benefits as of right, instead of as concessions.[26]

In November, Cabinet approved his plans to amend the Workman's Compensation Act 1934, 'and to provide for certain other matters connected with workmen's compensation . . . subject to the approval of the text of the Bill by the Taoiseach'.[27] The Act came into force in January 1949, and increased compensation from 37s 6d to 50s 0d (£1.87.5 to £2.50) per week.[28]

Norton told the Labour Party conference in September 1948 that the improvement in pensions was 'the result of Labour participation' in the inter-party government, adding: 'I went to the Cabinet with a plan costing £2.5 million and not one penny of it was cut. It has been suggested outside that Mr McGilligan cut down my plan for social services: that is not correct. On the contrary, I warned him, when I got my £2.5 million, that I will probably go beyond that, and I think I will.'[29]

Norton's touching tribute to his Cabinet colleague was rather undermined by the widespread belief that McGilligan was totally opposed to the extension of the social welfare system. His attitude was made explicit in a speech in March 1949, when he warned of the danger that, with the development of social services, people would lose their sense of independence. McGilligan added that the social services were not something to be proud of – they should be used like medicine, and kept in a locker until they were required to treat disease or illness. He also spoke against nationalisation.[30]

Norton reacted by assuring the Dáil that the government was committed to a comprehensive social security system, and that the White Paper on social security would be ready in April.[31] The evident disagreement between Norton and McGilligan was seen by one political correspondent as 'the first real basis for a dissolution of the government. Fine Gael cannot continue to get the unqualified support of the right and continue to yield to Labour pressure; Labour cannot continue to be the Labour Party and cease to press for ever greater social reform. Fine Gael may decide to give in gracefully; it has already been conditioned to such a step by its volte face on the question of the Republic. If it does not – well, your guess is as good as mine.'[32]

Norton's draft White Paper on social security was distributed to all departments on 8 April. By May, Seán Lemass was expressing disappointment that there was still no sign of the social welfare scheme.[33] At the beginning of June, Norton told the Post Office Workers' Union that the White Paper would be before Cabinet within a week,[34] and six days later it was submitted to the Department of the Taoiseach. The Departments of Justice, Defence, Education, Local Government, and Posts and Telegraphs all wanted staff under their jurisdiction excluded from the scheme, on the basis that they were already covered by their own schemes and would gain no advantage from Norton's proposals. However, Norton insisted that the scheme should be comprehensive, covering all employees. He also wanted prompt approval, reminding his colleagues that they were committed to introducing the scheme, and therefore 'it is imperative that early approval should be given by the government to the proposals contained in the White Paper so that necessary work can be put in hands without delay . . .'[35]

Norton's proposed scheme was to cost £11.6 million in the first year, rising to £17.8 million in the twentieth, with costs divided between employees, employers, and the state. Three new benefits (a contributory old age pension separate from the existing non-contributory pension, and grants at marriage and death) were to be added to the five existing benefits (covering disability, unemployment, maternity, orphans, and widows).[36]

In a memorandum to the Department of Social Welfare, Finance criticised the 'extreme rigidity' which the scheme would impart to the economy, and the 'ever increasing state intervention' and 'destruction of individual initiative and enterprise' it would entail. 'While some reform of existing insurance schemes may be necessary, the improvements proposed go much too far . . . The Minister considers the proposed scheme is unacceptable in its present form and he must urge that it be modified substantially . . .' Finance also pointed to the differences between Britain and Ireland: 90 per cent of workers who were employees compared to 50 per cent in Ireland; tax at £64 per head against £27; and a standard rate of income tax of 9s 0d (45 pence) in the pound compared to just 6s 6d (32.5 pence) in Ireland.[37]

Norton didn't pull his punches in his reply, stating that he had to interpret Finance's attitude 'as one of complete opposition to the principles and proposals in the draft White Paper', and speaking of 'a definite cleavage of opinion between the two Departments'.[38] He also insisted that he would not budge on the principle of comprehensive cover for all employees. He pointed out that it had been decided not to extend eligibility to insurance schemes beyond employees; therefore farmers couldn't participate in the new scheme. And all employees should be covered uniformly – so members of the Defence Forces, civil servants, gardaí, and teachers could not be treated differently.[39]

The White Paper was also attacked by Industry and Commerce (the benefits were too high and would discourage people from seeking work) and Agriculture (it was unfair to ask farmers to subsidise a higher standard of living for industrial workers, who earned more than them in the first place).[40] James Dillon was particularly virulent in his opposition, calling the proposals in the White Paper 'not only unrealistic but completely unjust. What would the government say if the Department of Agriculture proposed to relieve agricultural land from the onerous burden of rates by means of a levy on trade unionists?'[41] He claimed the result of the scheme would be the segregation of the Irish people 'into two warring factions of 500,000 working farmers on the one hand and 700,000 employed persons on the other'.[42] But at least Dillon accepted the need for a social security scheme, although one tilted more towards his own area of interest – he suggested that farmers should be allowed to gain pensions at the age of sixty-five if they assigned their land to their children (instead of having to go through a lengthy conveyancing procedure), a suggestion that was eventually to find favour with Norton.[43]

Even Seán MacBride expressed opposition to the scheme, on the grounds that it excluded farmers, who were half the working population. He also felt that the state should take responsibility for providing full employment, rather than insuring against unemployment. 'My objections are not to the magnitude of the scheme but to the approach. I feel that . . . the proposed White Paper is based upon the British scheme . . . which is open to many objections for a country such as ours which is in the main dependent upon agricultural production.'[44]

Less surprisingly, the secretary of the Department of Finance was also fighting a spirited rearguard action against the scheme, telling his minister that 'the cost . . . would run into staggering figures . . . if publication cannot be avoided or postponed, you should insist on . . . provisos being inserted which will make it clear that no commitment is involved. The White Paper will thus be of an expository character only.'[45]

Faced with this opposition, it was not surprising that approval for the White Paper was not immediately forthcoming; there were also other reasons for delay. A special Cabinet meeting arranged for 30 June was not held because Norton was in court for his libel action against the *Irish Press*.[46] Two special meetings were held, on 18 and 27 July, and after the second, a Cabinet committee of Costello, Norton, Dillon, McGilligan, Tom O'Higgins, Dan Morrissey, and Noël Browne was set up to consider the White Paper. The aim was for the committee to report back in time to publish the White Paper before the Dáil reconvened on 26 October.[47]

The following day, McGilligan resumed his criticism in the Seanad, saying there was much to be said for the view that the welfare state was 'a good step towards a servile system'. He said he was not against the amalgamation of services, or even their extension, but that 'if the services were to be extended to the point that we would be paying for benefits that some of us might not require, then a good deal of thought had to be given to the matter . . . the scheme would be produced when the government felt it had a scheme which it could stand over. The pace would not be accelerated in the slightest by any niggling questions going around, and it would appear when it was ready.'[48]

One political observer, not unsympathetic to Labour, commented that 'there is a deep sense of shock and confusion among Mr Norton's own rank and file supporters', emphasising that many of them only accepted participation in the inter-party government on the grounds that social security could be achieved. Norton was advised to assure the public that the scheme was going ahead, and the *Irish Times* acknowledged, with considerable understatement, that while McGilligan 'is not an ardent advocate of social security', Fine Gael said it recognised the public demand for the scheme 'and feels honour bound to carry it through'.[49] More than a year later, the same observer was able to state: 'Critics of Mr Norton cite his silence in the face of the McGilligan onslaught; admirers point to the fact that, in spite of the open displeasure of the Minister for Finance, the Social Security Bill forges ahead.'[50]

The Cabinet committee was also delayed in its work; the first meeting was due to be held on 11 August, but was cancelled due to the absence of Costello and Norton. It was further delayed because Norton was in Strasbourg later in the month for the Consultative Assembly of the Council of Europe. The committee met once at the end of August, but the second meeting, on 5 September, was attended only by Costello and Morrissey. While summer holidays undoubtedly played a part in all this delay, it is difficult not to agree with Noël Browne that the Fine Gael ministers were stalling the scheme. 'I noticed a number of queries, counterqueries, objections, tendering of memoranda on ideological grounds, which accumulated around Norton's proposals with each successive Cabinet meeting . . . This is one of the not-so-subtle ways in which the conservative majority party in a coalition can "legitimately" frustrate radical proposals submitted by the minority party. One wonders to what extent Norton had collaborated in the delay.'[51] In fairness to Norton, he had to draw up new legislation and get it through the Oireachtas in order to achieve his aim; Browne already had the legislative framework for the Mother and Child scheme, and also failed to introduce it.

While the Cabinet committee had clearly failed to come up with a winning formula, Costello continued discussions to reach an agreement. The White Paper was finally 'approved generally' by Cabinet on 11 October, but was subject to further consideration by a Cabinet committee of Costello, Norton, McGilligan, and O'Higgins.[52] The revised text was approved by Cabinet on 21 October[53] – but only after the most contentious issue was set aside for future decision. The new text left open the question of the inclusion of civil servants, gardaí, teachers, and members of the Defence Forces. Although Norton was not yet beaten, it was clear that the opposition to a fully comprehensive scheme was very strong.

The White Paper, entitled *Social Security*, was finally published on 25 October 1949. It proposed the replacement of all existing welfare and insurance schemes – national health insurance, unemployment, and widows and orphans pensions – with one comprehensive scheme with no means test. Workers earning more than £3 10s (£3.50) per week were to pay 3s 6d (men – 17.5 pence) or 2s 2d (women – 10.8 pence). Those earning less were to pay 2s 6d (men – 12.5 pence) or 1s 2d (women – 5.8 pence). Employers were to pay 3s 6d for men and 2s 2d for women in both categories. The state was to pay £4 million a year into the scheme.

The benefits were described in an *Irish Times* editorial as 'comprehensive and fairly generous'. A single person would get 24 shillings (£1.20) a week for disability or unemployment, with 12 shillings (60 pence) extra for men with a dependent wife, and 7 shillings (35 pence) for each of two children up to the age of sixteen. There was a separate scale for those in the lower income group, who were to get 18 shillings (90 pence) for a single person, with 9 shillings (45 pence) for a wife and 5 shillings (25 pence) a week for each of

two children. The White Paper pointed out that this would give a
married man with two children benefit of 50 shillings a week, or 37
shillings in the lower income group, against 22s 6d sickness benefit
under the current scheme (i.e. £2.50, or £1.85, compared to
£1.12.5).

Widows were to get 24 shillings a week (£1.20), plus 7 shillings
(35 pence) for each of two children. Orphans would get 10 shillings
(50 pence) a week. Women who were insured in their own right
would get a lump sum of £5 for maternity, plus 24 shillings (£1.20)
a week for the six weeks before and six weeks after giving birth,
while the wives of insured men would get the £5 lump sum as well
as 20 shillings (£1.00) a week for four weeks after giving birth. The
retirement pension was to be 24 shillings (£1.20) a week for a man
of sixty-five or a woman of sixty, with an extra 12 shillings (60
pence) for a dependent wife or husband. There were also grants
payable on the death of a contributor or a member of his or her
family, ranging from £6 for a child under three years, to £20 for a
person over twenty.

While these benefits were certainly an improvement, they were
not overgenerous when compared to wage rates. For instance, at
this time a turf worker employed by Bord na Móna earned between
£3 4s (£3.20) and £4 a week,[54] while building labourers got £4 13s
4d (£4.66.5).[55] Solicitors' typists would have been in the lower
income group, with their wages of just 25 shillings (£1.25) a week.[56]
It should be noted, though, that the benefits under Norton's scheme
were only marginally lower than those introduced in Britain shortly
before – 26 shillings (£1.30) in unemployment and sickness benefit,
25 shillings (£1.25) for a single pensioner, and 42 shillings (£2.10)
for a couple.[57] However, Norton's proposed lower scale of payments
did reduce the redistributive effects of his scheme compared to that
introduced by Jim Griffiths across the Irish Sea. Like the Irish
scheme, Britain's welfare provisions were based on the assumption
of 'high and stable employment' and consistent economic growth.[58]

Spending on benefits was forecast to rise from £9.3 million in
the first year to £11.2 million in the fifth, with administration costs
expected to rise from £1.2 million to £1.4 million, giving total
expenditure of £10.5 million in the first year and £12.6 million in
the fifth. Income was expected to be the same throughout the first

five years, with £3.25 million from employees, £4 million each from employers and the state, and dividend income of £350,000, giving a total income of £11.6 million a year. There would, therefore, be a deficit of £1 million by the fifth year, because people would be retiring before their contributions had built up a fund to generate enough interest to pay their pensions. The White Paper ducked this issue, suggesting that the government should wait five years before deciding if the system needed to be changed.

The *Irish Independent* criticised the White Paper as 'a painstaking attempt to adopt [*sic*] a British scheme to Irish conditions. Such an attempt, we think, is doomed to failure . . .'[59] The *Irish Times* suggested that Norton 'has made a genuine attempt to ensure for the Irish people a degree of social security in keeping with the Christian standards that ought to prevail in every civilised community. To that extent, at least, he deserves full credit.'[60]

Full credit was one thing that Norton was not going to get from the Catholic Church. The coadjutor bishop of Killaloe, Dr Joseph Rogers, said that 'state grants and social services, no matter how generous, are cold and impersonal and do not take into account the spiritual requirements of the recipient'.[61] The scheme was also criticised by other leading clergy, leading to a defence of the scheme from Aknefton in the *Irish Times*: 'The Papal Encyclicals have been quoted over and over again to prove that advanced and educated Catholic opinion is in the forefront of the struggle for social reform . . . it is . . . astonishing . . . that criticism of the Social Security White Paper should come, not from political conservatives, but from the Rev. E. Coyne, the noted Jesuit, and from the Rev. Phelim Ó Briain, the prominent Franciscan.'[62]

Political observers seemed astonished that Norton had got his way against McGilligan's public opposition, noting also that Fianna Fáil were unlikely to oppose the scheme for fear of being put to the right of Fine Gael.[63] Speaking to the Dublin Metropolitan branch of his party in December, Norton admitted that the White Paper 'does not represent perfection. It does not do all the things I would like it to do. But it represents a very creditable first effort.'[64]

In February 1950, the County Cork Farmers' Association (effectively the local branch of Clann na Talmhan) called on its TDs to withdraw support from the government if the White Paper was introduced as a Bill. The reason for their opposition was the exclusion of farmers and professionals from the scheme. One of the TDs, Patrick Lehane, described it as 'dangerous sectional legislation'. Lehane pointed out that there were 1.3 million people employed in the country, but only half of them would be covered by the benefits of the scheme. His colleague, Patrick Halliden, said the scheme was 'socially, morally and economically wrong'.[65]

Undaunted, Norton told a meeting in Bray that the White Paper was 'the Government's covenant with the people, and every effort will be made to implement it in the current year'.[66] Party leader Richard Mulcahy told the Fine Gael ard fheis in February that the social welfare scheme was 'a policy to which Fine Gael is committed, not only by the ten-point statement of inter-party government policy, but by every act and declaration of ours since we entered on the historic period in our history that brought us into politics. We offer all our thoughts and all our work in co-operation with the other parties in government to lay solid foundations for a comprehensive social security plan which will win the approval, the confidence and the support of our people.'[67] At the same conference, Costello said it was 'nonsense to suggest . . . that the White Paper proposals represent the first step on the road to totalitarian socialism. This attitude represents a confusion of thought that refuses to distinguish between genuine social security and the totalitarian Welfare State.'[68]

However, Norton was prepared to defend the welfare state, describing it as a place 'where Christian people under a Christian government, taking direction from Almighty God' provided benefits for the sick, the unemployed, widows, orphans, and the elderly. 'If that is the Welfare State . . . then I am an unrepentant admirer of the Welfare State. The Welfare State which does these things represents in my view the nearest and most practical approach to applied Christianity.'[69]

Norton, along with ministerial colleagues Joseph Blowick, Richard Mulcahy, and Seán MacEoin, and parliamentary secretary Brendan Corish, was at the time a member of the Knights of Saint Columbanus.[70] This was not unusual, as the Knights had a cross-party appeal – among other prominent members at one time or another were Seán T. O'Kelly, Gerald Boland, Lemass, and

MacEntee,[71] while Costello had been a member of the Columbians, an offshoot of the Ancient Order of Hibernians which merged with the Knights in the 1920s.[72] Norton's social welfare scheme was directly opposed to the policy of the Knights, and was denounced by many conservative Catholics. The historian of the organisation notes that 'not a single voice was raised in his favour from the ranks of his fellow-Knights'.[73]

Behind the scenes, the battle between Norton and the Fine Gael ministers continued. In a memorandum in the middle of May submitting a general scheme of the Bill to all departments, Norton reaffirmed 'his conviction that there should be no departure from the principle of comprehensiveness in relation to the employee class'.[74] In a sign of some movement, at the end of June Norton indicated that he was prepared to consider some modifications of the scheme where it applied to members of the Defence Forces – but he refused to even discuss the total exclusion of officers and chaplains demanded by the Minister for Defence, Tom O'Higgins.[75] For once, Norton's position as Tánaiste helped to speed matters up. In Costello's absence, he was able to insist on the circulation of this memorandum, despite objections by McGilligan, O'Higgins, and Dillon.[76]

The Minister for Defence was highly critical of Norton's refusal to discuss the exclusion of certain categories, adding that in his view 'the Government should not commit themselves . . . to the principle of comprehensiveness in the sense of making it impossible for any group of employees to be totally excluded from the application of the scheme'.[77] McGilligan also wanted exclusions from the scheme (and had clearly discussed the matter with his party colleagues). He felt that civil servants, gardaí, soldiers, and teachers should be left out of the scheme, as they were already covered for sickness and so would have to be paid double if they fell ill – which he thought would encourage malingering. McGilligan was also explicit about his ideological objections, claiming that although he accepted that a social security scheme was to be introduced, 'the scheme proposed by the Minister for Social Welfare is too costly and should be modified so as to reduce the burden of non-productive State expenditure which the scheme would involve'.[78]

Despite this opposition, Cabinet on 30 June authorised Norton to draft the long and short titles of a Bill embodying the White

Paper proposals, and to seek leave to introduce the Bill in the Dáil.[79] But the battle was far from over. On 14 July, a Cabinet committee of Costello, Norton, Dillon, McGilligan, O'Higgins, and Morrissey was set up to 'consider any points of controversy that may arise in connection with the Bill'.[80]

It seems that Norton overstepped the approval given to him by Cabinet, by actually introducing the Bill in the Dáil (on 7 July), by setting the second stage (for 18 October), and by arranging with the Attorney General for the drafting of the legislation.[81] However, Costello told his anxious civil servants that he had approved these arrangements 'informally' with Norton, 'with a view to facilitating consideration of any controversial points by the Cabinet Committee'.[82] On 5 October, the Department of Social Welfare was given permission to circulate the draft Bill 'without prejudice to any recommendation that may be made by the Cabinet committee or to any decisions that may be taken by the Government affecting the final text of the Bill'.[83]

Following a meeting of the Cabinet committee on 9 October, Norton finally admitted defeat, including in the draft Bill the power to exclude certain classes of employee (such as civil servants, teachers, gardaí, and soldiers) entirely, or to apply the scheme with modifications to them.[84] Four days later, the amended Bill was circulated to other departments for observations. In a clear sign of frustration, the memorandum accompanying the Bill noted that it followed the White Paper and the general scheme closely, and that 'the Minister anticipates that, having regard to the fact that these proposals have been before your Department for many months, the examination of this Bill . . . will be *completed rapidly*'.[85] Two weeks later, Norton was given permission to print the draft Bill.[86]

In December, the text of the Social Welfare (Insurance) Bill 1950 was finally approved, subject to two amendments dealing with farmers. Members of a farmers' co-operative who were not insured persons were to be treated as employees of the co-operative – thus bringing them within the ambit of the new scheme. And small farmers (i.e. those whose land had a rateable value of less than £30) were to qualify for old age pensions at the age of seventy, provided they assigned their farms to a child or children – the process of assignment being much simpler than conveyancing.[87]

The aims of the Bill were 'to replace the present separate codes by one co-ordinated scheme of social insurance; to extend the scope of the existing codes so as to bring an increased number of persons within the ambit of social insurance; to provide higher benefits than those payable at present under those codes, and to introduce new benefits'.[88] Its complexity is indicated by its length – it was fifty-four pages long, with eighty-two sections and six schedules. The explanatory memorandum alone was nine pages long.

Despite McGilligan's clear distaste for the scheme, Liam Cosgrave told a rally of young members of Fine Gael in Dublin in November that the party was not against it, because it provided a 'bulwark against Communism'.[89] This suggestion was echoed by Costello in December, when he told Wexford Chamber of Commerce that the scheme did not extend to state interference in personal or business life, would not involve the nationalisation of any commercial insurance body, and was not totalitarian, but rather a barrier against communism.[90]

The *Irish Independent* criticised the Bill because of its cost, the danger that benefits would be abused, the increase in the number of civil servants it would cause, and because it 'may still further weaken the spirit of self-reliance and thrift'.[91] The County Cavan Farmers' Trade Union executive requested the Independent TD it supported, Patrick O'Reilly, to vote against the Bill,[92] while Patrick Cogan described it as 'a slavish imitation of British Socialism'.[93] Patrick Lehane put down a Dáil motion opposing it 'until the views of the people have been ascertained',[94] while Fianna Fáil's Jim Ryan also tabled a motion rejecting it because it did not 'provide a comprehensive balanced scheme covering the needs of all sections of the community; it would impose greatly increased burdens on both employees and employers, while providing benefits little better than those now on offer'.[95] A third motion rejecting the Bill was tabled by John Flynn, the South Kerry Independent, because it did not provide for small farmers and casual workers.[96] Seán MacEoin told a Fine Gael meeting in Longford that if Fianna Fáil insisted on opposing the Bill, they might have to go to the country on it.[97]

However, Norton had another trick up his sleeve. He opened the second stage of the Bill on 2 March 1951 by announcing a number of amendments – all of which Independent deputies would find it hard to vote against. These changes included an increase in old age and blind pensions of 2s 6d (12.5 pence) a week, raising the maximum to 20 shillings (£1.00); and modifications to the means test to increase the number of people getting old age pensions.[98] In the Dáil, Norton said that the chief benefits of the new scheme were retirement pensions and death grants; the other benefits had existed since 1911, and it was hardly fair of the moral philosophers to suggest that 'we had been living in sin for 40 years'. Ryan said Fianna Fáil approved of the principle, but not the detail, of the plan. Patrick Lehane said the increase in the old age pension and the change in the means test met many of his objections, but he still wanted a plebiscite.[99]

In an editorial on the scheme, and Ryan's exposition of Fianna Fáil's alternative, the *Irish Times* noted that it left out farmers, who nevertheless as employers would have to pay contributions for their labourers, who in turn might seek higher wages to pay for their own contributions. 'If Mr Norton's scheme lends fresh encouragement to the almost universal demand for higher wages and salaries, it could be a very expensive luxury.' It also observed that the Fianna Fáil scheme would keep contributions at their present level, but would offer increased benefits through higher taxation. The editorial writer felt that this would not be welcome if it was financed entirely through direct taxation.[100]

With some justice, Lemass described the proposed pension increase as an attempt 'to bribe a few . . . back benchers to go into the Division Lobby' in support of the social security plan.[101] Its success was shown when four Independent TDs – Patrick Cogan, Patrick Lehane, Patrick O'Reilly, and William Sheldon – called on the government to proceed at once with a separate Bill to implement them.[102] This, of course, would have allowed them to support the proposals they favoured, while rejecting the substantive Bill.

Norton told the annual general meeting of the Kildare Labour Party in March that the pension increases and changes to the means test would cost £1.25 million,[103] an expensive purchase of Independent votes. McGilligan told the Seanad three days later that there was no provision in the Estimates for the scheme as it was not yet instituted, but warned that 'when provision is made, it will mean a very big increase for those who have to pay taxes', although he did say the increase would be less than under the alternative Fianna Fáil plan.[104]

During the second stage of the Bill in the Dáil on 11 April, Norton said that a lot of nonsense had been spoken about it. The Church's attitude to social welfare schemes, and the importance the Church attached to helping the weak and those in need of supplementary assistance, could be found in the encyclicals, and he preferred to depend on those than on lay theologians. De Valera said that Fianna Fáil did not consider the present method the best one for social welfare, while MacEntee insisted that it raised moral issues to which deputies were bound to have regard. Noël Browne – who that day had resigned with effect from midnight because of the Mother and Child crisis – voted with the government, while Lehane and Cogan voted against. The second stage was passed by seventy-one votes to sixty-six, after which government TDs shouted 'What about an election?', while the Fianna Fáil benches replied 'What about Dr Browne? You threw him to the Fine Gael wolves.'[105] However, by now an election had become inevitable, spelling the end of Norton's plans.

At its first meeting, the new Fianna Fáil government approved a Bill introducing the increases in pensions and the changes in the means test proposed by Norton.[106] The Social Welfare Act 1952 was brought in later. It contained many of the benefits of Norton's proposals,[107] although it did not introduce his planned retirement pension for men at sixty-five and women at sixty. It was not until 1961 that a contributory pension was introduced, and then only for men and women over seventy. Neither was a death benefit introduced, while those earning more than £600 a year were excluded from the Fianna Fáil scheme.[108] However, Jim Ryan did bring in social assistance benefits covering the self-employed, which dealt with one of the main criticisms advanced by Catholic theorists, that Norton's Bill 'violated distributive justice by doing nothing for self-employed people, such as small farmers'.[109] Whether a conscious attempt to get theologians on side, or (more likely) a gesture to small farmer support in the electorate and the Dáil, Fianna Fáil managed to get the measure through without serious opposition.[110]

The Labour Party's first experience in government was, then, rather mixed. On the plus side, the two wings of the party had reunited, largely thanks to sharing office. The work of Tim Murphy and Michael Keyes in housing had been first rate, and the party had successfully insisted on the nationalisation of CIÉ. However, the failure to introduce the social welfare scheme indicated that there were limits to what could be achieved when in power with a conservative partner, a point noted by commentators at the time. Aknefton, reflecting on the Social Welfare Bill, the prices 'freeze', and the Mother and Child scheme, concluded that 'while the progressive parties did mould legislation in its embryonic stages, other interests in the Cabinet have rendered their proposals completely ineffective'.[111] An editorial in *The Leader* some time later felt that while the government 'had worked well and loyally together . . . Fine Gael . . . had finally prevailed'.[112] Left-wing critics of Labour's participation in various coalitions would argue that this first experiment set the pattern for the rest.

SEVEN

THE CHURCH'S PROPER SPHERE

One day I was walking up to Bewley's for a coffee and a bun lunch and as usual I was accompanied by J.D. McCormack. I had been working all morning on the White Paper and it was very much on my mind . . . I said to J.D. quite suddenly 'I've got to name this thing. We'll call it the Mother and Child Service; that should sell it, no one could oppose a scheme with a name like that.'

James Deeny[1]

In the Dáil debate on Noël Browne's resignation as Minister for Health over the Mother and Child affair, John A. Costello concluded his contribution by complaining that the former minister 'has had a start of a whole day on me and no matter what I do I will never catch up with him to the end of my public life'.[2] For once, in a crisis that showed inept handling by all concerned, the Taoiseach was absolutely correct. The Mother and Child crisis has now entered political legend, a legend dominated by the romantic figure of the idealistic Noël Browne, fearlessly battling against the power of the Catholic hierarchy and the cowardice of his own colleagues. The truth is a little different: much of the blame for the crisis must rest on Browne himself; the power of the doctors has been consistently underestimated in the popular imagination; and the strains within Clann na Poblachta and the government itself have been somewhat overlooked.

That Browne should clash with his medical colleagues was hardly surprising, given his unorthodox views. 'I have always found the cash nexus between the patient and doctor indefensible . . . Being a doctor, with all its connotations of relieving human distress, was to

198

me such a privilege that I could not consider the need to take money from a patient.'[3] Browne himself pointed out that, as a 'Trinity Catholic', he left something to be desired as Minister for Health in the eyes of the hierarchy.[4] And then there was the question of his personality – in Joe Lee's memorable phrase, 'Browne was probably his own worst enemy, despite the competition from Costello, MacBride and McQuaid.'[5]

That said, it is important to note that the inter-party government, and particularly Costello, were more deferential to the hierarchy than Fianna Fáil had ever been. According to Patrick Lynch, the Taoiseach was 'a devout Catholic and placed his deep religious convictions above all else'.[6] This was demonstrated immediately after the new government was elected. Fianna Fáil had sent a message of 'respectful homage' to the Pope on assuming office in 1932.[7] Not to be outdone, on 23 February 1948, Costello sent the following message to Pope Pius XII: 'On the occasion of our assumption of office and our first Cabinet meeting, my colleagues and myself desire to repose at the feet of Your Holiness the assurance of our filial loyalty and devotion as well as our firm resolve to be guided in all our work by the teachings of Christ and to strive for the attainment of a social order in Ireland based on Christian principles.'[8] This message was sent despite the objections of the secretary of the Department of the Taoiseach, Maurice Moynihan, who felt the language was inappropriate, and that a civil power should not 'repose at the feet' of a Pope. He was overruled.[9]

The Pope received Joseph Walshe, the Irish ambassador to the Vatican, two days later to express his great satisfaction with the message and to convey his thanks to Costello.[10] On 29 February a more expansive written reply was sent to 'Our beloved son, John A. Costello', including thanks for the message, a reference to the 'lively Christian faith which your people have always jealously guarded', and 'Our earnest prayer that Almighty God may bless the praiseworthy intentions and zealous efforts of you and your Cabinet.'[11]

However, the relationship between the government and the Vatican was not entirely respectful, as can be seen from the strenuous attempts made to prevent the appointment of an Italian, Ettore Felici (a process described by Walshe as 'dumping [an] old . . . supernumerary from Secretariat'[12]), to replace Paschal Robinson as papal nuncio, a disagreement which Dermot Keogh characterised as 'the most serious crisis in Irish–Vatican relations since the foundation of the State'.[13] In the end, the Vatican 'calmly disregards all our most cogent and most important considerations . . . and answers in a manner which assumes that these considerations had never been formulated . . .'[14]

One might have expected the radical republican, MacBride, to be less obsequious towards the Church; one would have been wrong. Browne recalled a visit to Kylemore Abbey in 1948. 'There was a sudden movement beside me . . . For a moment I believed that he had been overcome by some sort of weakness and was about to collapse . . . Instead, with the ease and grace of a practised nobleman at the court of the Sun King at Versailles, he slid forward on one knee and gently, slowly and deferentially, bent his head to kiss the ring of office . . . I simply shook hands with the Abbess in the conventional way, and admired his capacity for the theatricals.'[15]

The attitude of leading politicians of all parties was revealed at the funeral of former President Douglas Hyde in 1949, when none entered St Patrick's Cathedral, except Erskine Childers of Fianna Fáil and Maurice Dockrell of Fine Gael, both Protestants.[16] While Costello had many Protestant friends, he had no insight into their thinking, and caused considerable offence with a reference in a speech in Trinity College Dublin to 'the so-called Reformation'. Costello personally added this reference to the speech, which had been drafted by Patrick Lynch, as an expression of his dislike for Trinity.[17]

It should also be noted that Catholic bishops at this time were extremely intolerant of any dissent. When Galway Corporation ruled out a site for a new school suggested by the local bishop, Dr Michael Browne, on traffic and public health grounds, he responded by accusing them of being communists![18] Needless to say, the school was eventually built on the site favoured by the bishop.[19]

As was seen in Chapter Six, a number of senior politicians (including at least four inter-party ministers) were members of the Knights of Saint Columbanus. However, while this organisation, then shrouded in secrecy, must have had significant influence in many areas, its members who were ministers sometimes ignored its policy. Even more surprising in this regard than Norton's social welfare scheme[20] was the controversy over adoption, which, with the obvious exception of the Mother and Child scheme, was the most serious issue in Church–state relations during the period under examination. In 1947, the supreme council of the Knights suggested it was high time that action was taken on legal adoption, and recommended that one of the members of the order in the Oireachtas should sponsor 'appropriate legislation for the purpose of protecting the welfare of the adopted children and the people adopting them'.[21] However, the two Knights who held the Justice portfolio in succession, Gerry Boland of Fianna Fáil and Seán MacEoin of Fine Gael, declined to do so.

Shortly after taking office, MacEoin informed Independent TD Alfie Byrne and Clann na Poblachta's John Timoney that the introduction of legal adoption was having 'his immediate, active and sympathetic consideration'.[22] But as the months passed with no action, despite repeated questioning in the Dáil, it became obvious that the minister had his doubts. Finally, in November 1950, Tom O'Higgins, replying on behalf of MacEoin, said he would not bring in legalised adoption, although he refused to say why.[23]

MacEoin gave a partial answer to the Fine Gael ard fheis in February 1951, saying that a law compelling a mother to waive her rights to her children for all time 'would be against charity and against the common law of justice'. He said that no parliamentary draftsman had been able to draw up a Bill which would 'meet the requirements of the ordinary Christian state', but that if such a Bill could be framed, he would be happy to introduce it. He denied that fears of proselytism or Catholic objections came into it.[24]

However, while the government was reluctant to legalise adoption, it not only sanctioned, but encouraged, the export of children for adoption in the United States, an issue that was to cause controversy when it came to widespread public attention in 1996. In December 1950, the consular section of the Department of External Affairs noted that about ten children a month were being granted passports to go to the USA for adoption. 'Up to some months ago the Catholic ecclesiastical authorities in the diocese of Dublin were opposed in principle to children being brought out of the diocese for adoption elsewhere. It is understood that they still maintain their opposition in principle but for some time past they have authorised institutions under their jurisdiction to surrender children to persons who have been vetted in the USA by Catholic organisations . . . the . . . procedure . . . is satisfactory from the Department's point of view [and] . . . the Section has been bringing it informally to the attention of other Catholic institutions throughout the state. The Department is satisfied that non-Catholic institutions are careful in surrendering children for adoption.'[25]

The adoption controversy also gave rise to an extraordinary outburst by the Attorney General, Charles Casey, at the Law Students Debating Society in February 1951. He claimed that the *Irish Times* was 'bitterly anti-Catholic' and attacked its views on adoption. Casey said that Ireland was a Catholic country, and while this did not mean that parliament should penalise other creeds, it did mean that parliament could not be asked to introduce legislation contrary to the teaching of that Church. He added that 'any influence of that Church on this, or any, government, will only be for good'.[26]

Noël Browne later claimed that 'the members of the first Coalition Government, all of them, believed . . . they were bound absolutely by the teachings of the Catholic Bishops. The first occasion was in respect of an Adoption Bill, and finally there was the matter of the Mother and Child scheme. I sought unsuccessfully to establish that a Cabinet Minister, in a nominally pluralist society, as a Catholic, could conscientiously hold one belief, yet, as a Minister in Cabinet, advocate and vote for, proposals and schemes in direct conflict with those conscientiously [held] beliefs.'[27]

Indeed, Browne claimed that his stand over the Mother and Child scheme was caused by his determination that there should not be a repeat of the Cabinet's cave-in on adoption, after 'being told that Dr McQuaid would not tolerate a proposed Adoption Act. I was determined that this type of thing was not going to happen again, that the bishops would not have the power of veto over Government decisions.'[28] This determination, along with the attitude of the leaders of Church and state, set the scene for the most serious crisis the inter-party government was to face.

Of course, Browne also brought to the crisis his reputation as a crusader for better health care, and his achievements in this area should not be underestimated, even though the plans for his success (as well as the seeds of his downfall, the Mother and Child scheme) were already in place when he moved into the Custom House – both in terms of work already done by civil servants and Fianna Fáil politicians,[29] and in a crucial agreement made at the time of the government's formation by Seán MacBride, as part of the price for his party's participation in the coalition, that money would be released from the Hospitals Trust Fund to pay for hospital building. The fund, which was set up to administer money raised by sweepstakes on horse races in the early 1930s, had mainly spent money on paying the deficits of voluntary hospitals up to this time. In the words of Ruth Barrington, 'Dr Browne had the good fortune to become Minister at the moment when the groundwork had been done and the system was already in motion.'[30]

Plans for improvements in the treatment of tuberculosis were made during the war, although by the time Fianna Fáil left office little progress had actually been made. In December 1944, the Minister for Local Government and Public Health, Seán MacEntee, along with his parliamentary secretary, Dr Con Ward, submitted to government a far-reaching memo, which recognised that 'very radical measures must be taken' in order to tackle the spread of TB, and that relying on the local authorities would lead to unacceptable delays. They proposed instead that the Minister for Local Government and Public Health should assume the powers of the local authorities, and that three regional sanatoria be built, providing 1,000 beds in Dublin, 680 in Cork, and 400 in Galway, with the costs being met from the Hospitals Trust Fund. The memo also recognised that building materials for this scheme were not available, and might not be for some time even after the end of the war.[31]

The Tuberculosis (Establishment of Sanatoria) Bill 1945 became law on 6 March 1945. During the passage of the Bill, Ward told the Dáil that the approximate cost of the three regional sanatoria would be £1.5 million.[32] The department published a White Paper on tuberculosis at the beginning of 1946, and began a short-term programme of bed acquisition for TB patients, including the use of empty fever hospitals, military hospitals, and district hospitals.[33]

With this programme beginning to get off the ground, the medical staff in the department were more than a little concerned at the arrival of Noël Browne, while some commentators doubted 'the prudence of entrusting so complex a Department . . . to a Deputy without previous parliamentary experience'.[34] The department's chief medical officer, Dr James Deeny, claimed he was telephoned by Tom O'Higgins and James Dillon to see if he would work with the new minister. 'If they sent along Satan himself I would work with him to end TB and to save babies' lives', he replied.[35]

The two men were to have their differences over policy, and Deeny was later to stress that plans were already in place when Browne took office. 'Different developments that we had planned and organised came about and he got the credit . . . Being a politician, and as was reasonable and to be expected, he exploited this situation very successfully.'[36] Indeed, years later, Browne acted as though he found a clean slate in the department. 'There was no need for a Commission of Inquiry into what needed to be done. Tuberculosis control had been a special study of mine since I had qualified as a doctor. The Department of Health was transformed into a battle headquarters. Since I had considered the need for an efficient tuber- culosis service for many years, a clear plan of action was quickly outlined.'[37]

In February 1948, Browne told the *Irish Times* that he was prepar- ing a plan for the reorganisation of the health service, including the use of films, newspapers, and radio to create interest in health issues. An immediate priority would be a review of accommodation for TB patients, and methods of making more beds available by using existing buildings and hospitals.[38] A few days later, the new minister outlined his 'emergency drive against tuberculosis', involving the immediate provision of two thousand places in temporary sanatoria; a panel of radio doctors; and better conditions for nurses. 'We must treat the problem as an emergency and we must be satisfied with certain conditions which, as a doctor and under other circum- stances, I could not possibly consider satisfactory. Our immediate aim is to provide sanatorium accommodation which will be better than the homes in which some patients live. It would be perfect if we could place them in modern sanatoria, but that would take a long time, and by then many of them would be dead.'[39]

The secretary of the Cabinet Economic Committee, Patrick Lynch, was asked in March 1948 to investigate the funds held by the Hospitals Trust Board.[40] He found that at the end of 1947, the balance in the fund was £9.7 million, of which £5.6 million was invested by the board, with the interest used to meet the working deficits of voluntary hospitals, leaving £4.1 million available for capital spending. 'The programme of the Department of Health for hospital building, extensions, etc., involves an estimated expenditure of £25 million . . . If the Sweepstakes continue operating on the present basis it is estimated that £1 million a year will accrue to the benefit of hospitals.'[41] Browne was not at the meeting which asked for the memo to be drawn up, nor was MacBride. Browne claimed that previous ministers had only spent the income from the interest on the capital, giving them £100,000 a year, while 'we decided to alter that policy radically, and proceeded to liquidate all the available assets in the Sweep funds . . . I decided further to pre-empt the income expected from the fund during the following seven year period.'[42] While the latter idea may well have been Browne's, the other decision had been insisted upon by MacBride during the formation of the government.

Despite all this, Browne had to fight hard for funds – Minister for Finance, Patrick McGilligan, did not, like Hugh Dalton in Britain, provide money for social services 'with a song in my heart'. For instance, in December 1948 Browne sought a small number of extra staff, warning that 'the carrying out of public policy in regard to the extension and development of health services will be detrimentally affected and considerably retarded unless an adequate staff is available'.[43] McGilligan replied with an attack on the scope of Browne's plans, complaining that Health was attempting 'to press forward with too many projects . . . at one time, with the inevitable results of considerable confusion and lack of real progress'. He stressed that he would not pay for the hospital building programme if the Hospitals Trust Fund ran out of money, and suggested that 'the comprehensive proposals of the Minister for Health for the improvement and extension of the health services . . . should be submitted to the Government for consideration in all their aspects and an agreed plan be approved which will not endanger other programmes such as housing . . . or throw a burden on the Exchequer which cannot, in present circumstances, be met.'[44]

This attempt by Finance to turn back the clock on his plans led to a furious response from Browne in February 1949 – so furious that civil servants in the Department of the Taoiseach complained about the language used.[45] In a rather petulant passage, Browne said that he 'did not enter public life because of his interest in politics. He did so because he was satisfied that our health services were scandalously inadequate . . . he would not agree to . . . a policy which was determined solely or mainly by financial considerations or which was in effect no more than a moderate advance on that of the late government.'[46] The matter was referred to the Cabinet Estimates Committee, and later in the year Browne got some of the extra staff he was seeking, but the incident demonstrated that the Minister for Health had to come close to threatening resignation before he got what he wanted.

Finance was concerned about the ever-increasing Health budget. In 1939/40, expenditure on health was just over £500,000. By 1947/8 it had risen to just under £900,000, and was estimated at £1.5 million for 1948/9 and £1.9 million for the following year. Finance pointed out that Browne also wanted the state to pay 70 per cent of the £20 million cost of upgrading county homes, as well as introducing the £700,000 Mother and Child scheme and meeting any costs for the building programme that the Hospitals Trust Fund couldn't meet.[47]

In May 1948, Frank Gallagher was appointed publicity director of the Department of Health and began work on a national advertising campaign designed to fight avoidable illness, using publications, posters, radio, and film.[48] A series of talks on Radio Éireann to promote health awareness, each Tuesday for five minutes before the 18.30 news, began in July.[49] Browne also started a competition for a slogan for the TB campaign; Myles na gCopaleen (Brian O'Nolan), a civil servant in the Department of Health, joked that he had won with the line 'TB is bad for you'![50] Another popular initiative from the new minister was his successful attempt to learn Irish and to use the language in broadcasts about TB. 'For the first and only time in the history of the state, a Minister was actually giving the language the importance in reality that the Constitution gave it in theory.'[51]

The question of publicity was crucial in the fight against the disease, and it was here that Browne made his greatest personal contribution. People were reluctant to admit to having the disease and to seek treatment; Browne managed to overcome this attitude with his 'mobilisation of the people's will to fight'.[52]

In July, Browne announced a seven-year, £15 million hospital construction programme in the Dáil.[53] By January 1949, the programme had increased in projected cost by nearly £3 million. The Hospitals Trust Fund was to provide £13.5 million of the funding. Browne conceded that these projects were not new, as 'the vast majority . . . had been under consideration for some years but could not be proceeded with owing to war and post-war difficulties . . . the promoters of the different types of hospital have been encouraged to revive and proceed with the greatest dispatch with the projects . . .'[54]

However, while Browne was proving a public success, things were not going so well inside the Custom House. James Deeny complained of 'a sort of Mafia which had not been seen before in the Irish civil service', which surrounded the minister, while the medical and administrative staff were excluded.[55] Browne also managed to upset the consultants, particularly with a speech to students at the Royal College of Surgeons, in which he warned that unless the best medical treatment was made available to every man and woman, irrespective of income, the Department of Health would have to discharge that reponsibility.[56] Doctors were also annoyed at the use of sweepstakes money for the regional hospital programme, which left the Dublin voluntary hospitals – the original beneficiaries of these funds – with financial problems.[57]

According to Deeny, Browne had initially 'had the general support of the Irish doctors, [but] he threw it away and for his own reasons antagonised them'.[58] However, it might be instructive to look at the problems faced by Aneurin Bevan as Minister for Health in Britain: 'No other Minister had had to interfere with the entrenched privileges and prejudices of a highly qualified body of middle-class professional people who, by the nature of their functions, were accustomed to ordering everybody about (politicians included) and who had always been at pains to surround themselves with an impenetrable cloud of awe and mystery.'[59]

In a progress report to Cabinet in June 1950, the Department of Health noted that the Hospitals Trust Fund's capital assets had been depreciating for years, and because of this and the demands of the building programme, an upper limit had been fixed on the deficits that would be paid for 1950, 1951, and 1952.[60] Browne was out of action from Easter 1950 to the following July because of a relapse of TB, during which time he conducted the business of his department from his bed.[61] On his return to the Dáil, he defended the policy of using the capital of the Hospitals Trust Fund, pointing out that it was being depreciated by inflation anyway. Fianna Fáil TD Bob Briscoe claimed it would be better to use the interest to pay for shortfalls in hospital budgets, which would otherwise be a charge on the public.[62]

In one incident which was later to be dragged up at the time of the Mother and Child crisis, Browne found himself in conflict with the Catholic hierarchy. In November 1948, Archbishop Joseph Walsh of Tuam informed the minister that he had been approached by Mayo County Council, who had asked for nursing sisters (i.e. nuns) to fill some posts in Castlebar County Hospital.[63] Browne responded that he would 'be delighted to see an all-religious staff' in any new hospital. He would even consider extra religious staff in existing hospitals, but couldn't do so in the case of Castlebar as it was to be a training centre for lay nurses. He added that he wanted to offer the maximum number of promotional opportunities to lay nurses to prevent them emigrating to England.[64]

There the minister obviously expected the matter to rest, but the following June the secretaries to the hierarchy (Bishops William MacNeely of Raphoe and James Staunton of Ferns) wrote a blistering letter to Costello, pointing out that Browne was a graduate of Trinity and that 'in the past, an ascendancy minority endeavoured to exclude religious from service in workhouse hospitals. We view the general attitude of the Minister in all this matter with concern.' They also claimed Browne's actions were 'a slight on the religious vocation and . . . savouring of secularism'.[65]

Costello's handwritten response employed his usual respectful terms when dealing with the hierarchy, but didn't make any concessions, simply assuring them that 'any policy savouring of unfair discrimination against Religious sisters in nursing or supervisory staff of Regional Hospitals is something that was never intended and which it is our fixed determination to avoid'. He added that the government would continue to utilise the services of the sisters to the best of its ability.[66]

Browne was able to point to considerable achievements during his term of office, including seven thousand hospital beds all over the country, the Cancer Council, the clean food code, the National Rehabilitation Organisation, BCG inoculation, the diphtheria vaccination scheme, mass radiography, and the Blood Transfusion Service.[67] In April 1951, just days before his fall from power, the Department of Health issued figures for deaths from TB and other infectious diseases. The figure for 1950 was the lowest ever recorded, at 2,353, compared to 2,712 in 1949, 3,103 in 1948, and an average of 3,649 for the years 1940 to 1949.[68] A couple of months later, his successor, Jim Ryan of Fianna Fáil, told the Dáil that work had been started or had been completed on 62 of the 128 hospitals affected by the building programme. Of the 37 totally new hospitals, 20 had been started or completed, while work was to start on another 16 by the end of 1951.[69] It was a stunning record.

But Browne had, as we have seen, a downside. He was impatient and intolerant of criticism, and while these traits undoubtedly helped to speed up the building programme, they were less helpful in other matters, particularly where delicate negotiations were required. Ruth Barrington has made the point that Browne 'had never had to compromise his ideals for party or national interest . . . [which] permitted him to cultivate the image of a knight in shining armour . . . By identifying himself so closely with policies which were not exclusively his, Dr Browne raised the political stakes surrounding his ministry and left himself vulnerable to personal attacks.'[70]

The seeds of the Mother and Child crisis lay in Fianna Fáil's attempt to reform health services for women and children. The first step was the 1945 Health Bill, which included provisions for the expansion, improvement, and unification of mother and child services, giving a unified, free scheme for mothers and children up to the age of sixteen, to be provided by dispensary doctors. The Bill also gave sweeping powers for the control of infectious diseases. Although other countries were introducing similarly comprehensive schemes at this time, the Irish initiative was different in a number of ways – there was no free choice of doctor, there was an emphasis on compulsion, and there was centralised control.[71]

In the Dáil in December 1945, leading figures in Fine Gael attacked the Bill. Richard Mulcahy said it introduced 'an unprecedented series of attacks on public liberty', and speculated that Dr Con Ward, the parliamentary secretary responsible for the measure, 'must be at loggerheads with the Church'. John A. Costello claimed the Bill was unconstitutional, while Patrick McGilligan said his opposition was based on the 'Christian tradition that there are individual rights which no State can take away'.[72] But in fact, the hierarchy had few objections. The archbishop of Dublin, John Charles McQuaid, wrote to Eamon de Valera on 1 January 1946 protesting about certain provisions of the Bill. Ward met him on 7 February as a result.[73] The archbishop appeared satisfied, writing two letters to Ward, one describing the Bill as satisfactory, the other calling it 'substantially good'. Even more surprising was the attitude of the Irish Medical Association (IMA), which also approved of the Bill.[74] After Ward's fall from grace,[75] the Bill was withdrawn while the government reorganised itself with the creation of two new departments, Health and Social Welfare. It was only when the Bill was reintroduced, substantially unchanged, in 1947 that the opposition became vocal.

The section of the 1947 Health Act which proved most controversial was only in the legislation by accident. The department's chief medical officer, James Deeny, wanted to introduce health education in schools, along the lines of a scheme in the United States. As there was no statutory basis for doing so, nor any funding, a section of the new Bill was drafted to allow for it. 'As the Bill was concerned with the establishment of a Mother and Child Scheme we had to relate the section on health education to education in respect of maternal and child health, which possibly gave it an ambiguous meaning . . .'[76]

Part of the explanation for the change in attitudes between 1945 and 1947 was the influence of James McPolin, the Limerick chief medical officer, on both the IMA and the Catholic hierarchy. McPolin attacked state medicine as 'interfering with the privacy of the family, as derogating from the responsibility of parents for their children, of the role and authority of parents, [and] of the family as a sacred unit'.[77] Deeny suggested that this approach was sold to the IMA, and thence to the bishops. Whatever about the hierarchy, the medical profession was probably glad of a theological basis for opposition to a scheme that could damage its economic standing. In Ruth Barrington's phrase, McPolin's role 'was to translate genuine medical objections to a state medical service into moral objections to state medicine which made sense to the more conservative elements of Irish public opinion'.[78] It is also important to note that it was not the IMA *per se*, but the Private Practitioners Group within that association that led the opposition to the scheme from 1946 until they reluctantly accepted Jim Ryan's final resolution of the controversy in 1953.[79]

In July 1947, the Attorney General advised that the Health Bill was not unconstitutional, while the Council of State advised the President a month later that he should sign it into law,[80] which he duly did on 13 August. But on 7 October, the hierarchy wrote to de Valera, expressing disapproval of parts of the Act, particularly those dealing with the Mother and Child scheme. Their main concern was directed at the section dealing with health education. Dr Cornelius Lucey, the bishop of Cork, was later to explain the reasons for this opposition: 'Certain practices and certain practitioners would counsel women that you shouldn't have any more babies, in other words that . . . would be a service . . . that could be used for promoting birth control practices . . .'[81] But in this letter, the hierarchy raised no complaint about the fact that the scheme was to be free and without a means test, the issues that were to dominate the debate in later years.[82] De Valera didn't reply to the hierarchy until 16 February 1948, two days before the change of government, on the grounds that the matter was before the courts – in December, James Dillon had begun a High Court challenge to the constitutionality of sections 21 to 28 of the Act.

Fine Gael made no bones about its position on health during the 1948 election campaign. Richard Mulcahy spoke in Limerick of 'the unconstitutional power which . . . [the government] desired to

take over family life under the Public Health Bill . . .'[83] More
surprising, perhaps, was the attitude of Clann na Poblachta. Noel
Hartnett pointed out that three Acts introduced by the government
had been declared unconstitutional by the Supreme Court – the
Trade Union, Sinn Féin Funds, and Education Acts. 'There was
now the Public Health Act which interfered with the Catholic
principles governing the rights of the State and of the family.'[84]
Ironically, Hartnett was to be blamed by MacBride for encouraging
Browne to take a stand against the Church on the scheme.[85]

In March, Dillon dropped his constitutional challenge to the
1947 Act 'in view of the decision of the Minister for Health . . . to
reconsider sections which had been the subject of controversy'.[86]
Setting up the Health Council two days later, Browne stressed that
one of its functions would be 'to advise on the recent Health Act,
with particular attention to certain clauses which have caused
disagreement in the past'.[87] On 19 March, the government approved
Browne's proposal to bring the outstanding sections of the 1947
Act into operation on 1 April, with the exception of the two controversial sections, 25 and 26, which dealt with compulsory medical
inspections of children. Browne had sought the advice of the
Attorney General as to the constitutionality of the Act. Cecil
Lavery advised him that only those two sections were potentially
unconstitutional.[88] At the first meeting of the Health Council,
Browne made the government's decision to bring in the remaining
sections of the Act public, and added: 'Controversial provisions
which were the subject of serious criticism or which are not in
accord with the policy of the present government will either not be
brought into operation or will be repealed or amended as the case
may be.'[89]

The crucial Cabinet meeting took place on 25 June 1948, with
all ministers in attendance, along with the Parliamentary Secretary
to the Taoiseach, Liam Cosgrave, and Cecil Lavery. Browne submitted a general scheme for a Bill to amend the 1947 Act, by
removing sections 25 and 26, along with some other technical
adjustments. The most far-reaching proposal, however, was a provision which would allow him to make regulations charging for
some of the services provided under the Mother and Child scheme,
to be paid either to the health authority or to the doctor providing

the service. Browne noted that under the 1947 Act 'it was proposed . . . that this service would be made available free of charge to all sections of the community' and that there was, therefore, no provision for charging fees.

'In the event of a decision to restrict the free service to certain categories a provision on the lines indicated . . . will empower the Minister to provide for payment by other classes availing of the service. On the other hand, the new provision will not prevent the Minister from providing a free service *should such be considered desirable in the future*.'[90] He added that the IMA had expressed opposition to a free scheme, and while he didn't intend at that stage to commit himself either way, the proposed amendment would reduce medical opposition.[91] The government approved the drafting of a Bill on the lines suggested, subject to the omission of the proposal to provide for the payment of fees.[92]

According to Browne, this decision 'in effect' committed the government to the provision of a free scheme, with no means test.[93] He later claimed that when Costello asked him what his preference was, he said he wanted to keep the free scheme contained in Fianna Fáil's 1947 Act. He was supported by Labour leader William Norton, and the free scheme was accepted by the government.[94] But Costello insisted that the government had only rejected the particular scheme for payment outlined by Browne, and had not dealt with the issue of the means test. 'I can say here and now that the scheme for the Mother and Child scheme – free for all and with no means test – which has been the cause of such acute controversy never came before the Government as a Government.'[95]

This is quite true – a minute prepared for Costello by his civil servants made it clear that 'we have no record of the submission to the government, at any time since the enactment of the Health Act, 1947, of proposals for the institution of the service'.[96] However, it is doubtful whether Browne was actually required to submit the scheme to the government (although details were sent to the Department of Finance for approval). Under section 28 of the 1947 Act, the Minister for Health was empowered to make regulations applicable to health authorities 'as to the manner in which, and the extent to which, they are to exercise their powers under Part III of the Act [which dealt with the Mother and Child service]. Such

Regulations, made by the Minister for Health, would, in effect, constitute a scheme for the Mother and Child Service under the Act.'[97] However, even if not required, it would have been advisable for Browne to ensure that he had full Cabinet support for the details of his scheme, as Jim Ryan had before him. His failure to do so, presumably the result of inexperience or a desire not to have the scheme pruned by McGilligan, made it easier for his colleagues to ditch him and his scheme when trouble arose.

Clearly, Browne felt that the decision of June 1948 closed discussion on the matter – the government had committed itself to a free scheme. However, Costello and his colleagues may have felt, from the terms of the memorandum quoted above, that no firm decision had been made in the Department of Health, and that an opportunity for further discussion would arise later. But because Browne already had the power to make the regulations which would establish the scheme, no such opportunity did arise. To suggest that ministers were not aware of Browne's proposals is untrue. McGilligan used the imminent introduction of the scheme as one of his arguments against Norton's social welfare proposals.[98] In June 1950 he wrote that 'having regard to the free maternity care service which will be provided under the Mother and Child ... Scheme ... there is no need for the Maternity Grant ...'[99] While this doesn't prove that Browne's Cabinet colleagues were *au fait* with the details of his proposals, they were certainly aware of the broad outlines.

In October 1948, Browne rejected IMA proposals for the amendment of the Act, and declined to meet a delegation from the association because the Act was being reconsidered within the department.[100] However, he assured the IMA on 17 November that 'consultations will be held ... before regulations of a major character ... are brought into force'.[101]

Alarm bells rang among the medical profession in March 1949, when the *Irish Times* ran a story that Browne was to make free medical treatment available 'for a large section of the community' under the Mother and Child sections of the 1947 Health Act.[102] In July, Fianna Fáil's Jim Ryan told Browne in the Dáil that he could see no reason for the delay in introducing the scheme.[103] By that time, detailed proposals for mother and child health services for Dublin and for areas outside the four county boroughs of Cork,

Galway, Limerick, and Waterford had been drawn up for Department of Finance approval.[104]

The president of the IMA, Dr P. Moran, told its annual meeting in July 1949 that while the association accepted that the best medical treatment should be available to all, 'we reject the thesis that this can best be done on mass production lines under state control'. On the Mother and Child scheme, he claimed that there was 'a real danger that it will pauperise the people and prostitute the profession . . . Pregnancy certainly should not be raised (or lowered) to the status of a dangerous disease.'[105]

There was no immediate reply from Browne, but in February 1950 he accused 'a section of the profession' of trying to 'stir up bitterness between the Minister and the medical profession', and warned that the forthcoming negotiations on the Mother and Child scheme could be jeopardised by this. He added that while the IMA appeared to believe that it should have a veto over any scheme, 'the Minister has responsibility to the people generally and must always consider the interests not merely of a section but of the community as a whole'.[106]

However, when the new president of the IMA, Dr P.T. O'Farrell, took office in July, he stressed the association's opposition to state control of the medical profession, and to the provision of free medical services for those who could afford to pay for them. 'We fear a general extension of state medicine which would make us civil servants, subservient to a soulless and oppressive bureaucracy.' He added that they opposed the Mother and Child scheme because it would be open to all, regardless of ability to pay, a development which would lead to the disappearance of private practice.[107]

A few days later, when the Dáil passed the Health Estimates without a division, Ryan claimed that some doctors were genuinely concerned that state medicine was to be introduced, and urged Browne to make a statement on the matter. The minister replied that he believed it was 'unworthy of members of the medical profession to try to confuse the simple matter of pounds, shillings and pence with questions of high principle and morality'. He assured the House that it was the government's intention to leave doctors with their autonomy and independence – as far as was humanly possible.[108]

Predictably, the IMA was outraged, referring to the proposal to make services available to all, regardless of ability to pay, as a 'form of socialised medicine and state control'. The association claimed that it had never been properly consulted, 'particularly in regard to safeguarding the liberties of the public and the profession from unnecessary intrusion by the state'.[109]

On 10 October, following a meeting of the hierarchy, McQuaid wrote to Browne seeking a meeting. The minister met the archbishop, along with Bishops Staunton and Browne, the following day in Drumcondra. Browne claimed that the prelates told him they were informing him of the hierarchy's objections to the Mother and Child scheme 'as a matter of courtesy'; a letter on the subject was being sent to Costello. After McQuaid read out the hierarchy's letter, Browne put forward his own views and gave 'answers and undertakings . . . in regard to the objections made by them' which he believed had satisfied them. The following day, McQuaid met Costello, and according to Browne, Costello gave no indication, when they discussed this meeting on 13 October, that the hierarchy remained unsatisfied. He said Costello gave him a copy of the hierarchy's letter on 9 or 10 November for his observations; believing he had already met the hierarchy's objections, Browne drafted a reply repeating the points he had made in Drumcondra, and forwarded it to the Taoiseach in mid-November for onward transmission to the bishops.[110]

Costello's version of events was very different. The Taoiseach said McQuaid told him that Browne refused to consider suggestions about the invalidity of the means test, accepting only that the hierarchy had a point about education, and then 'terminated the interview and walked out'. The Taoiseach told the archbishop that he would do his best to adjust matters between Browne and the hierarchy. Costello said that under these circumstances, he could hardly have confirmed Browne in his opinion that he had satisfied the hierarchy. Costello claimed that the hierarchy's letter was only given to him by McQuaid on 7 November, following the latter's return from a visit to Rome (despite the fact that it was dated 10 October and the two men had met on the 12th).

Following his meeting with McQuaid in November, Costello claimed he told Browne that he wanted to adjust matters between

him and the hierarchy, and that he would not reply to the letter immediately. He claimed Browne agreed to him acting in this way. The
Taoiseach further insisted that the letter given to him by Browne in
mid-November was not in a form that could be sent to the bishops.
(Clearly not – the letter from the hierarchy was addressed to Costello,
and therefore the reply would obviously come from him; Browne
was only making suggestions for the reply. Browne later claimed
that 'protocol insisted that a mere Cabinet minister had no direct
access to an Archbishop's office; it was my intention that with its
compromise proposals, the memorandum should and would be
transmitted to the Hierarchy for their detailed study'.[111]) Costello
further claimed that he had kept McQuaid informed of his efforts
to resolve the matter, but even on his own testimony those efforts
seemed less than vigorous.[112]

The IMA met Browne on 24 October, for what was later said to
be a 'friendly' encounter, at which it was agreed not to air differences
in public. The association had received details of the scheme in
June, which were sent to its 1,800 members and discussed in local
branches.[113] However, at the meeting, Browne told the IMA with
perhaps unnecessary frankness that his personal preference was for
a fully salaried medical profession. 'For the . . . Association it was a
confirmation of the fears of its members.'[114]

On 9 November, Browne and MacBride had dinner in the Russell
Hotel, one of the Clann leader's favourite haunts. MacBride claimed
that the purpose of the dinner was to get Browne's support before
Noel Hartnett, embittered by his party leader's failure to get him a
Seanad nomination, could 'get to him'.[115] Hartnett had certainly
expected a nomination to the Seanad, and MacBride's decision to
nominate Denis Ireland instead (as a gesture to the North) played
a part in his growing disillusion with his party leader,[116] although it
is doubtful if it was the only reason, as MacBride seemed to believe.
However, MacBride and his circle were convinced that Hartnett
'pulled Browne's strings' and directed the younger man's actions
against the party leader.[117]

At their meeting, according to MacBride, Browne made it clear
that he was dissatisfied with his leadership, with the Clann, and
with the government, threatening to 'break-up' both party and
coalition. He also allegedly told MacBride that he intended to pick

a public row with him, or resign from the party, as a way of bringing about a crisis, adding that he would have done so sooner had he not been anxious to bring in the Mother and Child scheme.[118] When he returned home that evening, MacBride dictated a detailed account of this discussion to his personal secretary,[119] and later circulated it to other members of the Cabinet, including Costello.[120] Browne allegedly repeated his intention of breaking up the government in January 1951 at another meeting with MacBride in Iveagh House.[121]

Also in November, the IMA announced that it was to ballot its members on the scheme.[122] Browne attacked the planned referendum, saying it was bound to be unfavourable. He repeated that the scheme would be introduced, that it would be free, with no means test, but with no compulsion on mothers, children, or doctors. 'This is a final decision of the Government, taken on behalf of the people, which the Medical Association or profession has no power to alter. Otherwise, . . . the scheme is in no way immutable or inflexible . . . I leave in these circumstances the Medical Association and the medical practitioners to return whatsoever referendum they may think fit, bearing in mind, as we all must, the best interests of our people. My actions are motivated solely by the dictates of my conscience, and no decision of a minority in the community can force or will induce me to impose on the majority the will of such a group.'[123]

Browne's claim that the referendum was weighted against the scheme was given some substance by the wording of the questions put to doctors: 'Do you agree to work a Mother and Child health scheme which includes free treatment for people who are able to pay for their own medical care? Do you agree to work a . . . scheme if private practitioners are excluded? Do you agree to work a . . . scheme which provides for free treatment for those who can afford to pay and if private practitioners are included?'[124]

The IMA members rejected the Mother and Child health scheme by around 80 per cent. On the first question, the margin was 80 per cent against, on the second 86 per cent, and on the third 75 per cent.[125] Several days later, Costello and Norton met an IMA delegation, with the Taoiseach 'acting as advocate on behalf of the Minister for Health . . . I put forward his views – views with which I did not agree . . .' Costello said that he wanted to come to some agreement with the medical profession which would allow some form of scheme – although not necessarily the one insisted on by Browne. He further claimed that after this meeting, MacBride spoke with Browne about 'the necessity for satisfying the Hierarchy's objections'.[126]

In February 1951, the IMA attacked as 'scurrilous' a document entitled *The Mother and Child Health Scheme – Is it Needed?*, which had been circulated widely, particularly in Dublin Corporation housing estates. The government and the Department of Health denied all knowledge of it.[127] However, Ruth Barrington received confirmation that Browne himself wrote the document,[128] and that the Minister for Defence, Tom O'Higgins, who retained office in the Irish Medical Association despite his Cabinet post, was at an IMA executive meeting where this was disclosed.[129] This helps explain the outspoken attack which O'Higgins launched on the pamphlet, claiming it was a 'foul piece of muddy-minded scurrility' and a 'lunatic libel' against doctors. However, speaking to the Dublin South-East executive of Fine Gael, he also praised Browne, saying he had discharged his duties 'energetically, enthusiastically and courageously. No one has ever given such intense devotion to health improvements.' O'Higgins said that while Fine Gael had opposed the 1947 Health Act, it had been supported not just by Fianna Fáil but by a wide range of other parties and TDs, and therefore could not be changed[130] – an unusual argument, to say the least.

In the middle of February, the IMA invited Browne and Clann na Poblachta to give an assurance that they were not involved in the distribution of the pamphlet.[131] The standing committee of the party denied that it was involved, and deplored the pamphlet's intemperate language. In a statement, Browne said he had resigned from the standing committee of Clann na Poblachta for 'personal and private reasons' – taken to be a reference to his workload and his health – and denied that there was a rift in the party.[132] The following day, a letter from Browne disowning the pamphlet was read to the committee of the IMA. He said he deplored anything which made negotiations more difficult, and said he had no knowledge of Clann involvement in it.[133] MacBride said in Cavan that there was no split in the party: 'None of the scares and alarms that our opponents seek to create will preclude the Clann from pursuing its own clear-cut policy.'[134]

However, two days later, the *Irish Times* political correspondent wrote that there was indeed a split, with MacBride wanting to keep the government going even at the expense of the Clann, while Browne and Hartnett wished to stick to party principles, even if it meant rows within the coalition. The story said that Browne was determined to press ahead with the Mother and Child scheme, which had the support of Fianna Fáil, Clann na Poblachta, and Labour, despite Fine Gael opposition – 'this is one issue on which Dr Browne has preferred to face the wrath of his Cabinet colleagues rather than desert his . . . principles'.[135] One commentator pointed out that MacBride was 'ready and willing to speak on foreign affairs, economics, and any and every other subject' but had not yet defended the Mother and Child scheme. 'The measure . . . is always known as "Dr Browne's scheme", not as "the Clann's scheme". Why? One would very much like to know.'[136]

Browne's patience with the IMA finally snapped in early March. He issued a statement on the 5th saying he had told the association on 23 February that further delay could not be justified, and had given them a deadline of 3 March to decide if they would enter talks – but the day before the deadline expired, the association said it would have to wait until its national council meeting on 8 March before deciding. 'The Minister has been forced to the conclusion that the Association is not prepared to accept the principles of the scheme, but is merely indulging in further delaying tactics. He cannot countenance any further delay in proceeding with measures for the introduction of the scheme.'[137]

As good as his word, Browne published the details of the scheme the following day, 6 March. For mothers before, during, and after the birth of children, it would provide free GP care; free specialist, consultant, and hospital treatment; free visits from a midwife at home; and free dental and eye treatment. For children up to sixteen years of age it would provide free medical treatment, including inoculations and injections, at school and at home, for all illnesses; free specialist, consultant, surgical, and hospital treatment; free home visits by public health nurses; and free dental and eye treatment. There would be a choice of doctor, including the family doctor if he or she came into the scheme. There would be no compulsion, no means test, and no contributions.[138]

Costello later claimed that this scheme had never been submitted to the Cabinet, and that the first time he saw it was when 'someone outside the government' sent him a copy that had been sent to 'some doctor' by Browne.[139] On 8 March, following the appearance of an advertisement for the scheme in the newspapers, McQuaid wrote to Browne, with a copy to Costello. Browne claimed that this was the first time he realised that the hierarchy's objections had not been met.[140]

The IMA, meanwhile, accused Browne of seeking 'to impose dictatorial terms', of breaking an agreement to set up a joint committee of the association and the Department of Health, and of failing to satisfactorily repudiate the anonymous pamphlet.[141]

More ominous were reports of a meeting attended by Costello, Norton, McGilligan, Mulcahy, MacBride, and Dillon to discuss the Mother and Child scheme. It was reported that 'the whole history of the scheme, and the attitude of the medical profession towards it, were under discussion ... some members of the Cabinet regarded the present situation with dissatisfaction'.[142] On 7 March, the Cabinet was reshuffled, but only Fine Gael ministers were involved (O'Higgins went to Industry and Commerce, MacEoin to Defence, and Morrissey to Justice). It was quite clear that although Browne survived his position was under threat, with 'extraordinary rumours in the lobbies ... concerned with the ... Minister for Health ... apart from the IMA criticism of the Minister's scheme ... there were suggestions that certain members of the government were not in complete agreement with the provisions of the proposal, and, as well as that, criticism had come from other influential quarters. For the present it would seem as if Dr Browne has weathered the storm but that is not to say that the scheme will also survive. During the day the Taoiseach had an interview with Dr Browne ...'[143]

An editorial in the *Irish Times* stated that the Mother and Child scheme had exceeded expectations, and commended Browne for not being discouraged by the opposition to it, while acknowledging that the doctors had 'been goaded into antagonism by the Minister's autocratic attitude, and by his lack of patience and tact'.[144]

In an apparently conciliatory move, the IMA national council called for a renewal of talks as soon as possible 'without preconditions'[145] – in other words, without a means test being excluded. However, over the weekend the association issued a lengthy statement attacking the scheme, claiming it would cost £12 million which would have to be met from taxation; that it would be over-bureaucratic and destructive of the medical profession; and that it would squander resources by paying for people who could afford to pay for their own treatment.[146] The Department of Health meanwhile took out half-page ads in the national papers, claiming the scheme would save the lives of many mothers and children.[147]

Browne wrote to the IMA welcoming the suggestion of talks, but reiterating his preconditions – that the scheme would be free, with no compulsion and no means test.[148] On 14 March, according to both men's later testimony, Costello appealed to Browne to accept a means test. Costello said that he had told the minister that 'whatever about fighting the doctors, I will not fight the bishops, and whatever about fighting the bishops, I will not fight the doctors and the bishops together'. He further told Browne that he would have to settle the differences with the hierarchy before he did anything else. Browne claimed in his resignation speech that he replied that if the Cabinet wished to reverse its decision of June 1948, it could do so and he would then 'take whatever action I considered fit in regard to my personal position'. He claimed Costello – as well as Dillon, O'Higgins, Norton, and MacBride, who had all been urging him to back down – refused to take this course.[149] On 21 March, Costello wrote to Browne suggesting that the 1950 Health Bill, which had been introduced in the Dáil in November 1950 to amend the 1947 Act but had progressed no further, should amend the section of the Act which referred to the education of women for motherhood.[150]

Browne next tried to appeal directly to the doctors. The latest half-page ad in the national papers set out the supposed benefits for doctors of the scheme, with an assured income and better facilities,[151] while a letter to all GPs asked them if they would participate in the scheme, warning that if they didn't the minister would base the scheme on the dispensary doctors, as originally planned. An IMA ad in the papers, in unusual language for such a body, characterised this as 'an invitation to scab on your profession. Do not reply to this contemptible letter . . . Do not be rushed into acceptance of bureaucratic control, destruction of professional secrecy and of the patient/doctor relationship . . .'[152]

A few days later, an IMA ad claimed that the 'million a month scheme' would do nothing to hit the real causes of infant mortality – bad housing, poor nutrition, accidents, and shortages of hospital beds.[153] The Minister for Finance, Patrick McGilligan, speaking in the Seanad the following day, gave a much lower estimate of the cost of the scheme – with £635,000 provided in the Estimates, and a total annual cost of £1.75 million when fully implemented.[154] At question time in the Dáil at the beginning of April, Browne told Patrick Cogan that the cost of the scheme would be around £2 million.[155] One estimate of the real cost, based on the British experience, was around £7 million.[156]

On 22 March, Browne met McQuaid to discuss the latter's objections to the Mother and Child scheme. The minister asked for a ruling from the whole hierarchy on whether the scheme was contrary to Catholic moral teaching, and agreed to abide by the result. As a result of his own consultations with at least one theologian, Browne felt that the scheme could only be criticised on the basis of social teaching, which would not be binding. He attempted to put this point of view across to a number of bishops in meetings in the run-up to a special meeting of the hierarchy on 3 and 4 April. McQuaid told the meeting that they had the doctors and every minister (except Browne) on their side, and if they rejected the scheme, 'we shall have saved the country from advancing a long way towards socialistic welfare. In particular, we shall have checked the efforts of Leftish Labour elements which are approaching the point of publicly ordering the Church to stand out of social life and confine herself to what they think is the Church's proper sphere.'[157]

The bishops ignored Browne's question about moral teaching and said the scheme was contrary to social teaching, evidently feeling this a strong enough condemnation.[158] McQuaid's view on this issue was simple: 'Catholic social teaching meant Catholic moral teaching in regard to things social.'[159]

It was not until after Browne's resignation that Clann na Poblachta released two motions passed at a meeting of its ard comhairle on the night of 31 March. The first expressed concern and disapproval at Browne's 'apparent disloyalty to the leadership of the party'; the second reiterated support for the Mother and Child scheme, but expressed concern that it would be jeopardised 'by the manner in which the whole problem is being handled by Dr Browne'. The Clann na Poblachta statement accompanying the two motions also claimed that up to this point, Browne had said his scheme had received the approval of the hierarchy. 'It was at this meeting that Dr Browne first gave an indication that this was not so.'[160]

According to Louie O'Brien, this loss of support within Clann na Poblachta was a decisive turning-point for Browne. Up to then, both the Old IRA group around Con Lehane and the supporters of the Minister for Health had been opposed to MacBride's leadership, partly at least because of frustrated ambitions on the part of Lehane and Hartnett. However, Lehane now realised that if MacBride was deposed, it would be Browne who would take over rather than him – and so he switched his support back to MacBride, removing any possibility that Browne and Hartnett could take control of the party.[161]

Browne's support at Cabinet was also evaporating. Maurice Moynihan alerted Costello when the Minister for Health attempted to write to the IMA stating that the free scheme was government policy; on 21 March, Costello ordered Moynihan to stop the letter being sent, as he did not accept Browne's assertion. He also telegraphed MacBride in the United States, asking him to return at once.[162] By this stage, the Taoiseach had come to the conclusion that there was no binding obligation on the government to introduce a free scheme with no means test,[163] because the only record of a government decision related to the June 1948 meeting.[164]

On Thursday, 5 April, McQuaid met Costello in Government Buildings for over an hour, explaining in great detail the decision reached by the hierarchy the previous day, that Browne's scheme was opposed to Catholic social teaching. 'The Taoiseach at once

and fully accepted our decision, as one would expect.'[165] The
Cabinet met for three hours the next day to consider the position.
All ministers attended, along with Cosgrave and Casey. The meeting
considered the hierarchy's letter outlining the result of its meeting.[166]
Browne has given a vivid portrait of the meeting, at which, following Costello's insistence that the bishops' letter must mean the
end of the scheme, he went round the table asking his colleagues for
their views. 'Michael Keyes . . . was the only one to demur meekly.
"They shouldn't be allowed to do this." But he too nodded his head.
. . . I reflected that one Judas was bad enough, but twelve of them
must be some kind of record, even in Ireland . . .'[167]

MacBride tried to have a memorandum setting out his views
included in the Cabinet minutes. Costello's civil servants advised
him that this would be unwise, as every minister would start doing
the same, leading to records of dissent from decisions, which they
viewed as being incompatible with the principle of collective
responsibility.[168] In the end, the memorandum was kept in the file
on the scheme.[169] As Browne sourly noted, 'it would have been
wiser for MacBride to have left his documentation of unconditional
surrender to a convenient wastepaper basket, and simply grunted
his approval with the rest'.[170]

The minutes of the meeting record the Cabinet decision to drop
the current scheme; to prepare a new scheme that would be in
conformity with Catholic social teaching and that would provide
the best facilities for those 'whose family wage or income does not
permit them to obtain, of themselves, the health care that is necessary for mothers and children'; and that the new Bill would include
any further amendments to the 1947 Act, in addition to those in
the Health Bill 1950, which were necessary.[171] Moynihan questioned
the wisdom of citing the objections by the hierarchy as the sole
reason for the decision, but both Costello and Norton insisted on
this: 'if Browne were to resign, the minutes had to place him in the
position of errant layman unwilling to show the same deference as
his colleagues to the views of the catholic church – an unfair position
considering his profuse assurances to the hierarchy throughout the
affair'.[172] Costello later claimed that the Cabinet had agreed to give
Browne as much time as he wanted to make up his mind on what
he wanted to do.[173] But the message was clear – if he would not

introduce the scheme demanded by the hierarchy and his Cabinet colleagues, he would have to resign.

The next day's *Irish Times* reported that Browne intended to resign because of opposition to the Mother and Child scheme,[174] but by the following Monday he was said to be having second thoughts after a meeting with a delegation from the Irish Trade Union Congress, who appeared to have been told by the minister of the objections of the Church. These objections were not yet public knowledge, but were alluded to in the *Irish Times*: 'In an effort to meet a growingly critical position, the government decided to invite the views of more influential authorities than the doctors, and it is understood that these have not been in favour of the scheme in the final draft.' Seán MacEoin also referred to the attitude of the hierarchy when he told a Fine Gael meeting in Cavan on Sunday that the Fianna Fáil government had been 'authoritatively' informed that parts of the 1947 Act were contrary to the moral law.[175]

The ard comhairle of Clann na Poblachta met for eleven hours from Sunday evening until after 3 a.m. on Monday morning. Browne described the proceedings as 'Kafkaesque', featuring detailed reports of his movements, which led him to believe that he had been followed by the Special Branch.[176] The meeting unanimously passed the following motion: 'That this Ard Comhairle again affirms its complete loyalty to Mr Seán MacBride as leader of the party, and that each member of it acknowledges the leader's right and the right of the party's executive bodies to take any action in accordance with the powers vested in them which is required to maintain party discipline and loyalty to the leader.'[177] This was an echo of the motion agreed before Captain Peadar Cowan was expelled from the party in July 1948.[178]

On Tuesday, 10 April, an ITUC delegation met William Norton with a proposal for a system of nominal contributions, which was not accepted by the government. Browne was not present in the Dáil for a division on the Local Government Bill, and his resignation was expected 'hourly'.[179] The decision was taken out of his hands by MacBride, who wrote to him asking for his resignation. He wrote a terse letter to Costello on Wednesday, informing him that 'as demanded by Mr MacBride, I hereby send you my resignation from the Government, to take effect from tomorrow'.[180]

Costello's reply was more friendly, noting that 'I myself and the other members of the Government who have been your colleagues during the past three years appreciate the work which you have done in the Department of Health, and regret that circumstances should have arisen that have made your resignation unavoidable.'[181]

According to Costello, he did not ask for Browne's resignation himself 'because I still hoped a satisfactory settlement could be achieved . . . I would have stayed my hand in that regard for a little while longer'.[182] Even sixteen years later, Costello claimed that if Browne had not resigned, a compromise could have been reached with the hierarchy.[183] However, he defended MacBride's action in asking for Browne's resignation in the Dáil, going so far as to stake his reputation as a constitutional lawyer on its accordance with procedure.[184] In fact, Costello had himself drafted a letter calling for Browne's resignation. It has been argued that MacBride felt it was up to him to seek the resignation, but that he delayed as long as possible, until he felt Costello was about to lose patience.[185]

Browne resigned with effect from midnight on 11 April. He sent his private secretary, Michael Mulvihill, in the early hours of the 12th to the newsrooms of the three national papers[186] with the full correspondence between himself, Costello, MacBride, and the bishops. It was printed in full. The civil service had to dig hard for precedents on ministerial resignations. The only previous one under the current constitution was that of P.J. Ruttledge on his appointment as General Solicitor for Wards of Court; the only situation similar to that of Browne was the resignation of Eoin MacNeill in 1925. It was noted that on that occasion, MacNeill made, by leave of the House, a personal statement for twenty minutes, following which the House considered the statement on the motion for the adjournment proposed by W.T. Cosgrave.[187] Browne refused to accompany Costello to Áras an Uachtaráin when the latter travelled there at 7 p.m. on the 11th to advise President O'Kelly to accept the resignation; he went alone to meet the President an hour and a half later.[188]

Costello assigned the Department of Health to himself; one of Browne's last official acts was to announce the rescinding of the Mother and Child scheme, saying 'As a Catholic I accept the rulings of their Lordships the Hierarchy without question.' In an editorial, the *Irish Times* claimed that 'the Roman Catholic Church would seem to be the effective government of this country'. The Dublin constituencies council of the Labour Party and the Irish Housewives' Association backed Browne, as did the Dublin South-East constituency council of Clann na Poblachta which severed all links with the party in protest. Cowan questioned the right of MacBride to demand Browne's resignation, and the Ceann Comhairle, Frank Fahy, agreed to raise the matter at the Committee on Procedures and Privileges.[189]

Browne made a personal statement on his resignation in the Dáil the following day. He said that, as a Catholic, he accepted 'unequivocally and unreservedly the Hierarchy's views on this matter', but that he did not accept the manner in which his former Cabinet colleagues had acted. He claimed that the government had authorised him in June 1948 to provide a mother and child health scheme; when 'the question of whether the Scheme should be free to all those anxious to use it was discussed ... the decision of the Government was, in effect, that there should be no means test'. Browne also explained that he believed that he had met the objections of the hierarchy at his meeting with McQuaid, Staunton and Browne on 11 October; and that Costello had done nothing to indicate otherwise when he discussed his own 'interview with McQuaid' (which took place the following day) with the minister on 13 October.[190]

In his reply, Costello insisted that a mother and child scheme without a means test had never been approved by the government; that the hierarchy's views should not have been made public, and 'would not have been if any reasonable person other than the Minister for Health was engaged at that time'; and that as a Catholic he obeyed his Church authorities, and would continue to do so 'in spite of the *Irish Times* or anyone else'. He regretted that the affair would be misrepresented in the North, but said that the hierarchy had confined themselves 'strictly to faith and morals' rather than trying to interfere in politics or the activities of government or state.

MacBride said that he regretted not getting rid of Browne before; that he had told Browne on a number of occasions that the views of the hierarchy would have to be met; that those members of the government who were Catholic were bound to accept their Church's teaching; and that 'for the last year, in my view, the Minister for Health has not been normal. I do not want to go into details.'

Captain Cowan said MacBride had deliberately sabotaged the scheme in order to get rid of Browne. One of the strongest defences of the former minister came, surprisingly, from Oliver J. Flanagan, who said he favoured a no means test scheme 'no matter who is for it or against it'.[191] De Valera ended the debate by saying simply: 'I think we have heard enough.'[192] His attitude has been called 'an unedifying example of political expediency and fence-sitting, and those who would ascribe Olympian statesmanship to his solitary remark . . . are either ingenuous or blinkered'.[193] Alexis Fitzgerald said that 'no one who was present at that debate (as I was) will forget the effect of the discipline of total silence he imposed on his party, or of that single contribution from himself'.[194]

Jack McQuillan resigned from the Clann, accusing the party's leaders of betraying the trust placed in them by those who elected them;[195] two thousand people attended a protest meeting in College Green; and the Northern Minister for Education, Harry Midgley, urged people to 'read, mark, and inwardly digest' the events south of the Border.[196] The *Belfast Telegraph* claimed the controversy proved that 'partition is a wise recognition of fundamental differences which are criss-crossed we believe by a radical difference of outlook between north and south in social reform'.[197] The Galway constituency council of Clann na Poblachta dissolved itself on 19 April, with several key members in the area leaving the party.[198]

At the end of April, McGilligan told a Fine Gael meeting in the Mansion House that the government was 'proud of what happened', adding that it would not let Browne's 'failure to produce a concrete scheme' stop it from bringing in a scheme quickly that would benefit Irish women and children and be 'within the confines of the moral laws'. He also insisted that the Cabinet had a right and a duty to consult the bishops about the moral law. 'I go to those who will guide me and I will take my instructions from them.'[199]

After the general election the following month, of which the Mother and Child crisis was at least partly the cause, the IMA in its annual report said that while the 'attempt to impose state-controlled medicine' had been abandoned, there were no grounds for complacency. 'Vigilance is as essential now as at any period of the trying months through which we have just passed.' The association also had a last blast at Browne, blaming his 'inflexible attitude' for the dispute between them.[200]

Seán Lemass later said he suspected that the crisis had been allowed to develop as a way of getting rid of Browne, 'who must have been a very difficult colleague', claiming that following the 1951 election one of the Fine Gael leaders said to him: 'Well, there's one good thing anyway, we got rid of that fellow, Browne, and MacBride.' However, Lemass placed most of the blame on Browne, whom he described as inept.[201]

Browne later termed the final Fianna Fáil-introduced scheme, which included a 'humiliating' means test and covered children only to the age of six weeks rather than sixteen years, as 'a pitifully inadequate parody of both our own, and the earlier Fianna Fáil, proposals', adding that he had rejected a settlement on similar terms when offered to him by his Cabinet colleagues on behalf of the medical profession.[202]

The new scheme – contained in the Health Act 1953 – was finally agreed between Fianna Fáil and the hierarchy because de Valera, apparently against the wishes of his Minister for Health, Jim Ryan, was prepared to go to great lengths to placate the bishops, who refused to approve the scheme even when a £600 income limit was in place.[203] De Valera's attitude to the hierarchy was indicated in a letter to Lemass, in which he suggested that each proposal 'to which objection was made' should be given to McQuaid, who could 'make a draft with the qualifications which would satisfy him. This draft could then be examined from our point of view, and amended if necessary, until an agreed text was arrived at. This is more or less what happened in regard to . . . the Constitution.'[204] If this was the kind of approach the bishops were used to, it is easy to see why Browne was unable to satisfy them.

James Deeny was happier with the final outcome. 'In the end we got more or less what we wanted. We were able to provide a good national ante-natal, delivery and post-natal service for most mothers and infants and the care included pre-school children. We got free medical care for school children requiring attention for anything discovered at school examinations . . . The important thing was that it covered the mothers and children of the poor and of those in large families.'[205] Perhaps this scheme could have been brought in by the inter-party government if Browne hadn't been forced to resign; perhaps a better scheme could have been arranged if politicians of all parties hadn't proved so weak in the face of Church and medical opposition.

Browne painted Tom O'Higgins, along with McQuaid, as one of the main personalities 'in the conspiracy to subvert my implementation of the free no-means-test mother and child scheme'.[206] O'Higgins's son, also Tom, who became Minister for Health in the second inter-party government, was later scathing in his criticism of Browne: 'If we were never Christians, Browne would have found a cross to nail himself to. Much of the mess I inherited as Minister for Health was because Noël Browne was a prima donna with a fugitive complex.'[207]

O'Higgins was not the only member of the Cabinet with contacts in the IMA. Costello's son-in-law, Alexis Fitzgerald, had two brothers who were prominent doctors, and both were close to the Taoiseach.[208] These contacts between Fine Gael and the IMA were vital, because the doctors knew that Browne did not have the full support of his Cabinet colleagues from an early stage – possibly before the truth had dawned on Browne himself.

The Knights of Saint Columbanus may also have played a role behind the scenes. Many prominent doctors were members of the order, as were a number of ministers. The order's historian, basing her conclusions on its minute books for the period, believes that the Supreme Knight, Stephen McKenzie, 'had been in possession of vital information since 1948' on the opposition to the scheme.[209] She also claims that Seán MacEoin had attended a meeting of the order's leadership in June 1948 at McKenzie's invitation and promised that 'every step possible would be taken to eliminate the threatening conflict between Church and State' over the scheme.[210] One would very much like to know how MacEoin and the Knights were aware of a 'threatening conflict' before it was apparently known to the minister responsible.

Nearly twenty years after the crisis, Costello maintained that he and his colleagues had been right. In a television interview he insisted that acceptance of the bishops' ruling was 'the correct attitude for any Catholic government to take . . . I would do the same again and I know the government would have to do it . . .'[211]

Summing up his discussion of the issue, one of the foremost students of Church–state relations, John Whyte, referred to the 'ill-informed' criticism that the actions of the hierarchy have been subjected to. Whyte maintained that the Mother and Child scheme had many objectionable features, principally relating to its overcentral-isation, and that the bishops were to some extent justified in their concern about growing state power. But he concluded that the hierarchy's intervention against the precise principles of a piece of legislation was unprecedented, and perhaps imprudent.[212] Certainly, it must have damaged the standing of the Church in the long run (and is even now used as an example of excessive interference in the affairs of state by the hierarchy). Whatever about that, the crisis put the survival of the government in serious doubt, as its Dáil majority melted away. It also demonstrated once again the limitations on minority parties in a coalition situation: all parties except Fine Gael were in favour of the Mother and Child scheme, but the opposition of the doctors, and even more of the hierarchy, allowed that party to frustrate the plans for its introduction.

EIGHT

THE BUSTED FLUSH

The first coalition failed because the head of Clann na Poblachta called
upon their nominee Dr Browne to resign ... [This] forced what Norton
used to call 'a yeasty condition' in the country and the Dáil and in which
circumstances I thought it better to consult the people on it.

John A. Costello[1]

The inter-party government's majority in the Dáil was always
extremely precarious; in order to survive, it had to maintain
the support of practically every TD in each of the five
parties that composed it, as well as the group of six Independents
supporting it. However, that support was slowly to slip away, with
both Clann na Poblachta and Clann na Talmhan losing TDs, while
a number of Independents also withdrew their support. While
personality was the main issue in some of the defections, policy also
proved a problem. The declaration of the Republic, the social
welfare scheme, and James Dillon's approach to agriculture were all
pay-offs to groups making up the government (Clann na Poblachta,
Labour, and Fine Gael respectively); but they also led to a splin-
tering of support in the Dáil. While the Mother and Child fiasco
made the government's defeat likely, it was actually a dispute over
the price of milk which led to its demise.

The first crack in the government's hold over the Dáil appeared
in the middle of May 1948, when Clann na Poblachta's Captain
Peadar Cowan moved an amendment at the committee stage of the
Local Elections Bill, to have the elections held in 1949 rather than
1950. He was supported by two other members of the party,
Patrick Kinnane and Joseph Brennan, but the Minister for Local
Government, Tim Murphy, refused the amendment, and a division

was called by Seán Lemass. Cowan voted with the opposition, although his two party colleagues supported the government, and the amendment was lost by sixty-six to fifty-one. Government spokesmen attempted to put the best possible gloss on Cowan's behaviour, telling the media that it was 'an illustration of the freedom of action which members associated with the inter-party government are entitled to exercise in matters in which they have a particular interest and in which the fate of the government is not immediately concerned'. It was not a good message to send out to backbenchers in such a tight parliamentary situation, despite the added warning that 'in a matter of confidence in the government it would, of course, be different'.[2]

The government's most significant Dáil defeat was over the Estimates for the Department of Posts and Telegraphs in July 1949. A Fianna Fáil motion to refer the Estimates back for further consideration was carried by sixty-two votes to fifty-nine. The issue was James Everett's proposal to limit the public's right to send correspondence to government departments without stamps. This had not been mentioned by P.J. Little, who was leading the debate for the opposition, but was suddenly brought up by backbencher Bob Briscoe, 'quite out of the blue'.[3] Three ministers – Richard Mulcahy, Dan Morrissey and William Norton – were away on official business and therefore couldn't vote. But also not voting were two Fine Gael deputies, six Labour, three Clann na Poblachta, one Clann na Talmhan, and five Independents.[4] The vote was taken close to the adjournment, and many deputies were in their cars when the division bell sounded, while at least one TD was locked in the toilet![5]

After a rather stunned two-hour meeting, the Cabinet decided to reintroduce the Estimates without amendment the following morning, with Patrick McGilligan moving the motion in the Dáil.[6] Noël Browne remembered that 'all of us were in differing states of shock at the unexpectedness of the defeat. We felt that there was too much work still waiting to be done in our departments. None of us was anxious for a general election yet.'[7] This time there was no mistake, and the government motion for leave to reintroduce the Estimates was passed by seventy-four votes to sixty-five. Lemass suggested that the government should either resign or hold a vote of confidence, while Eamon de Valera claimed that those deputies who were in the precincts of the House but did not vote clearly didn't approve of the Estimate. 'Is it not clear that what the government is trying to do is to force the estimate through against the majority opinion of the House?' Costello brazened the crisis out – on his election he had said he was not going to regard any snap decision as something that would necessarily involve the downfall of the government, and he was acting in that spirit.[8] The Estimate was passed the following week with no further trouble.[9]

A political commentator claimed that the Fianna Fáil victory had been accidental – a special parliamentary party meeting had been held shortly before to berate backbenchers for not turning up for non-vital votes. 'Inter-Party discipline has now been carried to severe lengths; no deputy may leave the House – even to buy a newspaper – until he has had permission from *all* the Inter-Party whips . . . the non-political deputies – and there are many – are left with an unholy hatred for the machinations of Fianna Fáil.'[10]

The first defection from the government ranks in the Dáil took place just five months after its formation, when Captain Cowan was expelled from Clann na Poblachta for alleged disloyalty. The party's ard comhairle voted by thirty-five to five in favour of Seán MacBride's motion to expel him and ask him to resign his seat in the Dáil.[11] The immediate cause for the expulsion was Cowan's decision to oppose the agreement between Ireland and the United States on Marshall Aid – the only deputy to do so when it was discussed on 1 July. Cowan claimed that the agreement contained a surrender of certain rights. While the US government was to be admired for its generosity to Europe, Marshall Aid was designed to promote the foreign policy of the US and to maintain that country's strength and stability.[12] Cowan claimed that a party meeting on 29 June had not come to a formal decision on the agreement, because MacBride, Browne, and Con Lehane (who he described as the party's deputy leader) were not present. He felt, therefore, that he was free to do as he wished in the Dáil.[13]

The standing committee of Clann na Poblachta didn't take kindly to Cowan's suggestion that he had been expelled because he refused to act as a 'yes-man'; they pointed out that the convention against which he spoke had been signed in April, that MacBride had made a statement to the Dáil about it in March, and that at no stage did Cowan indicate that he had any objection to it or to the Marshall Plan in general.[14]

The Cowan case is most interesting for the light it sheds on the internal workings of Clann na Poblachta. In a statement to the press, Cowan claimed that MacBride had secured the Departments of External Affairs and Health, and chosen himself and Browne to fill them, without consulting the parliamentary party. 'I believe we would have nominated Mr Con Lehane and Mr MacBride for ministerial office. I doubt very much that the parliamentary party would have decided to accept the Ministries that Mr MacBride favoured if we had been given the opportunity of coming to a decision on this question.'[15]

Although he was now outside the party, Cowan said that he would continue to 'press for the achievement of the aims, objectives and ideals' of Clann na Poblachta. But he refused to commit himself to continue supporting the government.[16] According to Jack McQuillan, the real surprise was that Cowan remained in the Clann as long as he did. 'Peadar and MacBride were very much at loggerheads – there was unquestionably a personality clash.' We have already seen the problems Cowan was to cause the government over the declaration of the Republic[17] and the private army he set up to invade the North.[18] In later life he was imprisoned on fraud charges and removed from his seat on Dublin Corporation as an undischarged bankrupt.[19]

However, a by-election victory in which Fine Gael took a seat from Fianna Fáil in November 1949 improved the government's stability. There had already been two by-elections, neither of which changed the balance of forces in the Dáil. Fianna Fáil's Neil Blaney had held the seat of his late father in Donegal East in December 1948, while Labour's William Murphy retained the Cork West seat left vacant by the death of his father, Minister for Local Government Tim Murphy, in May 1949. On 10 September 1949, the Fianna Fáil TD for Donegal West, Brian Brady, died.[20] Joseph Brennan was the Fianna Fáil candidate, while Fine Gael's Patrick O'Donnell was the 'Inter-Party' candidate. As in the other Donegal by-election, Clann na Poblachta put up a separate candidate, Alphonsus Canning.[21] MacBride said they would ask for second preferences from the other candidate supporting the government. 'Whatever happens we believe it necessary that the seat should be won by one or other of the parties supporting the government.' He added that the Clann candidature did not represent a split in the government, but was merely an expression of the party's identity.[22] De Valera told a crowd that every time he looked at the government at Dáil question time he was reminded of the Platypus, an animal he had seen in Canada with 'web feet, powerful claws, the bill of a duck and the tail of a lizard'.[23]

In the end, the inter-party candidate won by 771 votes. Fianna Fáil's Brennan got 47.4 per cent of the first preferences, to 42 per cent for O'Donnell and 10.5 per cent for Canning (who lost his deposit); 84.6 per cent of Canning's votes transferred to O'Donnell, while just 5.8 per cent went to Brennan.[24] While Fianna Fáil's vote had increased since the general election, at least partly at the expense of Clann na Poblachta, it was Fine Gael which saw the biggest rise, thanks to support from those who had voted for Independents in 1948 (none of the other parties had candidates in the general election). It was not long before observers began to draw the conclusions of Clann na Poblachta's poor performance, with one claiming that 'the Clann appears to be obliterated'.[25] Winning a seat from Fianna Fáil was a huge triumph for John A. Costello, who received a 'prolonged round of applause' from the government side in the Dáil in recognition of the achievement.[26]

The next defection from the government ranks came in September 1950, when Wexford TD Sir John Esmonde resigned from Fine Gael. He had offered his resignation on 31 July, but withheld the news until after polling in the local elections. A former Home Rule MP, having been elected to Westminster at the age of twenty-one, he later supported the Centre Party before joining Fine Gael.[27] He alleged that Fine Gael was moving away from its election promises and was not being run on democratic lines. 'I regret to say that . . . our bloc has not pushed our policies as vigorously in government circles . . . Perhaps we have been a little too polite to our colleagues in government by saying "there is no hurry, please look after your policies first".'

Esmonde claimed that Fine Gael was being run entirely by the former members of Cumann na nGaedheal. 'The policy pie is presented to us ready baked, but I personally have never had the experience of helping either in the choice of the ingredients, or the mixing of those chosen.' However, Esmonde gave every indication that he intended to continue supporting the government, saying 'I feel that I can only give it effective support and at the same time remain faithful to my election promises outside the ranks of the party.'[28] However, in May 1951 he resigned his seat in the Dáil, in protest at the decision by Wexford Fine Gael to run his younger brother Anthony as a candidate in the next general election.[29]

In December 1950, the Independent TD for Donegal East, William Sheldon, who represented Protestant opinion in the area, wrote to Costello saying he would no longer support the government, claiming that his 'feeling of uneasiness . . . [began] with the repeal of the External Relations Act and the ending of our association with the British Commonwealth. Since then, I have found myself at variance with other aspects of government policy, and ever more inclined to end the anomalous position in which I have been.' The issues he was most in disagreement with were the anti-partition campaign, which he felt would lead to bad feeling between North and South; compulsory Irish; the refusal to join NATO; 'extravagant' spending on foreign relations; encroaching state socialism; and the failure to address 'crushing' local taxation. 'As I have indicated, I am far from agreeing with the Opposition, and so no question of automatically opposing the government arises. I am merely returning to the position of Independent to which I was elected.'[30]

A few days later, the Independent TD for Wicklow, Patrick Cogan, who had already fallen out with James Dillon over agricultural policy, wrote to Costello saying he would not vote with the government until the 'wrong' of Baltinglass was righted.[31] And within a week, Patrick Lehane left Clann na Talmhan and withdrew his support from the government, claiming that he had 'found it increasingly difficult to give the unqualified support to some of the proposals and decisions of the government which it is entitled to expect from the members of the parties supporting it. Some of these decisions and proposals have been made without consultation with Deputies who, by their votes, are required to enact them.'[32]

The government's reliable majority was now down to four, and according to the *Irish Times* political correspondent, more of the Independents, including Oliver J. Flanagan, were disenchanted.[33]

The precarious situation in the Dáil was exacerbated by the death of Fine Gael TD Joseph 'Josie' Mongan of Galway West in the middle of March 1951. The *Irish Times* political correspondent noted shortly afterwards that 'several deputies . . . have become thoroughly dissatisfied with the government, mainly because they were unable to have carried out some scheme affecting their constituencies. In the past year the government has received many deputations from disgruntled deputies, and to some of them pretty strong language had to be used. It remains to be seen whether their feelings get the better of them to the extent that they will vote the government out of office. In the coming session there is likely to be plenty of opportunity for doing so . . .'[34]

Even after the departure of Noël Browne and Jack McQuillan over the Mother and Child crisis in mid-April, the government still had a strength of 75 out of 146, when Sheldon, Cogan, Lehane and Patrick O'Reilly, who voted against the Social Welfare Bill, were included. Although the social welfare issue had been declared closed, attention now turned to another area in which the government was vulnerable to the loss of Independent support – agriculture.

Farmers had been demanding increases of between 4d and 6d in the prices paid for milk, which were 1s 2d per gallon between May and October, and 1s 4d from November to April; the Minister for Agriculture, James Dillon, by contrast, actually wanted to reduce prices, to a flat rate of 1 shilling per gallon all year round, in order to save annual subsidies costing £3 million. He expected farmers to maintain income by increasing the volume of milk production,[35] and accused the Irish Creamery Milk Suppliers' Association of being 'a Fianna Fáil racket' when it insisted on increases.[36] One producer, commenting on reports that the Department of Agriculture would only offer a 1d increase, predicted 'a riot in the milk trade'.[37] But this was all the Cabinet offered.[38]

A Fianna Fáil attempt to force a division on the Agriculture Estimates, which would have had the support of a number of Independents, failed on 26 April, when Paddy Smith was named and suspended from the House for two weeks for calling Dillon a liar.[39] When the penny-a-gallon increase was announced,[40] the defections began. Patrick Finucane of Kerry resigned from Clann na Talmhan in protest at Dillon's treatment of the milk producers. With

Independent farmer TDs increasingly angry at the situation, the government's days were clearly numbered.[41] Patrick Halliden also left Clann na Talmhan to become an Independent, although he supported the Social Welfare Bill (which led to his expulsion from the County Cork Farmers' Association).[42]

In an attempt to avoid a defeat before the introduction of the Budget on 2 May, consideration of the Agriculture Estimates was deferred from 1 May to the following day.[43] On 1 May, Smith apologised for his remarks to Dillon and resumed his seat in the House. Cogan, O'Reilly and Finucane wrote to Costello asking for a clear government statement on a request for 'fair' prices. They also wanted farmer representatives to be consulted 'before important decisions are taken by the government affecting the agricultural industry'.[44]

On 2 May, Costello asked his civil servants for the possible alternative dates for a dissolution and general election, ranging from that day to the following Wednesday, 9 May.[45] Following a discussion with Costello, Nicholas Nolan, the assistant secretary at the Department of the Taoiseach, suggested a dissolution on the 7th, with polling on Wednesday, 30 May, and assembly of the new Dáil on 13 June.[46] Costello informed Maurice Moynihan and Nolan on the evening of 3 May that he had decided to follow this timetable – although he planned to inform the President on the 4th, the effective date of dissolution would be 7 May.[47] Costello told the government the same day that the President had decided not to leave the state in May and June as he had planned – obviously in order to appoint the new government.[48]

The government again avoided a defeat on the Agriculture Estimates by talking the matter out on 2 May. The House was adjourned until the following Tuesday, the 8th, but as expected, the 13th Dáil was dissolved in the interim.[49] After seeing the President on the afternoon of the 4th, Costello informed de Valera's secretary of his decision. He considered broadcasting a statement giving the reasons for the dissolution, but decided not to (presumably on the advice of his civil servants) 'in the light of the precedents against the making of party political broadcasts from Radio Éireann'.[50]

Each of the government parties was to run its own campaign, but urge supporters to continue their preferences for other inter-party candidates.[51] The close of nominations revealed the smallest number of candidates ever – 296 – as a result of an attempt to reduce competition between supporters of the government,[52] as well as a new sense of realism in Clann na Poblachta.

One political commentator reported all sides saying that this was the first election to be fought on purely 'bread and butter' issues – despite the Mother and Child fiasco, and thanks partly to the fact that 'the Republic' had been taken out of politics.[53]

On the coalition issue, Norton said the electorate had a choice between democratic, as opposed to 'one party, one man', government,[54] while Costello said that he would prefer to lead an inter-party, rather than a purely Fine Gael, government.[55] Lemass said a Fine Gael government would have been bad enough, and a Labour government might have been tolerable, but a government which was one thing one day and another the next could produce only confusion and ineffectiveness.[56] De Valera compared the policy of the coalition to a drunken man: 'He staggers forwards and backwards, left and right, and then finds himself flat in the mud.'[57] He complained that 'many of the men and many of the parties opposed to Fianna Fáil in the last election shamelessly deceived you. Are you going to believe these people again?'[58] Independent candidate Dr Michael ffrench-O'Carroll accused the inter-party government of being a 'tragic failure', with the smaller parties becoming 'mere Fine Gael subcommittees'.[59]

The economy was the single most important issue. De Valera claimed that when Fianna Fáil went out of office the total capital liability of the state was £100 million – now it was £192 million. In sixteen years, Fianna Fáil had borrowed £38 million for state purposes, while in three years the inter-party government borrowed £39 million, on top of $128 million in Marshall Aid loans and $18 million in grants.[60] Seán MacEntee attacked the 'vainglorious megalomania' of certain ministers, and said extravagant borrowing to provide for extravagant spending had given an illusion of prosperity, but the 'rake's progress' was now at an end.[61] Gerry Boland claimed that Fine Gael had let down its conservative supporters who expected tax cuts and retrenchment.[62]

Costello strongly defended the government's capital investment programme, adding that the only alternative to borrowing was to cut back on investment or increase taxation.[63] MacBride seized on the Fianna Fáil attacks, claiming that they would decrease spending on state capital projects.[64] McGilligan said that he would borrow more money if re-elected, for the benefit of the people and the country.[65] His own election literature stressed his reduction of income tax by 6d and removal of Fianna Fáil's Supplementary Budget taxes on tobacco, beer, and entertainment, and advised voters to support the Minister for Finance 'if *you* want – lower prices, less taxation and a better standard of wages and salaries'.[66]

Boland criticised Fine Gael for letting down Commonwealth supporters,[67] while MacEntee said the party had betrayed Protestants by pretending to favour the Commonwealth link. 'There is no plea of patriotism or political expediency which can justify such a breach of faith, whether it be done for 30 pieces of silver or to buy 10 votes in the Dáil.'[68] But Costello said he had no apology to make about the repeal of the External Relations Act and the declaration of the Republic, claiming it had given Ireland a new stature in world affairs and led to closer friendship with the Commonwealth and Britain.[69]

Not surprisingly, in view of the immediate cause of the election, agriculture was a major issue. Dillon claimed that farmers had never been better off, thanks to his success in securing profitable markets for whatever they produced.[70] Lemass announced halfway through the campaign that Fianna Fáil would not restore compulsory tillage unless there was another war.[71] Dillon claimed to have split Fianna Fáil over the issue, as those who said compulsory tillage would not be reintroduced – Lemass, Boland, Erskine Childers and Oscar Traynor – 'do not know one end of a bullock from another, or which end to milk a cow'.[72]

The Mother and Child crisis, while not central to the campaign, was also mentioned by speakers of all parties. Fine Gael's Michael O'Higgins expressed the hope that the right of Church leaders to express their views on legislation would be vindicated by the people, and said Fianna Fáil should have had the 'courage' to support the government against Browne.[73] MacBride asked if Fianna Fáil believed that the Catholic hierarchy was not entitled to express its

views, or that the government should ignore them.[74] Noël Browne
promised to continue his policies if elected, and attacked O'Higgins
for impugning his religious faith, 'which I cherish deeply'.[75]

Costello said family responsibility lay at the heart of the hierarchy's objections to the scheme. 'I could never understand . . . why
anybody should stand over a scheme which involved the Old Age
Pensioner in Connemara and the agricultural labourer in Laois–
Offaly paying for the rich lady in Foxrock when she was having her
children.'[76]

Browne claimed the Mother and Child scheme was defeated by
the IMA rather than the hierarchy, and suggested that unions
should be allowed to set their own rates of pay and conditions, as
that was what the doctors had done.[77] MacEntee used as an election
ad a *Sunday Independent* story from the previous October detailing
the Mother and Child scheme, alongside Costello's claims that he
had known nothing about the scheme, and with the slogan 'Sack
the lot!', a clear reference to the 'Put them out!' cry of the previous
election.[78]

It was important for the left-wing parties, and particularly Labour,
to stress the benefits of their period in government. Michael Keyes
claimed that Labour was implementing the ideals of Connolly on
work and decent wages for all.[79] James Larkin said working men
and women had benefited from Labour's participation in government, particularly with the repeal of Fianna Fáil's Supplementary
Budget and with wage increases. They could now secure the social
welfare scheme by voting for Labour.[80] In an important criticism of
his coalition partners as well as of Fianna Fáil, Larkin pointed out
that neither of the two major parties wanted price control, while
Labour would be fighting for more of it.[81] MacBride asked if
Fianna Fáil was going to reverse the gains made during the
government's term of office, by taking back the increases given to
pensioners, orphans, and the blind, scrapping the Social Welfare
Bill, and reintroducing taxes on cigarettes, cinema seats, and beer.[82]

Norton also pointed to Labour's success with house building. In
1948 there were 3,000 workers on local authority housing; this had
increased fourfold by the previous winter. In 1948, 3,068 houses
were under construction, while the present figure was 10,000. And
since 1948, 14,000 local authority houses had been completed, with

another 7,800 to be made available in 1951, compared to just 729 in the last year of the Fianna Fáil government.[83]

As in 1948, Fianna Fáil tried to have it both ways in the debate over the Labour Party. Major Vivion de Valera claimed that Fianna Fáil was the real labour party, as it was supported by the workers and the unions,[84] while MacEntee, trying to drum up a red scare, claimed that Norton was to be Taoiseach in a new government, with Costello becoming Minister for Justice in preparation for taking the next vacancy in the Supreme Court.[85]

Midway through the campaign, Liam Cosgrave pointed out that Fianna Fáil had changed policy on three important questions – the Wages Standstill Order, compulsory tillage, and increases for pensioners.[86] In fact, consistency didn't much matter, as Fianna Fáil had all the advantages of opposition – it was enough simply to oppose. One of the party's election ads featured a father and son advancing hand in hand against a background of a rainbow and sun emerging from clouds, under the title 'Look Ahead' and ending with the succinct phrase 'This time – Fianna Fáil'.[87]

As the campaign drew to a close, observers noted a slight increase in enthusiasm, with greater numbers at meetings and more heckling.[88] But the main memory of the campaign was of the public facing a difficult choice, 'the more difficult because of the absence of any real political issues between the main parties . . . enthusiasm is almost entirely absent'.[89] The campaign itself was 'one of the most uneventful in Irish history',[90] which could be seen as the result of the inter-party government's success in 'taking the gun out of politics' or, with more truth, as the inevitable outcome when two blocs were occupying much the same space on the political spectrum.

De Valera, at the age of sixty-nine, was 'still the hardiest of the campaigners. So long as he has the use of a microphone, three or even four meetings a day seem to impose no real strain on him, and even at midnight he will not hesitate to travel as far as 100 or 150 miles to the nearest city, have a meal before getting to bed about 3 a.m. and be on the move again at 8 a.m.'[91] He travelled more than 2,000 miles for forty meetings in fifteen counties, compared to Costello's 2,100 miles and twenty-seven meetings, which were marked by his 'over long' speeches (which gave the Taoiseach a bout of laryngitis). De Valera's campaign was judged 'easily the dullest' in ten years.[92] Fine Gael and Fianna Fáil finished their campaigns with rallies outside the GPO on successive days, but the attendance at both was judged to be smaller and less enthusiastic than in previous years.[93]

At dissolution, Fianna Fáil had sixty-seven TDs, having lost the Donegal West by-election. Fine Gael had thirty, their gain in Donegal West being offset by the death of Joseph Mongan and the resignation of Esmonde. The reunited Labour Party had twenty TDs, thanks to the arrival of Joseph Brennan from Clann na Poblachta. The Clann had only six deputies left, after the departure of Brennan, Cowan, Browne, and McQuillan, the latter three to the ranks of the Independents. Clann na Talmhan had also lost three TDs – Lehane, Halliden, and Finucane – to the Independents, leaving them with four deputies. The number of Independents had thus been boosted to eighteen. After the election on 30 May, the state of the parties was: Fianna Fáil, 69; Fine Gael, 40; Labour, 16; Clann na Poblachta, 2; Clann na Talmhan, 6; Independents, 14.

The inter-party grouping thus had sixty-four seats to Fianna Fáil's sixty-nine, with the balance of power again in the hands of fourteen Independents – the election had done nothing to clarify who should form the government. Added to MacBride's trauma as his party collapsed was his own difficulty in retaining his seat – he eventually got in on the tenth count. Seán Lemass later attributed the Clann's demise to its entry into government. He said of MacBride that 'he lost a very high percentage of his supporters by joining up with Fine Gael. Many of these supporters had been pro Fianna Fáil and came back again to Fianna Fáil in disgust. Secondly he appeared to be concerned only with his personal advancement and with getting a position in the Government . . . He may have seen political advantage in putting us out of office, but he did not have to take a role in Government to achieve it. It was this that destroyed him . . .'[94]

But it wasn't all bad news for the inter-party grouping. Despite a large increase in the Fianna Fáil vote, good inter-party transfers kept its gains down to one seat. Fianna Fáil did well in urban areas, and particularly Dublin where it won back much of the vote lost to Clann na Poblachta in 1948; Fine Gael did well in rural areas, a fact attributed by some to Dillon, and 'particularly to the obvious importance attached . . . to the alleviation of the problems of the small farmers of Ireland's poorest regions'.[95]

In a number of constituencies, Fianna Fáil won seats because of poor inter-party transfers. In Carlow–Kilkenny, Fianna Fáil had 48.5 per cent of the first preference vote and won three seats, compared to the two seats picked up by the inter-party bloc, with 51.5 per cent of the vote. The problem here was the inclusion of a second Labour candidate, Thomas Hayden, along with the sitting TD, James Pattison. Hayden had been a Labour loyalist while Pattison had joined National Labour, so running both was presumably a way of reuniting the organisation in the constituency, as well as providing a geographical spread between the two counties. However, they divided the Labour vote too evenly between them and the seat was lost. In Longford–Westmeath an Independent, Charles Fagan, took one seat, while Fianna Fáil won three with 44.7 per cent of the vote, compared to the one inter-party candidate elected from a vote of 37 per cent. In Louth, Labour's Roddy Connolly lost out, as Fianna Fáil won two seats with 49.3 per cent of the vote while just one Fine Gael TD was elected from the inter-party grouping's 50.6 per cent. Again, in Tipperary North, Fianna Fáil won two seats with 44.3 per cent of the vote, while only one inter-party candidate was elected with their 52.9 per cent share.[96]

However, twice as many seats – eight against four – were won as lost by inter-party transfers, particularly those from Clann na Poblachta. The party performed well in both Kerry constituencies, winning 12.6 per cent in North and 13.9 per cent in South. When these votes transferred they ended Fianna Fáil hopes of a second seat in each constituency. The 4.5 per cent won by Clann na Poblachta in Dublin County was vital, electing Labour and Fine Gael candidates who were just under a quota, ahead of a second Fianna Fáiler. In Tipperary South, Fine Gael took two seats, with 28.2 per cent of the vote, thanks to inter-party transfers, while Fianna Fáil also won two seats, with 50.7 per cent of the vote. In Galway North, Clann na Poblachta and Clann na Talmhan brought home the Fine Gael candidate instead of a second Fianna Fáil candidate. In Mayo North, excess Fine Gael votes and Clann na Poblachta transfers secured the last seat for Clann na Talmhan. In Roscommon, Clann na Talmhan, with 31.3 per cent of the vote, won two seats, while Fianna Fáil, with 37.4 per cent, only took one, thanks to the transfers of Fine Gael and Clann na Poblachta – which also benefited Independent Jack McQuillan. In Sligo–Leitrim, traditionally a Fine Gael heartland, an extra half a per cent of the vote (40.1 against 39.6 per cent) won Fine Gael three seats to Fianna Fáil's two, with transfers from Labour and Clann na Poblachta again proving vital.

The Fianna Fáil vote increased by four and a half percentage points, to 46.3 per cent, but the party gained just one more seat than in 1948. The biggest rise was in Dublin, where it received 46.4 per cent, an increase of seven and a half percentage points. This was closer to the normal Fianna Fáil vote in the capital than 1948, Clann na Poblachta's high point, or 1944, when the party won 51.8 per cent thanks to Labour's disarray. Fianna Fáil gained five percentage points in Leinster, almost four percentage points in Munster, and two and a half percentage points in Connaught–Ulster.

Fine Gael gained six percentage points on its 1948 tally, winning 25.7 per cent of the national vote and an extra nine seats, giving a total of forty. The most dramatic rises were in the more agricultural regions – 7.6 percentage points in Connaught–Ulster and 7.8 percentage points in Munster.

When the National Labour vote is included, Labour's vote increased by just one-tenth of one percentage point, to 11.4 per cent, and the combined number of TDs, sixteen, was three down. In Dublin, despite the eclipse of Clann na Poblachta, Labour gained less than half a percentage point, possibly a result of the Mother and Child debacle.

Once again, Clann na Talmhan's national vote was halved, from 5.6 to 2.9 per cent. However, this was largely because the party only contested constituencies in Connaught–Ulster, where it won 11.5 per cent of the vote, a marginal increase. They had won 7.5 per cent of the Munster vote and three seats in 1948, but all three TDs from the region had left the party by 1951. Patrick Halliden didn't run in Cork North, while Patrick Lehane in Cork South and Patrick

Finucane in Kerry North were re-elected as Independents. In fact, the party retained the four seats it held on dissolution in Connaught (single seats in Galway North and Roscommon, and two in Mayo South) and added a second seat in Roscommon as well as a new one in Mayo North. Clann na Talmhan only contested four constituencies, winning seats in all of them, with an average vote in those constituencies of 32.4 per cent.

The other Clann had a dismal election, winning just two seats compared to ten in 1948, with its vote falling by nine percentage points to 4.1 per cent. Its vote was down in every constituency except Cavan, with the worst fall in Dublin, its strongest area in 1948. Michael Gallagher has suggested that the figures imply that the Clann's 'socialist' supporters had been more alienated than the republicans[97] – but that could have been little comfort, given the scale of the rout. Of course part of this huge drop in vote was due to the fact that some constituencies had no Clann candidate – just twenty-six ran, compared to ninety-three in 1948. Again, a number of former Clann deputies were re-elected as Independents: Noël Browne, Peadar Cowan, and Jack McQuillan. In all, there were fourteen Independents in the new Dáil, an increase of two.

According to Cornelius O'Leary, 'so solidly did the voters for the various coalition parties support each other's candidates that the usual bonus won by the largest party was not forthcoming'.[98] O'Leary constructed an Index of Proportionality to demonstrate this bonus. A figure of 100 represents a 'perfect fit', in which a party won the number of seats it should have, proportionate to its vote. In 1948, Fianna Fáil won sixty-eight seats, whereas if the seats were apportioned according to the percentage of the vote, it should have won just sixty-one – the party had an Index of Proportionality figure of 110. But in 1951, that figure was 101 – Fianna Fáil won exactly the number of seats it deserved under strict proportionality. In a sense, then, the increase in the party's vote only served to bring its percentage of the vote and its number of seats into line. Fine Gael did slightly better, winning three more seats than it deserved and getting an Index figure of 107, while Labour got one less than it should, and a figure of 96. But the two smaller parties are most interesting – Clann na Talmhan, with its geographical concentration in the West, should have won just four seats, but in fact won six, translating to an Index of 141, while Clann na Poblachta did even worse than in 1948, when the party won nine seats less than it deserved and got an Index figure of 52. In 1951, it should have won six seats, but got only two, representing an Index figure of 34.[99] These figures demonstrate how unproportional the Irish system can be, especially for smaller parties.

When the government met on 1 June, Liam Cosgrave, Brendan Corish, and Michael Donnellan, who had lost office on the dissolution of the Dáil, were reappointed as parliamentary secretaries.[100] It remained to be seen how long they would retain their positions. De Valera pointed out that with five seats more than the inter-party grouping, 'it is evident that only Fianna Fáil can provide a stable government capable of lasting out the full term'.[101] Richard Mulcahy welcomed his party's gains, and pointed out that Fianna Fáil had failed to win the overall majority they had asked for, 'in spite of the fact that this election has taken place in circumstances favourable' to them.[102]

Following his humiliation at the polls, MacBride proposed a four-party government, of Fianna Fáil, Fine Gael, Labour, and Clann na Talmhan, to secure the reunification and economic reconstruction of the country. He ruled his party out of Cabinet representation. 'In the final analysis, apart from those who set out deliberately to wreck the Clann, the only people who can rejoice at [its] electoral weakening . . . are the enemies of the traditional ideals of the Irish people and those who are opposed to planned economic and social progress.'[103] In a farewell speech to the diplomatic corps at Iveagh House, he said he was 'in the happy position of knowing with certainty that whatever government takes over . . . I shall not be of it . . .'[104] He later declined to reconsider his refusal to join the Cabinet, writing to Costello that the electorate's decision was 'a repudiation of the policies I have been advocating and of my actions in the course of the last three years . . . That this decision was brought about by the treacherous or irresponsible actions of but a few people does not alter the realities which flow from the verdict of the people.'[105] Nearly twenty years later, it was clear who he blamed for the Clann's destruction. 'We felt we had done a good job and served our purpose well. In our party when you had two men like Noël Browne and Captain Peadar Cowan involved in controversy, which got a lot of publicity, naturally the party was harmed . . .'[106]

Some observers predicted that the majority of Independents would support Costello, and that a new inter-party government would therefore be formed. Part of the reason for this assumption was the expectation that if de Valera became Taoiseach he would call a snap general election in the short term (as he had done following inconclusive results in 1932, 1937, and 1943). But whatever government was formed was expected to be short-lived, and cautious, due to the dependence on Independent support.[107]

Of the fourteen Independents, James Dillon was of course going to support the outgoing government. Alfie and Alfred Byrne, Charles Fagan, and Oliver J. Flanagan agreed again to act as a group with him.[108] Patrick Lehane, Patrick Finucane, and William Sheldon were also expected to vote for Costello. This gave the inter-party grouping seventy-two votes to Fianna Fáil's sixty-nine, and left the decision in the hands of six non-aligned Independents – Browne, Cowan, Cogan, McQuillan, ffrench-O'Carroll, and John Flynn. The first four had voted for Costello in 1948, the fifth was a new TD, and the last had supported de Valera in the past. On 4 June Lemass wrote that 'what may happen . . . when the Dáil meets is still a very open matter . . . The position cannot be satisfactory no matter what happens, but the only prospect of some effective work being done is if Fianna Fáil can succeed in forming a government. Another Coalition, dependent on the support of nearly all these Independent deputies, offers a very depressing prospect.'[109]

After a meeting of the Fianna Fáil ard comhairle, de Valera said that if the party received the necessary support it would form a government and proceed at once to carry out its general programme, in accordance with its election pledges.[110] Noël Browne claimed that during this tense period, he had a secret meeting with Seán Lemass 'in a car outside the Harcourt Street laundry'. Lemass allegedly told him that he was not offering a deal, but that Fianna Fáil would try to introduce improvements in the health service. 'I had become bitterly disillusioned with the social policies of the coalition . . . Since health was the subject with which I had become most clearly associated, and in which I was most interested, I decided to support Fianna Fáil . . .'[111]

The Cabinet met on 5 June 'on the understanding that they will be staying in office'.[112] Two days later, Labour agreed to support a new inter-party government, subject to a number of conditions concerning social legislation and the composition of the new Cabinet. Clann na Talmhan met in Roscommon the following day and unanimously decided to continue the inter-party arrangement.[113]

Independent TD Patrick Cogan's preference was for a national government under de Valera. If this didn't happen, he said he would only support Fianna Fáil if there was no threat of an early election, no compulsory tillage (except in wartime), fair prices for agricultural produce, and a clarification of the party's position on proportional representation. He said he would support the inter-party alternative only if there were 'substantial changes in policy and membership' – the latter point clearly addressed at the Minister for Agriculture. He accused Dillon, after being put forward for membership of the Cabinet by the Independent TDs, of trying to 'liquidate' them and gain their seats for Fine Gael. 'The farmers of this country have a right to demand the appointment of a Minister for Agriculture who will understand their needs and will not try to misrepresent them.'[114]

By the time the Dáil met on 13 June, it was clear that Browne, ffrench-O'Carroll, Cogan, and Cowan were all to vote for de Valera, leaving only two undeclared TDs, McQuillan and Flynn. Only if both supported Costello would he be re-elected. Ministers made arrangements for vacating their offices, and rewarded their private secretaries with promotions, in case Fianna Fáil won power.[115]

Costello, Norton, and O'Higgins met ffrench-O'Carroll – at his request – in the early hours of the morning the Dáil met to explain what was being done about the Mother and Child scheme. O'Higgins later denied an accusation from Cowan that they had tried to pressurise the young TD,[116] while Costello was to deny that Cogan had been offered a parliamentary secretaryship shortly before the crucial vote.[117] The government met for the last time at 10 a.m. on the 13th for half an hour. All ministers were present, along with Cosgrave and Corish. No decisions were taken.[118] Civil servants concerned with the smooth transfer of power were again faced with a problem, because 'it was not until a sufficient number of the 14 Independent Deputies . . . had declared their attitude in the course of the actual debate on the nomination of the incoming Taoiseach in the Dáil on the 13th of June that it was definitely known that a change of administration would take place'.[119]

When the Dáil met, Labour's Paddy Hogan was unanimously elected Ceann Comhairle – leaving the inter-party grouping another vote down. Patrick Lehane demanded to know what promises had been made to Labour. After a meeting with Costello, Lehane supported the outgoing Taoiseach, so presumably he was given adequate reassurances on this point.[120] In the event, Costello was defeated by seventy-four votes to seventy-two; de Valera was elected by seventy-four to sixty-nine. Three Independents – Finucane, Lehane, and Sheldon – who voted for Costello did not vote against de Valera. Browne, ffrench-O'Carroll, Cogan, Cowan, and Flynn all voted against Costello and for de Valera; McQuillan supported the status quo, on the grounds that he could see no difference between the outgoing government and Fianna Fáil. Cogan accused Costello of 'lack of moral courage' over the Baltinglass and Browne affairs. Browne said that the inter-party government had only been able to make progress until a clash of ideologies was inevitable. Cowan said he had a solemn duty to release the Labour Party from the grip of the forces of reaction so that it could build its strength and work for a socialist Ireland. His sentiment was somewhat undermined by Labour TD Seán Keane's retort to Cogan's accusations of communism within the party – Keane said that in January 1937 he had been in charge of a group of 250 men planning to go to Spain to fight for Franco![121]

On 18 June, the new Taoiseach outlined the policy of his government at a press conference. He accepted the foreign policy of the previous administration, as it would be difficult to take any other line in the circumstances. The army would be expanded to 12,000 members, with extra reserves. The Social Welfare Bill would be dropped and a replacement brought in, and increased children's allowances would be considered.[122] The price of milk supplied to creameries, the immediate cause of the election, was increased by 1d per gallon,[123] doubling the increase given by the previous administration and thus appeasing some of the Independent deputies on whom de Valera now had to rely.

The new government, according to Tom O'Higgins, had 'a political tail studded with five feathers. Any passing breeze may blow from that tail one of these feathers, and even one feather lost can mean the end of this government.'[124] John A. Costello was later to claim that 'the people who formed the parties of the inter-party government got a majority . . . three or four of the people who had supported the inter-party government went over to Fianna Fáil . . . and became as Mr Dillon used to call them the "busted flush" . . .'[125] That the desertion of the 'busted flush' was largely the result of his own actions, and those of his government, was conveniently forgotten.

CONCLUSION

The basis of our present prosperity both in agriculture and in industry rests upon the policies and the initiatives of the inter-party governments . . . [B]ecause of the persistent and unjustifiable propaganda by . . . Fianna Fáil . . . people at present . . . haven't any idea of the achievements of the two inter-party governments . . .

John A. Costello[1]

With fifty years' hindsight, it is easy to see the weaknesses of the first inter-party government. Lax Cabinet discipline, while a boon to the historian, and even more to the journalist at the time, weakened the effectiveness of the government. So too did the strained relationship with the civil service, particularly the exclusion of Maurice Moynihan from Cabinet meetings. Whatever the rights and wrongs of the actual decision to declare a Republic – which, despite persistent claims, John A. Costello did not decide to do on the spur of the moment while in Canada – it cannot be denied that the government handled the affair rather badly. Their anti-partition policy was counterproductive. And a half-century's distance makes it harder to justify the attitudes of ministers towards the Catholic hierarchy, culminating of course with the shambles of the Mother and Child crisis.

But the government had much to its credit. The attempt to bring the social welfare system up to date, although in the end blocked by conservative elements, was a courageous one, given the antagonism from so many quarters. James Dillon did well in Agriculture, while the housing drive implemented under successive Ministers for Local Government was outstanding. And the advances made in economic policy, while modest in comparison to what was achieved a decade later, were nonetheless crucial first steps in the transformation of the Irish economy.

The first inter-party government also has much to tell us about coalitions involving a large number of players. Of course, later coalitions, with fewer members, relied in large measure on the chemistry between two party leaders – Liam Cosgrave and Brendan Corish sorted out problems over a glass of whiskey; Garret FitzGerald has written of how he and Dick Spring met frequently to iron out problems that were causing dissension in Cabinet; the same held true of subsequent arrangements involving Labour. The situation of the Progressive Democrats in their first coalition with Fianna Fáil was rather different, as both Charles Haughey and his successor Albert Reynolds appeared anxious to reduce the smaller party's input as much as possible. One result was that the PDs spent a great deal of energy in criticising the government (through the party chairman, Michael McDowell). At the time of writing, it appears that Bertie Ahern and Mary Harney have a much more productive relationship.

The first inter-party government was in a class of its own, partly because of the number of party leaders involved. However, it seems to be the case that in the later stages of the government, many important decisions were devolved, not to the party leaders, but to the Cabinet Estimates Committee. As has been pointed out in Chapter Two, this committee excluded Seán MacBride (as well as James Everett and Joseph Blowick, neither as important within the government as the other party leaders), and it has been argued that this indicated the diminution of the Clann leader's role within the government. While MacBride was highly thought of at the outset of the government, his Cabinet colleagues seemed to treat him less seriously as time went on. This may partly have been due to his many absences abroad, but the disintegration of his party was surely also crucial.

It is also true that Richard Mulcahy, as leader of the largest party, might have expected a greater input into policy formulation. But it seems, as we have seen in the discussion of the repeal of the External Relations Act and of economic policy, that in fact Costello, by virtue of his position as Taoiseach, called the shots as far as Fine Gael was concerned.[2] William Norton, however, had a very central role throughout the life of the government, a fact that Costello referred to on a number of occasions and that Seán Lemass confirmed during Norton's libel action against the *Irish Press*. Dillon was another figure vital to the workings of the Cabinet.

Some commentators have suggested that the first inter-party government survived as long as it did because it avoided divisive issues – an echo of Costello's suggestion that points that hadn't been agreed would be 'left in abeyance'.[3] Taking up this theory, Cornelius O'Leary has written that 'a modus vivendi was attained by avoiding any legislation that might involve the loss of even one deputy's support . . .'[4] Although this isn't strictly speaking true, as a number of measures brought in by the government led to the loss of support in the Dáil, notably the declaration of the Republic and the social welfare scheme, he goes on to point out that the government sought to introduce 'measures that were likely to enhance ministerial popularity, especially by increasing public expenditure'.[5] Here we have the explanation for the ready acceptance of Keynesian theory discussed in Chapter Five.

No other Taoiseach had to undertake as delicate a balancing act as that facing John A. Costello – trying to satisfy five parties and a mixed bag of Independents, some of them eccentric to say the least, was a task of monumental difficulty. Most observers expected the first inter-party government to last a year; the fact that it survived as long as it did is a tribute to Costello's skills as a chairman.[6] And it should also be noted that the government itself did not fall apart in 1951 – one of its constituent parties split, leading to the loss of a parliamentary majority. All of the parties appeared willing and eager to continue the experiment.

But Costello's style had its drawbacks. The Taoiseach took upon himself the role of mediator between ministers, interceding to try to reach a compromise which would ensure the government's survival. Often this resulted in victory for the more conservative elements in Fine Gael, because the time spent in endless discussion in Cabinet committees effectively killed proposals of which the larger party disapproved. Although the debacle over the Mother and Child scheme is the most obvious example of conservatism winning out, equally important, and more typical, was the failure to introduce Norton's social welfare plan, which formed part of the government's ten-point plan in 1948.

Even where Fine Gael appeared to sacrifice 'core values' in order to keep the government together, elements within the larger party actually favoured a radical approach – Costello believed in the repeal of the External Relations Act as much as MacBride, while Patrick McGilligan had been converted to Keynesian ideas before the formation of the government. The lesson for the smaller parties appeared to be that they would only succeed in pushing through their policies if they could persuade at least some members of the majority party of their value.

The electoral implications of coalition were more mixed. Labour has lost seats in every election following a period in government, apart from February 1982 when it retained its fifteen deputies. Clann na Poblachta in 1951, and Clann na Talmhan then and in 1957, lost seats; so too did Democratic Left in 1997. The PDs in 1992 were the only junior coalition partner to actually increase its number of seats. But it doesn't necessarily follow that the major party wins seats as a result of spending time in a coalition (as the conspiracy theorists on the left wing of the Labour Party used to believe). True, Fine Gael made significant electoral progress in 1951, and in 1997. But every other election following participation in a coalition led to the loss of seats. Fianna Fáil also lost seats in 1992 after its first experience of coalition.

But there is no denying the importance of the 1951 election for Fine Gael. Mulcahy recognised that Fine Gael had had a 'miraculous escape from near disaster'.[7] The party's vote had been in continuous decline for ten years, and dipped below 20 per cent in 1948. But after a spell in government it rapidly recovered, to nearly 26 per cent in 1951 and to 32 per cent in 1954.

How can this change be explained? Partly, of course, it was due to the renewed enthusiasm of party activists who felt they had a voice in government again. On his way back from the Fine Gael ard fheis in June 1948, after the change of government, James Dillon told Noël Browne that 'Last year, because Fine Gael was on its last legs in the country, it would have been possible for us to have held our Ard Fheis in Power's Hotel. This year, the Mansion House is full to the door with loyal members of the party.'[8] Dillon's status as an Independent was somewhat undermined by attendance at such functions, and he rejoined the party in 1952, the same year that

Oliver J. Flanagan entered Fine Gael for the first time.[9] The period in government also coincided with a more professional approach to party organisation, with the first national collection being held in 1949.[10]

Presumably, the party's return to government had re-established its credibility with the electorate. Two other factors might be mentioned. The improvement in the party's vote in agricultural areas of the country in 1951 (mentioned in Chapter Eight) implied that Dillon's work redounded heavily to the credit of the party he was to lead a decade later. Another point relates to the declaration of the Republic. Observers at the time felt that this would damage Fine Gael's image as the 'Commonwealth party'. But, as Nicholas Mansergh pointed out, 'the Commonwealth votes were on the other side of the Border'.[11] Even in the South, it seems that Protestants tended to vote for Independents,[12] not Fine Gael. In Chapter Three it was suggested that the repeal of the External Relations Act may have helped Fine Gael to lose the 'West Briton' tag it had laboured under for so long. Indeed, Seán MacEoin is reported to have thanked Michael Kelly, general secretary of Clann na Poblachta, 'for having removed the Union Jack which the "Long Fellow" . . . had wrapped around him and his Free State associates back in 1922'.[13]

As has been said, the results of government participation were more mixed for the smaller parties. The year 1948 marked a high point for those voting for neither Fianna Fáil nor Fine Gael – 38.3 per cent. The only election in which more voted for third parties was June 1927, when Labour, Farmers, and the National League all did well and the figure was 46.4 per cent. The only election since 1948 to come anywhere near was that of 1992, when Labour's Spring tide saw the proportion of those voting for neither of the two main parties rise to 36.4 per cent. But the decline of the two main parties seems to have been as temporary in 1992 as it was in 1948.

Apart from the electoral results, there were some advantages to the Labour Party in taking part in the inter-party government, principally the sorting out of internal difficulties which allowed the National Labour faction to return to the fold. But despite the successful housing drive and the limited advances made in social welfare, it was clear that the party had had only a peripheral influence on economic policy, and in the second inter-party government,

Norton became Minister for Industry and Commerce, one of the two engines of economic influence.

Clann na Talmhan, as we have seen, was reduced by 1951 to an entirely Connaught-based organisation, and although Joe Blowick was to participate as a minister in the second inter-party government, the party faded away in subsequent years. It could be argued that Blowick was not the best candidate for ministerial office, as he never projected a profile likely to attract extra support. The party's achievements in office were negligible, and its *raison d'être* was removed as prosperity increased and the nature of farming changed as the 1950s gave way to the 1960s.

But its decline was hardly as dramatic as that of the other Clann, which was from 1951 reduced to being a minor player in Irish political life. The destruction of Clann na Poblachta was well under way even before its second general election campaign: the parliamentary party had begun to disintegrate, with the loss of four TDs; with MacBride abroad so much on official business, the party organisation had not received the attention it needed; the loss of Noel Hartnett was a serious blow; and the support of the two main elements in the party had been lost – many republicans were disaffected by the decision to enter government with Fine Gael in the first place, while social radicals were naturally disappointed by the Mother and Child debacle. The party's historian has noted that none of the Clann TDs tried to consolidate their hold on their seats by contesting the local elections.[14] The party was reduced to two seats in 1951, rose to three in 1954, but subsequently returned only one deputy in each general election, finally being dissolved at a special ard fheis in 1965.[15]

It might well be asked, could the Clann have survived if it had spurned the chance to enter government in 1948? Richard Dunphy has suggested that such a course might have forced Fianna Fáil to continue in government, with the support of National Labour, while Fine Gael's decline continued, with Labour and Clann na Poblachta reaping the rewards, 'if the Clann's increasing maturity in these circumstances had enabled it to confront its internal contradictions'.[16] Such a counterfactual argument is, by definition, impossible to prove. But comparisons might be drawn with another party which attempted to 'break the mould' of Irish politics, although from precisely the opposite direction, four decades later.

Following a great deal of hype, and expectations that it could over-take Fine Gael as the second largest party, the Progressive Democrats won fourteen seats in the 1987 election. Although this was a very good result for a first attempt, it was a disappointment to many supporters – similar to that felt by Clann activists in 1948. The PDs remained in opposition, maintaining a high profile and promoting a radical (right-wing) agenda. But in 1989, it was reduced to six Dáil seats, and only a spell in government saved the party from a seemingly irreversible decline. There is no way of proving that the same would have happened in Clann na Poblachta's case, but certainly staying in opposition does not guarantee that a new party will prosper.

Labour has also been criticised for the decision to enter govern-ment in 1948, when, according to Peter Mair, 'the potential for long-term electoral growth was sacrificed in the interest of the short-term advantage of incumbency'.[17] The same author has sug-gested that Labour has continually 'drawn back from attempting to mobilise a genuine *political* alternative to mainstream Irish politics, and has instead opted for the more comfortable strategy of building *governmental* alternatives to Fianna Fáil'.[18] The process of entering coalition with Fine Gael was colourfully described by one Labour radical as choosing 'to sup with the devil without the proverbial long spoon'.[19] However, it is difficult not to have some sympathy with Labour politicians, offered their first chance of government, and it should be remembered that radical parties entering govern-ment at that time had the example of the wartime coalition in Britain, in which many Labour policies were implemented, paving the way for Clement Attlee's election victory in 1945.

Another interesting change brought about by the first inter-party government was on the one political grouping which didn't partici-pate in it. This was obvious at the level of party organisation, which was greatly strengthened during Fianna Fáil's period in opposition. But more fundamental was the shift in policy, which was greatly aided by Costello's government and was eventually to become evident during the Lemass era. Peter Mair has pointed to the difference between Fianna Fáil in 1932–48 and in 1957–73. In the first period, the party had a policy of 'economic autarky: the erection of tariff barriers, the discouragement of foreign investment, and the fostering of native industry behind a broad protective shield', while in the second it was devoted to an open economy, incentives to foreign capital, and membership of the Anglo-Irish Free Trade Area and the European Economic Community.[20] Mair explains this change by reference to 'a fundamental recasting of the nationalist discourse', changing from political, cultural, and economic isolation as the overriding national interest to a concern with economic well-being.[21] But it is certainly arguable that Fianna Fáil's transition (or more particularly, Lemass's attempt to change party policy) was helped by the inter-party interlude, which made Keynesianism and free trade central to political debate.

Elsewhere, Mair formulated his theory in different terms, suggesting that the primary cleavage in Irish politics was based on what he called 'ability to govern' rather than the persistence of Civil War divisions, and adding that the left–right dimension is secondary to this.[22] Richard Dunphy has criticised Mair for concentrating on political elites; he accepts that a 'new language of politics' came to be used by Fianna Fáil after the 1937 constitution marked the end of de Valera's dismantling of the 1922 settlement. But the new language was not about competence, it was about growth – Fianna Fáil could represent itself as the only party capable of delivering long-term growth for the Irish economy, a promise which gained it support among the growing sectors of the economy and allowed it to move out of the western heartland which nurtured the party in its early years. In Dunphy's words, Fianna Fáil 'succeeded in articulating the social project of the dominant groups – a project which, meeting the perceived needs of the whole society, is shared far beyond the confines of the dominant social groups alone'.[23] This thesis makes sense in terms of protectionism in the 1930s and self-sufficiency during 'the Emergency'. But in the later 1940s Fianna Fáil's offer of growth was becoming increasingly suspect. The credibility of a divided opposition was little stronger, but the discovery in government of the convenient language of Keynesianism allowed it to pursue its own growth strategy. It was only when Fianna Fáil adopted this strategy for itself that a further sixteen years in power became possible.

Even at the time, the conversion of political discourse was noted by T. Desmond Williams, writing in the *Statist* in 1953: 'For a very long time, the language of popular appeal in Irish politics was not an economic one. People . . . were more concerned with questions arising out of history and political science . . . The declaration of the Republic . . . finished a long chapter in modern Irish politics . . . Since that date, the politicians have adopted economics . . .'[24]

At the time of his resignation as leader of the opposition in 1959, Costello claimed that 'history will judge that the inter-party government of 1948 was the enterprise which finally proved that Irish democracy would efficiently work. Then, despite differences in party, despite indeed the historical antagonisms which divided some elements, in recognition of the undoubted desire of the people for a change of government, public men came together and gave the people the change they desired. The inter-party government did one thing even more important. It inaugurated the trend of events which has led to the present situation in which men are prepared to forget, and are forgetting, about the Civil War, when the relationships of public men are governed by many considerations other than the position they once occupied *vis-à-vis* that lamentable conflict.'[25] Although delivered with Costello's characteristic hyperbole, it is not a bad assessment of the government of which he was the head.

The first inter-party government, as Costello implied, was important for Irish politics simply because it existed; it proved that de Valera could be beaten, and ensured a change of government that was badly needed by all parties, including Fianna Fáil. But Costello's first administration is also important for what it tells us about coalitions. The large number of parties involved, and the range of ideologies they professed, suggest that policy was submerged by the desire to serve in office. However, an alternative view is that the parties' policy aims, while different, were not necessarily conflicting. As long as sufficient resources were available, all the parties could achieve some of their aims – Fine Gael's tax cuts, Labour's social welfare increases, Clann na Poblachta's hospital building programme. That is why the government was so keen to adopt Keynesian policies which justified borrowing; it allowed them all to win.

At the same time, this policy initiative helped to lay the groundwork for Fianna Fáil to change economic direction in the late

1950s. This alone would make the first Costello administration worthy of study, as would a number of other important initiatives, such as the declaration of the Republic. For all these reasons, it seems clear that the first inter-party government was far more than just a makeshift majority.

BIOGRAPHICAL NOTES

Acheson, Dean   US Secretary of State

Aiken, Frank   Fianna Fáil TD for Louth, 1923–73; various ministries, including Finance, 1945–8, and External Affairs, 1951–4

Andrews, C.S. ('Todd')   Managing Director, Bord na Móna

Blowick, Joseph   Clann na Talmhan TD for Mayo South, 1943–65; party leader, 1944–58; Minister for Lands, 1948–51 and 1954–7

Boland, F.H.   Secretary, Department of External Affairs

Boland, Gerald   Fianna Fáil TD for Roscommon, 1923–61; Minister for Justice, 1939–48 and 1951–4

Brennan, Joseph   Governor of the Central Bank

Brennan, Dr Joseph   Clann na Poblachta TD for Dún Laoghaire, 1948–51; unsuccessful Labour candidate, 1951

Briscoe, Bob   Fianna Fáil TD for Dublin South, 1927–65

Brook, Sir Norman   British Cabinet Secretary

Brooke, Sir Basil   Northern Ireland Prime Minister, 1943–63

Browne, Dr Noël   TD for Dublin South-East – Clann na Poblachta, 1948–51; Independent, 1951–4; unsuccessful Fianna Fáil candidate, 1954; Independent/National Progressive Democrat/Labour, 1957–65; Labour, 1969–73; Independent/Socialist Labour Party for Dublin Artane and Dublin North-Central, 1977–February 1982; Minister for Health, 1948–51

Burke, Thomas   Independent TD for Clare, 1937–51; a bonesetter and infrequent attender in the Dáil; supported de Valera in 1948

Byrne, Alfie   Independent TD for Dublin North-East, 1922–54

Byrne, Alfred Patrick, jun.   Independent TD for Dublin North-West, 1937–44 and 1948–54

Carrigan, Joseph   head of US Economic Co-operation Administration in Ireland, 1948–50

Casey, Charles Francis   Attorney General, 1950–1

Childers, Erskine   Fianna Fáil TD for Longford, 1938–73; Minister for Posts and Telegraphs, 1951–4

Chuter Ede, James British Home Secretary

Cogan, Patrick TD for Wicklow – Independent, 1938; Farmer, 1943; became deputy leader of Clann na Talmhan in 1943 and elected for that party in 1944; left in 1947; Farmer, 1948; Independent, 1951; defeated as Fianna Fáil candidate in 1954

Connolly, Roddy Labour TD for Louth, 1943–4 and 1948–51; former member of Socialist Party, Communist Party, Workers' Party, and Saor Éire

Corish, Brendan Labour TD for Wexford, 1945–81; Parliamentary Secretary to the Minister for Local Government, 1948–51

Cosgrave, Liam Fine Gael TD for Dún Laoghaire, 1943–81; Parliamentary Secretary to the Taoiseach and to the Minister for Industry and Commerce, 1948–51

Cowan, Captain Peadar TD for Dublin North-East – Clann na Poblachta, 1948; Independent (following expulsion from Clann na Poblachta in July 1948) 1948–54; former member of Saor Éire and Republican Congress; unsuccessful Labour candidate in four elections, 1937–44; expelled from Labour Party in 1945; joined Clann na Poblachta the following year

Cripps, Sir Stafford British Chancellor of the Exchequer

Davin, William Labour TD for Laois–Offaly, 1922–56

de Valera, Eamon Sinn Féin/Fianna Fáil TD for Clare, 1917–59; President 1959–73; Taoiseach and Minister for External Affairs 1932–48, Taoiseach 1951–4 and 1957–9

Deeny, Dr James Chief Medical Officer, Department of Health

Derrig, Tomás Fianna Fáil TD for Carlow–Kilkenny, 1927–57; Minister for Education, 1932–48, Minister for Lands 1951–4

Diamond, Harry Socialist Republican Stormont MP for the Falls

Dillon, James Independent/Centre Party/Fine Gael TD for Donegal 1932–7 and Monaghan 1937–69; voted for de Valera as Taoiseach in 1932; formed Centre Party 1932, Fine Gael 1933; left Fine Gael 1941 over neutrality, rejoined 1952; leader 1959–65; Minister for Agriculture, 1948–51 and 1954–7

Dockrell, Maurice Fine Gael TD for various Dublin constituencies, 1943–77

Donnellan, Michael Clann na Talmhan TD for Galway East, 1943–64; Parliamentary Secretary to the Minister for Finance, 1948–51

Esmonde, Sir John Home Rule MP for North Tipperary, 1915–18; Fine Gael TD for Wexford, 1937–44; re-elected 1948; left Fine Gael September 1950; resigned seat six months later

Evatt, Dr Herbert Australian Minister for External Affairs

Everett, James Labour/National Labour TD for Wicklow from 1922 until his death in 1967; Minister for Posts and Telegraphs, 1948–51; Minister for Justice, 1954–7

Fagan, Charles TD for Meath–Westmeath – Centre Party, 1933; Fine Gael, 1937–44; Independent, 1948–51; Fine Gael, 1954–61

Fahy, Frank Fianna Fáil TD for Galway, 1918–51; Ceann Comhairle, 1932–51

ffrench-O'Carroll, Dr Michael Clann na Poblachta councillor; elected Independent TD for Dublin South-West 1951; unsuccessful Fianna Fáil candidate, 1954

Finucane, Patrick TD for Kerry North – Farmer, 1943; Clann na Talmhan, 1944 and 1948; left party, April 1951; elected as Independent, 1951; Clann na Talmhan, 1954; Independent, 1957–69

Fitzgerald, Alexis John A. Costello's son-in-law and informal economic adviser

Fitzpatrick, Michael Clann na Poblachta TD for Dublin North-West, 1948–51

Flanagan, Oliver J. TD for Laois–Offaly, first as Monetary Reform in 1943; Fine Gael, 1952–87

Flynn, John Independent TD for Kerry South, 1948–54; Fianna Fáil 1954–7; supported de Valera 1948

Fraser, Peter New Zeland Prime Minister

Garrett, George US Minister in Dublin from July 1947; became Ambassador in April 1950 and retired in May 1951

Halliden, Patrick Clann na Talmhan TD for Cork North, 1943–51; at one stage chairman of party in Dáil, but left before 1951 election, which he did not contest

Hartnett, Noel Fianna Fáil activist who became involved in Clann na Poblachta; close to MacBride; left party over Battle of Baltinglass

Hickey, James Labour and National Labour TD for Cork City, 1938–43 and 1948–54

Hoffman, Paul head of US Economic Co-operation Administration

Hogan, Patrick Labour TD for Clare, 1923–68 (with some breaks); Leas Cheann Comhairle, 1948–51; Ceann Comhairle from 1951 until his death in 1968

Hogan, Sarsfield head of exchange control division, Department of Finance

Jowitt, Lord Benjamin British Lord Chancellor

Keyes, Michael Labour TD for Limerick East, 1932–57; Minister for Local Government, 1949–51, and for Posts and Telegraphs, 1954–7

Kinnane, Patrick Clann na Poblachta TD for Tipperary North, 1947 (by-election) to 1951

Laithwaite, Sir Gilbert British Representative in Dublin from April 1949; Ambassador from July 1950 to March 1951

Larkin, Jim, jun. Labour TD for Dublin South, 1943–8, and Dublin South-Central, 1948–57; educated at the Lenin School in Moscow for three years

Lavery, Cecil   Attorney General from 1948 until appointed to Supreme Court, April 1950

Legge, Hector   editor, *Sunday Independent*

Lehane, Con   Clann na Poblachta TD for Dublin South-Central, 1948–51

Lehane, Patrick   Clann na Talmhan TD for Cork South 1948; left party December 1950; Independent TD 1951–4

Lemass, Seán   Sinn Féin/Fianna Fáil TD for Dublin South and Dublin South-Central, 1924–69; Minister for Industry and Commerce, 1932–48, 1951–4, and 1957–9; Minister for Supplies, 1939–45; Taoiseach, 1959–66

Leydon, John   Secretary, Department of Industry and Commerce

Little, P.J.   Fianna Fáil TD for Waterford, 1927–51; Minister for Posts and Telegraphs, 1939–48

Lynch, Patrick   Department of Finance official; economic adviser and secretary to John A. Costello, 1948–51; later Professor of Economics at University College Dublin and Chairman of Aer Lingus

MacBride, Seán   Clann na Poblachta leader and TD for Dublin County and Dublin South-West, 1947–57; Minister for External Affairs, 1948–51

McCartan, Patrick   Independent Presidential candidate, 1945; Clann na Poblachta Senator, 1948–51

McElligott, James   Secretary, Department of Finance

MacEntee, Seán   Fianna Fáil TD for various Dublin constituencies, 1927–69; various ministries, including Local Government and Public Health, 1945–8, and Finance, 1951–4

MacEoin, Seán   Fine Gael TD for Longford, 1929–65; Minister for Justice, 1948–51, and for Defence, 1951

McGilligan, Patrick   Cumann na nGaedheal/Fine Gael TD for NUI/Dublin North-West/Dublin North-Central, 1923–65; Minister for Industry and Commerce, 1924–32, and for External Affairs, 1927–32; Minister for Finance, 1948–51; Attorney General, 1954–7

Mackenzie-King, William Lyon   Canadian Prime Minister, 1935–48

McQuillan, Jack   TD for Roscommon – Clann na Poblachta, 1948–51, Independent, 1951–65

Machtig, Sir Eric   British Permanent Secretary, Commonwealth Relations Office

Maguire, Ben   Independent TD for Sligo–Leitrim; supported de Valera 1948; defeated 1951

Miller, Paul E.   head of US Economic Co-operation Administration in Ireland from July 1950

Morrissey, Dan   TD for Tipperary – Labour, 1922–33, Fine Gael, 1933–57; Minister for Industry and Commerce, 1948–51, and for Justice, 1951

Moylan, Seán   Fianna Fáil TD for Cork North, 1932–57; Minister for Lands, 1943–8, and for Education, 1954–7

Moynihan, Maurice   Secretary, Department of the Taoiseach

Mulcahy, Richard   Sinn Féin/Cumann na nGaedheal/Fine Gael TD and Senator, 1918–61; Commander-in-Chief, Free State army, 1922; Minister for Defence, 1922–4; Minister for Local Government, 1927–32; Minister for Education, 1948–51 and 1954–7; Fine Gael leader, 1944–59

Murphy, T.J. (Tim)   Labour TD for Cork West, 1923–49; Minister for Local Government, 1948–9

Noel-Baker, Philip   British Commonwealth Secretary

Nolan, Dr Nicholas   Assistant Secretary, Department of the Taoiseach

Norton, William   Labour TD for Dublin County, June 1926–June 1927, and for Kildare/Carlow–Kildare, 1932–65; Labour leader, 1932–60; Tánaiste and Minister for Social Welfare, 1948–51; Tánaiste and Minister for Industry and Commerce, 1954–7

O'Brien, Louie   Seán MacBride's personal secretary

O'Donnell, Patrick   Fine Gael victor in Donegal West by-election, November 1949

O'Higgins, Michael   Fine Gael TD for Dublin South-West, 1948–51 and 1954–61, and for Wicklow, 1961–9

O'Higgins, Dr T.F. (Tom)   Cumann na nGaedheal and Fine Gael TD for various constituencies, 1929–54; Minister for Defence, 1948–51, and for Industry and Commerce, 1951

O'Higgins, Tom, jun.   Fine Gael TD for Laois–Offaly, 1948–73

O'Reilly, Patrick   Clann na Talmhan TD for Cavan, 1943–8; Independent, 1948–51

Pattison, James   Labour and National Labour TD for Carlow–Kilkenny, 1933–51 and 1954–7

Pearson, Lester   Canadian Minister for External Affairs

Pozzy, Col. Theodore   head of US Economic Co-operation Administration tourism section

Rugby, Lord   British Representative in Dublin, September 1939 to April 1949

Ryan, Dr Jim   Sinn Féin/Fianna Fáil TD for Wexford, 1918–65; various ministries, including Health and Social Welfare, 1947–8 and 1951–4

St Laurent, Louis   Canadian Prime Minister from November 1948

Sheehan, Michael   Independent TD for Cork Borough; voted for de Valera, 1948; defeated as Fine Gael candidate, 1951

Sheldon, William   TD for Donegal East – Clann na Talmhan, 1943; Farmer, 1944; Independent, 1948–61; represented Protestant vote

Smith, Paddy   Sinn Féin/Fianna Fáil TD for Cavan, 1923–77; various ministries, including Agriculture, 1947–8, and Local Government, 1951–4

Smyllie, R.M. (Bertie)   editor, *Irish Times*

Spring, Dan   Labour and National Labour TD for Kerry North, 1943–81

Sweetman, Gerard   Fine Gael TD for Kildare, 1948–70; party chief whip, 1948–51

Timoney, John   Clann na Poblachta TD for Tipperary South, 1948–51

Traynor, Oscar   Fianna Fáil TD for Dublin North-East, 1932–61; Minister for Defence, 1936–48

Tully, John   Clann na Poblachta TD for Cavan, 1948–65

Walsh, Thomas   Fianna Fáil TD for Carlow–Kilkenny, 1948–57; Minister for Agriculture, 1951–4

Ward, Dr Con   Fianna Fáil TD for Monaghan, 1927–48; Parliamentary Secretary to Minister for Local Government and Public Health, 1932–46

Whitaker, Dr T.K.   relatively junior, but influential, Department of Finance official

NOTES[*]

INTRODUCTION

1 Disraeli, 17/12/1852, quoted by Robert Blake, '1783–1902', in Butler (ed.), 1978, p. 1.
2 PR–STV was almost introduced in Britain after the First World War, when a Speaker's Conference recommended it for urban constituencies; David Lloyd George rejected the plan, a decision he was later to regret when the Liberals were replaced by Labour in the two-party system. See Bogdanor, 1984, pp. 75–6.
3 Details of the Maltese electoral system, and election results, are available on the Internet at http://www.maltadata.com/maltavot.htm.
4 Gallagher, 1986, p. 263.
5 Lijphart, 1984, p. 16.
6 Boston, Levine, McLeay and Roberts, p. 1.
7 During the protracted negotiations that led to the National/New Zeland First coalition, 'copies of several recent Irish coalition agreements were in circulation'. Prime Minister Jim Bolger had also sought information about the formation and management of coalition governments from, among others, Albert Reynolds. Boston, 1997, pp. 3 and 4.
8 See A.S. Cohan, 'Ireland: Coalitions Making a Virtue of Necessity', in Browne and Dreijmanis (eds), p. 280.
9 Maryann Valiulis, 'The Man They Could Never Forgive – The View of the Opposition: Eamon de Valera and the Civil War', in O'Carroll and Murphy (eds), p. 93.
10 Ibid.
11 This is clear from his private papers; see, for instance, a note dated 17/2/63, in Mulcahy Papers, UCDA, P7/D/2, referring to de Valera: 'He was himself directly responsible for the Civil War and its effects.'
12 Bruton interviewed on 'Farrell', RTÉ 1 Television, 15/5/94.

[*] Abbreviations used in the Notes are explained in the Bibliography.

ONE: PUT THEM OUT!

1 Lindsay, p. 152.
2 Cumann registration declined in both 1946 and 1947; John Horgan, 'Seán Lemass: A Man in a Hurry', in Hannon and Gallagher (eds), p. 40.
3 Donal Nevin, 'Industry and Labour', in Nowlan and Williams (eds), p. 97.
4 Ó hEithir, p. 115.
5 NAI, S 14153 A, D/T memo, 29/10/49.
6 NAI, S 14153, Tribunal report, dated 19/12/47.
7 NAI, S 14153, two telegrams from Flanagan to de Valera, dated 22/12/47.
8 *IT*, 6/2/48.
9 *IT*, 7/2/48.
10 Coogan, p. 636.
11 Mair, p. 52.
12 Quoted by Bell, p. 242.
13 Ibid., pp. 131ff.
14 Ibid., p. 122.
15 Ibid., p. 169.
16 RTÉ Archive Tape A 4184.
17 Information from Louie O'Brien.
18 NAI, S 13854, letter from Harry Diamond MP to de Valera, 30/4/46.
19 NAI, S 13854.
20 Bell, p. 243.
21 *DED*, Vol. 101, cols 1087–8, 29/5/46 – this line-up supports the view that Fine Gael was the least republican of the opposition parties.
22 NAI, S 13854.
23 Jordan, p. 84.
24 Information from Louie O'Brien.
25 *DED*, Vol. 101, col. 1129, 29/5/46 – his reference was to the inquest into the deaths of Tony D'Arcy and John McNeela on hunger strike in 1940; Boland described his cross-examination by MacBride at this inquest as 'one of the worst experiences I have ever had'; quoted in Fisk, p. 345.
26 *IP*, 24/6/46.
27 *IT*, 6/2/47.
28 Ibid.
29 Ibid.
30 Ibid.
31 Jordan, p. 93.
32 Robert M. Beaudry to Washington, 11/2/47, quoted in Cronin, pp. 183–4.
33 *II*, 26/5/47.
34 Browne, p. 100.
35 John A. Murphy, 'The Irish Party System, 1938–51', in Nowlan and Williams (eds), p. 149.
36 UK PRO, DO/130/84, record of conversation between de Valera and Noel-Baker, 4/11/47.

37   Maurice Manning, 'The Farmers', in Lee (ed.), 1979, p. 52.
38   *IP*, 27/7/44.
39   Gallagher, 1978, p. 18.
40   Mair, p. 25.
41   Dunphy, p. 287.
42   Rumpf and Hepburn, p. 147 – this explains the absence of a broad-based agrarian party in Ireland.
43   *The Leader*, 3/1/48, editorial.
44   See Gallagher, 1976, p. 54, and Garvin, 1981, p. 173, for analyses of Clann na Talmhan support demonstrating its appeal to small farmers.
45   Dunphy, p. 285.
46   See Gallagher, 1976, p. 55.
47   UCDA, McGilligan Papers, P35/207, Dillon to McGilligan.
48   Mulcahy interview, in Whyte, pp. 113 and 379.
49   Figures calculated from results in Walker (ed.).
50   Werner Moss, quoted in Gallagher, 1976, p. 10.
51   Information from Risteárd Mulcahy.
52   *IT*, 4 and 5/4/47.
53   UCDA, Mulcahy Papers, P7/D/123, Cosgrave to Mulcahy, 14/5/47.
54   The list is in UCDA, Mulcahy Papers, P7/b/115; the election results are in Walker (ed.).
55   Gallagher, 1978, p. 6.
56   Calculated from Walker (ed.); the constituency revision is discussed below.
57   See *IP*, 5/12/63, which describes the split as Norton's 'biggest crisis'.
58   ITGWU, p. 8.
59   Inglis, p. 172.
60   O'Higgins, p. 110.
61   Gallagher, 1978, pp. 15–17.
62   Stationery Office, Prl. 8624.
63   Gallagher, 1978, p. 17.
64   UCDA, Mulcahy Papers, P7/c/119, has both letters.
65   Information from Risteárd Mulcahy.
66   UCDA, Mulcahy Papers, P7/D/123, note of conversation with Dillon, 3/7/47 – other papers in this file outline the moves towards forming a new National Party.
67   Legation report, 20/11/47, quoted in Cronin, p. 184.
68   Legation report, 14/12/47, quoted in ibid., p. 185.
69   Coakley, 1980, p. 317.
70   Ibid., p. 298, Table 2.
71   *DED*, Vol. 108, cols 917–28, 23/10/47, quoted in ibid., p. 299.
72   *IT*, 12/1/48.
73   *IT*, 20/1/48.
74   *IT*, 2/1/48.
75   *IT*, 9/1/48.
76   *IT*, 23/1/48.

77 *IT*, 4/2/48.
78 The candidate figures, calculated from Walker (ed.), were Fianna Fáil 119; Clann na Poblachta 93; Fine Gael 82; Labour 43; Clann na Talmhan 25; National Labour 13; Independent 31.
79 Breakdown of candidate professions is in *IT*, 28/1/48.
80 See Garvin, 1981, p. 175.
81 *IT*, 10/1/48.
82 Quoted in Rumpf and Hepburn, p. 142.
83 *IT*, 27/1/48.
84 *IT*, 23/1/48.
85 *IT*, 10/1/48.
86 Election ad in *IT*, 10/1/48.
87 UCDA, McGilligan Papers, P35/258.
88 'Memories in Focus', RTÉ 1 Television, Tx 11/5/95.
89 *IT*, 3/2/48.
90 'Memories in Focus', film maker Liam O'Leary.
91 Both letters are in NAI, S 14204.
92 Leaflet reprinted in Mitchell and Ó Snodaigh (eds), p. 246.
93 *IT*, 13/1/48.
94 *IT*, 30/1/48.
95 *IT*, 4/2/48.
96 Rafter, p. 57.
97 *IT*, 2/2/48.
98 NAI, Govt 1, 19/2/48.
99 *IT*, 17/1/48.
100 *IT*, 3/2/48.
101 *IT*, 19/1/48.
102 Keatinge, 1978, p. 50.
103 *IT*, 19/1/48.
104 NAI, D/EA Secretary's files, P135, correspondence from Seán Nunan in Washington, 23/1/48 and 28/4/50.
105 *IT*, 20/1/48.
106 *IT*, 23/1/48.
107 *IT*, 2/4/50.
108 NAI, Cab 76, 13/3/49.
109 *IT*, 29/1/48.
110 *IT*, 22/1/48.
111 UK PRO, DO/130/93, Rugby to Machtig, 26/1/48.
112 *IT*, 28/1/48.
113 UK PRO, DO/130/93, Rugby to Machtig, 28/1/48.
114 Ibid., Rugby to Machtig, 9/2/48.
115 See below, Chapter Three.
116 Maurice Manning, 'The Farmers', in Lee (ed.), 1979, p. 51.
117 NAI, S 15422 A, Blythe to Cosgrave, 24/2/31; see below, Chapter Two.
118 Gallagher, 1976, p. 46.

119 *IT*, 2/1/48.
120 *IT*, 5/1/48.
121 *IT*, 6/1/48.
122 *IT*, 5/1/48.
123 NAI, S 14224, election leaflet; the reference was to Costello.
124 *IT*, 2/1/48.
125 *IT*, 22/1/48.
126 *IT*, 7/1/48.
127 *IT*, 20/1/48.
128 *IT*, 4/2/48.
129 Ibid.
130 Ibid.
131 *IT*, 6/2/48.
132 *IP*, 7/2/48.
133 All figures calculated from Walker (ed.).
134 Rafter, p. 60.
135 *The Leader*, 14/2/48, editorial.
136 *IT*, 7/2/48.
137 Gallagher, 1978, p. 19.
138 Ibid.
139 *IP*, 27/1/69.
140 *IT*, 9/2/48.
141 *IT*, 10/2/48.
142 UCDA, Mulcahy Papers, P7/D/116, Mulcahy to Costello, 17/7/67.
143 *IT*, 14/2/48.
144 Browne, p. 107; Patrick Lynch, 'Pages from a Memoir', in Lynch and Meenan (eds), p. 38, says Costello told him that Esmonde was MacBride's first choice.
145 *IT*, 9/2/48.
146 Information from Liam Cosgrave.
147 *IT*, 1/1/79.
148 Browne, p. 107.
149 Information from Risteárd Mulcahy.
150 UCDA Mulcahy Papers, P7/D/3, note on conversation with Commandant Vincent Byrne, 7/1/64.
151 Valiulis, p. 47.
152 Ibid., p. 3.
153 Jordan, p. 95.
154 FitzGerald, p. 45.
155 Information from Liam Cosgrave.
156 *IT*, 1/1/79.
157 Browne, p. 109.
158 *IT*, 16/2/48.
159 *IT*, 17/2/48.
160 *IT*, 16/2/48.

161 Ibid. – Dillon and Fagan were both former Fine Gael TDs; Cogan had been a member of Clann na Talmhan.

162 Liam Cosgrave, on RTÉ Archive Tape A 4184.

163 UCDA, Mulcahy Papers, P7/D/116, Mulcahy to Costello, 17/7/67.

164 Farrell, p. 43.

165 Patrick Lynch, 'Pages from a Memoir', in Lynch and Meenan (eds), p. 37; Norton had already asked that Costello be invited to the meetings 'for the purpose of . . . advice and help. There was a general feeling that you should be so asked.' UCDA, Mulcahy Papers, P7/D/116, Mulcahy to Costello, 17/7/67.

166 *IT*, 7/9/67.

167 Patrick Lynch, 'Pages from a Memoir', in Lynch and Meenan (eds), p. 37.

168 *IP*, 3/6/54.

169 *IT*, 6/7/67.

170 *IT*, 16/2/48.

171 Coakley, 1984, p. 413.

172 Brian Farrell, 'Coalitions and Political Institutions: The Irish Experience', in Bogdanor (ed.), 1983, p. 252.

173 NAI, S 14182; the Taoiseach nominates eleven of the sixty members of the incoming Seanad; in 1948 the eleven nominees were divided among the parties – four Fine Gael, two each for Clann na Poblachta and Labour, and one each for National Labour, Clann na Talmhan and Independents. McCabe, p. 28.

174 *IP*, 11 and 12/5/49.

175 Ronan Fanning in *SI*, 18/12/94.

176 *IT*, 4/9/67, John A. Costello remembers.

177 Maye, p. 310.

178 The conversation was overheard by Richard Mulcahy. UCDA, Mulcahy Papers, P7/D/116, Mulcahy to Costello, 29/4/69.

179 *IP*, 29/1/69.

180 NAI, S 9879 B, *passim*.

181 Deeny, p. 196.

182 Lindsay, p. 172.

183 Patrick Lynch, 'Pages from a Memoir', in Lynch and Meenan (eds), p. 40.

184 Everett, quoted in Ó Broin, 1985, p. 176.

185 *IT*, 17/2/48.

186 Browne, p. 109, ascribes the story to the *Irish Press*, but a similar list is in the *Irish Times*.

187 UCDA, McGilligan Papers, P35/208.

188 Information from Risteárd Mulcahy.

189 *IT*, 14/4/89, profile of McGilligan, by Garret FitzGerald.

190 *IT*, 7/2/48.

191 *IT*, 9/2/48.

192 *IT*, 17/2/48.

193 Thomas Johnson, quoted in Dunphy, p. 293.

194 Details from CIU annual report, in *IT,* 16/7/48.
195 *IT,* 7/9/67.
196 *IT,* 28/2/48.
197 Details from CIU annual report, in *IT,* 16/7/48.
198 *IT,* 18/2/48.
199 *IT,* 4/3/48.
200 *IT,* 11/3/48.
201 *IP,* 27/1/69.
202 NAI, S 10719 A, D/T memo, 31/3/48.
203 NAI, S 14165, statement of 17/2/48.
204 O'Reilly and Sheldon were both former Clann na Talmhan TDs; the latter represented the Protestant vote in Donegal.
205 *DED,* Vol. 110, cols 21–2, 18/2/48.
206 *IT,* 19/2/48.
207 Ibid.
208 The next paragraph is based on NAI, S 10719 A, D/T memo, 31/3/48.
209 NAI, S 14242.
210 *IT,* 19/2/48.
211 *IT,* 20/2/48.
212 *IT,* 22/4/50.
213 NAI, S 14169, 'Notes for the Taoiseach's discussion with the new Attorney General', 18/2/48.
214 Ibid., Moynihan note, 20/2/48.
215 Ibid., Moynihan note, 8/3/48.
216 Ibid., 'Notes for the Taoiseach's discussion with the new Attorney General', 18/2/48.
217 Ibid., Moynihan note, 20/2/48.
218 Ibid., Moynihan note, 6/1/50.
219 Ibid., Nolan note, 1/3/48.
220 NAI, Govt 1, 19/2/48.
221 NAI, S 10719 A, D/T memo, 31/3/48.
222 *IT,* 26/2/48.
223 *II,* 5/5/69.
224 Although his later exclusion from economic decision making was facilitated by his choice of portfolio; see below, Chapter Two.
225 *IT,* 23/2/48.
226 Horgan, p. 133.
227 *IT,* 15/6/49.
228 *IT,* 25/2/48.

TWO: ELASTIC GOVERNMENT

1 *DED,* Vol. 110, col. 77, 18/2/48.
2 *IT,* 13/2/50.

3   13.30 News, RTÉ Radio, 5/3/73.
4   Patrick Lynch, 'Pages from a Memoir', in Lynch and Meenan (eds), p. 42.
5   This Week, RTÉ Radio, 11/2/73.
6   Ibid.; see below for a discussion of majority voting in the Cabinet.
7   *IT*, 7/9/67.
8   Browne, p. 125.
9   NAI, S 5478 B – Cosgrave quoted by Lieutenant General Michael Joe Costello.
10 UCDA, Mulcahy Papers, P7/c/150, memo of a conversation between the two men in September 1959.
11 Lindsay, p. 157.
12 Information from Patrick Lynch.
13 Although McGilligan's liberal leanings did not extend to social welfare – see below, Chapter Six.
14 Lindsay, pp. 167–8.
15 Aknefton in *IT*, 18/3/50.
16 Information from Patrick Lynch.
17 RTÉ Archive Tape A 4184.
18 Quoted in *The Leader*, 25/10/52, profile of Norton.
19 Browne, p. 195.
20 Ó Broin, 1985, p. 164.
21 Interview with Morrissey, *IT*, 10/1/80.
22 Lemass to William Dwyer, 12/5/48, quoted in O'Sullivan, p. 116.
23 Browne, p. 127.
24 Information from Louie O'Brien.
25 Browne, p. 108.
26 Information from Louie O'Brien.
27 The film was reshown in 'Memories in Focus', RTÉ 1 Television, Tx 11/5/95.
28 This Week, RTÉ Radio, 27/4/69.
29 See *The Leader*, 25/10/52, profile of Norton.
30 *IT*, 9/10/67, Dr Noel Browne, a political portrait.
31 Browne, p. 190.
32 *IP*, 29/1/69.
33 *The Leader*, 25/10/52, profile of Norton.
34 Information from T.K. Whitaker.
35 Ibid.
36 Information from Patrick Lynch. McGilligan's poor health was not a figment of his imagination – he had been given six months to live while in his early twenties. Information from T.K. Whitaker.
37 *IP*, 12/4/79.
38 *IT*, 13/4/89, profile of McGilligan, by Garret FitzGerald.
39 *DED*, Vol. 9, col. 562, 30/10/24.
40 *DED*, Vol. 9, col. 551, 30/10/24.
41 NAI, S 10023, for biography.

42 Browne, p. 200.
43 *IT*, 6/9/67.
44 Information from T.K. Whitaker.
45 Quoted in Fanning, 1978, p. 458.
46 Information from Patrick Lynch.
47 Information from T.K. Whitaker.
48 Fanning, 1978, p. 459.
49 Browne, pp. 107–8.
50 Conor Cruise O'Brien's profile of MacBride was published anonymously in *The Leader*, 2/8/52, and was later reprinted in Akenson (ed.), 1994, pp. 6–10; quotation taken from p. 9.
51 CIA report, 'Ireland', dated 1/4/49, quoted in Cronin, p. 255.
52 Information from Patrick Lynch; the conversation took place on 8 October 1949.
53 *IT*, 14/6/51.
54 NAI, S 7870 A, extract from minutes for 11/8/22.
55 Ibid., extract from minutes for 26/8/22.
56 Ibid., Cosgrave to J.C. Meredith, 28/4/24.
57 Ibid.
58 NAI, S 11375 C, containing M/L memo, 26/7/48; M/F memo, 28/7/48; and Cabinet decision, 30/7/48.
59 Ibid., M/L memo, 4/11/48; M/F memo, 13/11/48; and Cabinet decision, 30/7/48.
60 Ibid., M/L memo, 27/11/48.
61 Ibid., M/F memo, 4/1/49; M/L memo, 6/12/49.
62 *DED*, Vol. 110, col. 2052, 25/5/48.
63 23/3/50, quoted in Brian Farrell, 'Coalitions and Political Institutions: The Irish Experience', in Bogdanor (ed.), 1983, p. 254.
64 Quoted in Ó Broin, 1982, pp. 157–8 – while this was illuminating on the government's attitude to collective responsibility, it did not answer Brennan's query.
65 *DED*, Vol. 113, cols 309–11, 24/11/48, quoted in Keatinge, 1973, pp. 48–9.
66 *IT*, 31/10/49.
67 *DED*, Vol. 117, col. 926, 14/7/49, quoted in Keatinge, 1973, p. 92.
68 *DED*, Vol. 113, col. 312, 24/11/48, quoted in Horgan, p. 143.
69 *IT*, 16/1/50.
70 *IT*, 19/1/50.
71 *IT*, 21/1/50.
72 *IT*, 30/1/50.
73 *IT*, 9/2/50.
74 *IT*, 15/2/50.
75 Ibid.
76 Details in *DED*, Vol. 119, cols 767–9, 23/2/50, and *IT*, 24/2/50.
77 *IT*, 24/2/50.
78 *IT*, 25/2/50.

79 *IT*, 17/3/51.
80 Although it should be noted that some civil servants believed the opposite to be the case. J.J. McElligott, secretary of the Department of Finance, apparently told Costello that the country 'had been a dictatorship under Fianna Fáil', with Lemass the dictator. Horgan, p. 134, based on a radio interview with Alexis Fitzgerald.
81 *II*, 19/6/71.
82 Browne, p. 121.
83 Keogh, 1994, p. 186.
84 UK PRO, DO/130/93, Rugby telegram to Machtig, 23/11/48.
85 NAI, S 10719 A, D/T memo, 31/3/48.
86 Information from Patrick Lynch.
87 Patrick Lynch, 'Pages from a Memoir', in Lynch and Meenan (eds), pp. 39–40.
88 Information from Patrick Lynch.
89 Ibid.; Reynolds was a close friend of Lemass, and was popularly believed to have kept a 'string of racehorses' at the Curragh in his own name on behalf of the Fianna Fáil politician – there is no evidence to support this allegation. Horgan, p. 102.
90 See Andrews, pp. 191–3.
91 *IT*, 1/3/51.
92 *IT*, 28/2/51, letter from O'Donovan.
93 *IT*, 20/2/51.
94 NAI, S 13988, Cab 240, 12/2/51.
95 NAI, Govt 207, 12/2/51.
96 *IT*, 22/2/51.
97 *IT*, 28/2/51.
98 All quotes from Ó Broin, 1982, p. 131.
99 See below.
100 *IT*, 2/3/51.
101 *IT*, 9/3/51.
102 *IT*, 14/2/51; see also NAI S 9404 A, memo of 30/11/36.
103 NAI, Govt 208, 16/2/51.
104 *IT*, 12/9/51.
105 NAI, S 13988 B/2 – Part B/1 of this file has been sealed until 2021.
106 NAI, S 4569 A, memo of 29/1/53.
107 NAI, S 13988 C, Moynihan note, 4/6/54, and O'Donovan letter to Moynihan, 3/6/54.
108 NAI, S 9404 A, Govt decision of 26/8/54.
109 NAI, S 1646/4 A, Moynihan to Costello, 17/2/49.
110 NAI, S 5052 B, Nolan to Foley, 8/3/49.
111 NAI, S 1646/4 A, Moynihan to Taoiseach, 20/1/49.
112 This later led to the setting up of the Industrial Development Authority – see below, Chapter Five.
113 NAI, S 3635, Moynihan to Taoiseach, 6/1/49.

114 Ibid., Moynihan memo, 6/1/49.
115 Ibid., Moynihan minute, 10/1/49.
116 NAI, S 5052 B, note by Foley, 23/8/50, with addition dated 24/8/50.
117 NAI, Cab 199, 15/8/50; Govt 169, 15/8/50.
118 Patrick Lynch, 'Pages from a Memoir', in Lynch and Meenan (eds), pp. 39–40.
119 See below, Chapter Six.
120 NAI, Cab 134, 22/11/49; S 12113 C/1, Costello's memorandum, 19/1/49.
121 Brian Farrell, 'Coalitions and Political Institutions: The Irish Experience', in Bogdanor (ed.), 1983, p. 255.
122 A.S. Cohan, 'Ireland: Coalitions Making a Virtue of Necessity', in Browne and Dreijmanis (eds), p. 276.
123 NAI, Cab 3, 27/2/48; see S 14252.
124 NAI, S 14293, minutes of first meeting, 2/3/48.
125 Ibid.
126 NAI, Cab 68, 11/2/49.
127 NAI, Cab 69, 18/2/49.
128 NAI, Cab 151, 3/2/50.
129 NAI, Cab 156, 24/2/50.
130 NAI, Cab 166, 4/4/50.
131 NAI, Cab 175, 12/5/50.
132 NAI, Cab 232, 2/1/51.
133 NAI, Cab 233, 5/1/51.
134 NAI, Cab 235, 16/1/51.
135 NAI, Cab 161, 14/3/50.
136 See below, Chapter Six.
137 John A. Murphy, 'The Irish Party System, 1938–51', in Nowlan and Williams (eds), p. 161. The three were Con Lehane, John Tully and Paddy Kinnane; Gregg, p. 64.
138 *IT*, 13/7/48.
139 Rafter, p. 96.
140 Gregg, p. 64.
141 UK PRO, DO/130/93, Rugby note of interview with MacBride, 23/2/48.
142 *IP*, 11/12/69.
143 *IT*, 1/1/79.
144 NAI, Govt 2, 24/2/48.
145 *IT*, 27/2/48.
146 NAI, Govt 5, 5/3/48.
147 For William Whelan and William Corbally, see NAI, Govt 8, 24/3/48; Martin Culligan, see Govt 11, 16/4/48; Patrick Shannon, see Govt 50, 31/12/48; and Patrick Woods and John Logan, see Govt 59, 4/2/49.
148 *DED*, Vol. 50, col. 2237, 28/2/34.
149 *IT*, 10/3/48.
150 NAI, Cab 30, 10/8/48.
151 NAI, S 14380.
152 NAI, S 15059 A, D/J progress report, 18/2/48 to 14/1/49.

153 Bell, p. 249.
154 Ó Broin, 1985, p. 164.
155 *IT*, 2/12/50.
156 *IT*, 6/12/50.
157 *IT*, 7/12/50.
158 *IT*, 9/12/50 – Cogan was already disaffected because of disagreements with Dillon over agricultural policy.
159 *IT*, 12/12/50.
160 *IT*, 13/12/50.
161 *IT*, 14/12/50.
162 Quoted in Earl, p. 130.
163 *IT*, 16/12/50.
164 *IT*, 19/12/50.
165 *IT*, 22/12/50.
166 *IT*, 29/12/50.
167 *IT*, 6/1/51; his successor, Erskine Childers, changed the procedure so that the board presented three names instead of one – Ó Broin, 1985, p. 165.
168 *IT*, 27/1/51.
169 F.S.L. Lyons, 'The Years of Readjustment, 1945–51', in Nowlan and Williams (eds), p. 79.
170 Letter published in *IP*, 16/4/51.
171 Information from Patrick Lynch.
172 *IP*, 27/1/69.
173 Quoted in O'Sullivan, p. 141.
174 John Healy, quoted in Akenson, 1994, p. 135.
175 *IT*, 27/2/48.
176 MacEntee, *IT*, 8/5/48.
177 *IT*, 31/5/48.
178 *IP*, 26/2/48.
179 *IP*, 27/1/69.
180 NAI, S 14518.
181 *IT*, 22/4/49.
182 *IT*, 1/7/49.
183 *IT*, 5/7/49.

THREE: STEALING THE LONG MAN'S CLOTHES

1 *IT*, 15/11/48, quoting Costello's interview with United Press.
2 *IT*, 20/4/49.
3 O'Higgins, pp. 132–3.
4 NAI, S 6412 A, Government decision of 25/6/48.
5 Ibid., letter of 2/7/48 to the Taoiseach from the National Union of Protestants (Hon. Sec. the Rev. Ian Paisley); the statue was taken down on 22 July and put into storage in Kilmainham. Attempts to sell it in Canada foundered on the question of transportation costs.

6 Speaking at Arbour Hill, quoted in Fisk, p. 24.
7 *DED*, Vol. 64, col. 1303, 11/12/36.
8 The text is reprinted in McCabe, p. 158.
9 UK PRO, DO/130/84, Rugby to Machtig, 16/10/47.
10 UK PRO, DO/130/93, Rugby telegram to Secretary of State, 21/2/48.
11 See above, Chapter One, referring to Rugby to Machtig, 28/1/48.
12 *IP*, 6/2/46.
13 Information from Patrick Lynch.
14 *IT*, 4/9/67, John A. Costello remembers – presumably a reference to the repressive Public Safety Act setting up military courts, which was introduced after the murder of Kevin O'Higgins in 1927. See Lee, 1989, p. 154.
15 Harkness, p. 133.
16 UK PRO, DO/130/93, Rugby to Machtig, 27/1/48.
17 *DED*, Vol. 110, col. 25, 18/2/48.
18 UK PRO, DO/130/93, Rugby to Machtig, 18/2/48.
19 Ibid., Rugby telegram to Secretary of State, 21/2/48.
20 *DED*, Vol. 110, cols 27–8, 18/2/48.
21 NAI, S 13760 A, memo by Aindrias Ó Caoimh, 10/10/60.
22 NAI, S 14387 C, note by F.H. Boland, 2/12/48.
23 Text in UCDA, McGilligan Papers, P35/215.
24 Text of speech in ibid.
25 Quoted in McCabe, p. 54.
26 UK PRO, DO/130/89, Home Office note, 9/11/48.
27 This decision was to have far-reaching consequences; the British Cabinet decided in 1951 not to change the Nationality Act in order to prevent immigration from the West Indies, on the grounds that such a move 'would have incalculable consequences for Britain's relations with her colonies and the Commonwealth in general, especially as the by now non-Commonwealth citizens from the Irish Republic would continue to enjoy unrestricted access to the UK'. Hennessy, p. 442.
28 *IT*, 23/4/48.
29 RTÉ Archive Tape A 4184.
30 *IT*, 22/7/48.
31 *IT*, 29/7/48.
32 *IT*, 6/8/48.
33 *DED*, Vol. 112, cols 2440–1, 6/8/48.
34 *DED*, Vol. 112, col. 2426, 6/8/48.
35 *IT*, 8/9/67.
36 RTÉ Archive Tape A 4184.
37 This Week, RTÉ Radio, 27/4/69.
38 See below, Chapter Five.
39 *IT*, 10/7/62.
40 Boland interview with Bruce Arnold, used in RTÉ Archive Tape A 4184.
41 *IT*, 1/1/79.
42 NAI, S 14210 B/1, M/EA memo, 24/7/48.

43 NAI, S 15067, D/EA progress report, 26/9/49.
44 McCabe, p. 33.
45 *IT*, 1/1/79.
46 UK PRO, DO/130/93, Rugby to Machtig, 30/9/48.
47 Ibid., Rugby to Machtig, 21/10/48.
48 Quoted by Harkness, p. 133.
49 *IT*, 5/9/67, John A. Costello remembers.
50 NAI, Cab 32, 19/8/48.
51 Patrick Lynch, 'Pages from a Memoir', in Lynch and Meenan (eds), p. 46.
52 UK PRO, DO/130/93, Rugby to Machtig, 16/8/48.
53 *IT*, 10/7/62.
54 *IT*, 28/8/48.
55 *IT*, 31/8/48.
56 *IT*, 8/9/67.
57 UK PRO, DO/130/93, Rugby to Machtig, 1/12/48.
58 *IT*, 8/9/67.
59 Patrick Lynch, 'Pages from a Memoir', in Lynch and Meenan (eds), p. 52.
60 *IT*, 10/7/62.
61 UK PRO, DO/130/94, Rugby to Machtig, 21/12/48.
62 Both letters quoted by Patrick Lynch, 'Pages from a Memoir', in Lynch and Meenan (eds), p. 51.
63 NAI, S 14387 A, extract of speech.
64 Quoted in Keogh, 1994, p. 189, based on Boland manuscript.
65 Patrick Lynch, 'Pages from a Memoir', in Lynch and Meenan (eds), p. 50.
66 Information from Risteárd Mulcahy.
67 *IT*, 8/9/67, John A. Costello remembers.
68 Costello's view recorded by Nicholas Mansergh in a note of a conversation with him in February 1952; reprinted in Mansergh (ed.), 1997, p. 187.
69 Letter to *IT*, 1/1/92.
70 Information from Louie O'Brien.
71 McCabe, p. 38, based on an interview with MacBride.
72 UK PRO, DO/130/93, Rugby to Machtig, 7/9/48.
73 This Week, RTÉ Radio, 27/4/69.
74 Patrick Lynch, 'Pages from a Memoir', in Lynch and Meenan (eds), p. 54.
75 Information from Patrick Lynch.
76 Information from Louie O'Brien.
77 *II*, 8/9/49.
78 Information from Patrick Lynch.
79 *II*, 8/9/49.
80 Information from Patrick Lynch.
81 Boland manuscript, quoted in Keogh, 1994, p. 190.
82 Ibid.
83 Ibid.; see also Lord Rugby in *IT*, 10/7/62.
84 *IT*, 4/7/62, Lord Rugby remembers.
85 *IT*, 1/1/79.

86 UK PRO, DO/130/93, Rugby telegram to Secretary of State, 9/9/48.
87 Attlee, p. 190.
88 UK PRO, DO/130/93, Rugby to Machtig, 30/9/48.
89 UK PRO, DO/130/94, Rugby to Machtig, 21/12/48.
90 UK PRO, DO/130/93, Rugby to Machtig, 9/8/48, containing record of meeting, 5/8/48.
91 NAI, S 14387 E, H.J. Dowd to Moynihan, 22/7/57.
92 Browne, p. 129.
93 The letter, which was dated 11/9/48, was reprinted in the *Irish Times* on 3/1/79. Mackenzie King retired as Prime Minister in November.
94 NAI, S 9429 B, M/EA memo and draft Bill, both dated 9/9/48.
95 NAI, S 14387 A, Form A (Certificate of Urgency), 9/9/48.
96 NAI, Cab 35, 9/9/48.
97 Information from Patrick Lynch.
98 *IT*, 2/10/48.
99 Browne indicated the meeting was held on a Sunday, but added that it was the evening of the day Costello received the British *aide-mémoire* (discussed below), which was Thursday, 7 October. See Browne, p. 130.
100 Browne, p. 130.
101 RTÉ Archive Tape A 4184.
102 McCabe, p. 55, based on S 14331.
103 NAI, S 14470 A, note by Nolan.
104 UK PRO, DO/130/93, Rugby telegram to Secretary of State, 7/10/48 – the private member was presumably Captain Cowan.
105 Ibid., Rugby telegram to Secretary of State, 15/10/48.
106 NAI, Cab 38, 11/10/48.
107 NAI, S 14387 A, for the British *aide-mémoire*, which is undated, unsigned and on unheaded notepaper. Most favoured nation clauses committed the British to give the same trade rights to a number of foreign countries. If Ireland left the Commonwealth, these countries could in theory demand the same access to British markets.
108 NAI, Cab 38, 11/10/48.
109 NAI, S 14387 A, Attlee to Costello, 14/10/48.
110 Ibid., draft reply to British invitation.
111 Ibid., Costello to Attlee, 15/10/48.
112 Quoted in McCabe, p. 58.
113 Fanning, 1981, gives a full account of the meeting, based on records in UK PRO, CAB 129/30/147–149.
114 *IT*, 1/1/79.
115 UK PRO, DO/130/93, Pritchard to Archer (CRO).
116 NAI, Cab 41, 20/10/48.
117 *II*, 21/10/48.
118 *IT*, 22/10/48.
119 *IT*, 27/10/48.
120 *IT*, 23/10/48.

121 *IT*, 26/10/48.

122 Ibid.

123 UK PRO, DO/130/93, Rugby to Machtig, 26/10/48.

124 *IT*, 26/10/48.

125 *IT*, 9/11/48.

126 FitzGerald, p. 45.

127 NAI, S 14387 A, draft Bill, 30/10/48.

128 NAI, S 14387 B, Moynihan note, 8/11/48.

129 Ibid., M/EA submission to government, 8/11/48.

130 Ibid., for Costello's copy of the Bill, complete with largely incomprehensible notes. The phrase 'description' was used to avoid clashing with the constitution, which says the 'name' of the state is Ireland or Éire. However, despite this legal footwork, it could be argued that the government's action was unconstitutional, a view held by a later Attorney General. See NAI, S 14387 E, note by Aindrias Ó Caoimh, 2/5/59.

131 NAI, Cab 46, 9/11/48.

132 NAI, S 14387 E, memo by Aindrias Ó Caoimh, 2/6/59, detailing the sequence of events.

133 UK PRO, DO/130/93.

134 Ibid., summary of events from 13 to 18 November, marked 'Secret'.

135 NAI, Cab 48, 14/11/48.

136 *IT*, 1/1/79.

137 UK PRO, DO/130/93, summary of events.

138 Ibid., Secretary of State telegram to Rugby, 18/10/48.

139 *IT*, 1/1/79.

140 Fanning, 1981, p. 103, quoting CAB 128/13/143–144.

141 UK PRO, DO/130/93, Machtig telegram to Rugby, 19/11/48.

142 NAI, S 14387 B, note by Nolan, 15/11/48.

143 Browne, p. 133. MacBride was at a banquet in Chicago organised by the Irish Fellowship Club when the Act came into force – NAI, S 15067 A, D/EA progress report, 9/6/49.

144 Patrick Lynch, 'Pages from a Memoir', in Lynch and Meenan (eds), p. 62.

145 *IT*, 18/11/48.

146 *IT*, 25/11/48.

147 UK PRO, DO/130/93, Rugby to Machtig, 25/11/48.

148 *IT*, 25/11/48.

149 Ibid.

150 *IT*, 26/11/48.

151 Ibid.

152 *IT*, 27/11/48.

153 *IT*, 3/12/48.

154 *IT*, 16/12/48.

155 *IT*, 22/12/48.

156 Quoted in *IP*, 2/1/79.

157 NAI, S 14387 D, M/EA memo for government, 2/3/49.

158 Quoted in McCabe, p. 130.
159 NAI, Cab 81, 5/4/49.
160 *IT*, 13/4/49.
161 *IT*, 18/4/49.
162 *IT*, 19/4/49.
163 NAI, S 2818.
164 *IT*, 20/4/49.
165 Burridge, p. 288.
166 *IT*, 28/4/49.
167 Hennessy, p. 237 – Peter Fraser of New Zealand was the most opposed to the idea, as he felt it could lead to the break-up of the Commonwealth, but eventually agreed.
168 Churchill's views quoted in letter of Attlee to the King, reprinted in Williams, p. 218.
169 Attlee, p. 186 – an interesting contrast to de Valera in 1922.
170 Ibid., p. 187. In fact, de Valera said in private that if he had been in office, he 'would have striven' for the Indian solution, i.e. a republic within the Commonwealth. Note by Nicholas Mansergh of a conversation with de Valera in February 1952; Mansergh (ed.), 1997, p. 185.
171 Thomas Davis lecture, first broadcast 1966, reprinted in Mansergh (ed.), 1997, p. 101.
172 *IT*, 31/5/49.
173 Quoted in McEvoy, p. 522.
174 *IT*, 26/1/50.
175 NAI, S 5669 B, M/EA memo for government, 16/5/50.
176 *IT*, 27/7/50.
177 NAI, S 15067 A, D/EA progress report, 30/9/50.
178 *IT*, 29/10/48.
179 PRONI, CAB 4/769/11, Cabinet conclusions, 25/11/48.
180 PRONI, CAB 4/773/5, memo by Permanent Secretary, 20/12/48.
181 PRONI, CAB 4/773/6, Cabinet conclusions, 23/12/48.
182 *Belfast News Letter*, 4/2/48.
183 Harris, pp. 3 and 42.
184 *Belfast News Letter*, 21/2/48, reporting Brooke's speech to the Ulster Unionist Council – apart from any other considerations, dominion status would have meant financial ruin.
185 Burridge, p. 323.
186 NAI, Cab 59, 7/1/49.
187 McCabe, p. 127, quoting note of meeting.
188 PRONI, CAB 4/776/5, Cabinet conclusions, 19/1/49.
189 PRONI, CAB 9B/267/6, extract from Hansard, 8/2/49.
190 Ibid., Ross to Brooke, 17/2/49.
191 Ibid., McWilliam to Ross, 18/2/49.
192 Ibid., Brooke to Attlee, 18/2/49.
193 Ibid., Attlee to Brooke, 21/3/49.

194 Ibid., Brooke to Attlee, 30/3/49.
195 *Daily Express*, 31/7/48.
196 UK PRO, DO/130/92, James to Pritchard, 20/8/48.
197 Ibid., Pritchard to Maclennan, 27/11/48.
198 *SED*, Vol. 36, col. 325, 15/12/48.
199 UK PRO, DO/130/92, Rugby to Machtig, 13/12/48.
200 NAI, S 10467 B, M/EA memorandum on the description of the state, 12/9/49.
201 Ibid., Moynihan to Leo McCauley, 23/9/49.
202 *IT*, 2/5/49.
203 UK PRO, DO/130/99, Rugby to Liesching, 2/5/49.
204 *IT*, 4/5/49.
205 Ibid.
206 *IT*, 6/5/49.
207 NAI, Cab 90, 7/5/49.
208 *IT*, 9/5/49.
209 McCabe, p. 195.
210 *IT*, 10/5/49.
211 *IT*, 14/5/49.
212 UK PRO, DO/130/100, Pritchard to Maclennan, 19/5/49.
213 *IT*, 11/5/49.
214 Quoted in McCabe, p. 139.
215 Information from Patrick Lynch.
216 UK PRO, DO/130/99, Laithwaite to CRO, 19/5/49 – this note was circulated to the Cabinet, and later printed and distributed to UK high commissioners abroad.
217 *IT*, 12/5/49.
218 *IT*, 23/5/49.
219 *IT*, 26/5/49.
220 Ibid.

FOUR: A SUPERFICIAL SUAVITY

1 Quoted in Gray, p. 147.
 2 NAI, S 15067 A, D/EA progress report, 14/1/49.
 3 *IT*, 10/3/48.
 4 *IT*, 11/3/48 – it should be noted that Truman was unable to find the time to meet either Costello or Brooke on their tours of the US.
 5 Ibid.
 6 *IT*, 17/3/48.
 7 *IT*, 18/3/48.
 8 *IT*, 20/3/48.
 9 *IT*, 8/4/48.
10 *IT*, 30/4/48.

11 *IT*, 25/5/48.
12 *IT*, 4/6/48.
13 PRONI, CAB 9F/123/11, note of meeting, 29/4/48.
14 *IT*, 24/7/48.
15 *IT*, 31/7/48.
16 *IT*, 11/8/48.
17 McCabe, p. 36, based on an interview with Browne.
18 RTÉ Archive Tape A 4184.
19 *IT*, 16/8/48.
20 Cole, p. 11.
21 Ibid., p. 10.
22 *IT*, 21/8/48.
23 Attlee, p. 160.
24 Ibid., p. 459.
25 PRONI, CAB 9B/201/5, minutes of Publicity Committee, 30/7/48.
26 Ibid., Northwood to Adams, 28/7/48.
27 See above, Chapter Three.
28 NAI, Cab 94, 20/5/49.
29 *IT*, 17/6/49.
30 *IT*, 27/6/49.
31 Douglas Gageby, 'The Media, 1945–70', in Lee (ed.), 1979, p. 130 – Gageby was editorial chief of the agency until he became editor of the new *Evening Press* in 1954.
32 Akenson, 1994, p. 137.
33 *IT*, 24/1/51.
34 PRONI, CAB 9CD/286/2, note of meeting, 30/1/51.
35 Ibid., Attlee to Brooke, 1/2/51.
36 *IT*, 14/2/49.
37 NAI, S 2910 A.
38 Ibid.
39 *IP*, 4/1/81.
40 *IP*, 18/1/87.
41 Michael Farrell, 'The extraordinary life and times of Seán MacBride', *Magill*, January 1983, p. 31.
42 *IT*, 6/10/48.
43 *IT*, 21/1/49.
44 *IT*, 25/1/49.
45 *IT*, 26/1/49.
46 NAI, S 9361, M/EA memo for government.
47 *IT*, 28/1/49.
48 *IT*, 29/1/49.
49 *IT*, 31/1/49.
50 *IT*, 3/2/49.
51 *IT*, 4/2/49.
52 Cornelius O'Leary, 'Northern Ireland, 1945–72', in Lee (ed.), 1979, p. 156.

53 Terry Cradden, 'The Trade Union Movement in Northern Ireland', in Nevin (ed.), p. 77.
54 NAI, Cab 76, 15/3/49.
55 *IT*, 11/4/49.
56 *IT*, 24/10/49.
57 McCabe, p. 148.
58 NAI, S 15067 A, D/EA progress report, 31/3/50.
59 *IT*, 31/10/49.
60 *IT*, 17/2/50.
61 NAI, Cab 155, 21/2/50.
62 *IT*, 17/2/50.
63 *IT*, 25/5/50.
64 Ibid.
65 *IT*, 1/11/50.
66 T. Ryle Dwyer, 'Eamon de Valera and the Partition Question', in O'Carroll and Murphy (eds), p. 88.
67 *IT*, 6/5/49.
68 *IT*, 8/3/48.
69 *IT*, 15/3/48.
70 PRONI, CAB 9F/140/28, Maginess memo, 23/5/49.
71 Ibid., Cabinet conclusions, 25/5/49.
72 *IT*, 18/9/49.
73 PRONI, CAB 9F/140/28, McCleery memo, 9/8/50; see also Pope to McCleery, 5 and 10/12/49; Brooke to McWilliam, 9/2/50; and memo on Attorney General's view, 15/8/50.
74 *IT*, 22/4/50.
75 PRONI, CAB 9F/140/28, summary of report, 2/5/50.
76 Ibid., McCleery memo, 20/5/50.
77 Ibid., Cabinet conclusions, 25/5/50.
78 *IT*, 23/8/50.
79 PRONI, CAB 9F/140/28, minute of meeting, 30/5/50.
80 Ibid., Cabinet conclusions, 14/8/50.
81 *IT*, 23/8/50.
82 PRONI, CAB 9F/140/28, McWilliam to Brooke, outlining McCleery's initial report, 23/8/50.
83 PRONI, CAB 9F/140/29, McCleery's report of meeting, 17/11/50.
84 Ibid., Cabinet conclusions, 23/11/50.
85 NAI, Cab 223, 24/11/50.
86 PRONI, CAB 9F/140/29, Cabinet conclusions, 28/11/50.
87 Ibid., Cosgrave to McCleery, 2/12/50.
88 Ibid., note of meeting, 11/12/50; Cosgrave to McCleery, 16/12/50; McCleery to Cosgrave, 19/12/50.
89 See ibid.
90 *IT*, 6/1/51.
91 *IT*, 9/1/51.

92 PRONI, CAB 9F/140/29, record of meetings, 8 and 9/1/51.
93 NAI, Cab 234, 9/1/51.
94 PRONI, CAB 9F/140/29, Cabinet conclusions, 8/3/51.
95 PRONI, CAB 9A/37/18, see draft speech, 28/1/49.
96 *IT*, 9/5/50.
97 *IT*, 17/5/50.
98 *IT*, 10/7/50.
99 NAI, S 14414 A, Curran to Lavery, 4/4/49.
100 NAI, Cab 139, 6/12/49.
101 NAI, S 14414 A, secret memo of 10/6/50.
102 NAI, Cab 189, 4/7/50.
103 McCabe, pp. 125–6.
104 Ibid., p. 167, quoting Lords of the Admiralty to the Under Secretary of State at the Home Office, 22/6/50.
105 Ibid., p. 129.
106 *IT*, 7/2/51.
107 *IT*, 22/5/51.
108 NAI, S 6390 A, for copy of memo.
109 *IT*, 8/3/48.
110 Information from Louie O'Brien.
111 *IT*, 15/2/49.
112 *IT*, 16/2/49.
113 *DED*, Vol. 114, cols 313–14, 23/2/49.
114 NAI, S 6390 A, Iremonger to Moynihan, 19/3/49.
115 *IP*, 4/3/49.
116 NAI, S 6390 A, M/EA memo to government, 9/3/49.
117 Ibid., Conlon to Costello.
118 *DED*, Vol. 117, cols 1 and 2, 5/7/49.
119 NAI, S 6390 A, MacBride memo, 20/5/50.
120 Ibid. – there is a note on file indicating that the withdrawal was not to be communicated, presumably so as not to draw MacBride's attention to it.
121 *DED*, Vol. 122, col. 407, 4/7/50.
122 NAI, S 6390 A, memo on meeting, 31/7/50.
123 Ibid., Costello to McNally, 13/9/50.
124 *IT*, 26/10/50.
125 *IT*, 8/12/50.
126 *IT*, 16/12/50.
127 NAI, S 6390 A, McNally to Costello, 26/2/51.
128 Ibid., Moynihan memo, 27/2/51.
129 *IT*, 2/3/51.
130 NAI, S 6390 A, both letters are dated 4/5/51.
131 *IP*, 6/6/49 for ard fheis report.
132 *IP*, 4/2/50.
133 *IT*, 16/5/50.
134 NAI, S 14850, note by Nolan.

135 Ibid., text of Dáil question received 21/6/50.
136 Ibid., draft reply, 26/6/50.
137 Ibid., reply approved on 27/6/50.
138 *IT*, 28/6/50.
139 *IT*, 7/7/50.
140 *IT*, 12/7/50.
141 *IT*, 15/11/50.
142 *IT*, 16/2/49.
143 *IT*, 13/7/50.
144 NAI, S 15067 A, D/EA progress report, 29/4/49.
145 Ibid., 24/10/49.
146 Ibid., 30/9/50 and 31/3/51.
147 Keatinge, 1973, p. 309.
148 Information from Louie O'Brien.
149 Inglis described his accent as 'excruciating', and claimed that it irritated
    French and non-French speakers alike; p. 174.
150 NAI, Cab 67, 8/2/49.
151 *IT*, 4/5/49.
152 *IT*, 10/8/49.
153 *IT*, 11/8/49.
154 *IT*, 13/8/49.
155 *IT*, 15/8/49.
156 *IT*, 17/8/49.
157 UK PRO, DO/130/99, Laithwaite note of discussion with MacBride,
    19/8/49.
158 *IT*, 1/9/49.
159 *IT*, 18/8/49.
160 Ibid.
161 Ibid.
162 *IT*, 20/8/49.
163 *IT*, 12/8/50.
164 *SP*, 14/8/50.
165 O'Higgins, pp. 144–5.
166 *IT*, 15/3/48.
167 *IT*, 17/3/48.
168 *IT*, 14/9/49.
169 UK PRO, DO/130/84, record of conversation between de Valera and
    Noel-Baker, 4/11/47.
170 *IT*, 21/7/48.
171 *IT*, 2/5/49.
172 *IT*, 6/7/50.
173 *IT*, 11/9/50.
174 *DED*, Vol. 102, col. 1374, 24/7/46.
175 NAI, S 14291 Λ/1, Belton to Secretary, D/EA, 8/4/48.
176 McCabe, p. 31, quoting Hickerson to Garrett, 4/5/48, National Archives,
    Washington, 841D.00/3–2448.

177 Based on ibid., p. 106.
178 Ibid., p. 107.
179 Ibid., p. 64, quoting decision of 28/10/48.
180 Fanning, 1981, p. 111, quoting Cab 128/13/2A–3A.
181 Keogh, 1994, p. 193, quoting Boland manuscript.
182 Garrett to Washington, 21/1/49, quoted in Cronin, p. 229.
183 Garrett to Washington, 26/1/49, quoted in ibid., p. 232.
184 Quoted in McCabe, p. 108
185 NAI, Cab 67, 8/2/49.
186 Keogh, 1994, p. 193.
187 Fisk, Chapter Six.
188 NAI, S 14291 A, D/EA memorandum for the Taoiseach, quoted in McCabe, p. 109.
189 Hickerson to Garrett, 10/1/49, quoted in Cronin, p. 227.
190 Keogh, 1994, p. 194, based on *Foreign Relations of the United States*, 1949, Vol. IV.
191 Keatinge, 1978, p. 112.
192 CIA report, 'Ireland', dated 1/4/49, quoted in Cronin, p. 254.
193 *IT*, 30/3/49.
194 *IT*, 5/4/49.
195 *IT*, 9/3/50.
196 PRONI, CAB 9F/123/27, William Simpson to Brooke, 10/6/49.
197 *IT*, 7 and 8/4/50.
198 PRONI, CAB 9F/123/27, Gransden to Hill, 9/2/50.
199 *IT*, 10/4/50.
200 *IT*, 12/4/50.
201 *IT*, 18/5/50.
202 *IT*, 24/6/50.
203 Quoted in Fanning, 1979, p. 39.
204 McQuillan on RTÉ Archive Tape A 4184.
205 Quoted in Fanning, 1979, pp. 41–2.
206 Quoted in ibid., pp. 42–3.
207 *IT*, 9/10/50.
208 *IT*, 19/3/51.
209 *IT*, 15/3/51.
210 *IP*, 20/3/51.
211 NAI, S 9361, Moynihan minute, 22/3/51.
212 Information from Liam Cosgrave.
213 Geoffrey Troy memorandum of conversation with William Christiansen, US Press Attaché, 2/4/51, quoted in Cronin, p. 279.
214 Acheson memo of meeting, quoted in Fanning, 1979, p. 45.
215 *IT*, 23 and 24/3/51.
216 Bowman, p. 275.

FIVE: THE COURSE OF LEAST DISADVANTAGE

1 *DED*, Vol. 110, col. 253, 9/3/48.
2 *DED*, Vol. 143, cols 769–80, 26/11/52.
3 Patrick Lynch, 'The Irish Economy Since the War, 1946–51', in Nowlan and Williams (eds), p. 187.
4 *DED*, Vol. 124, col. 1163, 6/3/51.
5 Information from Patrick Lynch; McGilligan managed to prevent this matter being raised at Cabinet.
6 Ó Broin, 1982, p. 99 – McGilligan, then private secretary to Kevin O'Higgins, introduced Brennan to Collins.
7 NAI, S 14261, Costello to each minister, 3/3/48.
8 NAI, Cab 2, 24/2/48.
9 *IT*, 6/3/48 – these Estimates were circulated by the new government with a note disclaiming any responsibility for them.
10 *IT*, 5/5/48.
11 Ibid.
12 NAI, S 14261, for McGilligan's memo of 15/4/48; the decisions are in Cab 15, 14/5/48.
13 NAI, S 14261, Costello to each minister, 12/6/48.
14 Ibid., M/F memo for government, 6/7/48.
15 UCDA, McGilligan Papers, P35/a/57, D/D memo.
16 UCDA, McGilligan Papers, P35/a/59, McElligott to McGilligan, 3/11/48.
17 UCDA, McGilligan Papers, P35/a/61, memorandum for government, 11/12/48.
18 *IT*, 14/3/49.
19 UCDA, McGilligan Papers, P35/a/82, McElligott to McGilligan, 1/5/49.
20 NAI, S 14464, D/F circular 25/49, 12/10/49.
21 UCDA, McGilligan Papers, P35/a/77, McElligott to McGilligan, 24/2/49. Emphasis added.
22 UCDA, McGilligan Papers, P35/a/86, McElligott to McGilligan, 9/9/49.
23 UCDA, McGilligan Papers, P35/a/104, McElligott to McGilligan, 26/1/50. Emphasis added.
24 Information from T.K. Whitaker.
25 *IT*, 12/3/48.
26 *IT*, 3/3/49.
27 *IT*, 9/9/50.
28 Whelan, p. 65. Marshall Aid funds made up 49.5 per cent of the state's £81.8 million capital spending in this period.
29 Information from Patrick Lynch.
30 Information from T.K. Whitaker.
31 Lee, 1989, p. 312.
32 Central Bank report for year ended 31/3/49, p. 17.
33 Moynihan, p. 352.

34 Ibid., p. 341.
35 NAI, Govt 131, 31/1/50.
36 Fanning, 1978, p. 455, quoting MacBride to Costello, 30/1/50.
37 Ó Broin, 1982, p. 159.
38 Central Bank report for year ended 31/3/50, pp. 12–13.
39 UCDA, McGilligan Papers, P35/a/110, Brennan to McGilligan, 11/1/50.
40 Ibid., McGilligan to Brennan, January 1950.
41 Ibid., Dillon memorandum, undated.
42 *IT*, 21/11/49.
43 Patrick Lynch, 'Pages from a Memoir', in Lynch and Meenan (eds), p. 36.
44 Ibid., p. 37.
45 Fanning, 1978, pp. 457–8.
46 Girvin, p. 170.
47 Information from T.K. Whitaker.
48 Information from Patrick Lynch.
49 Information from T.K. Whitaker.
50 Whitaker, 1983, p. 84.
51 Ibid., p. 288.
52 Information from Patrick Lynch.
53 NAI, S 14106, M/EA memo for government, 23/8/50.
54 *IT*, 4/5/50.
55 O'Hagan, p. 31.
56 Based on O'Hagan, Table 1, p. 19, and Table 3, p. 22.
57 See Whitaker, 1983, p. 86.
58 NAI, S 15065, calculated from figures in various D/P&T progress reports.
59 NAI, Cab 29, 30/7/48.
60 NAI, Cab 72, 25/2/49.
61 NAI, S 14478 A, various memos from M/F.
62 NAI, S 15066, D/L progress reports.
63 *IT*, 12/3/49.
64 NAI, S 15058 A, D/LG progress reports.
65 Kennedy and Dowling, p. 172.
66 NAI, S 13059 C, D/F view quoted in M/LG memo to government, 21/10/49.
67 IBEC report, quoted in Rumpf and Hepburn, p. 128.
68 Kennedy, Giblin and McHugh, p. 58.
69 Kennedy and Dowling, pp. 208–10. However, see the views of T.K. Whitaker, quoted above, suggesting that without Marshall Aid the state had no source of funding to continue such a policy.
70 Whitaker, 1983, p. 164.
71 Quoted in Bew, Hazelkorn and Patterson, p. 83.
72 *IT*, 13/4/50.
73 Dunphy, p. 234.
74 Horgan, p. 354.

75 Quoted in John F. McCarthy, 'Ireland's Turnaround: Whitaker and the 1958 Plan for Economic Development', in McCarthy (ed.), p. 27.
76 NAI, Cab 14, 7/5/48.
77 NAI, S 15061 A, D/F progress report, 30/6/51.
78 NAI, S 14106 B, M/EA memo to government, 9/5/48.
79 Ibid., M/A memo, 12/5/48.
80 NAI, S 15061 A, calculated from D/F progress report, 30/6/50.
81 *IT*, 7/5/48.
82 NAI, S 14106 B, M/EA memo, 9/5/48.
83 *IT*, 19/5/48.
84 *IT*, 20/5/48.
85 Cronin, p. 197, quoting Hickerson to Secretary of State, 20/5/48.
86 Brian Girvin, 'Ireland and the Marshall Plan', in Griffiths (ed.), p. 67.
87 Ibid.
88 NAI, S 13831 A, M/F memo, 22/4/48.
89 NAI, S 14106 C, M/F memo, 8/6/48.
90 Ibid., M/EA memo, 8/6/48.
91 NAI, S 14106 G/1, D/F memo, 8/6/50.
92 NAI, Cab 19, 11/6/48.
93 NAI, Cab 20, 25/6/48.
94 Fanning, 1978, p. 427.
95 Whelan, p. 60.
96 *IT*, 20/7/48.
97 NAI, S 14106 C, D/EA memo, 30/7/48.
98 Ibid., M/F memo, 27/9/48.
99 Ibid., note of meeting, 22/10/48.
100 NAI, schedule attached to Cab 55, 17/12/48.
101 *IT*, 29/12/48.
102 Quoted in Coogan, p. 660.
103 J.J. Lee, 'Economic Development in Historical Perspective', in McCarthy (ed.), p. 116.
104 John F. McCarthy, 'Ireland's Turnaround: Whitaker and the 1958 Plan for Economic Development', in McCarthy (ed.), p. 21.
105 Information from T.K. Whitaker.
106 NAI, S 14106 E, progress report, 21/2/49, recording meeting between Costello, MacBride and McGilligan on 5 February, and Cabinet meeting of 8 February; the report noted that the Cabinet's decision was not formally recorded.
107 NAI, S 15061 A, D/F progress report, 31/3/49.
108 NAI, Cab 142, 16/12/49.
109 NAI, S 14106 G/1, M/F memo, 8/6/50.
110 Ibid., M/EA memo, 10/7/50.
111 NAI, Cab 194, 18/7/50; see below.
112 *IT*, 14/7/50.
113 NAI, S 14106 G/1, Miller to Costello, 30/11/50.

114 *IT*, 14/12/50.
115 NAI, S 14106 G/1, M/EA memo, 28/12/50.
116 NAI, S 14106 G/2, MacBride to Miller, 23/1/51.
117 NAI, S 15067 B, D/EA progress report, 31/3/51; the *aide-mémoire* is in S 14106 G/2.
118 *IT*, 3/5/51.
119 NAI, S 15061 A, D/F progress report, 30/6/51.
120 See, for example, John F. McCarthy, 'Ireland's Turnaround: Whitaker and the 1958 Plan for Economic Development', in McCarthy (ed.), p. 20.
121 *IT*, 3/1/49.
122 *IT*, 23/2/48.
123 NAI, S 15062 A, D/A progress report, 17/1/49.
124 *IT*, 19/3/48.
125 *IT*, 17/6/48.
126 *IT*, 23/6/48.
127 *IT*, 24/6/48.
128 *II*, 5/5/69.
129 *IT*, 4 and 11/4/49.
130 See NAI, S 15067 A, D/EA progress report, 31/3/51.
131 *IT*, 22/2/49.
132 NAI, Cab 70, 22/2/49.
133 UCDA, Mulcahy Papers, P7/c/106, report by New Zealand expert G.A. Holmes on Irish pasture land.
134 *IT*, 12/4/49.
135 NAI, S 6614 B, contains all statistics.
136 *IT* editorial, 2/6/51.
137 Ó hEithir, p. 121.
138 Daly, p. 162. See also Kieran Kennedy, 'The Context of Economic Development', in Goldthorpe and Whelan (eds).
139 *IT*, 7/6/48.
140 *IT*, 6/9/48 and 26/11/49.
141 *IT*, 23/7/49.
142 *IT*, 12/8/49.
143 *IT*, 1/6/49.
144 *IT*, 8/6/49.
145 NAI, S 5472 B, M/I&C memo for government, 17/10/49.
146 Ibid., Moynihan to Private Secretary, M/I&C.
147 NAI, S 14106 F/1, M/EA memo, 11/11/49, containing extract of a letter from Hugh McCann, Counsellor of the Irish Legation in Washington.
148 NAI, S 14106 G/1, Carrigan to MacBride, 7/12/49.
149 Ibid., M/EA memo, 4/5/50.
150 NAI, Cab 174, 9/5/50; see also D/F memo, 8/5/50, in S 14106 G/1.
151 *IT*, 8/6/50.
152 NAI, S 14708, minutes of meeting, 29/3/50.
153 Coogan, p. 660.

154 NAI, S 14061 G/1, M/EA memo, 9/5/50.
155 Ibid., M/A memo, 11/5/50.
156 Ibid., M/EA memo on conversation with Pozzy, 27/7/50.
157 *IT*, 30/8/50.
158 NAI, S 8814 C, minutes of meeting, 14/9/49.
159 Ibid., M/I&C memo to government, 20/10/49.
160 Ibid., MacBride to Garrett, 13/1/50.
161 Ibid., Garrett to MacBride, 17/2/50.
162 Ibid., M/I&C memo, 13/3/50.
163 Ibid., MacBride memo, 13/7/50.
164 Ibid., M/F and M/I&C memos of 17/7/50.
165 *IT*, 3/10/50.
166 NAI, S 15067 B, D/EA progress report, 31/12/50.
167 Kennedy, p. 319.
168 NAI, S 14617 A, M/F memo, 13/6/49.
169 Ibid., M/EA memo, 23/6/49.
170 Ibid.
171 NAI, S 15061 A, D/F progress report, 31/7/49.
172 NAI, S 14617 A, Attlee to Costello, 17/9/49.
173 NAI, Cab 119, 17–18/9/49 for times of meetings; *IT*, 19/9/49 for reference to Cushing.
174 NAI, S 14617 A, note by Moynihan.
175 The British Cabinet had only (reluctantly) decided to devalue on 29 August, so the Department of Finance were quick off the mark with the new memorandum. See Hennessy, p. 374.
176 NAI, S 14617 A, M/F memo, 3/9/49.
177 Ibid., draft statement.
178 Information from T.K. Whitaker.
179 Fanning, 1978, pp. 448–9.
180 Ibid.
181 Information from T.K. Whitaker.
182 NAI, S 14617 A, M/I&C memo, 24/9/49.
183 Ibid., M/F memo, 24/9/49.
184 Ibid., M/A memo, 27/9/49.
185 Ibid., M/EA memo, 27/9/49.
186 Ibid., M/EA memo, 27/9/49.
187 NAI, Cab 122, 28/9/49.
188 NAI, S 14617 A, AG's opinion, circulated to government on 6/10/49.
189 Ibid., M/I&C memo, 12/10/49.
190 Ibid., M/EA memo, 28/10/49.
191 Ibid., M/A memo, 7/11/49.
192 Ibid., M/I&C memo, 14/11/49.
193 Ibid., note, 18/10/49.
194 Ibid., Moynihan note, 11/2/50.
195 Ibid., Government decision, 4/10/49.

196 NAI, S 14617 B, memo by Whitaker, 25/3/58.
197 *IT*, 18/10/49.
198 *IP*, 19/10/49.
199 Moynihan, p. 361; see above, Chapter Two, for Costello's response.
200 Fanning, 1978, p. 454.
201 Information from Patrick Lynch; see above, Chapter Two.
202 Kennedy and Dowling, p. 35.
203 Whitaker, 1983, p. 86.
204 Patrick Lynch, 'The Irish Economy Since the War, 1946–51', in Nowlan and Williams (eds), p. 196.
205 Kennedy and Dowling, pp. 49–50.
206 See, for example, NAI, S 10959 C, Irish Banks Standing Committee to Costello.
207 Whitaker, 1949, p. 204.
208 *IT*, 20/4/48.
209 NAI, S 10959 C, M/F memo, 30/7/48.
210 NAI, Cab 34, 31/8/48.
211 NAI, S 10959 C, M/I&C memo, 30/9/48.
212 *IT*, 7/10/48.
213 NAI, S 10959 C, M/F memo, 6/10/48.
214 Ibid., note of meeting, 12/11/48.
215 *IT*, 20/1/49, quoting Liam Cosgrave.
216 *IT*, 7/2/49.
217 Ibid.
218 Kennedy and Dowling, p. 203.
219 Ibid., p. 207.
220 Ibid., p. 212.
221 Information from T.K. Whitaker.
222 Patrick Lynch, 'The Irish Economy Since the War', in Nowlan and Williams (eds), p. 194.
223 Ronan Fanning, 'The Genesis of Economic Development', in McCarthy (ed.), p. 118, quoting D/F memo, 31/12/48, in UCDA, McGilligan Papers, P35B/75.
224 NAI, Cab 68, 11/2/49.
225 NAI, S 14474 A, GIB statement, 12/2/49.
226 *IT*, 19/3/49.
227 *IT*, 1/6/49.
228 *IT*, 6/9/49.
229 NAI, Govt 210, 2/3/51.
230 See NAI, S 14474 A.
231 Ibid., M/EA memo for government, 9/11/50.
232 Ibid.
233 Donal Nevin, 'Industry and Labour', in Nowlan and Williams (eds), p. 108.
234 C. Brock, 'Public Policy and Private Industrial Development', in Bristow and Tait (eds), p. 154.

235   Central Bank report for year ended 31/3/51, p. 10.
236   *IT*, 14/10/50
237   *IT*, 27/10/50.
238   Niamh Hardiman, 'Pay Bargaining – Confrontation and Consensus', in Nevin (ed.), p. 150.
239   *IT*, 19/5/50.
240   See Aknefton in *IT*, 28/10/50.
241   NAI, Cab 213, 24/10/50.
242   NAI, S 14280, memo for government, 11/10/50.
243   *IT*, 31/1/51.
244   *IT*, 10/11/50.
245   *IT*, 3/11/50.
246   *IT*, 1 and 4/11/50.
247   NAI, S 14955, PLP resolution, 30/11/50.
248   UCDA, Mulcahy Papers, P7/c/123, for text of speech.
249   *DED*, Vol. 123, cols 1277–8, 23/11/50.
250   *DED*, Vol. 123, cols 1809–10, 6/12/50.
251   *DED*, Vol. 124, col. 1172, 6/3/51.
252   *The Leader*, 25/10/52, profile of Norton.
253   *IT*, 20/12/50.
254   *IT*, 3/1/51.
255   NAI, S 14955, Ó Broin to Moynihan, 3/1/51.
256   *IT*, 8/1/51.
257   *IT*, 22/2/51.
258   Ibid.
259   *IT*, 29/1/51.
260   NAI, S 14955, note of meeting, 2/2/51.
261   *IT*, 3/3/51.
262   *DED*, Vol. 124, col. 1172, 6/3/51.
263   *IT*, 16/6/51.

SIX: A DEFINITE CLEAVAGE OF OPINION

1   *IP*, 2/12/48.
2   *IP*, 1/7/48.
3   *IP*, 24/12/48.
4   NAI, Cab 66, 4/2/49.
5   *IT*, 26/5/50.
6   *IT*, 22/1/48.
7   See NAI, S 13749 C.
8   *IT*, 5/12/49.
9   *IT*, 8/12/49.
10   UCDA, McGilligan Papers, P35/208.
11   *DED*, Vol. 108, col. 20, 8/10/47.

12 *IT*, 11/6/48.
13 NAI, S 13384 A/2, M/SW memo, 10/6/48.
14 Ibid., M/F memo, 12/7/48.
15 NAI, Cab 23, 12/7/48.
16 NAI, Cab 141, 13/12/49.
17 NAI, Cab 145, 13/1/50.
18 NAI, Cab 159, 7/3/50.
19 *IT*, 25/5/50.
20 NAI, Govt 155, 6/6/50.
21 *IT*, 22/7/48.
22 The figures in brackets are decimal equivalents.
23 *IT*, 24/7/48.
24 NAI, S 15069 A, D/SW progress report.
25 *IT*, 30/7/48.
26 *IT*, 6/8/48.
27 NAI, Cab 49, 19/11/48.
28 NAI, S 15069 A, D/SW progress report.
29 *IT*, 18/9/48.
30 *IT*, 19/3/49.
31 *IT*, 24/3/49.
32 *IT*, 26/3/49.
33 *IT*, 5/5/49.
34 *IT*, 3/6/49.
35 NAI, S 13384 B, M/SW memo, 8/6/49.
36 Ibid., M/SW memo, 27/6/49.
37 Ibid., McElligott to O'Donovan, 7/6/49.
38 Ibid., M/SW memo, 10/6/49.
39 Ibid., M/SW memo, 27/6/49.
40 Ibid., M/SW memo, 25/6/49.
41 Ibid., M/A memo, 29/6/49.
42 Ibid., M/A memo, 25/8/49.
43 Ibid., M/A memo, 29/6/49.
44 Ibid., M/EA memo, 24/9/49.
45 UCDA, McGilligan Papers, P35/a/86, McElligott to McGilligan, 9/9/49.
46 See above, Chapter Two.
47 NAI, Cab 112, 27/7/49.
48 *IT*, 29/7/49 – his remarks could also be read as a criticism of Browne's Mother and Child proposals.
49 Aknefton, *IT*, 6/8/49.
50 *IT*, 7/10/50.
51 Browne, p. 191.
52 NAI, S 13384 B, note dated 11/10/49.
53 NAI, Cab 126, 21/10/49.
54 *DED*, Vol. 123, col. 890, 16/11/50.
55 *DED*, Vol. 121, col. 1638, 14/6/50.

56 *DED*, Vol. 119, col. 1581, 9/3/50.
57 Hennessy, p. 130.
58 Ibid., p. 182.
59 *II*, 26/10/49.
60 *IT*, 26/10/49.
61 Ibid.
62 *IT*, 17/12/49.
63 Aknefton, *IT*, 29/10/49.
64 *IT*, 13/12/49.
65 *IT*, 6/2/50.
66 *IT*, 28/2/50.
67 UCDA, Mulcahy Papers, P7/c/123.
68 *IT*, 15/2/50.
69 NAI, S 15069 A, transcript of speech in Newbridge, 12/5/50.
70 Bolster, pp. 95–6.
71 Ibid., pp. 48 and 71.
72 Ibid., p. 14.
73 Ibid., p. 98.
74 NAI, S 13384 C, M/SW memo, 12/5/50.
75 NAI, S 13384 D, M/SW memo, 27/6/50.
76 Ibid., note by Foley, 29/6/50.
77 Ibid., M/D memo, 29/6/50.
78 Ibid., M/F memo, 29/6/50.
79 NAI, Cab 187, 30/6/50.
80 NAI, Cab 193, 14/7/50 – this line-up was extremely unfavourable to Norton, as it contained four Fine Gael members, along with Dillon.
81 NAI, S 13384 D, Moynihan note, 25/9/50.
82 Ibid., Moynihan note, 27/9/50 – the fact remains that the usual procedures had been ignored.
83 Ibid., Moynihan to Private Secretary, M/SW, 5/10/50.
84 Ibid., O'Donovan to Moynihan, 11/10/50.
85 Ibid., D/SW memo, 13/10/50. Emphasis in the original.
86 NAI, Cab 214, 27/10/50.
87 NAI, Cab 225, 1/12/50.
88 NAI, S 13409 B, explanatory memorandum.
89 *IT*, 15/11/50.
90 *IT*, 13/12/50.
91 *II*, 11/12/50.
92 *II*, 6/2/51.
93 *IP*, 10/2/51.
94 *IT*, 8/2/51.
95 *IT*, 12/2/51.
96 *IT*, 21/2/51.
97 *IT*, 26/2/51.
98 NAI, Cab 243, 2/3/51.

 99 *IT*, 3/3/51.
100 *IT*, 5/3/51.
101 *DED*, Vol. 124, col. 1162, 6/3/51.
102 NAI, S 13384 E, petition to government, 7/3/51.
103 *IT*, 19/3/51.
104 *IT*, 22/3/51.
105 *IT*, 12/4/51.
106 NAI, S 13384 E, note of meeting, 14/6/51.
107 Philip O'Connell and David Rottman, 'The Irish Welfare State in Comparative Perspective', in Goldthorpe and Whelan (eds), p. 230.
108 Kaim-Caudle, p. 40.
109 Whyte, p. 274.
110 Ibid.
111 *IT*, 5/5/51.
112 *The Leader*, 9/2/52.

SEVEN: THE CHURCH'S PROPER SPHERE

 1 Deeny, p. 116.
 2 *IP*, 13/4/51.
 3 Browne, p. 82.
 4 Ibid., p. 142.
 5 Lee, 1989, p. 318.
 6 Patrick Lynch, 'Pages from a Memoir', in Lynch and Meenan (eds), p. 41.
 7 Bew, Hazelkorn and Patterson, p. 209.
 8 NAI, S 9469 A, for text of message.
 9 Keogh, 1995, p. 232.
10 NAI, S 9469 A, note by Nolan, 25/2/48.
11 Ibid., Pius XII to Costello, 29/2/48.
12 NAI, D/EA Secretary's files, P 126/1, coded telegram, 7/9/48.
13 Keogh, 1995, p. 252 – a very full account of the controversy is given by Keogh.
14 NAI, D/EA Secretary's files, P 126/1, Walshe to MacBride, 6/9/49.
15 Browne, p. 96.
16 *IT*, 15/7/49. There may have been some confusion about attending the actual service. Nicholas Nolan, in a note for ministers and other senior political figures (dated 13/7/49, in S 9783 A), advised that those wishing 'to attend the funeral should arrive in their cars not later than 9.15 a.m. at St Patrick's Cathedral, where they may remain until the cortege moves off'. It is not clear whether he was referring to the people, or just the cars, remaining in St Patrick's Close.
17 Information from Patrick Lynch.
18 See *IT*, 19 and 20/8/49.
19 *IT*, 10/6/50.

20 See above, Chapter Six.
21 Bolster, p. 94.
22 *IT*, 10/3/48.
23 *IT*, 30/11/50.
24 *IT*, 8/2/51.
25 NAI, S 15067 A, D/EA progress report, 31/12/50.
26 *IT*, 14/2/51.
27 Letter to *IP*, 8/1/83 – it should be noted in this regard that Browne went to a great deal of trouble to try to show that his Mother and Child scheme was *not* contrary to Catholic teaching.
28 *EP*, 4/2/78.
29 Browne accepted this point, referring to the Health Act brought in by his predecessor as 'magnificent'. *IT*, 9/10/67, Noël Browne, a political portrait.
30 Barrington, p. 197.
31 NAI, S 13603 A, M/LG&PH memo, 23/12/44.
32 Ibid., for details of Dáil debate.
33 Deeny, pp. 128–9.
34 *The Leader*, editorial, 28/2/48.
35 Deeny, p. 165.
36 Ibid., p. 166.
37 Browne, p. 110.
38 *IT*, 23/2/48.
39 *IT*, 26/2/48.
40 NAI, S 14293, minutes of meeting of Cabinet Economic Committee, 15/3/48.
41 NAI, S 14298, for Lynch memo.
42 Browne, p. 115.
43 NAI, S 14152 B, M/H memo, 30/12/48.
44 Ibid., M/F memo, 6/1/49.
45 See above, Chapter Two.
46 NAI, S 14152 B, M/H memo, 16/2/49.
47 NAI, S 13831 A, M/F memo, 31/12/48.
48 *IT*, 22/5/48.
49 *IT*, 21/7/48.
50 Deeny, p. 172.
51 Ó hEithir, p. 128.
52 Barrington, p. 198.
53 *IT*, 7/7/48.
54 NAI, S 15068 A, D/H progress report, 15/1/49.
55 Deeny, p. 168.
56 *IT*, 8/11/48.
57 Deeny, p. 169.
58 Ibid., p. 170.
59 Seaman, p. 447.
60 NAI, S 15068 A, D/H progress report, 30/6/50.

61 *IT*, 10/10/67, Noël Browne, a political portrait.
62 *IT*, 5/7/50.
63 NAI, S 15008, Walsh to Browne, 13/11/48.
64 Ibid., Browne to Walsh, 2/12/48.
65 Ibid., MacNeely and Staunton to Costello, 30/6/49.
66 Ibid., Costello to MacNeely and Staunton, 16/9/49.
67 Browne, pp. 111–15.
68 *IT*, 6/4/51.
69 Barrington, p. 224.
70 Ibid., p. 198.
71 Whyte, pp. 130–3.
72 All quoted in ibid., p. 136.
73 McKee, p. 168.
74 Whyte, pp. 137–8.
75 See above, Chapter One.
76 Deeny, pp. 119–20.
77 Ibid., p. 177.
78 Barrington, p. 181.
79 McKee, pp. 172–3.
80 See Barrington, p. 185.
81 Interview on RTÉ Archive Tape A 1519.
82 See Barrington, p. 187.
83 UCDA, Mulcahy Papers, P7/c/122, for text of speech delivered on 19/1/48.
84 *IT*, 15/1/48.
85 Information from Louie O'Brien.
86 *IT*, 6/3/48.
87 *IT*, 8/3/48.
88 NAI, S 13444 G, M/H memo, 16/3/48.
89 *IT*, 20/3/48.
90 NAI, S 13444 G, M/H memo, 9/6/48. Emphasis added.
91 Ibid.
92 NAI, Cab 20, 25/6/48.
93 *IP*, 13/4/51, resignation speech.
94 Browne on RTÉ Archive Tape A 1519.
95 *IP*, 13/4/51, speech on Browne's resignation.
96 NAI, S 13444 G, Moynihan minute for Costello, 27/3/51.
97 Ibid., D/T memo, 2/4/51.
98 See above, Chapter Six.
99 NAI, S 13384 D, M/F memo, 29/6/50.
100 *IT*, 8/10/48.
101 NAI, S 15068 A, D/H progress report, 15/1/49.
102 *IT*, 5/3/49.
103 *IT*, 6/7/49.
104 NAI, S 15068 A, D/H progress report, 31/7/49.
105 *IT*, 8/7/49.

106 *IT*, 6/2/50.
107 *IT*, 6/7/50.
108 *IT*, 12/7/50.
109 *IT*, 13/7/50.
110 Browne gave his version of events in his resignation speech in the Dáil, *IP*, 13/4/51.
111 Browne, p. 162.
112 Costello's reply to Browne in the Dáil, *IP*, 13/4/51.
113 IMA statement quoted in *IT*, 15/11/50.
114 McKee, p. 175.
115 *SP*, 7/12/86, MacBride interview.
116 Information from Louie O'Brien; see above, Chapter Four.
117 Ibid.
118 *SP*, 7/12/86, MacBride interview.
119 Information from Louie O'Brien.
120 *SP*, 7/12/86, MacBride interview.
121 McKee, p. 181, quoting memorandum by MacBride, dated 4/1/51, in McGilligan Papers.
122 *IT*, 3/11/50.
123 *IT*, 14/11/50.
124 *IT*, 18/11/50, questionaire quoted by Aknefton.
125 *IT*, 24/11/50.
126 *IP*, 13/4/51.
127 *IT*, 9/2/51.
128 Barrington, p. 208 and note 61, p. 314.
129 Ibid., p. 209 and note 68, p. 314.
130 *IT*, 12/2/51.
131 *IT*, 13/2/51.
132 *IT*, 15/2/51.
133 *IT*, 16/2/51.
134 *IT*, 19/2/51.
135 *IT*, 21/2/51.
136 Aknefton in *IT*, 3/3/51.
137 *IT*, 6/3/51.
138 *IT*, 7/3/51.
139 *IP*, 13/4/51.
140 Ibid.
141 *IT*, 7/3/51.
142 Ibid.
143 *IT*, 8/3/51.
144 Ibid.
145 *IT*, 9/3/51.
146 *IT*, 12/3/51.
147 Ibid. – the ad seemed to be pitched towards men: 'It may save the life of your family'; another ad two days later stressed what the scheme would bring 'to your wife' and 'to your child', *IT*, 14/3/51.

148 *IT*, 14/3/51.
149 *IP*, 13/4/51.
150 Barrington, p. 212, quoting Costello to Browne, 21/3/51, in NAI, S 14497 A.
151 *IT*, 16/3/51.
152 *IT*, 17/3/51.
153 *IT*, 21/3/51.
154 *IT*, 22/3/51.
155 *IT*, 6/4/51.
156 Alexis Fitzgerald, 'The problem of finance', in *Studies*, Vol. 40 (June 1951), p. 154.
157 Quoted by Cooney, *IT*, 6/4/98.
158 See Barrington, pp. 216–17.
159 McQuaid quoted by Cooney, *IT*, 6/4/98.
160 *IP*, 13/4/51.
161 Information from Louie O'Brien.
162 McKee, p. 185, quoting Moynihan note of 21/3/51 in NAI, S 14997 A.
163 See Barrington, p. 213.
164 NAI, S 13444 G, notes by D/T officials for Costello on 13/2/50, 27/3/51 and 2/4/51.
165 McQuaid quoted by Cooney, *IT*, 6/4/98.
166 NAI, Cab 247, 6/4/51.
167 Browne, p. 177.
168 NAI, S 7870 A.
169 NAI, S 14997.
170 Browne, p. 177.
171 NAI, Cab 247, 6/4/51 – the effect of this was to do away with the 'free' scheme and provide for a means test.
172 McKee, p. 188.
173 Costello interview on RTÉ Archive Tape A 1519.
174 *IT*, 7/4/51.
175 *IT*, 9/4/51.
176 Browne, p. 180.
177 *IT*, 10/4/51.
178 See below, Chapter Eight.
179 *IT*, 11/4/51.
180 NAI, S 14165, Browne to Costello, 11/4/51.
181 Ibid., Costello to Browne, 11/4/51.
182 Costello in Dáil, *IP*, 13/4/51.
183 *IT*, 7/9/67.
184 *IP*, 13/4/51.
185 McKee, p. 189, concludes that the draft was Costello's, both from its contents and from handwritten amendments.
186 Gregg, p. 78, quoting Mulvihill interview.
187 NAI, S 10719 B, note by M. Ó Conaill, 11/4/51.

188 Ibid., memo, 20/4/51.
189 *IT*, 12/4/51.
190 *IP*, 13/4/51.
191 Quoted in *IT*, 11/10/67, Noël Browne, a political portrait.
192 *IT*, 13/4/51.
193 John A. Murphy, 'The Achievement of Eamon de Valera', in O'Carroll and Murphy (eds), p. 8.
194 Alexis Fitzgerald, 'Eamon de Valera', in Lynch and Meenan (eds), p. 220.
195 *IP*, 13/4/51.
196 *IT*, 13/4/51.
197 *Belfast Telegraph*, 14/4/51.
198 *IT*, 20/4/51.
199 *IT*, 1/5/51.
200 *IT*, 4/6/51.
201 *IP*, 27/1/69.
202 *IP*, 8/1/83, Browne letter.
203 Ronan Fanning in *IT*, 13 and 14/2/85, 'Fianna Fáil and the Bishops'.
204 De Valera to Lemass, 9/11/52, quoted in Horgan, p. 151; the Taoiseach was out of the country receiving treatment from an eye specialist.
205 Deeny, p. 189.
206 Browne, p. 150.
207 *IT*, 7/10/91.
208 Information from Patrick Lynch.
209 Bolster, p. 101.
210 Ibid., p. 97.
211 Seven Days Special, RTÉ Television, Tx 24/6/69.
212 Whyte, pp. 260–1.

EIGHT: THE BUSTED FLUSH

1 This Week, RTÉ Radio, 27/4/69.
2 *IT*, 21/5/48.
3 Ó Broin, 1985, p. 163.
4 *IT*, 8/7/49.
5 O'Higgins, p. 138.
6 NAI, Cab 106, 7/7/49.
7 Browne, p. 195.
8 *IT*, 9/7/49.
9 *IT*, 13/7/49.
10 Aknefton in *IT*, 16/7/49.
11 *IT*, 5/7/48.
12 *DED*, Vol. 111, cols 2031–40, 1/7/48, for Cowan's speech. The question was put and agreed without a division.
13 *IT*, 5/7/48.

14   *IT*, 12/7/48.
15   *IT*, 13/7/48.
16   *IT*, 5/7/48.
17   See Chapter Three.
18   See Chapter Four.
19   NAI, S 16584.
20   *IT*, 12/9/49.
21   *IT*, 17/10/49.
22   *IT*, 24/10/49.
23   *IT*, 15/11/49.
24   *IT*, 18/11/49.
25   Aknefton in *IT*, 19/11/49 – Canning had done much better than the
     Clann candidate in the other Donegal by-election, who got just 4 per
     cent of the vote.
26   *IT*, 18/11/49.
27   *IT*, 21/9/50.
28   *IT*, 25/9/50.
29   *IT*, 2/5/51. The elder Esmonde didn't run in 1951 – the seat was retained
     by his brother for Fine Gael.
30   *IT*, 2/12/50.
31   *IT*, 9/12/50; see above, Chapter Two.
32   *IT*, 13/12/50.
33   Ibid.
34   *IT*, 27/3/51.
35   NAI, S 14627 A/1, M/A memos, 2/11/49 and 8/12/50.
36   *IT*, 5/4/51.
37   *IT*, 6/4/51.
38   NAI, S 14627 A/1, D/T memo, 27/4/51.
39   *IT*, 27/4/51.
40   *IT*, 28/4/51.
41   *IT*, 30/4/51.
42   Ibid.
43   *IT*, 1/5/51.
44   *IT*, 2/5/51.
45   NAI, S 15017, D/T minute, 2/5/51.
46   Ibid., Nolan note, 3/5/51.
47   Ibid., Nolan note, 3/5/51.
48   NAI, Govt 218, 3/5/51.
49   *IT*, 3 and 5/5/51.
50   NAI, S 15017, note on file, 4/5/51.
51   *IT*, 7/5/51.
52   Based on figures in *IT*, 18/5/51.
53   Aknefton in *IT*, 19/5/51.
54   *IT*, 7/5/51.

55 *IT*, 8/5/51.
56 *IT*, 7/5/51.
57 *IT*, 16/5/51.
58 *IT*, 14/5/51.
59 *IT*, 9/5/51.
60 *IT*, 7/5/51.
61 Ibid.
62 Ibid.
63 *IT*, 16/5/51.
64 Ibid.
65 *IT*, 22/5/51.
66 UCDA, McGilligan Papers, P35/258, for a selection of election literature.
67 *IT*, 7/5/51.
68 *IT*, 16/5/51.
69 *IT*, 8/5/51.
70 *IT*, 7/5/51.
71 *IT*, 14/5/51.
72 *IT*, 24/5/51.
73 *IT*, 7/5/51.
74 Ibid.
75 *IT*, 9/5/51.
76 *IT*, 14/5/51.
77 *IT*, 19/5/51.
78 See ad in *IT*, 24/5/51.
79 *IT*, 7/5/51.
80 *IT*, 16/5/51.
81 *IT*, 17/5/51.
82 *IT*, 7/5/51.
83 *IT*, 17/5/51.
84 Ibid.
85 Ibid.
86 *IT*, 15/5/51.
87 See ad in *IT*, 26/5/51.
88 *IT*, 23/5/51 – it is perhaps significant of Irish political campaigns at this date that the absence of hecklers was taken to indicate a lack of interest!
89 *IT*, 26/5/51.
90 *IT*, 29/5/51.
91 *IT*, 12/5/51.
92 *IT*, 29/5/51.
93 *IT*, 29 and 30/5/51.
94 *IP*, 27/1/69.
95 Gallagher, 1976, p. 55.
96 All calculated from figures in Walker (ed.).
97 Gallagher, 1976, p. 57.
98 O'Leary, p. 42.

99 Ibid, p. 103.
100 NAI, Govt 221, 1/6/51.
101 *IT*, 2/6/51.
102 *IT*, 4/6/51.
103 Ibid.
104 *IT*, 12/6/51.
105 UCDA, Mulcahy Papers, P7/c/106, MacBride to Costello, 7/6/51.
106 *IP*, 11/12/69.
107 *IT*, 2/6/51.
108 *IT*, 13/6/51.
109 O'Sullivan, p. 124, quoting Lemass to Harrison, 4/6/51.
110 *IT*, 5/6/51.
111 Browne, p. 210.
112 *IT*, 5/6/51.
113 *IT*, 9/6/51.
114 *IT*, 8/6/51 – one wonders if he had himself in mind!
115 *IT*, 13/6/51.
116 *IT*, 14/6/51, quoting O'Higgins in the Dáil.
117 *IT*, 20/6/51.
118 NAI, S 14470 A, note of meeting.
119 NAI, S 10719 A, note on the change of government.
120 *IT*, 14/6/51.
121 Ibid., Dáil report.
122 *IT*, 19/6/51.
123 *IT*, 28/6/51.
124 *IT*, 18/6/51.
125 Costello speaking on This Week, RTÉ Radio, 11/2/73.

CONCLUSION

1 This Week, RTÉ Radio, 11/2/73.
2 Costello was later to say that Mulcahy 'was quietly efficient and never intruded that he was leader of Fine Gael'. *IT*, 7/9/67, John A. Costello remembers.
3 See epigraph to Chapter Two.
4 O'Leary, p. 40.
5 Ibid.
6 His role can be compared to that of Attlee: 'His governments bristled with able and articulate individuals who thrived on conflict: he rightly regarded his ability to "adjust relations" between them as one of his major achievements.' Burridge, p. 188.
7 Mulcahy to Costello, 15/5/67, in UCDA, Mulcahy Papers, P7/D/116.
8 Browne, p. 97.
9 Maye, p. 96.

10 Ibid., p. 102.
11 Mansergh, 1958, p. 297.
12 Gallagher, 1976, p. 61.
13 Kelleher, p. 6.
14 Rafter, p. 120.
15 Ibid., p. 190; see also table on p. 201.
16 Dunphy, p. 309.
17 Peter Mair, 'Explaining the Absence of Class Politics in Ireland', in Goldthorpe and Whelan (eds), p. 408.
18 Ibid.
19 Kelleher, pp. 2–3.
20 Mair, p. 182.
21 Ibid.
22 See Peter Mair, 'Ireland 1948–81: Issues, Parties, Strategies', in Budge, Robertson and Hearl (eds), p. 137.
23 Dunphy, p. 317.
24 Quoted in Ronan Fanning, 'Economists and Governments: Ireland 1932–52', in Antoin Murphy (ed.), p. 138.
25 UCDA, Mulcahy Papers, P7/c/151, text of Costello's speech to Dublin South-East Fine Gael branches, Morehampton Hotel, 20/11/59.

BIBLIOGRAPHY

PRIMARY SOURCES

(a) Archives

The various archives consulted are referred to in the Notes as follows:

NAI – National Archives of Ireland, Dublin. Unless otherwise stated, all files
are from the Department of the Taoiseach. 'Cab' and 'Govt' refer to the
minutes of Cabinet and Government meetings; in the Notes the reference
is followed by the number of the meeting and the date.
UK PRO – British Public Record Office, Kew, London
PRONI – Public Record Office of Northern Ireland, Belfast
UCDA – Archives Department, University College Dublin

(b) Newspapers

The main sources were the *Irish Press* cuttings library and microfilm of the
Irish Times in UCD library. The following abbreviations are used in the Notes:

EP – Evening Press
II – Irish Independent
IP – Irish Press
IT – Irish Times
SI – Sunday Independent
SP – Sunday Press

The following have been particularly helpful:

ITGWU pamphlet, *ITGWU and the Labour Party: The Union's Reply to the
Labour Party's Statement*
Studies, Vol. 40 (June 1951), pp. 129–59, articles on the Mother and Child
scheme by Edward Coyne SJ, John F. Cunningham and Alexis Fitzgerald
IT, 3 to 5/7/62 – Lord Rugby remembers, by Terence de Vere White

IT, 4 to 8/9/67 – John A. Costello remembers, by Michael McInerney

IT, 9 to 11/10/67 – Dr Noël Browne, a political portrait, by Michael McInerney

IP, 27 to 29/1/69 – Profile of Seán Lemass, by Michael Mills

II, 5 and 6/5/69 – Interview with James Dillon

Magill, January 1983, 'The Extraordinary Life and Times of Seán MacBride, Part Two', by Michael Farrell

IT, 13 and 14/2/85 – 'Fianna Fáil and the Bishops', by Ronan Fanning

IT, 12 to 14/4/89 – Profile of Patrick McGilligan, by Garret FitzGerald

IT, 6/4/98 – Discussion of McQuaid's role in the Mother and Child crisis, based on his private papers, by John Cooney

(c) Official publications

DED – Official reports, Dáil Éireann Debates

SED – Official reports, Seanad Éireann Debates

Central Bank – Reports for various years, published by the Stationery Office, Dublin

Stationery Office, Prl. 8624, *Results of Presidential Elections and Referenda, 1937–79*

(d) Interviews and correspondence

Liam Cosgrave

Patrick Lynch

Risteárd Mulcahy

Louie O'Brien

T.K. Whitaker

(e) RTÉ Archives

As well as various programme tapes referred to in the Notes, the following were used:

Archive Tape 20/68, Review of 1951, Tx 31/12/51

Archive Tape A 1519, 'Mother and Child Scheme', Tx 7/10/80

Archive Tape A 4184, 'The Republic of Ireland Act, 1948', Tx 26/3/89

Archive Tape B 1444, clips of Noël Browne

'Memories in Focus', Programme Three: 'The War Years and After', RTÉ 1 Television, Tx 11/5/95

Seven Days Special, Tx 24/6/69, interview with John A. Costello by David Thornley

SECONDARY SOURCES

Akenson, Donald Harman, 1994, *Conor: A Biography of Conor Cruise O'Brien*, McGill-Queen's University Press, Montreal and Kingston

Akenson, Donald Harman (ed.), 1994, *Conor: A Biography of Conor Cruise O'Brien; Volume II – Anthology*, McGill-Queen's University Press, Montreal and Kingston

Andrews, C.S., 1982, *Man of No Property*, Mercier Press, Dublin and Cork

Attlee, Clement, 1954, *As it Happened*, William Heinemann, London

Barrington, Ruth, 1987, *Health, Medicine and Politics in Ireland, 1900–1970*, Institute of Public Administration, Dublin

Bartolini, Stefano, and Peter Mair, 1990, *Identity, Competition and Electoral Availability: The Stabilisation of European Electorates, 1885–1985*, Cambridge University Press

Barton, Brian, 1988, *Brookeborough: The Making of a Prime Minister*, Queen's University Belfast

Bell, J. Bowyer, 1990, *The Secret Army: The IRA 1916–1979*, Poolbeg Press, Dublin

Bew, Paul, Ellen Hazelkorn and Henry Patterson, 1989, *The Dynamics of Irish Politics*, Lawrence and Wishart, London

Blondel, Jean, and Ferdinand Muller-Rommel (eds), 1988, *Cabinets in Western Europe*, Macmillan, London

Bogdanor, Vernon (ed.), 1983, *Coalition Government in Western Europe*, Heinemann Educational Books, London

Bogdanor, Vernon, 1984, *What is Proportional Representation? A Guide to the Issues*, Martin Robertson, London

Bolster, Evelyn, 1979, *The Knights of Saint Columbanus*, Gill & Macmillan, Dublin

Boston, Jonathan, 1997, 'Learning the Art of Government Formation under Proportional Representation: Recent New Zealand Experience', paper delivered to British Political Science Association conference, available on the Internet at http://www.vuw.ac.nz/pols/nzpcp/BPSA/April_1997/text.html

Boston, Jonathan, Stephen Levine, Elizabeth McLeay and Nigel S. Roberts, 'The 1996 General Election in New Zealand: Proportional Representation and Political Change', *Australian Quarterly*, available on the Internet at http://www/vuw.ac.nz/pols/nzpcp/australian-quarterly_text.html

Bowman, John, 1989, *De Valera and the Ulster Question, 1917–1973*, Oxford University Press

Bristow, J.A., and A.A. Tait (eds), 1968, *Economic Policy in Ireland*, Institute of Public Administration, Dublin

Browne, Eric C., and John Dreijmanis (eds), 1982, *Government Coalitions in Western Democracies*, Longman, London and New York

Browne, Noël, *Against the Tide*, Gill & Macmillan, Dublin

Budge, Ian, David Robertson and Derek Hearl (eds), 1987, *Ideology, Strategy and Party Change: Spatial Analyses of Post-war Election Programmes in 19 Democracies*, Cambridge University Press

Budge, Ian, and Hans Keman, 1990, *Parties and Democracy: Coalition Formation and Government Functioning in 20 States*, Oxford University Press

Burridge, Trevor, 1985, *Clement Attlee: A Political Biography*, Jonathan Cape, London

Butler, David (ed.), 1978, *Coalitions in British Politics*, Macmillan, London

Butler, David, Howard R. Penniman and Austin Ranney (eds), 1981, *Democracy at the Polls: A Comparative Study of Competitive National Elections*, American Enterprise Institute for Public Policy Research, Washington and London

Chubb, Basil, and Patrick Lynch (eds), 1969, *Economic Development and Planning*, Institute of Public Administration, Dublin

Chubb, Basil, 1974, *Cabinet Government in Ireland*, Institute of Public Administration, Dublin

Chubb, Basil, 1982, *The Government and Politics of Ireland*, 2nd edn, Longman, London and New York

Coakley, John, 1980, 'Constituency Boundary Revision and Seat Redistribution in the Irish Parliamentary Tradition', *Administration*, Vol. 28, No. 3, pp. 291–328

Coakley, John, 1984, 'Selecting a Prime Minister: The Irish Experience', *Parliamentary Affairs*, Vol. 37, No. 4, pp. 403–17

Coakley, John, 1990, 'Minor Parties in Irish Political Life, 1922–89', *Economic and Social Review*, Vol. 21, No. 3 (April), pp. 269–97

Coakley, John, and Michael Gallagher (eds), 1992, *Politics in the Republic of Ireland*, PSAI Press, Galway

Cohan, A.S., 1972, *The Irish Political Elite*, Gill & Macmillan, Dublin

Cohan, A.S., 1979, 'The Open Coalition in the Closed Society: The Strange Pattern of Government Formation in Ireland', *Comparative Politics*, Vol. 11, No. 2 (April), pp. 319–38

Cole, John, 1996, *As It Seemed to Me*, rev. edn, Phoenix, London

Collins, Stephen, 1996, *The Cosgrave Legacy*, Blackwater Press, Dublin

Coogan, Tim Pat, 1993, *De Valera: Long Fellow, Long Shadow*, Hutchinson, London

Cooney, John, 1986, *The Crozier and the Dáil: Church and State in Ireland, 1922–86*, Mercier Press, Cork

Cronin, Seán, 1987, *Washington's Irish Policy, 1916–86*, Anvil Books, Dublin

Daly, Mary E., 1981, *Social and Economic History of Ireland Since 1800*, Educational Company, Dublin

Deeny, James, 1989, *To Cure and to Care: Memoirs of a Chief Medical Officer*, Glendale Press, Dún Laoghaire

Dunphy, Richard, 1995, *The Making of Fianna Fáil Power in Ireland, 1923–1948*, Clarendon Press, Oxford

Earl, Lawrence, 1952, *The Battle of Baltinglass*, George Harap, London

Fanning, Ronan, 1978, *The Irish Department of Finance, 1922–58*, Institute of Public Administration, Dublin

Fanning, Ronan, 1979, 'The United States and Irish participation in NATO: The Debate of 1950', *Irish Studies in International Affairs*, Vol. 1, No. 1, pp. 38–48

Fanning, Ronan, 1981,'The Response of the London and Belfast Governments to the Declaration of the Republic of Ireland, 1948–49', *International Affairs*, Vol. 58, No. 1 (Winter), pp. 95–114

Farrell, Brian, 1971, *Chairman or Chief? The Role of Taoiseach in Irish Government*, Gill & Macmillan, Dublin

Farren, Seán, 1995, *The Politics of Irish Education, 1920–65*, Queen's University Belfast

Fisk, Robert, 1983, *In Time of War*, Paladin, London

FitzGerald, Garret, 1992, *All in a Life*, Papermac, London

Flora, Peter (ed.), 1987, *Growth to Limits: The Western European Welfare State Since World War II*, Vol. IV, Walter de Gruyter, Berlin and New York

Gallagher, Michael, 1976, *Electoral Support for Irish Political Parties, 1923–1973*, SAGE professional papers in contemporary political sociology, 06–017, SAGE Publications, London and Beverly Hills

Gallagher, Michael, 1978, 'Party Solidarity, Exclusivity and Inter-Party Relationships in Ireland, 1922–77: The Evidence of Transfers', *Economic and Social Review*, Vol. 10, No. 1 (October), pp. 1–22

Gallagher, Michael, 1985, *Political Parties in the Republic of Ireland*, Gill & Macmillan, Dublin

Gallagher, Michael, 1986, 'The Political Consequences of the Electoral System in the Republic of Ireland', *Electoral Studies*, Vol. 5, No. 3, pp. 253–75

Gallagher, Michael, Michael Laver and Peter Mair, 1992, *Representative Government in Western Europe*, McGraw-Hill, New York

Gallagher, Tom, and James O'Connell (eds), 1983, *Contemporary Irish Studies*, Manchester University Press

Garvin, Tom, 1981, *The Evolution of Irish Nationalist Politics*, Gill & Macmillan, Dublin

Garvin, Tom, 1996, *1922 – The Birth of Irish Democracy*, Gill & Macmillan, Dublin

Girvin, Brian, 1989, *Between Two Worlds: Politics and Economy in Independent Ireland*, Gill & Macmillan, Dublin

Goldthorpe, J.H, and C.T. Whelan (eds), 1992, *The Development of Industrial Society in Ireland: Proceedings of the British Academy, 79*, Oxford University Press

Gray, Tony, 1994, *Ireland This Century*, Little, Brown and Company, London

Gregg, Gerard, 1981, 'Dr Noël Browne: Irish Political Maverick', MA thesis, University College Dublin

Griffiths, Richard T. (ed.), 1997, *Explorations in OEEC History*, OECD, Paris

Hannon, Philip, and Jackie Gallagher (eds), 1996, *Taking the Long View: 70 Years of Fianna Fáil*, Blackwater Press, Dublin

Harkness, David, 1979, 'Patrick McGilligan: Man of Commonwealth', *Journal of Imperial and Commonwealth History*, Vol. 8, No. 1, pp. 117–35

Harris, Kenneth, 1982, *Attlee*, Weidenfeld and Nicolson, London

Hennessy, Peter, 1992, *Never Again: Britain 1945–51*, Jonathan Cape, London

Horgan, John, 1997, *Seán Lemass: The Enigmatic Patriot*, Gill & Macmillan, Dublin

Inglis, Brian, 1990, *Downstart*, Chatto and Windus, London

Jordan, Anthony J., 1993, *Seán MacBride: A Biography*, Blackwater Press, Dublin

Kaim-Caudle, P.R., 1967, *Social Policy in the Irish Republic*, Routledge and Kegan Paul, London

Keatinge, Patrick, 1973, *The Formulation of Irish Foreign Policy*, Institute of Public Administration, Dublin

Keatinge, Patrick, 1978, *A Place Among the Nations*, Institute of Public Administration, Dublin

Kelleher, Derry, 1984, *Coalition: Labour's Scourge or Rigor Mortis*, Justice Books, Greystones, Co. Wicklow

Kennedy, Kieran A., and Brendan Dowling, 1975, *Economic Growth in Ireland: The Experience Since 1947*, Gill & Macmillan, Dublin

Kennedy, Kieran, Thomas Giblin and Deirdre McHugh, 1988, *The Economic Development of Ireland in the Twentieth Century*, Routledge, London and New York

Kennedy, Paul, 1981, *The Realities Behind Diplomacy*, Fontana, London

Keogh, Dermot, 1988, *Ireland and Europe, 1919–1948*, Gill & Macmillan, Dublin/Barnes & Noble Books, Totowa, New Jersey

Keogh, Dermot, 1994, *Twentieth-Century Ireland: Nation and State*, Gill & Macmillan, Dublin

Keogh, Dermot, 1995, *Ireland and the Vatican*, Cork University Press

Laver, Michael, and Norman Schofield, 1990, *Multiparty Government: The Politics of Coalition in Europe*, Oxford University Press

Laver, Michael, and Kenneth Shepsle, 1990, 'Coalitions and Cabinet Government', *American Political Science Review*, Vol. 84, No. 3, pp. 873–90

Laver, Michael, and Ian Budge (eds), 1992, *Party Policy and Government Coalitions*, St Martin's Press, New York

Laver, Michael, and Ben Hunt, 1992, *Policy and Party Competition*, Routledge, New York and London

Laver, Michael, and Kenneth A. Shepsle (eds), 1994, *Cabinet Ministers and Parliamentary Government*, Cambridge University Press

Lee, J.J. (ed.), 1979, *Ireland, 1945–70* (RTÉ Thomas Davis Lectures), Gill & Macmillan, Dublin/Barnes and Noble Books, New York

Lee, J.J., 1989, *Ireland 1912–1985: Politics and Society*, Cambridge University Press

Lijphart, Arend, 1984, *Democracies – Patterns of Majoritarian and Consensus Government in 21 Countries*, Yale University Press, New Haven and London

Lijphart, Arend, 1994, *Electoral Systems and Party Systems*, Oxford University Press

Lindsay, Patrick J., 1992, *Memories*, Blackwater Press, Dublin

Luebbert, Gregory, 1986, *Comparative Democracy: Policymaking and Governing Coalitions in Europe and Israel*, Columbia University Press, New York

Lynch, Patrick, and James Meenan (eds), 1987, *Essays in Memory of Alexis Fitzgerald*, Incorporated Law Society of Ireland, Dublin

Lyons, F.S.L., 1973, *Ireland Since the Famine*, Fontana, London

McCabe, Ian, 1991, *A Diplomatic History of Ireland, 1948–49: The Republic, the Commonwealth and NATO*, Irish Academic Press, Dublin

McCague, Eugene, 1994, *Arthur Cox, 1891–1965*, Gill & Macmillan, Dublin

McCarthy, John F. (ed.), 1990, *Planning Ireland's Future: The Legacy of T.K. Whitaker*, Glendale, Dublin

McEvoy, F.J., 1985, 'Canada, Ireland, and the Commonwealth: The Declaration of the Irish Republic, 1948–49', *Irish Historical Studies*, Vol. 24, No. 96 (November), pp. 506–27

McKee, Eamonn, 1986, 'Church–State Relations and the Development of Irish Health Policy: The Mother and Child Scheme, 1944–53', *Irish Historical Studies*, Vol. 25, No. 98 (November), pp. 159–94

Mair, Peter, 1987, *The Changing Irish Party System*, Pinter Publishers, London

Mansergh, Diana (ed.), 1997, *Nationalism and Independence: Selected Irish Papers by Nicholas Mansergh*, Cork University Press

Mansergh, Nicholas, 1958, *Survey of British Commonwealth Affairs: Problems of Wartime Co-operation and Post-war Change, 1939–52*, Oxford University Press

Mansergh, Nicholas, 1982, *The Commonwealth Experience, Vol. II: From British to Multiracial Commonwealth*, Macmillan, London

Maye, Brian, 1993, *Fine Gael, 1923–1987*, Blackwater Press, Dublin

Mitchell, Arthur, and Pádraig Ó Snodaigh (eds), 1985, *Irish Political Documents, 1916–49*, Irish Academic Press, Dublin

Moynihan, Maurice, 1975, *Currency and Central Banking in Ireland, 1922–60*, Central Bank of Ireland and Gill & Macmillan, Dublin

Murphy, Antoin E. (ed.), 1984, *Economists and the Irish Economy*, Irish Academic Press, Dublin

Nevin, Donal (ed.), 1994, *Trade Union Century*, Mercier Press, Cork and Dublin

Nowlan, Kevin B., and T. Desmond Williams (eds), 1969, *Ireland in the War Years and After, 1939–51*, Gill & Macmillan, Dublin

Ó Broin, Leon, 1982, *No Man's Man: A Biographical Memoir of Joseph Brennan*, Institute of Public Administration, Dublin

Ó Broin, Leon, 1985, *Just Like Yesterday*, Gill & Macmillan, Dublin

O' Carroll, John P., and John A. Murphy (eds), 1986, *De Valera and His Times*, Cork University Press

O' Connor, Emmet, 1992, *A Labour History of Ireland*, Gill & Macmillan, Dublin

O' Driscoll, Robert (ed.), 1981, *The Celtic Consciousness*, Dolmen Press, Dublin

Ó Gráda, Cormac, 1997, *A Rocky Road: The Irish Economy Since the 1920s*, Manchester University Press, Manchester and New York

O'Hagan, J.W., 1980, 'An Analysis of the Relative Size of the Government Sector: Ireland 1926–52', *Economic and Social Review*, Vol. 12, No. 1 (October), pp. 17–35

Ó hEithir, Breandán, 1986, *The Begrudger's Guide to Irish Politics*, Poolbeg Press, Dublin

O' Higgins, T.F., 1996, *A Double Life*, Town House, Dublin

O'Leary, Cornelius, 1979, *Irish Elections, 1918–77*, Gill & Macmillan, Dublin

O'Sullivan, Michael, 1994, *Seán Lemass: A Biography*, Blackwater Press, Dublin

Penniman, Howard, and Brian Farrell (eds), 1987, *Ireland at the Polls, 1981, 1982 and 1987: A Study of Four General Elections*, Duke University Press, Durham, North Carolina

Pridham, Geoffrey (ed.), 1986, *Coalitional Behaviour in Theory and Practice: An Inductive Model for Western Europe*, Cambridge University Press

Rafter, Kevin, 1996, *The Clann: The Story of Clann na Poblachta*, Mercier Press, Cork and Dublin

Raymond, Raymond James, 1985, 'The Marshall Plan and Ireland, 1947–52', in P.J. Drudy (ed.), *The Irish in America*, Irish Studies 4, Cambridge University Press

Rumpf, E., and A.C. Hepburn, 1977, *Nationalism and Socialism in Twentieth-Century Ireland*, Liverpool University Press

Savage, Roland Burke, SJ, 1965, 'The Church in Dublin, 1940–65', *Studies*, Vol. 54 (Winter), pp. 295–338

Seaman, L.C.B., 1966, *Post-Victorian Britain, 1902–1951*, Metheun, New York and London

Valiulis, Maryann Gialanella, 1992, *Portrait of a Revolutionary: General Richard Mulcahy and the Founding of the Irish Free State*, Irish Academic Press, Dublin

Walker, Brian M. (ed.), 1992, *Parliamentary Election Results in Ireland, 1918–92*, A New History of Ireland Ancilliary Publication V, Royal Irish Academy, Dublin and Queen's University Belfast

Walsh, Dick, 1986, *The Party: Inside Fianna Fáil*, Gill & Macmillan, Dublin

Weller, Patrick, 1985, *First Among Equals: Prime Ministers in Westminster Systems*, George Allen and Unwin, Sydney

Whelan, Bernadette, 1992, 'Ireland and the Marshall Plan', *Irish Economic and Social History*, Vol. 9, pp. 49–70

Whitaker, T.K., 1949, 'Ireland's External Assets', paper read to the Statistical and Social Inquiry Society, 29 April, copy lent by the author

Whitaker, T.K., 1983, *Interests*, Institute of Public Administration, Dublin

Whyte, J.H., 1980, *Church and State in Modern Ireland, 1923–1979,* 2nd edn, Gill & Macmillan, Dublin

Williams, Francis, 1961, *A Prime Minister Remembers*, Heinemann, London

INDEX